LIFESKILLS
A Handbook

LIFESKILLS
A Handbook

Richard Nelson-Jones

CASSELL

Cassell Educational Limited
Villiers House, 41/47 Strand, London WC2N 5JE

First published 1991

British Library Cataloguing in Publication Data
Nelson-Jones, Richard, *1936–*
Lifeskills: a handbook.
1. Counselling
I. Title
361.323

ISBN 0-304-32400-0 (hardback)
ISBN 0-304-32396-9 (paperback)

Typeset by Selectmove Ltd, London
Printed and bound in Great Britain by
Dotesios Ltd, Trowbridge, Wilts.

CONTENTS

EXERCISES

Preface

This book focuses on the central skills of leading training or lifeskills groups. Training groups are time-limited, structured, psychological education groups focused on helping participants to develop one or more lifeskills: for example, parenting, stress management or assertion skills. Training groups are now perhaps the most common way that helpers work in groups.

This book is written for group leaders who either will be or are in roles where they train others in lifeskills. Such people may be in various areas: counselling, teaching, parent education, marriage guidance, social work, nursing, health care, rehabilitation, career work, youth work, correctional work, community relations, personnel work, and working as training officers in business, industry and the public service. The book may be used to train such people as part of group leadership courses at postgraduate, undergraduate and further education levels. Also, trainers forced to acquire training skills on the job may find the book useful. In addition, the book, with its comprehensive detail, may be used by trainers and others as a resource for reference.

A number of assumptions underlie the book. First, my theoretical position integrates both cognitive-behavioural and existential-humanistic insights. Second, lifeskills are self-help skills. Lifeskills training groups teach participants to fish for themselves. Third, effective training involves both teaching and group interaction. Consequently, lifeskills group leaders require both good facilitative and good didactic skills. Fourth, I have an optimistic approach to the human condition. Though all of us to a greater or lesser degree have acquired some lifeskills weaknesses, we can choose not to sustain them. Well-led training groups help numerous people to reclaim and develop more of their human potential.

What are the book's contents? Chapter 1 places training groups in the context of different kinds of groups and further clarifies their characteristics. Chapter 2 overviews how people not only acquire, but also maintain, both lifeskills strengths and weaknesses. Then follow eleven chapters on 'how to': prepare training groups; design lifeskills programmes; assess participants and help self-assessment; facilitate training groups; speak in public; demonstrate lifeskills; manage structured activities; prepare and lead sessions; consolidate trained skills and end groups; evaluate and research training groups; and maintain and develop your training group leader skills.

This book is a manual of trainer choices. Training group leader skills are viewed as choices that you may make either well or poorly. Sometimes trainer choices are presented in list form to highlight different options. Though the book may be read from cover to cover, readers are more likely to develop skills if they work through it section by section. When read as a whole, the amount of detail may be off-putting. However, when approached chapter by chapter the detail should be both manageable and appropriate. The book's learning by doing or 'hands-on' emphasis is highlighted by the inclusion of numerous exercises. Furthermore, session outlines, programme outlines and training examples illustrate skills. Each chapter starts with Chapter Questions, to let readers know what is coming and ends with Chapter Highlights, for review and revision purposes. Throughout I have attempted to use simple, clear English.

A word about myself. I have a long history of participating in groups, leading groups, and training group leaders. A few illustrations. When I was a graduate student at Stanford University in the early to mid-1960s I participated in three psychotherapy groups at the Stanford Medical Centre, one of which was co-led by Professor Irvin Yalom. I have attended numerous workshops on various approaches to group work. In the early 1970s I was leading person-centred interactional groups with undergraduates and with graduate counsellor trainees. Since then, my interests have moved much more into leading lifeskills training groups. Currently, I lead undergraduate groups in the areas of relationship skills and thinking skills. In addition, I train graduate counsellor trainees in both facilitative and didactic group leader skills.

I express appreciation to the following people: Naomi Roth, for commissioning the book; Michael Carroll for his thoughtful review; and last but not least, all those practitioners, theorists and researchers who have written about groups and whose names form a roll of honour in the bibliography.

I hope that you find your time with this book an interesting and rewarding experience. I wish you good skills when you lead training groups.

Richard Nelson-Jones
MELBOURNE, AUSTRALIA

ONE
An Introduction to Training Groups

Give a person a fish, and you feed them for a day.
Teach a person to fish, and you feed them for a lifetime.
Chinese proverb (Non-sexist adaptation)

CHAPTER QUESTIONS

How do training groups differ from other groups?

Why the growth of training groups?

What sorts of training groups are there?

What are lifeskills?

What is the leader role in training groups?

What are some criticisms and reservations about training groups?

INTRODUCTION

As we approach the twenty-first century, leading training groups is likely to become an increasingly large part of the work of many helpers. Attempts to help people to acquire the skills to manage their lives better are nothing new. However, as psychological knowledge has developed, so have systematic attempts to use psychological insights and principles to train people to be more effective in all aspects of their lives. Terms like psycho-education (Ivey, 1976), human resource development (Carkhuff, 1971a), lifeskills teaching (Hopson and Scally, 1981), lifeskills training (Gazda, 1989), deliberate psychological education (Mosher & Sprinthall, 1970; Sprinthall & Scott, 1989) and developmental education (Nelson-Jones, 1988a) have been used to describe this movement. The growth in the training function of group helpers has not been paralleled by the growth in books about how to train. The major focus of most books on group leadership is still on interactional groups rather than training groups (for instance, Corey, 1990; Corey *et al.*, 1988a; Gazda, 1989; Jacobs *et al.*, 1988; Ohlsen *et al.*, 1988). There were no books with the word 'training' in their titles or subtitles in the content area of group theory and practice in a survey of the leading textbooks used in counsellor education programmes throughout the United States (Sampson & Liberty, 1989). This book attempts to redress the balance by taking group leader as trainer skills as its major focus.

HOW DO TRAINING GROUPS DIFFER FROM OTHER GROUPS?

There are many ways that leaders can work with groups. Below is a listing of some of the main kinds of groups, each with a brief descriptive paragraph. Though an oversimplification, this listing may help you to place training groups within the broad context of other groups. Needless to say, there is overlap between the different groups.

Discussion groups

Discussion groups focus on specific topics, such as how to deal with AIDS sufferers, whether or not to legalize pot, and whether religion is helpful or harmful. Discussion groups are topic-centred rather than centred either on the relationships between discussion group members or on the systematic development of specific lifeskills. Discussion groups aim to get participants involved and to broaden their knowledge and understanding of stipulated topics.

Information groups

Information groups impart specific information. Though information may be provided by members to each other, usually the group leader is the main source of information. Information groups cover such areas as occupational information, sex education, and drug and alcohol education. Information groups have the educational purpose of helping people to acquire specific knowledge. Such groups tend to have developmental and preventive rather than remedial goals.

Task-orientated groups

Here the task rather than the topic is the group's major focus. Task groups go beyond talking to action, or at least to deciding on and planning proposed courses of action. Usually task-orientated groups have specific and clear goals. Examples of task-orientated groups include: deciding on the rules in a nursing home for the elderly, planning how to market a new product, working as part of a research team, and being on the committee of a social club. The personal development of task group members is tangential to performing the group's tasks. If and when these tasks are completed, such groups are likely to disband.

Growth groups

Growth groups come under many different titles: encounter groups, sensitivity groups, T-groups, experiential groups, human relations groups and so on. Rogers defines an encounter group as follows: 'This tends to emphasize personal growth and the development and improvement of interpersonal communication and relationships through an experiential process' (Rogers, 1970, pp. 4, 5). Central values for growth groups include dropping social façades, openness and honesty, working in the 'here-and-now', getting in touch with and expressing feelings, and working through blocks to make genuine person-to-person contact with other members. Yalom observes that the goals of such groups are often vague (Yalom, 1985). Participants in growth groups tend to be self-selected. Participants tend not to view themselves as 'clients' or 'patients', but rather as people in search of higher levels of self-actualization. Growth groups are often time-limited, for instance a weekend marathon group.

Counselling groups

In counselling groups, group interaction and relationships are used by leaders to help members to attain personal goals. Members of counselling groups tend to be 'clients' who use group counselling after, concurrently with, or instead of individual counselling. Ohlsen views group counselling as enabling clients to: (a) discuss what really worries them; (b) define desired new behaviours; (c) practise essential interpersonal skills; and (d) implement new behaviours (Ohlsen, 1977). Though group counsellees undoubtedly have their anxieties and personal difficulties, there is a basic assumption that these concerns are not so debilitating as to require extensive personality change (Gazda, 1989; Ohlsen et al., 1988). Counselling groups are frequently time-limited. However, they tend to last for months rather than for a weekend or a few weeks. For instance, Mahler suggests that about ten sessions should be the minimum for most group counselling programmes held in schools (Mahler, 1969).

Psychotherapy groups

Psychotherapy groups tend to be different from counselling groups and encounter groups in a number of ways. First, the purposes of therapy groups are almost invariably remedial rather than developmental or preventive. Second, the clientele tends to be 'relatively seriously emotionally disturbed . . .' (Gazda, 1989, p. 45) or 'persons who are in need of or desire a personality restructuring, who are so debilitated not to be able to function effectively in their day-to-day lives' (Ohlsen et al., 1988, p. 14). Yalom observes that therapy groups are often composed of people who cannot cope with minor everyday stress without discomfort (Yalom, 1985).

Basic interpersonal competencies and the ability to send and receive messages without much distortion cannot be assumed. Third, because of their lower self-esteem and self-awareness, therapy group members are more closed, defensive and concerned with their psychological survival. Especially at the start of psychotherapy groups, they are less open to questioning themselves and less willing to learn from new experiences. Fourth, the training of psychotherapy group leaders tends more to be 'intensive psychological and/or medical at the doctoral level' (Gazda, 1989, p. 45). Fifth, the distortions contained in members' transference relationships with the leader are likely to be explored in greater depth than in counselling or encounter groups, where they may not be explored at all. In sum, psychotherapy groups are intensive and often long-term group experiences, frequently held in psychiatric in-patient and out-patient settings, for people with highly debilitating emotional problems and interpersonal skills weaknesses.

Self-help groups

Self-help groups go by other names, such as peer support groups, mutual support groups and mutual sharing groups. Huge numbers of self-help groups exist. For example, about a decade ago, there were approximately half a million self-help groups in the United States with a membership of 15 million (Katz, 1981; Riordan & Beggs, 1987). The range of self-help groups is vast: women's groups; men's groups; gay groups; Alcoholics Anonymous; widows' groups; bereaved parents' groups; groups for relatives of people suffering from schizophrenia or senility; Overeaters Anonymous and Mended Hearts (coronary surgery patients), among many others. Self-help groups often evolve their leadership from within their own members. However, groups may still have experts on call as consultants. Self-help groups have a heavy emphasis on sharing and on mutual support.

Support networks

All people exist with various degrees of connectedness to others who can support them (Acock & Hurlbert, 1990). In reality, individuals' support networks comprise participation in many different networks: family, friends, work colleagues, clubs, church, school and so on. When people seek help from professionals, it is often a sign that their own helping or support networks are inadequate (Murgatroyd, 1985). Support networks provide groups of varying degrees of extension to which people may or may not be adequately connected. In a sense, support networks are informal rather than formal self-help groups. Many people of varying degrees of disturbance may need to appreciate more the importance of support networks. Also, they may need to develop their skills of expanding, participating in and using their networks (Conn & Peterson, 1989).

Training groups

Training groups, lifeskills groups or lifeskills training groups are time-limited structured groups with specific and predetermined learning goals and programmes. There is often no assumption of mental unwellness for participation in a training group. Social skills are perhaps the most common focus of training groups: for example, assertion groups, managing-anger groups, and managing-conflict groups. However, lifeskills training groups take place in many other areas of living: for example, health, studying and work. Training group leaders use both didactic and facilitative skills to help participants to develop skills and then transfer and maintain them after the programmes end.

Below are some examples of people participating in training groups.

- Nancy, 43, goes along to a weekend workshop, run by a social worker in private practice, on assertion skills.

- John and Valerie, both in their early 30s, attend weekly sessions in effective parenting at their local Community Centre.

- Khalid, 9, participates in a class at his primary school to develop children's friendship skills.

- Julie, 17, has some classroom periods at her secondary school in which the curriculum covers career decision-making skills.

- Angus, 63, attends a series of seminars, offered by his company's personnel department, on preparing for retirement.

- Stephen, 18, attends a skills group at his university counselling service on managing exam anxiety.

- Dorothy, 21, attends a course in human relations skills as part of her teacher training.

WHY THE GROWTH IN TRAINING GROUPS?

Some reasons for the growing emphasis on training groups include the following. Problems of living are widespread. The world is full of people failing to maximize their human potential. The statistics on marital breakdown provide one indication of this. In the early 1980s the divorce rate for first marriages in the United States was 49 per cent (Glick, 1984). In the period 1971 to 1985 the number of divorces in England and Wales more than doubled from 75 000 to 154 000 (Office of Population Census and Surveys, 1987). In Australia, the percentage of marriages ending in divorce increased from 14 per cent in 1971 to 35 per cent in 1986 (McDonald, 1988). The above figures partly reflect the fact that obtaining a divorce has become easier. Also, divorce is less socially stigmatized. Nevertheless, the figures underestimate the extent of marital breakdown. If the figures for the separated population were added to those of the divorced population to form a 'dissolution index', the statistics for marital breakdown would be considerably higher. Add the many couples who remain neither separated nor divorced, but unhappy, and the extent of marital distress, with its repercussions for children, becomes even more apparent. Keeping relationships happy and intact is just one among many problems of living that numerous people experience.

Training groups have both developmental and preventive objectives. You do not have to admit mental disturbance to participate in a training group. The goal of lifeskills training in an ideal world would be for everyone to possess the requisite skills to meet all developmental tasks throughout their lives. Distinctions between remedial, preventive and developmental emphases are seldom clear-cut. Daws (1973), writing of the need for preventive work in schools, argues that the strongest expression of the preventive principle is work devoted to the personal and social education of *all* students in such a way that it anticipates their developmental needs. Drug and alcohol education and AIDS education are further examples of preventive training.

Increased pressures for helper accountability provide another impetus for running training groups. Some helpers consider that their cost-effectiveness is much greater if they actively engage in developmental and preventive interventions, like training groups, rather than passively wait in their offices for clients requiring remedial help. These helpers seek ways to benefit as many people as possible. Also, they wish to better justify the services they offer to budget setters and other influential people.

Successful training groups can both save and make money. Low-functioning people cost money, and high-functioning people can make money. For instance, good communicators in business and commerce are more likely to contribute to income and profits than are bad communicators. Skilled supervisors and managers are conducive to developing and maintaining competitiveness (Goldstein & Gilliam, 1990). On the other hand, employees whose functioning is impaired through stress, substance abuse or other emotional problems are often costly.

The increased influence of cognitive-behaviourism has been a major stimulus for people to run training groups. The theoretical foundations for training groups rest on the behavioural (actions-focused) revolution in helping of the 1960s and the cognitive (thinking-focused) revolution of the 1970s. The cognitive-behavioural model is basically a lifeskills training model. Many, if not most, training groups now focus on both thinking and action skills.

WHAT SORTS OF TRAINING GROUPS ARE THERE?

Broad areas for training groups

The scope of lifeskills training is vast. Training groups can be run both with helping-service clients and also with non-helping-service client participants. The following are four broad areas in which training groups may be fruitfully conducted with non-client participants. First, there is the area of developmental education. Developmental education entails training children through to old people in the psychological lifeskills appropriate to their developmental stages (Havighurst, 1972). The second broad area is that of training specific clienteles to handle better their problems of living. Examples of this include training groups in: coping with dual career skills for married couples (Amatea & Cross, 1983); emotional expressiveness skills for men (Moore & Haverkamp, 1989); assertion skills for women (Butler, 1981); and coping with unemployment skills for the unemployed and those facing job loss (Azrin *et al.*, 1975).

The third broad area for lifeskills training groups is that of work-related training. Work-related training groups can be run on either a pre-service or in-service basis. In-service training programmes include: relationship skills for teachers and doctors; anger management skills for police officers; and supervisory skills for newly promoted supervisors. Helper training is a fourth broad area for training groups. Much helper practical skills training takes place in groups, for example training counsellors and social workers in listening skills.

Settings for training groups

Lifeskills training groups are run in many different settings and skills areas. Below are some of the main settings, with examples of illustrative groups.

PRIMARY AND SECONDARY SCHOOLS

Lifeskills training takes place in both primary and secondary schools. Training groups can be run both within and outside the formal curriculum (Martin, 1983). Morgan describes a kindergarten to 6th-grade guidance curriculum in an Oregon school district (Morgan, 1984). The programme's objectives were clustered into such skills areas as: awareness of feelings, valuing, listening, cooperation and conflict resolution, and occupational and educational decision-making. Another programme attempted to train visually impaired primary schoolchildren in social skills (Sacks & Gaylord-Ross, 1989).

Four of the main areas in which training groups can be conducted in secondary schools are: study skills, relationship skills, career education and staff development. Study skills groups cover both study techniques and managing test anxiety. Illustrative relationship skills groups include Mosher and Sprinthall's seminar and practicum format for teaching empathy in high schools (Mosher and Sprinthall, 1971; Sprinthall, 1973, 1980) and Hatch and Guerney's (1975) pupil relationship enhancement programme (PREP). PREP focuses on training pupils to enhance their skills as speakers (expressive mode) and as listeners (responder mode) in two-person relationships. Some lifeskills training groups have focused on control of anger and aggression both in the classroom and towards teachers (Pentz & Kadzin, 1982; Huey & Rank, 1984). Other topics for relationship skills groups in schools include overcoming shyness and making friends, assertion, managing conflict, cross-cultural communication skills, integration of sexuality and sex-role education. Such training may be either focused on pupils in general or targeted on specific groups, for example, gifted and talented adolescents (Barnette, 1989). Adolescents have also been taught stress reduction skills to raise their self-esteem and lower their proneness to anxiety and anger (Hains & Szyjakowski, 1990). Other training groups relevant to relationships include drug and alcohol education (Dorn & South, 1986; Wragg, 1986), AIDS education, and groups for children and adolescents whose parents are getting divorced.

Career education training groups in schools can have a number of objectives, including: self-awareness, opportunity awareness, decision making (Savikas, 1990), information-seeking skills, interview skills, and learning how to cope with transition (Amatea *et al.*, 1984; Roessler, 1988). Additional objectives of career education groups include handling unemployment, leisure skills education, and helping disabled students to make a successful transition from secondary programmes to employment and independent living (Brolin & Gysbers, 1989).

Staff development training groups in schools can cover such areas as: counselling skills, relationship skills, and classroom and behaviour management skills. Some staff may also gain from training groups to reduce stress and avoid burnout.

COLLEGES AND UNIVERSITIES

Training groups in colleges and universities can be targeted on at least three groups: students, staff and helping-service trainees. Training groups targeted at students include remedial, preventive and developmental interventions across a number of lifeskills areas. Sometimes these are taught by lecturers within the curriculum, for instance relationship skills programmes. Often, training groups are run by counselling service staff outside the curriculum. The range of training groups includes those on: study skills; managing test anxiety; relationship skills; career development skills (Swain, 1984; Garis & Niles, 1990); anxiety and stress management skills (Romano, 1984); and effective thinking skills (Barrow and Moore, 1983; Heppner *et al.*, 1984). There are also specific training groups aimed at the problems of new students, minority groups, females, males, homosexual or bisexual students, singles and couples, among others. Some training interventions, such as drug prevention courses (Gonzalez, 1990) and date-rape seminars, may be targeted at large numbers of students.

Training groups for staff include those in helping and tutoring skills (Thorne & Da Costa, 1976; Ratigan, 1986). Sometimes these groups go beyond training staff for their teaching roles to aid them in becoming counselling-service assistants. Lecturers can also be trained to identify their own self-defeating attitudes and behaviours. For instance, Thurman (1984, 1985) ran a training group to reduce coronary-inducing 'Type A' thinking and behaviours among university lecturers. He focused both on altering irrational beliefs and on anger management. Relationship skills and retirement planning are further areas for staff lifeskills training groups.

Helping-service trainees include those on courses for counsellors, social workers, applied psychologists, pastoral carers, personnel managers, community health workers, doctors, nurses, health paraprofessionals, rehabilitation workers, career officers, youth workers and teachers. Training groups for such people can focus on skills in: counselling and helping, group facilitation, relationships, behaviour management, team building and leadership. In addition, helping-service trainees can be trained as training group leaders.

MEDICAL SETTINGS

Training groups in medical settings are conducted with two main categories of participants: patients and their families and also health professionals and paraprofessionals. Patient groups can be run in National Health Service hospitals and out-patient clinics in numerous skills areas, including: anxiety management; stress management; preventing and managing heart attacks; managing tension headaches (Martin *et al.*, 1989; Murphy *et al.*, 1990); pain management (Keefe *et al.*, 1990; Turner & Clancy, 1988); relationship skills; social phobia (Heimberg *et al.*, 1990); alcohol and drug rehabilitation; overcoming obesity (Kalodner & De Lucia, 1990); coping with depression (Brown & Lewinsohn, 1984); coping with physical disabilities; overcoming insomnia (Morawetz, 1989; Morin & Azrin, 1987); and making the transition back to the community after hospitalization. Training groups can also be conducted with family caregivers (Abramowitz & Coursey, 1989; Lovett & Gallagher, 1988). Groups on death and dying can be run for relatives of terminally ill patients, and groups on how to cope for relatives of patients who have illnesses such as schizophrenia, Down's syndrome, or Altzheimer's disease. Sometimes, as in the case of coping with AIDS, the scope of training groups is extended beyond blood relatives to include lovers and friends.

Lifeskills training groups can be run on both pre-service and in-service bases for health professionals and paraprofessionals. One-to-one helping skills may be taught to medical residents through to support staff, for instance hospital receptionists. There is a widespread need for relationship skills training for health workers. Training groups can be run in hospitals and nursing homes to sensitize staff both to each other's and to residents' needs (Allred, 1988). Additionally, medical staff can be trained to recognize patients who should be referred to psychologists or psychiatrists. Furthermore, training groups can be run to help health workers to cope with work-related problems and stresses, for instance on how to avoid burnout and on how to work through feelings about being with badly disfigured or dying patients.

BUSINESS AND INDUSTRY

Lifeskills training groups in business and industry are big business. Toomer (1982) writes of the American scene: 'it has been suggested that industry spends more money on education and training than the public service does on educating and training students in elementary and secondary school' (p. 20). Much of this training is in non-psychological work skills. However, there is still a considerable amount of psychological lifeskills training aimed both at improving efficiency and morale and also at preventing psychological health problems.

Three broad areas for lifeskills training groups in business and industry are: career development, communication skills and mental wellness. Training groups in the career development area can be on such topics as: career planning, job enrichment, preparation for transfer to a new location, coping with job loss and retirement skills. Effective communication is important within organizations and also in delivering customer services (Georges, 1989; Goldstein & Gilliam, 1990). Lifeskills training groups for within-organization communication skills encompass: management and leadership, supervision, team building, negotiation, managing conflict, assertion, cross-cultural communication, counselling, expressing appreciation, creative problem-solving, conducting effective meetings, and public speaking. Training groups for delivering customer services can focus on skills of: listening, negotiating, sending clear messages, and managing anger and conflict.

The cost of psychological problems both to business and industry and to individuals is substantial. For the employer the negative effects include absenteeism, industrial accidents, underachievement and interpersonal conflict. Such problems can involve the costs of under-utilization of plant, sick pay, absenteeism/overtime and replacement training (Osipow, 1982). A high proportion of those losing jobs in business and industry are dismissed because of communication problems, substance abuse and other psychological problems. Training groups for mental and physical wellness include: stress management, weight control, smoking cessation, alcohol and drug education, marital and family relationship skills and physical fitness (Wilbur & Vermilyea, 1982; Blanchard, 1989). These groups can be targeted at all levels, for instance managers, supervisors, production-line employees and sales staff.

MARRIAGE AND FAMILY AGENCIES

Lifeskills training groups for marital and family competencies do not fit neatly into any single setting. Partner relationship skills and parenting skills are the two main emphases. Such groups may be run in out-patient clinics, counselling services, churches, voluntary agencies such as Relate, and privately. Nowadays numerous people live in *de facto* relationships, either temporarily, or prior to or instead of marriage. Consequently, partner relationship skills are important for both unmarried and married people. Such skills include: listening, self-disclosing, asserting yourself and helping your partner to do likewise, expressing caring, identifying and engaging in joint rewarding activities, cooperative decision making, building trust, managing anger, managing conflict and sexual-relating skills (Nelson-Jones, 1990). Also, training groups sometimes focus on the sex-role expectations and behaviours of partners and on the problems of dual-career couples (Amatea & Cross, 1983).

Numerous training groups exist for effective parenting skills. A prime example is Gordon's parent effectiveness training (Gordon, 1970). This programme focuses on the skills of active listening, and sending 'I' messages, and on his 'no-lose' method of resolving conflicts. Other skills for parent training groups include: increasing the exchange of rewarding behaviours in parent–child conflicts (Raue & Spence, 1985), assertion (Clifford, 1987), managing anger (Nomellini & Katz, 1983), behaviour management skills for dealing with children (Webster-Stratton *et al.*, 1989), fathering skills (Resnik *et al.*, 1978) and learning how to be sexuality educators (Bundy & White, 1990).

MISCELLANEOUS SETTINGS

Other than those listed above, there are many further settings for lifeskills training groups. These include the following:

- *Voluntary agencies*. Voluntary agencies cover an enormous range of activities. Examples of training groups run in voluntary agencies include: coping with grief and bereavement, coping with homosexuality, and providing care in a church community.

- *Government agencies*. Many of the lifeskills training groups run in business and industry are also relevant for people in local and national government. They are also pertinent to armed forces personnel of all ranks.

- *Career and employment services*. The kinds of lifeskills training groups run in career services include: knowledge of the world of work, decision making, information seeking and interview skills.

- *Prisons*. Training groups can be run for prison officers, for instance managing stress or anger. Groups may also be run for adult prisoners and juvenile delinquents, for example on relationship skills (Sarason, 1976), anger and aggression management (Schlichter & Horan, 1981), and finding and keeping employment (Weissman, 1985).

- *Private practices*. Helping-service professionals often provide consultation and training groups for social service agencies, schools, courts, clergy, police and other community service agencies. Private practitioners may also, on their own premises, run training groups for the public: for example, on relationship or stress management skills.

- *Retirement communities and nursing homes*. Quality of life is a very important issue for old people. Training groups can focus on such issues as adapting to a retirement or nursing home community and making friends (Plesma & Flanagan, 1986), assertion skills (sometimes in relation to dealing with grasping offspring), use of leisure skills, values clarification, coping with physical changes, and dying and survivorship.

WHAT ARE LIFESKILLS?

What are skills?

The meanings of the word *skill* include proficiency, competence and expertise in some activity. However, the essential element of any skill is the ability to make and implement a sequence of choices to achieve a desired objective. For instance, if you are to be good at asserting yourself or managing stress, you have to make and implement effective choices in these lifeskills areas. Also, if you are to be good as a training group leader, you have to make and implement effective choices in leader skills such as facilitating groups, speaking well in public and demonstrating skills clearly.

The concept of skills is best viewed not as an either/or matter in which you either possess or do not possess a skill. Rather, it is preferable to think of yourself as possessing *skills strengths* or *weaknesses* or a mixture of the two. If you make good choices in a skills area, this is a skills strength. If you make poor choices, this is a skills weakness. Put simply, the criterion for good or poor choices is whether they help or hinder you in assuming personal responsibility for your happiness and fulfilment.

In all lifeskills areas you are likely to possess both skills strengths and weaknesses in varying degrees. For instance, in the skills area of listening, you may be good at understanding talkers, but poor at showing them that you have actually understood. The object of lifeskills training groups is to help participants, in one or more skills areas, to shift the balance of their strengths and weaknesses more in the direction of strengths. The object of training lifeskills group leaders is the same, but in regard to training skills rather than lifeskills. In both instances those being trained are helped to affirm themselves and others by becoming *better choosers*.

Defining lifeskills

There are a number of ways to approach a positive definition of lifeskills. Some of these are explored below.

Lifeskills entail *personally responsible choices*. When people are being personally responsible they are in the process of making the choices that maximize their happiness and fulfilment. Personal responsibility is a positive concept whereby people are responsible for their well-being and making their own choices. Lifeskills are the component skills by means of which people assume rather than avoid personal responsibility for their lives. Lifeskills are also *self-help skills*. They are competencies that enable people to help themselves. As such they empower rather than depower or weaken people (Hopson & Scally, 1981).

Lifeskills are conducive to *mental wellness*. People who are stunted in their possession of lifeskills are less able to fulfil their potential and meet their needs than those more skilled. Psychological distress both reflects and results from deficiencies in lifeskills. However, this is less true for biologically influenced disorders, for instance schizophrenia (Lazarus, 1989). Lifeskills possess a *psychological component*. Virtually any skill, for instance tying a shoelace, might be viewed as a lifeskill. However, almost all the lifeskills mentioned in this book have a large 'mind' component in them. Thus, even though many lifeskills are stated as specific observable behaviours, they usually heavily involve people's thoughts and feelings as well.

Lifeskills are *processes*. They are not static, but are processes requiring effective sequences of choices. Throughout their lives people are choosers. Humans can never escape the need to choose among possibilities (Frankl, 1969). People who possess a lifeskill make the choices involved in implementing that lifeskill. People require a *repertoire* of lifeskills. To attain their full human potential, people require a repertoire of lifeskills in a number of different areas. These lifeskills need to be appropriate both to their developmental tasks at any particular stage of their life-span and also to any special problems of living, challenges or transitions that they may face.

Below, some of the above threads are drawn together into a definition of lifeskills for this book.

> Lifeskills are personally responsible sequences of choices in specific psychological skills areas conducive to mental wellness. People require a repertoire of lifeskills according to their developmental tasks and specific problems of living.

Attitude, knowledge and skills

It can be helpful to think of specific lifeskills as comprising three dimensions: attitude, knowledge and skills.

- *Attitude.* An appropriate attitude to any lifeskill is that you assume personal responsibility for acquiring, maintaining, using and developing it. You may lose some or all of a lifeskill if you fail to work at using and developing it. A personally responsible attitude is the motivational or 'wanting to do it' dimension of a lifeskill.

- *Knowledge.* Any lifeskill involves knowledge concerning what are the correct choices to make. People who have been exposed to good examples, for instance by their parents' behaviour, may possess the required knowledge implicitly rather than explicitly. People with skills weaknesses are likely to need the relevant knowledge clearly 'spelled out' so that they can instruct themselves. Knowledge is the 'knowing how to do it' dimension of a lifeskill.

- *Skill.* The skill dimension entails the application of attitude and knowledge to practice. Skills can be the 'inner game', focusing on feeling and thinking, as well as the 'outer game', focusing on observable actions. In appropriate circumstances, you translate your 'wanting to do it' and 'knowing how to do it' into 'actually doing it'.

Some specific lifeskills

In the section on the scope of lifeskills groups, many different skills areas were identified. Here a comprehensive list of lifeskills for all settings and stages of the human life-span is not provided: rather, a list of some central lifeskills for most people is given. Other writers have attempted to divide lifeskills into different categories. For instance, Egan and Cowan have six categories of skills relating to: (1) physical development; (2) intellectual development; (3) self-management; (4) value-clarification; (5) interpersonal involvement; and (6) small-group involvement (Egan & Cowan, 1979). Hopson and Scally discuss lifeskills training in relation to five specific situations: (1) education; (2) work; (3) home; (4) leisure; and (5) the community (Hopson & Scally, 1981). Below, lifeskills are categorized into seven areas: (1) feeling; (2) thinking; (3) relationships; (4) study; (5) work; (6) leisure; and (7) health. If anything, the feeling and thinking categories contain the fundamental psychological skills. They are highly relevant to the other five categories, which represent areas of human functioning. The list of lifeskills has been incorporated into Exercise 1. This exercise asks you to rate yourself on different skills. The idea behind the exercise is to create interest by encouraging you both to look at your own lifeskills and also to identify lifeskills areas in which you might lead groups.

Exercise 1 Assess your lifeskills

INSTRUCTIONS

The questionnaire that follows lists a number of lifeskills in seven broad areas. Rate how satisfied you are with your lifeskills by using the rating scale below.

3   *much* need for improvement
2   *moderate* need for improvement
1   *slight* need for improvement
0   *no* need for improvement

Put a question mark (?) rather than a rating by any lifeskill whose meaning is not clear to you. If a lifeskills area is not relevant to you, for example study, you may choose not to respond in that area.

YOUR RATING	LIFESKILLS
	1. FEELING
....	Acknowledging the importance of your feelings
....	Awareness of and openness to your feelings
....	Awareness of your wants and wishes
....	Inner empathy/ability to 'tune in to' and explore feelings
....	Awareness of your body sensations
....	Capacity to experience your sensuality
....	Capacity for spontaneity
....	Full awareness of the parameters of existence: for example, death, suffering, fate
	2. THINKING
....	Possessing a realistic conceptual framework
....	Assuming personal responsibility for the choices that 'make' your life
....	Using coping self-talk
....	Choosing your personal rules
....	Choosing how you perceive
....	Attributing cause accurately
....	Predicting risk and reward
....	Setting personal goals

.... Using visualizing skills
.... Decision-making skills
.... Managing-problems skills

3. RELATIONSHIPS
.... Ability to own your thoughts, feelings and
actions in relationships
.... Disclosing personal information
.... Expressing feelings appropriately
.... Sending good voice messages
.... Sending good body messages
.... Sending good touch messages
.... Overcoming your shyness
.... Making initial contact skills
.... Conversational skills
.... Good listening
.... Helpful responding
.... Asserting yourself
.... Showing caring
.... Relating sexually
.... Managing anger
.... Managing conflict
.... Awareness of sex-role issues
.... Awareness of cross-cultural issues
.... Skills for specific roles: for example, parenting,
dealing with elderly relatives (stipulate
role and skills) ....
....

4. STUDY
.... Making educational choices wisely
.... Setting goals
.... Managing time effectively
.... Ability to meet deadlines
.... Effective reading
.... Writing skills
.... Coping with achievement/examination anxiety
.... Coping with maths/statistics anxiety
.... Ability to be creative
.... Ability to think critically
.... Participating in groups
.... Speaking in public

5. WORK

.... Accurately identifying your values
.... Accurately identifying your interests
.... Realistically appraising your abilities and skills
.... Awareness of opportunities
.... Information-gathering skills
.... Decision-making skills
.... Written self-presentation skills
.... Job interview skills
.... Skills for constructively evaluating feedback
.... Preparing for and handling transitions skills
.... Ability to develop/make the most of your work setting
.... Teamwork skills
.... Business/money-related skills
.... Skills for specific roles; for example, managing, supervising, providing customer services (stipulate role and skills) ....

....

6. LEISURE

.... Ability to value leisure time highly
.... Awareness of personally rewarding interests and activities
.... Information-gathering skills
.... Decision-making skills
.... Willingness to develop skills in specific activities
.... Ability for passive relaxation
.... Having adequate and enjoyable holidays

7. HEALTH

.... Assuming responsibility for your health
.... Eating nutritionally and in moderation
.... Adequate control of alcohol consumption
.... Avoidance of smoking
.... Avoidance of addictive drugs
.... Keeping physically fit
.... Managing stress well
.... Observing a good balance between work, relationship, family and recreational activities

Conclude the exercise by writing out a summary statement that identifies as specifically as possible the areas in which you might:

1.   develop your own lifeskills; and
2.   be a lifeskills trainer.

LEADERSHIP ROLE AND STYLE

As the name suggests, the leader role in training groups is that of trainer. Though lifeskills groups may involve releasing participants' existing potentials, their major emphasis is on systematically instructing them in skills. The word trainer is used because it has stronger connotations than the word teacher with respect to three important aspects of acquiring and developing lifeskills. First, training emphasizes the learning of practical rather than intellectual skills. Second, training suggests experiential learning or 'hands-on' learning-by-doing. Third, training entails participatory learning – the learner is an active participant in setting and achieving goals. Throughout this book, to emphasize the importance of participatory learning, members of training groups are called participants.

Didactic and facilitative leadership styles

Despite the wide variety of group approaches, there are basically two main styles of leading groups. Each style consists of a cluster of leadership skills. Stating the two extreme positions, the leader may be either didactic or facilitative. Let us look in turn at each of these extreme leadership styles.

The adjective 'didactic' means instructing or having the manner of a teacher. Didactic group leaders are highly task-orientated. Achieving the teaching or training goals of the group comes first, with the fostering of group interaction and relationships coming a poor second. Didactic leaders are the experts who know best how to impart knowledge and skills. It is a jug-and-mug approach to group work. The leader keeps control of what is poured into participants, how and when. Didactic lifeskills group leaders have developed or decided upon the content of their programmes in advance. These leaders do not allow participants to share in decisions on goals and methods. What experiential component they allow in their groups involves coaching, rehearsal and feedback, with little time for discussion. At all times, teacher knows best.

The adjective 'facilitative' means making easy or easier, assisting or helping. Facilitative group leaders are more concerned with the quality of relationships in the group and with helping participants to explore and experience their feelings than with any systematic training in specific skills. Much time is spent working to improve the here-and-now relationships in the group and on trying to release the group's healing potential. The facilitative leader shares responsibility with the participants for how the group develops. Though the leader may give feedback, this is more in response to material generated in the group than any systematic attempt to impart skills. Participants are free to accept or reject the leader's comments. A major agenda of the facilitative leader is helping participants to drop their social masks and thus engage in genuine encounters both with themselves and with each other.

Plotting the way a leader works on a simple two-dimensional continuum is an unsatisfactory way to look at lifeskills group leadership style.

Didactic .... Facilitative

Most training group leaders use both didactic and facilitative skills. In any group a tension almost invariably exists between how much they emphasize each cluster of skills. Training group leaders may alter the balance with regard to either the particular needs of different clienteles or to the particular needs of a group at any given moment. Skilled training group leaders possess both good didactic skills and good facilitative skills that they use flexibly to attain group goals. Figure 1.1 is a four-dimensional framework for looking at training group leadership style.

High facilitative skills	Low facilitative skills
High didactic skills	High didactic skills
High facilitative skills	Low facilitative skills
Low didactic skills	Low didactic skills

Figure 1.1 *A four-dimensional framework for viewing training group leadership style*

The probability is that training group leaders possessing and using both high didactic and high facilitative training skills are generally more effective. Nevertheless, leaders exhibiting one of the two cross-over styles — high facilitative–low didactic and low facilitative–high didactic — may also do good work. For instance, leaders may have much scope for using didactic skills and little scope for using facilitative skills in large lifeskills training groups which, by force of numbers, are heavily focused on imparting information. On the other hand, leaders exhibiting high facilitative and low didactic training skills may be good at helping participants to learn from one another, if less good at helping participants to learn from them. Leaders combining low didactic with low facilitative training skills are to be avoided at all costs.

Defining training groups

This book heavily emphasizes the notion of *training group leaders as choosers*. Leaders must try to make the choices that best suit their goals and those of the group's participants. To do this adequately, the leader requires a repertoire of skills. Earlier, a definition of lifeskills was provided. A definition of training groups for this book is now given.

> Training groups are time-limited structured groups in which one or more leaders use a repertoire of didactic and facilitative skills to help participants to develop and maintain one

or more specific lifeskills. Important features of training groups include: no assumption of psychological disturbance, systematic instruction, experiential learning by doing, and a high degree of participant involvement.

SOME CRITICISMS AND RESERVATIONS

Lifeskills training groups are not magic. They are open to criticism from both professionals and participants. Much of this criticism relates to inadequate leader behaviour rather than to training groups as such. Below, some criticisms that might be made of lifeskills training groups are answered.

Effectiveness

Criticism: Training groups are of varying degrees of effectiveness.

Answer: There are many considerations that make for an effective training group: leader skills, the state of readiness and degree of motivation of participants, the time available and so on. Systematically run training groups, based on theory and research, are still a relatively recent development. Furthermore, there has been a dearth of skilled leaders. One reason for this is that helping-service training programmes, when they teach groupwork, are more inclined to focus on leading counselling groups than leading training groups. Unfortunately, some leaders have made exaggerated claims for lifeskills groups. This may partly reflect ethical shortcomings, for instance wanting to 'make a quick quid'. Also, some leaders inadequately acknowledge that lifeskills training is a matter not just of participants learning new skills strengths, but of unlearning old, and sometimes rigidly held, skills weaknesses.

Leading a training group is difficult, not easy. Lifeskills training requires more work on its theoretical underpinning: for instance, psychology is weaker on theories of optimum as contrasted with abnormal functioning (Maslow, 1962, 1970). Further development and research validation of training skills is also desirable. Particular attention should be paid to considerations related to assisting the transfer and maintenance of lifeskills to real-life settings. Furthermore, potential training group leaders require systematic training by skilled trainers rather than being left to 'fly by the seat of their pants'.

Trainability

Criticism: People vary in their suitability for training groups.

Answer: This is correct. Joining a lifeskills training group is not a universal panacea. Some people, particularly those who have been unfortunate enough to have received a severe lack of nurturing when growing up, may be better off in individual counselling. Either concurrently or later they may join a training group. Others may resist joining training groups or not commit themselves to them if they do join.

Some people are threatened by any group approach to helping. Others may find the concept of lifeskills hard to grasp. They may consider that lifeskills are inherent rather than learned. Also, some may find it difficult to admit that they require lifeskills training. It means acknowledging that they have room for improvement.

Another problem, common to much of education, is that lifeskills training groups may insufficiently take into account individuals' needs and states of readiness. A further problem where training groups are prescribed, for instance as part of a school curriculum, is that not everyone wants to be there. For instance, some boys may think it 'sissy' to be trained in relationship skills. Furthermore, they may then disrupt the class in ways that interfere with the learning of interested peers (Nelson-Jones, 1986). In short, the issue of trainability is a complex one. The improvement of both training group content and of leaders' skills may make it less of a problem in future.

Depersonalization and superficiality

Criticism: People are more than skills, and just focusing on their lifeskills is superficial.

Answer: Arbuckle (1976) observes that the history of trying to teach a person to be a more effective human being is about as dismal as the history of traditional psychoanalysis in curing a person of sickness. He adds that he has known many ineffective people who possessed many of the mechanical skills of being an effective person. On the other hand, there are innumerable people who fail to actualize their human potential because they mechanically repeat learned patterns of ineffective behaviour. Poorly designed and led training groups can be superficial and depersonalize. However, well-designed and led training groups are advocated here. As much as possible, these groups should be based on good theory, take into account their participants' states of readiness and stages of psychological development, and focus on feelings as well as on thinking and acting. Low-functioning people, possibly unawares, can depersonalize both themselves and others by being highly manipulative. Well-designed training groups can help to give them skills to meet their needs without resorting to mechanical and superficial manipulation.

Conformity

Criticism: Training groups insufficiently prize participants' individuality.

Answer: There can be a danger in moving away from a counselling model, with its emphasis on uncovering and bringing out people's existing potentials, to a training model, with an emphasis on skills education. This danger may be represented by words like brainwashing and conformity. There are risks that, instead of encouraging personal responsibility and autonomy, training group leaders tell people how they should be. Consequently, participants may replace one set of externally based 'musts', 'oughts' and 'shoulds' with another. This may be an especial risk in areas where there can be a deep sense of injustice, for instance in some women's and homosexual groups. An answer to this is better selection and training of leaders. The fact that training groups are sometimes poorly conducted is not a reason for abandoning them altogether. Effective training groups can provide people with the skills both of getting more deeply in touch with what they think and feel and of expressing this assertively. Fostering such skills is the opposite of encouraging conformity.

YOUR GROUP LEADER AS TRAINER SKILLS: INITIAL ASSESSMENT

To end this chapter, you are requested to give an initial assessment of your skills strengths and weaknesses as a lifeskills training group leader. You will be asked to reassess yourself with the same questionnaire at the book's end. The initial presentation of this questionnaire is meant to get you thinking in a self-referent way about what are the central skills of being a training group leader.

Exercise 2 Assess your skills strengths and weaknesses as a training group leader

Using the following format, make a worksheet for assessing your skills strengths and weaknesses for leading lifeskills training groups. Answer each category as best you can at this stage of the book.

SKILLS AREA	MY STRENGTHS	MY WEAKNESSES
Prepare training groups		
Design lifeskills programmes		
Assess and help self-assessment		
Facilitate training groups		
Speak in public		
Demonstrate lifeskills		
Design and implement structured activities		
Prepare and manage individual training sessions		
Consolidate self-help skills and end training groups		
Evaluate and research training groups		

Make a list of your main skills strengths and weaknesses. Hopefully, working with this book will help you to shift the balance more in the direction of skills strengths. You may wish to refer back to your initial assessment when, at the book's end, you reassess your group leader as trainer skills.

CHAPTER HIGHLIGHTS

Terms like psychological education, human resource development, lifeskills teaching, and personal and social education have been used to describe lifeskills training.

The scope for training groups is vast. Settings for training groups include: elementary and high schools; colleges and universities; medical settings; business and industry; marriage and family agencies; and many others.

Lifeskills are personally responsible sequences of choices in specific psychological skills areas conducive to mental wellness. People require a repertoire of lifeskills according to their developmental tasks and specific problems of living.

Categories of lifeskills include: feeling; thinking; relationships; study; work; leisure; and health.

The group leader as trainer requires good didactic and facilitative skills.

Training groups are time-limited structured groups in which one or more leaders use a repertoire of didactic and facilitative skills to help participants to develop and maintain one or more specific lifeskills. Important features of training groups include: no assumption of psychological disturbance, systematic instruction, experiential learning by doing, and a high degree of participant involvement.

Reservations about training groups include: their effectiveness; the degree to which lifeskills are trainable; whether they are superficial and depersonalize participants; and whether they erode personal responsibility and encourage conformity.

TWO
Acquiring and Maintaining Lifeskills: An Overview

If we do not change our direction, we are likely to end up where we are headed.

Chinese proverb

CHAPTER QUESTIONS

How do people learn lifeskills strengths and weaknesses?

How do some become successful in coping with life's tasks, whereas others lead stunted and unproductive lives?

What inner and outer factors influence how people acquire lifeskills?

What inner and outer factors influence how people maintain lifeskills?

INTRODUCTION

Given that humans are only weakly programmed by their instincts (Maslow, 1962, 1970), what are the processes by which they acquire lifeskills? Below, some factors influencing how people acquire lifeskills strengths and weaknesses are suggested. However, it is insufficient only to discuss how people learn lifeskills in the first place, because they may either maintain or fail to maintain what they have learned. There is an important distinction between *acquisition* and *maintenance*. Consequently, there follows a discussion of how people maintain their lifeskills strengths and weaknesses. More often than not, as a lifeskills group leader you work with people who already have skills weaknesses that they maintain. Thus, lifeskills training partly helps people to unlearn skills weaknesses as well as to learn different and better skills strengths.

This overview does not claim to be a comprehensive presentation of personality and developmental psychology. Nevertheless, attention is paid to how people acquire and maintain lifeskills for a number of reasons. First, highlighting the processes by which people acquire and maintain lifeskills before they enter training groups suggests processes and practices that leaders might either encourage or avoid in such groups. Whether explicit or implicit, all leaders operate from theoretical assumptions. They possess models of how people can be trained. Ideally, their models of how people learn and maintain skills strengths and weaknesses before training correspond with their models of how they can use training to help people to develop different and better skills. Second, the integrative theoretical position taken in this book is indicated. This position does not restrict itself to cognitive-behavioural theory, but also draws upon humanistic and existential insights (Nelson-Jones, 1984). Third, raising awareness about the learning histories that people bring into training groups can protect leaders against a naïve Pollyannaism. People who enter lifeskills groups at 10, 30 and 50 years of age have had respectively 10, 30 and 50 years of prior living. In varying degrees they will have built up a pattern of skills strengths and weaknesses. Leaders need to work from 'where people are at'. Participants' starting points can include considerable lack of awareness, faulty prior learning, and resistance to change.

SOME FACTORS IN ACQUIRING LIFESKILLS

Below are some important and somewhat overlapping factors that influence whether people acquire good or poor lifeskills.

Supportive relationships

People are active explorers of their environments not just passive receptacles. Bowlby (1979) talks of the concept of a secure base or attachment figure. He observes that there is accumulating evidence that humans of all ages are happiest and able to function most effectively when they feel that there is a trusted person who will come to their aid should difficulties arise. Rogers also stresses supportive relationships for releasing people's 'actualizing tendency' (Raskin & Rogers, 1989; Rogers, 1959, 1980) or inherent capacity to maintain, enhance and develop themselves. In particular, Rogers has focused on supporting others through empathy. Empathy entails not only sensitively and accurately understanding the inner worlds of others, but also communicating your understanding back to them so that they feel understood. Empathy helps others to listen better to themselves and get more in touch with their wants and wishes. Furthermore, people may now become freer to manifest lifeskills previously latent in their repertoire.

The role of supportive relationships when growing up goes far beyond the acquisition of specific lifeskills. The presence or absence of supportive relationships can either affirm or fail to confirm a person's core of personhood. Children may either feel themselves of value and possess the confidence to interact with the world or they may become inhibited, withdrawn and afraid to take risks. This lack of self-esteem may stop them from both learning and using lifeskills.

Role models

Bandura has been a prominent psychologist drawing attention to the power of learning from observing others' behaviour (Bandura, 1969, 1977, 1986). Skills weaknesses as well as strengths are frequently learned this way. Learning from observing others is pervasive. Observational learning is potentially insidious because much of it is unconscious. You learn and yet remain unaware that you have learned. Below are some examples of learning from others' examples.

- Kate, 23, grew up in a home where many significant feelings were neither acknowledged nor openly expressed. Now she has a boyfriend Robert, who says he would prefer it if she would let him know when she was angry rather than bottle it up.

- Carolyn, 15, observes her parents arguing a lot. Each parent is quick to blame the other. When someone criticizes Carolyn, however gently, she bristles and gets defensively aggressive.

- Ronald, 43, had a dad who was a workaholic and who died of a heart attack in his mid-fifties. Recently Ronald, who has similar work patterns to his dad, has been having chest pains. Ronald wonders if he should ease up before it is too late.

- Amanda, 36, worked for a supervisor, Maggie, who was good both at making her supervisees feel understood by her and at getting good work out of them. Amanda thinks that, by observing Maggie, she has picked up some effective supervision skills, for instance active listening and giving clear instructions.

Skills strengths and weaknesses in the areas of feeling, thinking and action can be learned from observing role models. For instance, Kate was helped to acquire the skills weakness of having trouble acknowledging her feelings from the absence of demonstration in her family. Her parents' examples also helped her to acquire the thinking skills weaknesses of thinking that she would never gain approval if she were to be more open. Furthermore, by not expressing some of her feelings, she acts in a closed way that mirrors her parents' behaviour.

Rewarding consequences

Learning lifeskills from observing role models is often intermingled with learning from rewarding or unrewarding consequences. For instance, in the above example, Kate's family, in addition to not disclosing their own feelings, may have sent unrewarding verbal and/or non-verbal messages that discouraged her from talking about her feelings to them. One of the factors affecting the influence of models is whether their behaviours bring about consequences perceived by observers as rewarding (Bandura, 1977).

Rewarding consequences can be either primary or secondary. Primary rewarding consequences are those that people find rewarding independent of their learning history: for instance, food, shelter, sex and human warmth. Skinner (1971) considers that all rewards eventually derive their power from evolutionary selection and that it is part of 'human nature' to be rewarded by particular things. However, he considers only a small part of behaviour to be immediately reinforced by rewards of evident biological significance. Most behaviour is manifested in response to secondary rewards, for example approval or money, that have become associated with or conditioned to primary rewards.

The role of rewarding consequences in helping or hindering people in acquiring lifeskills is immense. Virtually from the moment of birth, humans are given messages about how 'good' or 'bad' their actions are. Usually, with the best of intentions, adults try to reward children for developing the skills necessary to cope with the world. However, the rewards they provide are often deficient in various ways. For example, most people learn their relationship and thinking skills from a mixture of observing others, unsystematic feedback and trial-and-error. People are rarely systematically rewarded as they develop these lifeskills, either inside or outside the home. Furthermore, children are sometimes rewarded for exhibiting skills weaknesses rather than strengths. For example, they may find that they are more likely to get their way if they shout aggressively rather than take a more reasonable approach.

Another major problem in the use of external rewards is that people may continually look outside for a locus of evaluation rather than think through and get in touch with what they themselves think and feel (Raskin & Rogers, 1989; Rogers, 1959). Consequently, they may lack a secure sense of their own identity. An associated complication is that those receiving positive or negative rewarding consequences from others may sometimes fail to make the distinction between their specific behaviours being good or bad and their whole personhood being good or bad. Failure to make this distinction can undermine their self-esteem in at least two ways. On the one hand, because someone else thinks they have behaved badly, they may wrongly perceive themselves as bad. On the other hand, because someone else thinks that their behaviour is good, they may become dependent on that person's approval to maintain their fragile self-esteem. However, despite the above cautions, provision of rewarding consequences by others is central to how people learn to provide rewarding consequences for themselves.

Instruction

Much instruction in lifeskills is informal and takes place in the home. Some of this is very basic: for instance, asking children to say 'please' and 'thank you'. Children are often told by their parents and others how to relate, how to study, how to look after their health and so on. There are three important issues here. First, do the people giving the informal instruction have an adequate conceptual framework and understanding of the skills that they are attempting to pass on? It is possible to misinstructed as well as to instruct. For instance, children may be misinstructed both to be prejudiced against people who differ from them in various characteristics and also to deal with all perceived provocations on an 'eye for an eye, tooth for a tooth' basis. Second, do the instructors have an adequate model of instruction? Children are notorious for not listening to their parents. Attempts to impart lifeskills may falter either because children feel talked down to or because they do not see the relevance of the instruction. Third, to what extent are children then able to instruct themselves in the lifeskills that others have attempted to impart? Arguably, if learners do not know how to talk themselves through the sequences of choices involved in the skills, many lifeskills have been inadequately learned. Much instruction falls far short of this self-instructional objective.

In Chapter 1 mention was made of some systematic attempts in schools to train people in lifeskills. To date, these kinds of lifeskills groups are probably the exception rather than the rule. Inside and outside education there is still a widespread assumption that the main role of educational institutions is academic rather than practical. Allied to this is the assumption that the home is the main arena for acquiring lifeskills. Some parents may see attempts to teach lifeskills in the schools as usurping their roles. Furthermore, conflicts can arise between lifeskills taught in schools and those espoused in the home. For instance, argumentative parents may not like being told by their children that in school they are being taught that the best way to handle conflicts is by assuming a cooperative rather than a competitive attitude. Doubts about the effectiveness of lifeskills training and about the skills, qualifications and experience of leaders also work against the adoption of lifeskills groups in schools.

A further problem in lifeskills instruction is that the idea of skills in certain areas is alien to many. For instance, it is common for people to talk about work skills, study skills or even health maintenance skills. However, it is much less common for them to talk about feeling, thinking and relationship skills. Difficulties in instructing people in lifeskills are created when they fail to acknowledge that the concept of skills is applicable and provides them with 'handles' to work in many important areas of their lives.

Self-instruction

Self-instruction is another important way in which people acquire lifeskills. Self-instruction can help people to consolidate lifeskills in which they may have received either formal or informal instruction. For instance, people who have received instruction in interview skills can then rehearse and practise them by instructing themselves as they visualize using the skills in an imaginary interview. Another way in which self-instruction helps to consolidate skills entails drawing conclusions from their application. As a result of learning from practice, people can instruct themselves in better ways to apply the skills to particular situations that they confront.

Many people try to improve their lifeskills through reading self-instructional books. Popular examples of such books include Norman Vincent Peale's *The*

Power of Positive Thinking (Peale, 1953), Wayne Dyer's *Your Erroneous Zones* (Dyer, 1977) and Alberti and Emmons's *Your Perfect Right: A Guide to Assertive Living* (1986). These self-instructional books can help people to acquire a richer conceptual framework for understanding the skills they need for their lives. However, sometimes the understanding of lifeskills acquired from books falls far short of that required to apply the skills. Also, self-instructional books may insufficiently motivate people to use and practise the skills.

Information

People need adequate information if they are to develop lifeskills. For instance, keeping them in ignorance about basic facts of death and sexuality impedes their self-awareness and capacity for emotional responsiveness. Human beings often relate to their children on the basis of lies, omissions of truth and partial truths (Steiner, 1974). Adults may protect themselves in the eyes of their children in ways that blunt their children's awareness of the world. Also, children are heavily dependent on the amount and accuracy of information available from significant adults. For example, an adult who does not understand the concept of anxiety may mislabel a child's social anxiety as 'wimpishness' or 'being difficult', thus blocking the child's self-understanding and harming the child's self-esteem.

Opportunity

Children, adolescents and adults all need the availability of adequate opportunities in line with their maturation to test out and develop their lifeskills. However, many people's chances of exploring themselves and developing a sense of their own competencies in areas such as relationships, study, work or leisure are restricted. Below are some examples.

- Darren, 17, is very worried about his relationship skills. He has had little experience of girls since he has three younger brothers and no sisters and also his parents sent him to a single-sex boarding school out in the countryside.

- Fiona, 25, thinks that she lacks public speaking skills. She has just been appointed a polytechnic lecturer after completing her PhD. She has never taken a class and admits to having been very nervous on the few occasions she was asked to give seminar papers as a student.

- Andrew, 39, would like to develop his leisure skills by taking up golf. However, there are no public courses where he lives and the private golf clubs in his area are far beyond his budget.

- Hanif, 16, would like to acquire cooking skills. However, there are no cooking classes available in his secondary school.

- Anne, 17, never received help for her exam anxiety when at secondary school because no one knew how to help her. She hopes that at university she can learn better skills for coping with her debilitating exam anxiety.

Challenge and confrontation

People are challenged by life to develop skills. Challenge is implicit in any learning. Learning entails risking giving up the safety of the known to acquire better skills. Transition points in people's lives, such as moving to a new area, school or job or having one's first child, frequently act as a stimulus for skills development. However, sometimes these challenges are met in ways that reactivate previous skills weaknesses, like social withdrawal, rather than in positive ways. Adversity and pain can also help people to acquire lifeskills. Though adversity can erode some people's confidence, others rise above it. The break-up of a relationship, unexpected loss of a job, or coming to terms with an illness or injury, can each be opportunities for personal growth. Frankl (1959) writes of how, even in Nazi concentration camps, some people were able to use their suffering as an opportunity for personal growth.

People exist in the world of their perceptions (Beck & Weishaar, 1989; Combs *et al.*, 1976; Ellis, 1962, 1980, 1989). These perceptions are of varying degrees of accuracy. For instance, parents may assume that all is well in the family yet suddenly be confronted with the acute distress of one of their children, for instance by a suicide gesture. One response to such a confrontation is to externalize it – the child is the problem. Another response is to use the confrontation as an opportunity to explore their own behaviour towards the child. Where this degree of openness exists, confrontations can not only enlarge people's perceptions, but can also provide them with the opportunity to develop their lifeskills. There are many instances in most people's lives where they are confronted with negative or positive feedback that, for good or ill, they may use to develop their skills.

Peer group interaction

Peer groups provide one of the main avenues for learning lifeskills strengths and weaknesses. Peer groups can provide presence or absence of supportive relationships, role models, rewarding consequences, instruction, information, opportunity, challenge and confrontation. Below are some examples of people acquiring lifeskills through social interaction in a peer group.

- Sally and Daniel are parents of two pre-school children. Sally and Daniel mix a lot with parents of other pre-schoolers and find it mutually helpful to exchange information on how best to deal with their children.

- Matthew has just been appointed a bank manager. Matthew has made friends with a number of other bank managers so that they can learn from each other's experience.

- Alice was blinded in an industrial accident six months ago. Alice meets weekly with a self-help group of other recently blinded people for emotional support and also so that they can exchange coping strategies.

- Michelle is one of a group of medical students who discuss how best to survive the onslaught of the extremely heavy workload.

- Lisa's husband died recently. Lisa has a support network whose members have also had to cope with the death of a loved one. Lisa has learned from her friends many skills, both for coming to terms with grief and for surviving on her own.

Learning from peer group interaction can be for good or ill. Every peer group has its rules or norms of varying degrees of explicitness concerning appropriate behaviour on the part of its members. In each of the above examples, people probably learned more skills strengths than weaknesses from their peer groups. However, other peer groups may have norms, for instance hatred of people who are racially different or heavy participation in substance abuse, that are lifeskills weaknesses. Also, there is the danger that participants in any peer groups, whether their norms are constructive or destructive, allow the members to do their thinking for them. Insufficient autonomous thought is a major lifeskills weakness.

Thinking skills

Thinking skills are important lifeskills to be acquired both in their own right and because they contribute to learning and using other lifeskills (Beck & Weishaar, 1989; Ellis, 1989; Nelson-Jones, 1989). Mention has already been made that people who do not realize that skills are involved in various areas of their lives, for instance in their relationships, are less likely to have 'handles' for developing competencies than those acknowledging that specific skills are desirable. Also, the idea that skills are sequences of choices can help people to work on developing them. They can identify the choices involved in the skills and then choose whether or not to make them.

The thinking skill that you are personally responsible for developing and using the lifeskills conducive to your survival, happiness and fulfilment is an overriding lifeskill (May & Yalom, 1989; Nelson-Jones, 1984). The extent to which people acquire this attribution of assuming responsibility for making their lives influences how motivated they may be to acquire and develop their lifeskills. Assuming personal responsibility goes deeper than verbal acknowledgement of it. Your feeling, thinking and action choices need to be clearly based on this assumption, too. You need not only to 'talk the talk' but also to 'walk the walk'. Below are examples of people either assuming or avoiding personal responsibility for acquiring and developing their lifeskills.

- Philip has an unhappy relationship with his 12-year-old son Stuart. Philip locates the problems in Stuart and thinks 'Stuart has to learn to grow up before we can be happy together'. Philip's inability to assume responsibility for acquiring better parenting skills helps to keep both Stuart and himself stuck in their repetitive cycles of negative behaviour.

- Linda is manager of a shop selling office equipment. A year ago she became aware that many of the 30 employees who worked in the shop were unhappy in their work. Linda had a series of conversations with her staff to find out the reasons for their dissatisfaction. Feedback about her behaviour included the facts that some staff found her offhand and that also she rarely expressed appreciation to anyone. Linda accepted these criticisms and worked on avoiding 'put-downs' and her expressing-appreciation skills. Once Linda acquired better managerial skills, both morale and sales in the shop noticeably improved.

The capacity to be realistic about the role of mistakes and setbacks during the process of acquiring a lifeskill is another important thinking skill. The assumption that acquiring a lifeskill involves continuous improvement is erroneous, causing people to become discouraged when inevitable mistakes and setbacks occur. Sometimes, when initially acquiring a skill, learners may appear to get worse before getting better. For example, shy adolescents starting dating may be highly conscious of their inadequacies. If they tell themselves 'Mistakes and setbacks are terrible and I will never be any good', they may give up. However, if they tell themselves 'Mistakes and setbacks are uncomfortable, but I'm learning all the time and starting to do better', they are more likely to help themselves through the sometimes awkward period of trying out new behaviours. Usually, acquiring lifeskills is best represented by a jagged rather than a straight learning curve.

Another important thinking skill relevant to acquiring lifeskills is the ability to perceive your behaviour accurately. In the earlier examples of Philip and Linda, Linda was able to perceive her behaviour accurately and, hence, to initiate learning, whereas Philip was able to do neither. Perceiving your behaviour accurately is also important during learning. You can erode your confidence if you selectively focus on your weaknesses and difficulties at the expense of acknowledging your strengths and successes. On the other hand, you can erroneously think that you make more progress than the facts justify.

Anxiety

Thinking skills are also highly relevant to managing unhelpful as contrasted with helpful anxiety. In his book *The Inner Game of Tennis*, Gallwey observes that every game is composed of two parts: the outer game of playing your opponent and the inner game that takes place in the mind of each player. This inner game 'is played against such obstacles as lapses in concentration, nervousness, self-doubt and self-condemnation. In short, it is played to overcome all habits of mind which inhibit excellence in performance' (Gallwey, 1974, p. 11). Similarly, acquiring and maintaining lifeskills involves an inner game to deal with thinking skills weaknesses interfering with learning and performance. Gallwey focuses on teaching people the art of 'relaxed concentration'. Learning any lifeskill is best achieved when the mind is alert yet relaxed enough to devote all its energies to the task at hand.

Children grow up having both helpful and harmful experiences with respect to their self-esteem. The fortunate ones acquire a level of anxiety that acts both as a protection against actual dangers and as a motivator for realistic levels of achievement. Unfortunately adults, through their role modelling and the faulty examples provided for children's behaviours, often pass on and contribute to significant debilitating anxieties. These anxieties can be both the cause and effect of children's – and later adults' – thinking skills weaknesses. These weaknesses include: reluctance to assume responsibility for their lives; difficulty in facing reality; low tolerance of mistakes and setbacks; and inability to evaluate performance accurately. Other ways in which anxiety can interfere with skills acquisition and performance are: not hearing instructions clearly; insufficient awareness of significant information from practical learning situations; difficulty concentrating; thought blocking; feeling confused; and mentally and emotionally freezing. Since people's inner mental games are disrupted by anxiety, correspondingly their outer games of observable behaviour tend to suffer. Deficient behaviours resulting from, as well as manifesting, anxiety include: unwillingness to take realistic risks; tense and nervous rather than relaxed skills performance; a heightened tendency to say and do the wrong things; unnecessary aggression; excessive seeking of approval; and the combination of overstriving and underachieving.

Learning lifeskills entails learning not to let anxiety get in the way of acquiring and using the skills. People who either are helped to or who help themselves to acquire anxiety management skills may learn other skills more easily than those without anxiety management skills. Some anxiety management skills, for instance tensing and relaxing one's muscles or breathing slowly and regularly, help people to manage the physiological arousal associated with anxiety. Many anxiety management skills entail learning to think more effectively. These thinking skills include: choosing personal rules for one's own and for others' behaviour that are realistic rather than perfectionist (Ellis, 1980, 1989); using coping rather than anxiety-engendering self-talk (Meichenbaum, 1983; Meichenbaum & Deffenbacher, 1988); not jumping to unwarranted perceptual conclusions (Beck & Emery, 1985; Beck & Weishaar, 1989; Emery, 1982); and using good visualizing skills (Lazarus, 1977; Nelson-Jones, 1989).

Acquiring and using good lifeskills builds confidence and lowers anxiety, which in turn may help future lifeskills learning. Conversely, being highly anxious may impede the learning of some lifeskills and lead to poor performance in them. This poor performance may further raise anxiety and make future lifeskills learning even more difficult.

Sex-role considerations

This is a period in which traditional sex-roles are being challenged and changed. Nevertheless, males and females are still often brought up with different emphases in their lifeskills. In Western societies, certain psychological characteristics have traditionally been viewed as either 'feminine' or 'masculine'. Feminine characteristics have included being: affectionate, gentle, sensitive to the needs of others, tender and warm. Masculine characteristics have included being: aggressive, ambitious, assertive, analytical and dominant (Bem, 1974). The predominant traditional roles of women have been those of nurturers and social harmonizers. Men's traditional roles have focused on being breadwinners and disciplinarians.

Because of differing views about their psychological characteristics and sex-roles, males and females have been encouraged to develop different lifeskills strengths and weaknesses. With regard to relationship skills, Argyle (1984) states that the research evidence suggests that there are a number of areas where females may be more socially competent than males. These areas include: being better at sending and receiving body language, being more rewarding and polite, and disclosing more and forming closer friendships. However, Argyle notes that assertion is an area in which women appear to have more problems than men. Other areas where males and females may have been brought up with different lifeskills include the following:

- *Sexual relationships.* The male has traditionally been expected to be more of the initiator and to be more open about acknowledging and expressing sexuality than the female (Alberti & Emmons, 1986; Masters & Johnson, 1975).

- *Parenting.* Child care was mainly the responsibility of the female and hence it was less important for the male to learn parenting skills.

- *Home maintenance.* Females developed more skills in looking after the inside of the house, whereas males developed more skills in looking after the outside of the house, including the garden and car. Purchasing and preparation of food was mainly a female responsibility.

- *Education.* Where funds were limited in a family, it was more important to educate males than females, since homemaking was the main role of females. Male educational achievement was more valued than that of females.

- *Work.* The idea of having a career applied more to males than females. There were certain traditional feminine occupations – nursing, teaching, secretarial work – which reflected women's nurturing nature. Entrepreneurship and senior management required 'masculine' skills.

- *Leisure.* Female leisure interests traditionally centred more around the home and family than did those of the male with his pubs and clubs. In some respects the female was the social secretary to the male, doing much of his private and business entertaining.

Currently there are huge changes under way in how sex-roles are defined, negotiated and end up in practice. There has been an increase in talk about psychological androgyny. The androgynous male or female 'is flexible masculine or feminine as circumstances warrant' (Bem, 1981, p. 362). Thus males and females could be brought up with a range of lifeskills independently of whether they were traditionally regarded as 'masculine' or 'feminine'.

Perhaps enough has been said to indicate that in the past people's acquisition of lifeskills has been heavily influenced by their biological sex. Though sex-roles are changing, there are still numerous areas in which, subtly or not, males and females learn lifeskills differently.

Culture

Lifeskills learning is heavily influenced by the culture in which it takes place. Culture refers to the predominant patterns of behaviour and rules for living of a given group during a given period. Here are a few examples. Argyle conducted a study on the rules for social relationships in Britain, Italy, Hong Kong and Japan. He found that in the Eastern cultures, especially in Japan, there were more rules about obedience, avoiding loss of face, maintaining harmonious relationships in groups and restraining emotional expression (Argyle, 1986). Gaze, or looking at other people in the area of their faces, is perceived differently according to culture. In the 'contact cultures' of the Arab world, Latin America and Southern Europe, the amount of gaze is high. Too little gaze is seen as impolite and insincere. However, in 'non-contact' cultures like North America, Northern Europe and Asia, too much gaze is seen as threatening. Gestures have different meanings in different cultures, so misunderstanding body language can lead to embarrassing cross-cultural misunderstandings. In Greece, people toss their heads back to say 'no'. The 'A-Okay' sign in North America of thumb and forefinger in a circle means in France and Belgium 'You're worth nothing', and in southern Italy either means 'You asshole' or signifies that you desire anal sex (Ekman *et al.*, 1984). Level of self-disclosure may also differ according to culture. For example, British female undergraduate students have been found to disclose less than their American counterparts (Jourard, 1971). Language is an obvious manifestation of culture and cultural difference.

In Britain, there is a majority British culture that contains many subcultures within it. However, in addition, there are the cultures of numerous ethnic minority groups. During the 1984–1986 period, the size of Britain's ethnic minority population was around 2.4 million or 4.5 per cent of the total population of 54.2 million. Together, South Asians – Indians, Pakistanis and Bangladeshis – were 52 per cent of the total ethnic minority population; the West Indian and African groups, 26 per cent; the population of mixed origins, 10 per cent; the Chinese, about 5 per cent; and the Arabs about two and a half per cent. Some 57 per cent of the ethnic minority population had been born outside of the United Kingdom (Shaw, 1988). As Britain draws closer to Europe, numerous Britons are likely to have far more exposure to European cultures.

Social class

Lifeskills learning is also heavily influenced by social class considerations. Income, educational attainment and occupational status are three of the main ways in which social class is measured in Britain. Other indicators of social class include where you live, what school you attended, and your accent. Poverty, overcrowding, disease, lack of educational opportunity and support for educational aspirations work against people breaking out of lower-class constraints. Slum dweller lifeskills can be very different from those required at top public schools. Also, the skills required by the working class to relate to colleagues are different from those required in middle-class professions. Communication tends to be blunter and more direct amongst workers.

All people are shaped by their learning histories. People bring their learning histories into training groups. Above, 14 factors influencing how people acquire lifeskills have been presented. This listing is far from exhaustive.

SOME FACTORS MAINTAINING LIFESKILLS

There is an old story about someone asking for a pay rise on the basis of 19 years' experience and being told: 'You have had one year's experience which you have repeated eighteen times.' Once acquired, lifeskills strengths may be maintained and developed. Alternatively, these strengths may be transformed into weaknesses. Lifeskills weaknesses, once acquired, may also be maintained. Their continuation is sometimes at great personal cost. Paradoxically, people frequently choose to repeat behaviours that are unrewarding for themselves and others.

The challenge to maintain lifeskills strengths will be addressed at many points in the book. This section focuses on how people maintain lifeskills weaknesses. Especially with children, acquiring lifeskills strengths and weaknesses is more a matter of 'what the environment does to me' than 'what I do to myself'. Young people are frequently at the mercy of their elders. However, maintaining lifeskills strengths and weaknesses is a different matter to acquiring them initially. Here, partly because they are maintained into adulthood, the balance of attribution of cause shifts more in the direction of 'what I do to myself' than 'what the environment does to me'. The buck stops much more with the individual.

What people do to themselves

Below are some of the processes by which people maintain their lifeskills weaknesses. These processes focus heavily on thinking skills weaknesses.

ATTRIBUTIONAL DEFICIENCIES

How people assign cause greatly influences the degree to which they maintain lifeskills weaknesses. Earlier, mention was made that assuming responsibility for developing and using lifeskills was an overriding lifeskill. Assuming this responsibility consists of at least two areas: first, overall responsibility for making your life (Frankl, 1959; May & Yalom, 1989); and second, responsibility in specific situations.

Attributions of responsibility and cause are explanations that people give themselves to make sense of what happens in their lives. Faulty attributions are those which explain responsibility and cause inaccurately. Below are some potential attribution errors that people may use to sustain lifeskills weaknesses.

- 'It's my nature.' People may block themselves from change by saying that characteristics like laziness or excessive anger are their nature. They fail to realize that such lifeskills weaknesses are learned and then maintained.

- 'It's my unfortunate past.' People may blame their parents and others in their pasts for not being as they would like to be now. These attributions of inadequate upbringing may or may not be accurate perceptions of how their skills weaknesses were initially acquired. However, for people who have left home, they are largely irrelevant to how they maintain their skills weaknesses in the present.

- 'It's my bad luck.' People often make their luck. For example, a woman who keeps choosing inadequate partners may erroneously attribute her difficulties to bad luck rather than to her failure to develop choosing-partner lifeskills.

- 'It's my poor environment.' Undoubtedly, adverse social conditions like poverty, overcrowding, and poor housing may make it more difficult to develop certain lifeskills. However, many people have learned to overcome the skills weaknesses contributed to by their poor environments.

- 'It's all your fault.' This absolutist attribution of blame is possibly the most common reason why people stay stuck with managing-anger and conflict skills weaknesses. Why bother to develop your lifeskills when it is always someone else's fault? Responsibility for negative events is conveniently externalized.

- 'It's all my fault.' Blaming oneself all the time can also interfere with overcoming lifeskills weaknesses. Quite apart from cause being inaccurately identified, self-blame may erode the confidence that people need to deal with the realistic difficulties in their lives. Guilt can be a constructive emotion if it leads to better lifeskills. However, guilt can be destructive if it brings about self-disparagement rather than self-improvement. Overinternalizing responsibility for negative events is a characteristic of very depressed people (Weishaar & Beck, 1986).

UNREALISTIC PERSONAL RULES

Personal rules are the 'do's' and the 'don'ts' by which people lead their lives. Each person has an inner rulebook of standards for themselves and for others. Sometimes these standards are realistic and appropriately flexible. On other occasions the standards may be unrealistic and inappropriately rigid. Ellis has coined the term 'mustabation' to refer to rigid internal rules characterized by 'musts', 'oughts', and 'shoulds' (Ellis, 1980, 1989). Below are illustrations of mustabatory personal rules in different lifeskills areas. These unrealistic rules are not only lifeskills weaknesses in themselves, but also maintain other lifeskills weaknesses. For example, the feeling area rule that 'I shouldn't have negative feelings about other people' may interfere with open and honest communication necessary for intimacy. Other unrealistic personal rules include the following.

- Thinking. 'I must not think for myself.'

- Relationships. 'I must always be liked by everyone.'

- Study. 'I must always learn without making mistakes.'

- Work. 'I must always feel fulfilled in my work.'

- Leisure. 'Work must come before leisure.'

- Health. 'I must not acknowledge when my body feels stressed.'

FAULTY SELF-PERCEPTIONS

People can maintain lifeskills weaknesses if they erroneously think that their skills are adequate. Here are some examples.

- Andrew used to think that he looked after his health adequately until one day he had a heart attack. He then realized that he had adopted an 'It can't happen to me' attitude that had allowed him to keep smoking and eating too much.

- Carol thinks that she is a very affectionate person, though others do not find her so.

- Whenever her daughter Susan says that she is unhappy with their relationship, Mary says that she has done everything she can for her.

- Brian thinks of himself as an adequate public speaker. He does not seem to notice how bored his audience becomes when he speaks.

- Richard sees himself as a good lover who does not need to develop his skills. Others tell a different tale.

- Anita sees herself as an inadequate student, despite getting good marks. She is afraid to go on to university though her teachers tell her she has the ability to do well there.

In each of the above illustrations, people were seeing only what they wanted to see. They were giving way to the Nelson-Jones Reality Principle: 'If you cannot accept reality, create it' (Nelson-Jones, 1989). 'Defence mechanisms', 'defences' or 'security operations' are terms for the ways that people operate on incoming information that differs from their existing self-pictures (Arlow, 1989; Freud, 1936; Maslow, 1962, 1970; Sullivan, 1953). As in the case of Anita, it is possible to operate on positive feedback to sustain a negative self-picture as well as on negative feedback to sustain a positive self-picture (Rogers, 1959). In either instance, the faulty self-perceptions are likely to contribute to the individual maintaining lifeskills weaknesses.

Defensive perceptions involve people in diminishing their awareness of life in order to remain more psychologically comfortable in the short term. Below are some defensive processes.

- *Denial.* Totally warding off from conscious awareness feelings, thoughts and behaviours regarded as too frightening or threatening: for instance, homosexual feelings or clear evidence of your own hypocrisy.

- *Distortion.* Altering feedback that you do not like to make it more acceptable to you; for instance, perceiving that you would have received better marks if your teacher had read your paper more thoroughly when all the evidence points to the teacher being conscientious.

- *Rationalization.* Providing excuses when your behaviour causes you anxiety; for instance, making out that the reason why you have never developed adequate parenting skills is that you have always been so busy at work. Rationalizations differ from excuses in that people do not have full insight into their behaviour. In short, they deceive themselves as well as attempt to deceive others.

- *Avoidance.* Avoidance is a common manifestation of denial: for example, by remaining unaware that you avoid developing lifeskills in areas, for example confronting people, that you find difficult.

- *Externalizing responsibility.* Blaming other people rather than acknowledging your own responsibility for failing to develop your lifeskills.

- *Attack.* 'Attack is the best method of defence.' Attacking and intimidating others who either provide or might provide negative feedback about one or more of your lifeskills. Going for their jugular vein or disparaging their personality. Making up stories about yourself and others that make you seem in the right and them seem in the wrong.

- *Projection.* Projection entails externalizing something that is internal; for instance, experiencing difficulty in the lifeskill of controlling your sexuality and setting yourself up as a guardian of public morality. In such instances people would do better to work on their own lifeskills.

- *Defences against the good.* Blocking off and diluting both the awareness of and also the manifestation of positive qualities such as generosity and concern for others. Being out of touch with prosocial feelings maintains egocentricity. Possibly, humans are just as threatened by acknowledging their altruistic feelings as their less altruistic ones.

Negative self-labelling is another way in which people may sustain lifeskills weaknesses. Instead of perceiving themselves in a balanced fashion, they over-emphasize their negative points and underemphasize their positive points. The outcome of negative self-labelling may be twofold. First, people may undermine their overall level of self-esteem. Second, they may erode their confidence and motivation to improve specific lifeskills weaknesses.

NEGATIVE SELF-TALK

Negative self-talk may be contrasted with coping self-talk (Meichenbaum, 1977, 1983, 1985, 1986; Meichenbaum & Deffenbacher, 1988). Coping self-talk has two main functions: calming and coaching yourself. A sample calming self-instruction might be: 'Keep calm'. A sample coaching self-instruction might be: 'Break the task down and take one step at a time'. Below are some illustrative negative self-talk statements:

- 'I'm never going to be able to do it.'

- 'If I make a mistake it will be terrible.'

- 'I'm starting to feel anxious and this is a signal that things may get out of control.'

- 'The future is hopeless.'

- 'I can't stand setbacks.'

- 'I've tried before without success.'

The above are negative self-talk statements that may inhibit people from working on a range of lifeskills weaknesses. Negative self-talk may also refer to specific lifeskills weaknesses: for example, 'Learning to control my anger is far too difficult a task.'

FEAR OF CHANGE

Once acquired, lifeskills weaknesses can become well-established habits. People may become very resistant to giving them up (Ellis, 1985, 1987; Greiger, 1989). The following are seven possible components of fear of change. First, there is fear of the unknown. Changing a lifeskills weakness into a strength requires risking new behaviours. There is no longer the safety and certainty of the old habits. The unknown becomes a negative consequence in its own right, even though a realistic appraisal would indicate otherwise. Second, there is fear of making an effort. Changing some lifeskills weaknesses may be perceived to require the discomfort of effort. It may seem easier to stay as you are rather than make this effort. Third, there is fear of losing payoffs. There may be rewards and payoffs from maintaining lifeskills weaknesses. For instance, you may get your way if you are violent in the home and perceive a more reasonable approach as losing your influence.

Fourth, there is fear of others' disapproval. Giving up lifeskills weaknesses may bring you into conflict with other people. For instance, others may prefer you to be quiet, docile and nice rather than assertive. Fifth, there is fear of inner conflict. Overcoming lifeskills weaknesses may create an inner conflict between how you were and how you are becoming. During the transition you may experience a painful conflict between your previous and emerging self-pictures. Sixth, there is fear of failure. Failure can be defined in many ways, both objectively and subjectively. Fear of failure can consist of two elements: fear of the occurrence of negative consequences and fear about your ability to cope with negative consequences if they occur. Seventh, there is fear of success. People who succeed in overcoming lifeskills weaknesses have to face the consequences. For example, they may have to handle the consequences of obtaining a promotion, being asked out a lot, getting high marks and facing other demands that go with being successful. They may start getting afraid about their ability to cope with their new status.

What the environment does to people

Lifeskills weaknesses are usually maintained both by what people do to themselves and by what the environment keeps doing to them. Many of the factors mentioned in the section on how people acquire lifeskills can help them to maintain their lifeskills weaknesses. For example, people may continue to: have inadequate supportive relationships; lack good role models; receive inappropriate rewarding consequences from others; lack sound instruction in specific lifeskills; have insufficient or faulty information; lack suitable opportunities to develop their skills; not receive appropriate challenges and confrontations; belong to unhelpful rather than to helpful peer groups; be restricted by sex-role expectations and rules; possess cultural blinkers; and undergo socio-economic and social class deprivations. People have varying degrees of choice about how they can cope with and, if possible, overcome these external factors. For example, it may be possible to find good role models, to choose friends who offer more appropriate rewarding consequences and to create opportunities for learning that might not seem immediately apparent. Sometimes external factors are relatively immutable, perhaps especially for young people living at home. Even so, there may be some lifeskills that they can develop to survive living in what may be emotionally inclement environments.

CONCLUDING COMMENT

Trainers in lifeskills groups cannot change how participants originally acquired their lifeskills weaknesses. To change direction, trainers must help participants to alter the thinking and action skills weaknesses that presently maintain their ineffective behaviours. Also, at risk of repetition, trainers need to realize that participants entering training groups have often had years of faulty learning and self-instruction.

CHAPTER HIGHLIGHTS

All training group leaders work on theoretical assumptions of varying degrees of explicitness.

Participants entering lifeskills groups have built up patterns of skills strengths and weaknesses. Consequently, leaders need to guard against a naïve optimism concerning change.

An important distinction exists between how people initially acquired lifeskills strengths and weaknesses and how they maintain them.

Factors influencing initial acquisition of lifeskills include: supportive relationships; role models; rewarding consequences; instruction; self-instruction; information; opportunity; challenge and confrontation; peer group interaction; thinking skills; anxiety; sex-role considerations; culture; and social class.

Maintaining lifeskills strengths and weaknesses consists both of 'what people do to themselves' and 'what the environment does to people'.

The inner processes by which people maintain their lifeskills weaknesses include: attributional deficiencies; unrealistic personal rules; faulty self-perceptions; negative self-talk; and fear of change.

Many external factors influencing the initial acquisition of lifeskills weaknesses continue to influence their maintenance. These factors include: insufficient supportive relationships; inadequate role models; inappropriate rewarding consequences; inadequate instruction; insufficient information; insufficient opportunity; peer group interaction; and sex-role, cultural and social class considerations.

THREE
How to Prepare Training Groups

In all things success depends upon previous preparation,
and without such preparation there is sure to be failure.

Confucius

CHAPTER QUESTIONS

What are the stages in training groups?

How can you find time to lead training groups?

What are the skills of working within your environmental context?

How do you state goals and sub-goals for training groups?

What should you consider when preparing training groups?

What are some of the ethical issues in running training groups?

STAGES OF TRAINING GROUPS

This chapter looks at many of the choices that leaders make when they prepare training groups. The importance of preparing a lifeskills group thoroughly cannot be emphasized enough. Leaders foolishly rushing in unprepared court disaster. Below is a limerick that tries to make this point.

> A training group leader from Yale
> Had leadership skills that were frail;
> He gave little care
> When he came to prepare
> So his sessions were boring as jail!

Training groups can be viewed as having four main, albeit overlapping, stages:

1. The preparatory stage.

2. The initial stage.

3. The working stage.

4. The ending stage.

The *preparatory stage* is what goes on before the group meets. This starts with either the creative glint in the leader's eye or with an external request for a lifeskills training group. Numerous leader choices exist at this stage. These choices include: whether or not to have a co-leader; setting goals; length of programme and frequency and duration of sessions; location, physical setting and facilities; availability of resource material; group composition; advertising; and whether or not and how to make a contract with group participants. Often a further set of choices is that of how best to work within the environmental context in which the group is to be run. Last, but not least, leaders have to design the training programmes they offer.

The *initial stage* starts from when the training group first meets together. This stage may last for the whole of the first session and, sometimes, extends into subsequent sessions. The initial stage has both relationship-building and also task-orientation functions. The participants start getting to know the leader and each other. The leader requires initial structuring, ice-breaking and group facilitation skills to help along this process. Participants may be orientated to the tasks of the group in at least two ways. First, the training programme may be further outlined to them – they are already likely to have some idea about it when they enter. Second, participants may be encouraged to assess their skills strengths and weaknesses in the areas covered by the group. Initial self-assessment and setting of personal goals may not only motivate participants, but also provide them with yardsticks for assessing subsequent progress.

The *working stage* covers most of the remainder of the group sessions. Though the participants may engage in social relationships outside, inside the group they are encouraged to engage in working relationships. The leader uses facilitation skills to help participants to learn from each other, both by talking about themselves and by giving feedback. Additionally, the leader attempts to attain specific training goals by using didactic skills such as: carefully designed individual sessions; presentations; coaching, rehearsal and feedback; using different group formats creatively; using exercises and games; and setting and reviewing homework.

The *ending stage* focuses on issues of closure of the training group and on the transfer, maintenance and development outside the group of the lifeskills learned inside it. Most training groups run for fixed terms, so participants have few illusions about when the group will end. Nevertheless, leaders may need to help participants to handle feelings concerned with the break-up of the group. Above all, leaders need to focus on the consolidation of the lifeskills learned in the group as self-help skills for afterwards. From their inception, well-designed training programmes are sensitive to issues of transfer of learning. Ways of consolidating self-help skills at the end of a group include: ensuring that participants have an adequate grasp of the self-talk necessary to guide their behaviour in the skills areas; helping them to assess their strengths and weaknesses; developing action plans for maintaining and developing their skills, including anticipating setbacks; and, where appropriate, arranging for one or more booster sessions.

DECIDE YOUR ROLE

A journey of a thousand miles must begin with a single step.
Lao-tse

Helpers and other potential lifeskills group leaders are always being confronted with role decisions about how best to spend their time (Morrill *et al.*, 1974; Watkins *et al.*, 1986). Those considering leading training groups require the skills of making good role decisions. Helpers must be clear about both their objectives with regard to their overall role and the objectives of their specific interventions. Three aspects of helper interventions are their clientele, their objectives and their method. The clientele for an intervention may be an individual, a group, or an institution or community. The objectives of an intervention may be remedying moderate to severe psychological disturbance, preventing disturbance, or developing the lifeskills of 'normal' people. The method of an intervention may be individual counselling, group counselling, training or consultation.

Some people are appointed to positions in which their training function is primary. Others may have the opportunity to develop their helping or other roles to include lifeskills training interventions. Such training may be in one or more skills areas for one or more clienteles. Figure 3.1 is a simplified pie diagram of two different ways in which helpers might distribute their time between individual counselling, group counselling, training groups and consultation. Time spent on administration, which may be as much as a quarter of total helper time (Troy & Magoon, 1979), is excluded here. Helpers may have more scope than they acknowledge to develop their roles to encompass lifeskills training groups. If helpers can develop a vision of how they would like to perform, they may then be in a stronger position to achieve their goals. Helpers may still need to negotiate their roles within their institutions.

Exercise 3, on making role decisions, has been included because this is an important practical skill of people considering conducting training groups. If you have not thoroughly thought through your role, you may miss the opportunity to lead lifeskills training groups.

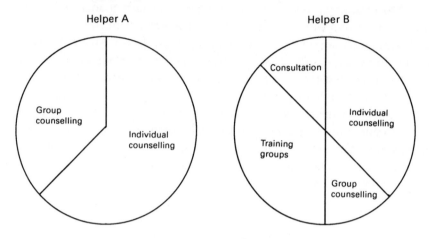

Figure 3.1 *Pie diagram of how two helpers might distribute their time*

Exercise 3 Make role decisions: allocate your time

The first part of this exercise is for 'loosening up', so try to get as many ideas down as possible. Make up a worksheet with the following three headings:

CLIENTELES	OBJECTIVES	METHODS

With regard to your present or future work role, fill in your worksheet, indicating the following:

(a) the possible clienteles for your work

(b) the kinds of objectives you might have for each clientele

(c) the methods you might use with each clientele – in particular take into account any opportunities you may have for leading lifeskills training groups, including being specific about the skills focused on in possible training groups.

This second part of the exercise is for 'tightening up'.

Based on your responses to your clienteles/objectives/methods worksheet:

(a) make a listing of your priorities among the activities you might realistically do

(b) indicate how much of your time you might spend on each of these activities.

To what extent has this exercise altered your perception of how you might perform your role to include more of a focus on training groups? If you are part of a work team, the above can be done as a group exercise.

WORK WITHIN YOUR ENVIRONMENTAL CONTEXT

All lifeskills training groups, with the exception of those within private practices, are planned and led within institutional or agency settings. Consequently, it is critical that you show sensitivity to the institutional or agency perspective. One reason for showing such sensitivity is to avoid unwanted interference in what you try to do. Brown (1986) cites the example of how prison officers tried to thwart a group that was run within a prison wing. For instance, on arrival to start the first session, the leader found that the officers 'didn't know' about it. During the session prison officers opened the door from time to time and stared through the window. At the end of the session, both members and leader heard a senior officer remark in a voice easy to hear that 'You're wasting your bloody time with these buggers, they'll never change'. Perhaps the leader might have spent more time preparing the ground with the prison officers to prevent them from trying to sabotage the group. The same type of sabotage may take place in other institutions, such as hospitals, schools and businesses. For example, if some teachers feel that their 'turf' is being infringed upon, they may try to block a lifeskills group from getting started or, once started, make derogatory remarks about it to pupils and parents.

Quite apart from heading off sabotage attempts, positive reasons exist for gaining support within your institution. If, as is likely, you work in a hierarchy, it can be diplomatic to let your superior(s) and colleagues know what you plan to do and address any reservations they have. You can develop a one- or two-page typed outline, clearly communicating what you have in mind. Institutions have their codes of etiquette which, if infringed, can create problems. On the other hand, following etiquette can engender goodwill. Furthermore, your efforts at consultation and securing the necessary 'permissions' may identify supporters as well as gain their support. Benefits of institutional support can include: being allocated resources, be they time, money, access to participants or physical facilities; having your work affirmed by others making positive rather than negative comments about it to participants and potential participants; being supported in the event of misunderstandings over your group; and feeling that you are appreciated for what you do.

Institutions and agencies may have their 'hidden agendas' for their interest in training groups. These agendas may either work to your advantage, or place you in a position of role conflict, or a mixture of the two. Costley and Moore provide the following examples of organizational hidden agendas: conducting stress management training to provide protection for legal liability arising from stress-related accidents; running women in management seminars 'to project a positive image of equal rights for women in this organization and to get women's groups off our back' (p 102); and teaching employees communication skills in such a way that they know that if they continue to receive customer complaints they will be forced to go on more training programmes on their own time (Costley & Moore, 1986). In business and industry, training groups can be selection tools for easing out poor employees.

Consultation skills for gaining institutional support include: the ability to analyse the environmental context and to identify where best to look for support; sensitivity to institutional practices and codes of etiquette; skills of clear and non-threatening communication regarding what you wish to do; responsive skills that show that you understand others' viewpoints and reservations and, where feasible, will address them; and taking the time and effort to prepare the ground as a team member who works with the institution rather than a 'lone ranger' who can all too easily be seen as a threat. A further consultation skill is that of finding out what training groups other people in the institution may want run by someone. If others request your group leadership services, you start off from a position of support.

There is also an 'inner game' to working within an institutional or agency context. It is very easy to get paranoid and to overreact to any perceived resistance to what you want to do (Whitaker, 1985). Some otherwise talented people in the helping professions sabotage their work by inadequately coping with their own thoughts and feelings. Here are two examples of potential lifeskills group leaders not handling their inner game as well as they might.

- Eileen is a primary school teacher/counsellor who has proposed a making-friends lifeskills group to her school head. When the head expresses misgivings over how some parents might react, Eileen misperceives this as an unnecessary objection rather than a genuine reservation that she could help the head to work through.

- Joe is a social worker in a psychiatric hospital. He wants to run a transition skills group for adult patients who have recently returned to the community. His hospital sees his role as dealing with in-patients rather than out-patients. Joe gets extremely angry over his superiors not seeing things his way. Joe cannot take 'no' for an answer and gets their backs up through continuing to push aggressively for what he thinks should be a clear need 'even to a seven-year-old'.

What are some of the inner game thinking skills that might help you to work effectively within an institutional context? These thinking skills include formulating realistic personal rules. You can make self-defeating 'mustabatory' demands both on yourself and others (Ellis, 1980, 1989). For instance, you may think: 'If others do not give me what I want straight away, then they are unreasonable and I am a failure'. Joe is an example of someone who translates unrealistic inner demandingness into counterproductive outer demands. Eileen is an example of someone too quick to attribute negative intentions to another. Jumping to perceptual conclusions before checking whether there are more accurate ways of viewing others' positions is another thinking skills weakness (Beck & Weishaar, 1989).

You can learn to talk to yourself in ways that help you to stay calm and focused on achieving what you want (Meichenbaum, 1977; Meichenbaum & Deffenbacher, 1988). For instance, you may be nervous about going before a management group to present a proposal for a training group and then make matters worse by using anxiety-engendering rather than calming self-talk. Your obvious anxiety weakens your presentation's effect.

Exercise 4 Explore your working within the environmental context skills

Think of a specific lifeskills group that you might offer in an institution or agency of your choice. Write out your answers for each of the following tasks.

1. Perform an environmental context analysis that, as specifically as possible, identifies:

   (a) where and what support you are likely to find for your group
   (b) where and what resistance you are likely to find to your group
   (c) institutional practices and codes of etiquette that you need to take into account in planning and running your group.

2. Assess your own skills in dealing with the environmental context regarding your proposed lifeskills group. Such skills might include:

   (a) relationship and communication skills: for instance, clearly expressing what you want to do, and understanding others' perspectives and responding adequately to their reservations
   (b) thinking skills: for instance, perceiving others' perspectives accurately and not jumping to unwarranted conclusions about their motivation; possessing realistic personal rules; and using coping rather than anxiety-evoking self-talk.

3. Develop a plan for working effectively to have your lifeskills group accepted and supported within your institution or agency. Your plan should specify what are your goals and how you intend attaining each one of them.

FURTHER PREPARATORY CONSIDERATIONS

Know the subject matter

A distinction exists between training group leaders' knowledge of subject matter and their delivery skills. If you are going to run successful lifeskills programmes it is essential to have a good grasp of your subject matter. For example, a study conducted for the British Manpower Services Commission asked trainers and managers in large organizations with training programmes which characteristics they would expect an effective trainer to have (Leduchowicz & Bennett, 1983). The three characteristics most associated with trainer credibility were, in rank order: knowledge of subject matter; good communication skills; and good planning and preparation.

It is unethical to run training groups if you are unfamiliar with your subject. In reality, there are degrees of familiarity with subject matter. Many leaders will have a good working knowledge of a lifeskills area, but still need to update their information from time to time. Other leaders may originally have obtained a reasonable working knowledge of a lifeskills area, but have failed to keep up with its relevant research and practitioner literature. Still others may be reaching beyond their grasp, since they have never adequately mastered the area in which they attempt to train.

Take a typical area for a lifeskills group: for instance, parenting skills or problem-solving skills. For each lifeskills area, there are three main kinds of subject matter knowledge that leaders require. First, there is *theoretical* knowledge. Theoretical knowledge involves familiarity with explanations of how people acquire, maintain and can change their lifeskills both in general and in any specific lifeskills area for which a training group is envisaged. Second, there is *research* knowledge. What is the relevant research that has been conducted in the lifeskills area and what is its relevance to designing and leading your training group? Third, there is *experiential* knowledge. For example, a leader running a training group for parents and adolescents on managing parent–adolescent conflict may have a fund of 'case knowledge' derived from working with such problems both in family counselling and in previous groups. Additionally, that leader may have received initial training on running training groups plus further supervision.

Apart from the obvious point that if you do not know your subject, you are unlikely to be able to train participants in it well, there are a number of other reasons for possessing a good knowledge base. First, knowing your subject releases time and energy for concentrating on how best to put it across. Second, you are more likely to be confident if you know your material. A side-effect of this confidence is that you handle the relationships in the group better. Third, you are more likely to be a source of influence for participants if they perceive you as having expertise (French & Raven, 1959). As a leader trying to develop participants' lifeskills, you are in the influence business. You cannot afford needlessly to erode your influence base. In Leduchowicz and Bennett's study, the two items mentioned most frequently as characterizing non-credible trainers were: pompous, sees self as superior; and lack of subject matter knowledge (Leduchowicz & Bennett, 1983). Possibly, being pompous and seeing oneself as superior is a compensatory mechanism for inadequate knowledge of the subject.

Clarify and state goals and sub-goals

A distinction may be made between the overall goal or goals for a lifeskills group and the division of that goal or goals into cognitive-behavioural or operational sub-goals. This distinction is between the focus of the group stated in broad terms and a narrower 'how-to-do-it' working definition of those skills. Training groups that do not have clear goals and sub-goals are at risk from many directions. These risks include: lack of specificity in programme design; wasting participants' time through ill-thought-through sessions; and lowered motivation on the part of both leader and participants, since neither have a clear sense of direction. Successful training groups set out clearly both their overall goal and also their specific sub-goals.

Many considerations – from leader, potential participant and institutional perspectives – may influence the overall goals that leaders set for their lifeskills training groups. There are also practical considerations like the amount of time and resources that can be devoted to the group. Defining the overall scope of lifeskills groups involves becoming more specific as to their content. For example, a leader may have eight weekly two-hour sessions to run an assertion group. However, this begs the question of what he or she means by assertion in this context. Possible meanings of assertion include training participants in the skills of: expressing wants and wishes, taking initiatives, showing appreciation, stating their opinions, handling aggressive criticism, setting limits and saying no, standing up for their rights and making assertive requests for behaviour change. From these and other possible goals within the broad area of assertion, the leader needs to choose the specific goals for the lifeskills group. At the preparatory stage, it is the leader who chooses the goals. However, once the group meets, these goals may be modified in light of participants' feedback.

Having set out the broad skills focus of the lifeskills group, the leader still needs to break these skills down into operational or working sub-goals. Say the overall goals of an assertion group are to develop participants' skills in setting limits and saying no and in making assertive requests for behaviour change. Participants still do not know how to work towards these goals. Consequently, the leader needs to identify what thinking and action skills are relevant to attaining them. Basically, when leaders state sub-goals in working terms, they state the specific steps in helping participants to attain the overall goals. Trainers in business and industry often use the term 'task analysis' for the process of reviewing each task selected for training. Cook (1986) observes: 'The output of this process is a list of the steps required to perform the task' (p. 106). An example of how to state goals and sub-goals is provided in the next chapter on designing training programmes.

Choose the number of leaders

You may conduct lifeskills training groups on your own or with others. If you choose to work with another leader or leaders, all preparatory-stage considerations listed in this chapter should be discussed together. The size of training groups can vary, thus affecting the desirable number of leaders. Four ways in which you may lead training groups with others are as follows:

- *Co-equal leading.* You work with one other leader on an equal footing. You share responsibility for the success of the group fairly evenly. Neither leader feels that they have to defer to the other one.

- *Supervisory co-leading.* This is an unequal 'apprenticeship' model where one leader learns leader skills from another who acts in a supervisory role.

- *Team leading.* There are more than two leaders involved in running the group.

- *Using leader's aides.* One or more people are brought in to support the leader: for instance, the leader might give a whole-group presentation followed by skills-building sub-groups led by leader's aides. Leader's aides may also be used where there are two or more leaders. Sometimes leader's aides include technicians who work the audiovisual equipment.

Some of the potential advantages for participants of having more than one group leader include the following. Leaders may differ in basic characteristics, for instance age, gender and race. In lifeskills areas such as managing marital conflict participants may benefit from having female and male leaders. Co-leading also allows for differences in leader personality, thus increasing the likelihood that participants will feel comfortable with at least one leader. Further reasons for having more than one leader are that it increases the range of available resources, especially where leaders have different training strengths, and that individual participants may get more leader attention.

There are also potential advantages for group leaders in working together. Working with another, you may offer lifeskills programmes to larger groups of participants than if training on your own. Some leaders prefer working with another leader. Co-leading can lessen feelings of isolation both within the training group and within the leaders' institution or agency. Leaders can support each other both emotionally and in the mechanics of planning, designing and running their group. Mutual support may lessen the chances of burnout where leaders carry a heavy training load. Leaders may also decide to perform different functions within the group: for instance, one may be more task-orientated while the other is more sensitive to relationship issues and to individual participants' anxieties and difficulties in acquiring skills. Either as co-equals or in the 'apprenticeship' model leaders may learn from each other. This learning may take place both by observing and by discussion and feedback between group sessions.

The issue of whether, from institutional perspectives, co-leading is more expensive is not clear-cut. On the surface, if two leaders are allocated to training the same number of participants as a single leader, running the group is roughly twice as expensive. However, this does not take into account the group's outcomes which may justify some, if not all, of the extra expense. Economies of scale are possible from co-leading or team leading. For instance, where leaders take turns in giving presentations, they save preparation time. However, ultimately participants are likely to require some degree of individual attention as they develop their skills, thus placing limits on the possibilities for economies of scale.

There can also be problems and conflicts in leading training groups with another or others. Whitaker observes: 'There is little else so unpleasant as trying to work with an uncongenial co-leader' (Whitaker, 1985, p. 95). However, differences of opinion can be handled constructively as well as destructively.

Rather than only focusing on the problems, below are *some guidelines for effective co-leading*.

1. Work with leaders who have compatible theoretical positions and values to yourself.

2. Work with leaders whose training skills and experience you respect.

3. Work with leaders with whom you feel you can engage in frank discussion and with whom you can have a collaborative rather than a competitive relationship.

4. Leaders need to share in all aspects of the planning and running of the group, even if you decide on a division of labour.

5. Leaders need to commit time and energy to working with each other both before the group starts and also between sessions.

6. The status and role relationships between leaders need to be clearly understood by each. If the leaders wish to perform different functions in the training group, you should agree on this. If one of the leaders is to exercise more power and authority, the other leader(s) should be comfortable about this.

Decide on group size

Many considerations are relevant to group size. First, what is an optimum size for didactic training purposes? Second, what is a good size for participants to learn from and receive feedback and support from each other? Third, what are the practicalities of the training situation, including the resources available to the group?

From four to eight members is a good size for a training group. The group is small enough for leaders to give time and attention to building the skills of individual participants. For instance, a training sequence may include coaching, video-recorded role-play, and playback accompanied by participant and trainer feedback. In a large group, going through this experiential learning sequence with individual participants would be far too time-consuming and repetitious. Because experiential learning is difficult to arrange, there can be a pressure in large groups for the leader to lecture about a lifeskill rather than to impart it in a practical 'how-to' way. Also, in settings such as schools, large groups may be more prone to disruption from participants not feeling actively involved.

Four to eight participants is also a good size for learning from interacting with other members. Yalom observes: 'My own experience and a consensus of the clinical literature suggests that the ideal size of an interactional therapy group is approximately seven or eight, with an acceptable range of five to ten members' (Yalom, 1985, p. 283). If the group becomes too large it is hard for individual participants to have their say, especially the shyer ones. Since the scope for person-to-person interaction is reduced, developing relationships may also be more difficult. Consequently, the cohesiveness and attraction of the group to participants may be lessened.

In reality, practical considerations often determine how large are lifeskills training groups. For instance, if the group is being run for a school class or an army platoon, its numbers could be in the region of 30. If a business organization is only prepared to allocate limited resources to the training function, this may create a pressure for training groups larger than eight participants. On the other hand, if an institution or agency is prepared to offer sufficient resources to allow for co-leading, team leading or using leader's aides, the overall size of an effective lifeskills group could even be upwards of 30, with individual attention to building skills and to small-group interaction taking place in sub-groups. Another set of practical considerations influencing group size has to do with the leader's confidence and skills. For example, a confident leader with good skills of using a group creatively through various forms of sub-grouping may be better able to take on more than eight participants than someone less confident and skilled.

Decide on open versus closed group

An open group may take in new participants during its life, whereas a closed group will not. The vast majority of lifeskills training groups are closed. This is for two main reasons. First, training groups are usually time-limited, say six to ten weeks, rather than being spread out over a long period of time, say six months to a year. Consequently, there is less likelihood of the group losing many participants. Second, participants in training groups, unlike those in interactional counselling groups, receive cumulative instruction in specific skills. Participants are usually not allowed to enter late because they have missed out on earlier steps.

Decide on group composition

In almost all textbooks on group counselling, the issue of whether to have a heterogeneous or a homogeneous group is raised and debated. The participants in heterogeneous groups differ in such characteristics as styles of relating, age, sex, and presenting concerns. Homogeneous groups are characterized more by the similarities in their participants than their differences. There is a much stronger emphasis on homogeneity in lifeskills training groups than in interactional counselling groups. Lifeskills training groups, which invariably include their specific skills focus in their titles, by definition have a high degree of homogeneity. Training groups often target specific clienteles, for example stressed executives or prospective fathers. A further way in which training groups can be homogeneous is in the level at which they are offered: for example, training in public speaking skills can be either basic or more advanced. Entry to the more advanced programme might be conditional on successful completion of the less advanced programme.

Some training groups are more likely to attain their goals if their participants are somewhat heterogeneous. Examples include: a dating skills group composed of both females and males; a cross-cultural awareness and communication group composed of participants from different cultures; an interracial communications group composed of participants from different races; a coping with death and dying group composed of those dying as well as of those living; a hospital group on interprofessional communication composed of participants from different professions, for example doctors and nurses; and a managing-conflict group in industry composed of representatives from unions and management.

Decide on group selection

Group selection and composition are interrelated in that you try to select according to your criteria for group composition. There are five main ways of selecting participants for lifeskills training groups, albeit they are sometimes interrelated. First there is *self-selection*. A training group may be advertised and filled on a 'first-come-first-served' basis. Participants have decided on their own accord that they need to develop their skills. Sometimes self-selection includes having sufficient finances to pay for the group.

Second, there is *leader selection*. Leaders have their own criteria for inclusion and exclusion. They may conduct intake interviews in which they and potential participants can assess their mutual suitability.

Third, there is *third party selection*. An example of selection by a third party is that of salespeople sent on effective-communication courses by their sales managers. Third party selection is common in business and industry and may be viewed as either reward or punishment.

Fourth, there is *compulsory whole-category selection*. Sometimes training is required for whole categories of people: for example, a company may have a policy that all newly appointed supervisors should attend supervisory skills training groups.

Fifth, there is *compulsory whole-group selection*. An example of this would be career education offered to all pupils as part of a secondary school curriculum.

A number of the above methods of selection contain elements of compulsion. Though it is possible to select people to be physically present in training groups, they select themselves to be psychologically present. Many leaders would much prefer not to have unwilling participants in their groups. However, often the leaders too are part of systems that restrict choice.

Conduct intake interviews if feasible

Intake interviews are individual interviews conducted by the leader with prospective participants prior to starting a group. The main disadvantage of conducting intake interviews is that they are time-consuming. However, especially where the group size is not going to be large, intake interviews have advantages that may outweigh their disadvantages. First, intake interviews allow the leader to apply criteria for inclusion and exclusion. Leaders can increase the chances that those joining need to improve their skills in the areas of their groups and at the levels at which they are offered. Potential participants who are either too advanced or not ready can be excluded. The motivation of participants to work hard can be assessed. Also, decisions can be made as to whether to exclude participants with characteristics likely to be disruptive to the group: for example, monopolizing and excessive hostility. Second, intake interviews are a two-way process that allow potential participants to ask questions and to decide whether the training group is going to meet their needs.

Third, intake interviews allow leaders and participants to get to know one another. Leaders may get a clearer idea of individual participants' skills strengths and weaknesses. Additionally, intake interviews allow participants to feel that they have a relationship with leaders. This feeling may make joining the group a less threatening experience and possibly contribute to participants 'staying the course'. Fourth, intake interviews allow leaders to orientate prospective participants. For instance, leaders can clarify expectations by discussing the group's formal or informal contract. Also, participants may be encouraged to engage in pre-group preparation. Such preparation may include: doing relevant reading; keeping a daily record monitoring their skills; answering a pre-group questionnaire; and watching a videocassette demonstrating desirable participant behaviours.

Decide how to advertise

Advertising is not required for those lifeskills training groups that are compulsory or whose participants are known to the leader, for instance previous or current counselling clients. Leaders whose theoretical position is built around a single lifeskill may find it particularly easy to compose a training group from counselling clients: to a large degree, they operationalize all their clients' problems in the same way. For instance, group rational-emotive therapy is essentially lifeskills training in the central skill of identifying and disputing irrational beliefs. Minimal advertising is required when leaders can obtain sufficient participants by notifying colleagues that they will be running a specific kind of lifeskills group. The nature and duration of such lifeskills groups may even have been joint decisions amongst colleagues, for instance staff in a college counselling service.

Sometimes more extensive advertising will be necessary to get the numbers for lifeskills groups. Methods of advertising training groups, albeit interrelated, include the following.

- *Word of mouth.* Letting your group be known to colleagues and other relevant people in an institution or agency. This may be done on a one-to-one basis or by giving talks about it.

- *Satisfied customers.* People who have received benefits from previous lifeskills groups provide another important 'word of mouth' method of advertising.

- *Establishing a referral network.* Over a period of time, getting to know people who might refer participants to you as and when you notify them that you intend running a training group.

- *Brochures and hand-outs.* Compiling and disseminating appropriate literature about your proposed group.

- *Posters.* Displaying well-designed posters that provide stimulating and interesting information about your proposed group.

- *Advertising in professional journals and newsletters.* This kind of advertising is especially relevant if you wish to target professional and paraprofessional participants.

- *Advertising in institutional publications.* For example, college counselling services might advertise their lifeskills training groups in institutional publications, such as newsletters and handbooks.

- *Advertising in the public press.* Since advertising in the public press is likely to be expensive, the advertisements need to more than pay for themselves in terms of participants' fees.

- *Radio advertising.* Sometimes this can be free, for instance if there is a talk-show host interested in the area of your lifeskills group.

- *Running outreach programmes.* Running lifeskills groups on different people's 'turfs' rather than in central training locations. Such groups may engender local interest both when first being run and also, if successful, subsequently.

Successful training group leaders may need to develop marketing skills in the best sense. Even though they may not charge money, if leaders believe in their product they should devise ways of bringing it to the attention of those who might benefit from it.

Settle on format and length of group

Leaders have to make choices concerning the formats and lengths of their training groups. Writing of developments in social work, Brown observes that, in recent years, the shift in casework to brief task-focused interventions has also taken place in groupwork 'from groups that last for years, to ones that are much briefer in duration (say six to twelve sessions over a three- to six-month period) and specific in intent' (Brown, 1986, p. 41). Though longer-term group counselling and therapy is still practised and may be valuable to some, the shift to briefer and more focused groups is much more widespread than in just social work.

Though issues of format and length of lifeskills group and of frequency and duration of sessions overlap, here the former will be discussed first. Basically, there are three main formats for training groups: massed, spaced, and massed-spaced combinations. Issues of post-programme follow-up and support are relevant to each of these formats. *Massed* lifeskills training groups are intensive in that all the sessions are massed together over a relatively brief period of time. Participants attend full-time. Sometimes massed training groups are called workshops. Examples of massed training groups include: a two-day workshop on public speaking skills run by a large corporation; a one-week training course on leadership skills for newly appointed supervisors; and a two-week training course on counselling and helping skills for health paraprofessionals.

In *spaced* lifeskills training groups the individual training sessions are spaced out. For example, sessions may be held bi-weekly, weekly, fortnightly or monthly. Since they are less intensive, spaced groups tend to take place over a longer time period than massed groups: say, from a month to six months. Examples of spaced training groups include: a one session a week group on parenting skills lasting for three months; a twice-weekly career education course for secondary school students lasting for one term; and a training group on assertion skills for women that lasts for eight weekly sessions.

In *massed-spaced combinations*, the massed element may come either at the start of or during the training group, but rarely at the end. The massed section gives participants an intensive exposure to skills that then get consolidated and developed in spaced sessions and practice. Examples of massed-spaced programmes include: a weekend workshop followed by once-weekly sessions for six weeks for training telephone counsellors for the suicidal and depressed; a 10-week lifeskills group for young people, run by a church minister, on relationship skills – sessions are held one weekday evening per week and the group goes away for a weekend retreat half-way through the programme; and a one-week intensive course on people management skills for bank managers followed by four sessions at monthly intervals.

The dividing line is not always a clean one between a lifeskills training group and provisions, if any, for follow-up and support. A major theme of this book is the need for leaders to pay great attention to issues of transfer and maintenance of skills. Booster sessions, say three months after the group ends, may not only help participants' motivation but also assist them to overcome difficulties in implementing their skills. Additionally, the environments from which participants come can reinforce their skills development. For instance, participants in a corporation who have been on public speaking courses can be given managerial support and opportunities to use and develop their speaking skills.

Both practical and teaching considerations influence the length of training groups. Practical considerations influencing length include the availability of participants. For example, a group run in a prison on transition-to-the-community skills must take into account the remaining sentences of participants. Other practical considerations include: the cost of sending participants on the training group; the time framework in which participants are available, for example school terms; the urgency of acquiring the skills, for example job-seeking skills for the short-term unemployed; and the availability of leaders. Teaching considerations influencing the length of lifeskills groups centre on whether the group can achieve its goals in the time available. Related considerations include: the complexity and difficulty of these goals; the starting-off points of participants; and whether or not the group is part of a sequence.

Practical and teaching considerations also determine the format of training groups. Many leaders do not have a choice over format: they work in environments geared to either massed or spaced training. For example, schools and colleges may lend themselves to spaced training, whereas business and industry training groups are often massed, with participants being taken out of their normal work settings. The main teaching consideration related to massed or spaced groups is which is most conducive to skills acquisition, maintenance and development. Massed groups may give participants a thorough introduction to the skill and the chance to get to know each other in a brief period of time. However, unlike spaced groups, massed groups can have the major drawback of allowing participants insufficient time to learn and practise the skills so that they become part of their daily living. Also, massed groups may be too intense for the motivation and attention span of some categories of participants, for instance primary schoolchildren. Though generalizations are risky, a massed-spaced combination format often has much to recommend it.

Settle on frequency and duration of sessions

Even for massed groups, leaders must make choices concerning frequency and duration of sessions. For example, in a two-day workshop on public speaking skills, how many periods should there be; should they all be the same length, despite some sessions having different objectives; and when and how long should the breaks be? Sessions in which participants acquire skills by means of an initial leader presentation that includes demonstration of skills, followed by coaching rehearsal and feedback, are time-consuming. Such practical training sessions may last two to three hours. Usually, the final choice concerning length of sessions represents a compromise between practical and teaching considerations. For instance, despite the advantages of flexibility, there may be limits to the extent that breaks can be altered.

For spaced groups, a number of practical and teaching considerations may influence the frequency and duration of sessions. Ideally, length of session should take into account such factors as the purposes of the session and the motivation and attention span of participants. However, such flexibility is not always possible. For instance, lifeskills groups that are run in schools and further education colleges as part of the formal curriculum may need to adhere to the normal length of classroom periods. Practical considerations may also influence frequency of sessions. For example, educational institutions may only be willing to allocate one period a week to a training group or the leader may only be available weekly. Participants' ability to pay may also affect how many sessions they want to afford in a given period. Teaching considerations relevant to frequency of sessions include: the need to maintain momentum – this may be easier if sessions are bi-weekly rather than weekly or longer; and allowing participants realistic opportunities for between-session homework – bi-weekly sessions may leave insufficient time for homework. Leaders make trade-offs and compromises all the time in deciding both on format and length of training groups and also on frequency and duration of sessions.

Decide location, physical setting and facilities

Where are you going to run your training group? If you are in private practice you may either use your own facilities or rent them elsewhere. Here the focus is on running lifeskills training groups in institutional, organizational and agency contexts. There are at least four principal locations for such groups. First, there is the no-choice or limited-choice setting. Here leaders have to work with the facilities that they have, whether they like them or not. For instance, school teachers may have to run lifeskills groups in the classrooms allocated to them. In running a relationship skills group for 25 undergraduates as part of my college's general education programme, I was once assigned a classroom where the departmental chairperson maintained that the desks had to remain in rows! His big concession was that students might turn their chairs towards each other. Since flexibility of space is important, a more congenial environment was looked for and, happily, found.

Second, the institution or agency may have its own training facility. For instance, a large corporation may have both a central training facility in town and a further facility in the countryside. Colleges and schools may have specially designed areas for lifeskills training groups – so may other organizations, such as hospitals. Central institutional training facilities tend to mean that participants leave their own 'turf' and, by doing so, mix with participants from other parts of the organization. For instance, secretaries from different parts of a company may be brought together to acquire assertion skills. Travelling 'abroad' in this way may free them to take more risks than they might if they had stayed in their work setting.

Third, there are outreach settings. Here leaders, who may or may not possess their own training facilities, go out to run 'on-the-spot' lifeskills groups to meet local needs in different parts of an institution. Leading on from the previous example, the training of secretaries in assertion skills may take place in the various parts of the company in which they work. Outreach lifeskills groups can have the advantage of being more readily tailor-made to meet local needs. Also, outreach groups are more visible than groups run in central settings. Furthermore, once the group ends, it may be easier for participants drawn from the same setting to support each other in maintaining and developing their skills.

Fourth, training groups may be run outside institutional settings. Leaders may choose to organize lifeskills training groups in locations that have no connection with their employing institutions, organizations, or agencies. Such groups may be run in hotels and training facilities that are either local or distant – or even overseas. The advantages of moving outside of the organizational 'turf' include: the long hours that participants are able to spend without home and work distractions; the opportunity to develop social relationships and to improve morale; the increased possibility for fresh thinking in a different setting; and the chance for fun and a holiday.

Where they have a choice, there are a number of questions that leaders might ask themselves regarding the location, physical setting and facilities options that they consider. Below is a simple 12-point checklist of relevant questions.

1. If necessary, can I obtain permission to use the location?

2. Will I be able to use the same location for the whole of my training group?

3. Is the location easily accessible?

4. Are the physical facilities the right size?

5. Does the location offer suitable privacy?

6. Is the location free from undue noise and other unnecessary distractions?

7. Are the heating, cooling, lighting and ventilation adequate?

8. Is the decor pleasant?

9. Can the space be used flexibly?

10. Are the audiovisual facilities good?

11. Is the furniture conducive to the tasks of my group?

12. If necessary, are there adequate refreshment, toilet and parking facilities?

The above checklist is illustrative rather than exhaustive. Many training group leaders are forced to accept physical facilities that are far from ideal. Hopefully, the quality of your work will shine through!

Decide on training methods and materials

The design of lifeskills programmes and of individual sessions is covered later in the book. Suffice it for now to indicate that leaders, in their preparation, need to take into account what training methods and materials they intend using. For example, if leaders intend to use demonstrations, are these going to be live or pre-recorded? If the demonstrations are pre-recorded, does the recording already exist or will the leader have to make it up? The main methods used in systematic lifeskills training include: lecturettes; facilitated self-assessment; demonstrations; coaching, rehearsal and feedback; worksheets; exercises and games; group discussion; feedback; graduated practice; and homework.

Lifeskills training groups may involve extensive use of audiovisual aids. For example, audiocassettes may be used to present information and to demonstrate skills. Furthermore, audiocassettes may be used to develop participants' skills in self-instruction, for instance in the skills of either problem-solving or progressive muscular relaxation. Visual aids include: whiteboards; blackboards; flip-charts; posters; pre-recorded training videos and films; and live video-recording and playback. Additionally, leaders may wish to audio- or video-record sessions for supervision purposes.

Lifeskills training groups can also involve extensive use of written aids. Written aids for assessment and self-assessment include: questionnaires, standardized tests, and behaviour-monitoring sheets. Written aids for training include books, training manuals, training packages (for instance, trainer manual, manuals for participants, and audiovisual aids), and hand-outs. A basic choice for leaders is whether they build their group around an existing training manual or package, or independently or collectively design their own material. Numerous commercial training manuals and packages exist. Leaders are advised to familiarize themselves with the existing training materials in the areas of proposed programmes. This advice does not mean that you have to adopt them either in whole or in part. There is much to be said for the freshness and extra relevance that comes from creating your own material.

Decide whether or not to use contracts

A number of different kinds of contract are relevant to lifeskills training groups. First, there is the pre-group contract that ideally clearly states what the group offers and what is expected from participants. Second, there are the working agreements made between leader and participants during the life of the group. Unlike the pre-group contract, such agreements may be negotiated. Third, there are individual learning contracts in which participants set themselves personal goals for all or parts of the group (Corey & Corey, 1982; Wehrenberg, 1988). Fourth, there are contracts of varying degrees of explicitness that leaders may have about a training group with representatives of the institution or agency in which it is to be held.

The focus here is the pre-group contract or working agreement between leader and participants. Many advantages accrue from having clear pre-group contracts. Participants know what they are getting into. Consequently, they are more likely to be motivated and less likely to drop out. Employers and others who send participants to groups also know the skills they can expect their people to develop. This knowledge helps them to select participants and also increases their understanding of the experience of those attending training groups. Pre-group contracts can be a good marketing and public relations strategy. Clear pre-group contracts also force leaders to think through issues connected with offering training groups. Such contracts also minimize the chance of unfortunate misunderstandings with participants, for instance with regard to matters such as workload or fees. Furthermore, clear contracts help leaders to fulfil their ethical obligation to obtain informed consent from participants.

What might the contents be for a pre-group contract? Areas requiring clarification include the following.

- What the training group offers participants:

(a) The goals and sub-goals of the group. 'At the end of this training group participants should have the following skills . . .'

(b) Brief detail(s) of leaders. What is their relevant background and experience?

(c) Structural details. These details include: format and length of group and frequency and length of sessions.

(d) Location.

(e) Group size and composition.

(f) Training methods. Training methods may include: demonstrations, lecturettes, role-plays, video feedback and so on.

(g) Training materials. Key learning resources might be indicated, for instance a particular training manual.

(h) Confidentiality. Any limitations on confidentiality should be stated, for instance communication about participants with sponsoring employers.

(i) Release arrangements. Within an organization, it can be important to know how being sent on a lifeskills group affects job and income.

(j) Certificates etc. Does participation in the lifeskills group lead to any formal recognition such as a certificate?

• What the training group expects from participants:

(a) Attendance requirements.

(b) Outside-of-session commitment. For example, will weekly homework be assigned and, if so, how much time is it likely to take?

(c) During-session participation. For example, active participation in working at personal goals and helping others is frequently a requirement.

(d) Fees. Details of any fees and when they are due.

The above list of suggestions for a pre-group contract is not exhaustive. Also, the list assumes that leaders are working with adults. Each pre-group contract requires careful drafting in light of local needs and circumstances. Leaders are more likely to achieve their objectives of using pre-group contracts if they have clear writing and presentation skills.

Sometimes pre-group contracts have the word 'contract' implicit rather than explicit in them. For instance, a hand-out or brochure may state expectations for leaders and participants. On other occasions the hand-out or brochure may use the word 'contract' and resemble a legal contract. Some leaders may even get such contracts signed and countersigned by both parties. There can be various levels at which expectancies and working arrangements get clarified. For example, at a preliminary level a brochure suggests what the broad details of a lifeskills training group might be, but then this may get further clarified and codified for those joining the group. My preference is for expectations to be stated clearly without requiring signatures. However, those of you earning your living by running training groups may consider that you require the extra protection of signed contracts.

Review how to assess and evaluate the group

Since issues of assessment and evaluation are covered in some detail elsewhere in the book, the topic is only briefly mentioned here. Many areas exist in which you may make evaluation choices prior to starting your lifeskills training group. These choice areas include how to assess participants' skills before, during and at the end of the group and how to help them assess their own skills. Additionally, you may wish to assess the effectiveness of individual sessions and of specific training interventions. If you are under supervision you also need to work out with your supervisor how best to assess your training skills. A further assessment consideration is whether you are required to submit grades or reports to third parties. For instance, if you run a training group as part of a formal school or college curriculum, you may need to decide how to assign grades.

Make a time commitment

Especially with groups being run for the first time, lifeskills training can be very time-consuming. The following tasks, both individually and collectively, may take up much group leader time: first, gaining permissions and engaging in the negotiations to run the group; second, designing the overall programme; third, designing individual sessions; fourth, creating your own training materials; fifth, obtaining and selecting participants; and sixth, reviewing participants' self-assessments and worksheets. In addition, there are likely to be further tasks and commitments not listed above. Also, you may conduct training groups either in the evenings or at weekends, so you need to take into account the impact of these hours on you. In sum, an absolutely fundamental preparatory consideration for leaders is whether you are prepared to commit the time to run your proposed lifeskills training groups properly.

Exercise 5 Prepare a lifeskills training group

For a lifeskills training group that you may wish to lead, write out the choices you make concerning each of the following preparatory considerations. Refer back to the text if you are in doubt about the meaning of any of the categories.

- Number of leaders

- Group size

- Open versus closed group

- Group composition

- Group selection

- Intake interviewing

- Advertising

- Format and length of group

- Frequency and duration of sessions

- Location, physical setting and facilities

- Training methods and materials

- Contracts

- Assessment and evaluation

- Time commitment

- Other considerations not listed above

Summarize what seem to be the major considerations in preparing your lifeskills group.

ETHICAL ISSUES

As with group counselling and psychotherapy (Corey *et al.*, 1988b), there are numerous ethical issues connected with running lifeskills training groups. Professional associations to which group leaders belong are likely to have their own codes of ethics. For example, the British Association for Counselling has published a *Code of Ethics and Practice for Counsellors* and the British Psychological Society a *Code of Conduct, Ethical Principles & Guidelines* (British Association for Counselling, 1990; British Psychological Society, 1991). The American Association for Counseling and Development has published its ethical standards (Allen *et al.*, 1988; American

Association for Counseling and Development, 1988). Leaders are encouraged to familiarize themselves with the relevant sections of codes of ethics put out by associations to which they belong.

What are some of the many ethical issues that might be pertinent to lifeskills training groups that you run? Below are some suggestions.

- *Leader competence.* Leaders should possess the personal maturity, psychological knowledge, training skills and experience to be effective in the role. Where leaders are learning group training skills, it is important that they work under adequate supervision.

- *Leader's personal agendas, needs and values.* At all times leaders must show respect for the personal integrity of participants. They should refrain from imposing their own agendas, unfinished business, needs and values on participants.

- *Assessment and diagnostic labelling.* Training group leaders operating within a cognitive-behavioural lifeskills framework are likely to share their assessments with clients. Ethical issues surround the degree of accuracy of such assessments and the extent to which they are imposed on participants. In general, an assumption of skills-training groups is that leaders refrain from applying psychiatric diagnostic labels to clients. However, in certain in-patient and out-patient hospital settings, this assumption may be untenable: participants may both fit into psychiatric diagnostic categories and have their skills strengths and weaknesses assessed in targeted areas.

- *Emotional and sexual relationships.* Leaders should endeavour to pay equal attention to each participant. Emotional and sexual relationships with participants are unethical. Corey *et al.* (1988b) observe: 'most of the ethical codes caution against dual relationships and point to the need to avoid exploitation of clients out of the therapist's needs' (p. 173).

- *Informed consent.* The importance of a clear contract for potential participants has already been stressed. Also, during training groups, leaders should ensure that participants are clear about the activities in which they engage prior to engaging in them.

- *Advertising.* Advertising should accord with the rules of professional associations to which you belong. Overselling of programme content and outcomes is to be avoided.

- *Psychological risk.* Though lifeskills training groups, because of their focused and time-limited nature, tend to be less emotionally charged than psychotherapy or counselling groups, participants may still require leader protection from certain psychological risks: for example, excessive group hostility or inappropriate group pressure. Additionally, where necessary, leaders should arrange appropriate psychological support for people whose coping resources are being overwhelmed either inside or outside of the group.

- *Termination issues.* Issues involved in the ethical termination of training groups include: adequate preparation of participants to handle setbacks and relapses; arranging for follow-up support, possibly including booster sessions; letting participants know where and how they might further develop their skills; and to what extent and how to evaluate the group's processes and outcomes.

- *Confidentiality.* Where there are limitations on confidentiality, participants have a right to this knowledge. In specific instances that cannot always be anticipated, for instance physical danger to third parties, leaders may have a duty to warn and protect. Such decisions may be based on legal requirements and not just on ethical considerations. Participants' records should always be kept securely.

- *Cassette or video-recording of sessions.* Leaders may want to audio- or video-record sessions for their own feedback, training and supervision purposes. Where possible, participants should be informed of this wish before or during the initial session. Leaders should be honest about why the recordings are being made, who will have access to them, where they will be stored and how they will be used.

- *Undue pressure.* Leaders should respect the rights of participants not to disclose themselves more than they want. Also, leaders should refrain from forcing participants to do exercises and games with which they are uncomfortable.

- *Issues regarding minors.* There are numerous ethical issues regarding minors: for example, whether or not parental consent should be required for children to participate in a lifeskills group; the reporting of alleged sexual, physical or psychological abuse committed on children outside of the group; and children's rights to confidentiality.

- *Cross-cultural sensitivity.* Leaders need to be sensitive to differences in the meaning of behaviours between cultures. For example, in a multicultural society, there is a risk of mislabelling behaviours as skills weaknesses from the viewpoint of the dominant culture when they may have a different meaning within a minority culture.

- *Financial exploitation.* If there is to be a training group fee, on what basis should it be set? There should be no hidden costs.

- *Rights of employing agencies.* What rights do organizations and agencies employing the leader have? How should group leaders behave where there are conflicts of interest?

- *Rights of other professionals*. If a participant or potential participant is receiving related services, for example psychotherapy, from another professional, how should the leader behave?

The above are just some of the ethical issues pertinent to leading lifeskills training groups. You may be able to think of other important issues. From the moment you start preparing your group, you require sensitivity to the ethical implications of your choices. If necessary, talk these through with either trusted colleagues or a supervisor. Some ethical issues may be emotionally and intellectually difficult for you. Nevertheless, you must confront these issues.

CHAPTER HIGHLIGHTS

Lifeskills training groups require thorough preparation.

Training groups have four major, albeit overlapping, stages: preparatory, initial, working, and ending.

Helpers and others incorporating lifeskills training groups into their work require good skills for defining their roles and allocating their time.

Leaders require adequate knowledge of the subject matter of any training groups they run. There are three main kinds of subject matter knowledge: theoretical, research and experiential.

Training group leaders require both sensitivity to and skills in working with their environmental contexts.

Goals for lifeskills groups should first be stated in broad terms and then operationalized into clear and specific sub-goals. These sub-goals should focus on the specific thinking and action skills required for attaining overall training group goals.

Preparatory choices for lifeskills training groups include: number of leaders; group size; open versus closed group; group composition; group selection; whether or not to conduct intake interviews; format and length of group; frequency and length of sessions; location, physical setting and facilities; training methods and materials; contracts; assessment and evaluation; and time commitment.

Group leaders must always be conscious of the ethical implications of their training group choices.

FOUR

How to Design Lifeskills Training Programmes

*There is always an easy solution to every human problem
– neat, plausible and wrong.*

H.L. Mencken

CHAPTER QUESTIONS

What approaches are there to designing training programmes?

What are some of the main programme design considerations?

What is a good format for outlining training programmes?

INTRODUCTION

Programme design is always a major task of the preparatory stage of lifeskills training groups. Many of the component skills of designing and leading individual lifeskills sessions are described in more detail in later chapters. In designing lifeskills training programmes, leaders are hypothesis makers and testers. Each programme represents a series of 'If . . . then . . .' statements relating process and content to desired outcomes. Most lifeskills group leaders do not evaluate their hypotheses by means of rigorous research designs. Nevertheless, leaders always need to be conscious that, in designing and running their training groups, they are applied scientists conducting behavioural experiments.

APPROACHES TO PROGRAMME DESIGN

Training group leaders have the final responsibility of putting their lifeskills training programmes together and implementing them. Different approaches exist to constructing programmes. For instance, leaders can design lifeskills programmes around existing training manuals/packages. Usually it is worth researching what, if any, training manuals and packages already exist in your lifeskills areas of interest. If you can locate suitable training material, some of the work of designing programmes will be done for you. However, you still need to adapt existing material to the specific needs of your groups. Another option is for leaders to design lifeskills programmes by working closely with those requesting or paying for the programme. Leaders may do this either within their organizations or as outside consultants. In both instances leaders require consultancy skills such as clarifying others' goals and then formulating programme outlines and content with them.

As a training group leader you can design all aspects of your lifeskills programmes on your own. This model is assumed in this chapter. However, leaders may also design lifeskills programmes working as part of a team. The team approach to lifeskills programme design may range from working with co-leaders to large-scale curriculum design projects. Another possibility is to design your lifeskills programmes in consultation with participants. Such consultation may take place at the start of and during your training groups. One approach is to design the whole programme as a group exercise. Here, the leader acts as a resource person helping the group to construct a curriculum geared to attaining participants' personal and collective goals. Another approach is to allow for flexibility within programmes designed by you in advance. For example, programmes may be altered after feedback and consultation with participants. Furthermore, in most lifeskills programmes, there is a role for individuals working towards personal goals as well as towards group goals. Hence, some degree of latitude is required to cater for individual needs.

PROGRAMME DESIGN CONSIDERATIONS

Many considerations relevant to designing training programmes are discussed in greater detail elsewhere in the book. Consequently, the present discussion is restricted to an overview of programme design considerations. The following are some questions that leaders might ask themselves when designing lifeskills training programmes.

What are my goals?

Training group leaders require goals stated at three levels of specificity: overall programme goals, broad skills goals, and skills goals broken down into sub-goals. Lifeskills groups have overall or programme goals expressed in general terms: for example, 'for delinquent boys to enter the workforce and keep out of jail', 'for women to develop assertion skills', 'for drug addicts to get off and stay off drugs' or 'for psychiatric out-patients to develop social skills'.

Overall goals then need to be broken down into the broad skills goals targeted by the programme. For example, a lifeskills programme on anger management may have as an overall or programme goal 'to help participants to manage their anger better'. This programme goal says nothing about what skills the leader intends to instil to help participants manage their anger better. The leader then decides that the broad skills goals are as follows (Nelson-Jones, 1990):

THINKING SKILLS	ACTION SKILLS
Owning responsibility for anger	Assertion skills
Choosing realistic personal rules	• expressing anger constructively
Perceiving provocations differently	• requesting behaviour changes
Coping self-talk	Handling aggressive criticism
Using visualization	Using relaxation

The above list of broad skills goals may be sufficient for the leader to start outlining a programme. However, even more detail is required of the component sub-goals of each of the broad skills goals before the leader can decide how much time is necessary for training for each skill and what each session's content should be.

For example, sub-goals for the broad anger management *thinking* skills goal of choosing realistic personal rules might be:

• understanding how thinking influences feeling and action;

• the ability to identify anger-generating unrealistic personal rules;

• the ability to dispute unrealistic rules;

• the ability to reformulate self-oppressing unrealistic rules into self-supporting rules.

Sub-goals of the broad anger management *action* skills goal of using relaxation might be:

• understanding that relaxation may be used as an anger management self-help skill;

• developing the skill of progressive muscular relaxation;

• developing the skill of using visual images to relax;

- developing brief relaxation self-help skills, for example, controlled breathing;

- developing relaxing recreational outlets.

Depending on the length and complexity of the programme, leaders may end up with a long list of goals and sub-goals. Then leaders may be faced with the choice of how many skills they can train for in the group's life. A little done thoroughly tends to be much preferable to too much done superficially.

What is the knowledge base for my programme?

Earlier it was mentioned that there are three main kinds of knowledge that lifeskills group leaders require: theoretical, research and experiential. Leaders need to know the relevant theoretical and research literature for their skills groups. For instance, the above broad goals and sub-goals for managing anger were derived from interventions described in the managing-anger literature (for example, Deffenbacher *et al.*, 1988; Feindler *et al.*, 1984). Also, if available, a further useful source of ideas is from programmes designed by others. For instance, Glick and Goldstein outlined three 10-week aggression-replacement training programmes entitled structured learning training, anger-control training and moral education (Glick & Goldstein, 1987). Leaders who are open to their experience and who have previously run similar lifeskills groups can learn from what happened.

What are the structural parameters of my programme?

Training group leaders, though they sometimes have little choice when designing programmes, always have to take structural parameters into account. Structural parameters described in the previous chapter include: whether or not to have an open or closed group; group composition; the group's format and length; the frequency and duration of sessions; and the group's location, physical setting and facilities.

What environmental considerations do I need to take into account?

Leaders may design programmes in consultation with third parties sponsoring or paying for programmes. In designing programmes, leaders must be mindful of how the content is likely to be perceived by significant others in their environments: for example, with training groups run in schools, head teachers, other teachers and parents. In some instances, even if others are not actively involved, it may pay you to check your programme's content with them. Constructive suggestions and support may be positive outcomes from checking. Unwanted pressure to edit your programme may be a negative outcome.

What management of learning considerations do I need to take into account?

Most, if not all, of the considerations relevant to planning individual lifeskills group sessions are relevant to planning whole programmes. As a designer and manager of lifeskills group learning you should take into account: clearly articulated initial, working and ending stages; the sequencing of content across sessions; starting from where participants are; self-referent learning; involvement through participation; learning by hearing, observing and doing; balancing facilitation with didactic input; adequate variety; realistic homework; availability of audiovisual materials and equipment; and suitable written training materials.

How does my programme help participants to consolidate learned skills as self-help skills?

Ultimately the effectiveness of a training group lies in what happens afterwards. The crucial issue of how to consolidate the skills that your programme targets as self-help skills is explored in some detail in Chapter 11.

How am I going to evaluate my programme?

Leaders should always evaluate their training programmes. Suggestions for evaluating lifeskills programmes are provided in Chapter 12.

How much time do I have for developing this programme?

Leader commitment of time can be a critical variable in designing training group programmes. Preparing written, verbal and audiovisual materials consumes time. What you can do is heavily determined by the time and energy you either have or make available for this purpose. For example, if you lead any lifeskills group for the first time, you are going to have to commit much more time if you develop your own material than if using existing materials. You may even have to exclude topics that you neither have time to develop nor can find suitable existing material for.

OUTLINE LIFESKILLS TRAINING PROGRAMMES

> *Everybody who is incapable of learning has taken to teaching.*
>
> Oscar Wilde

Training group leaders require the skills of developing and writing up lifeskills programmes. Once goals are articulated, there are varying levels of detail in designing programmes to attain the goals. Designing training programmes is a journey from the general to the specific. Designs for programmes can start with a one-sentence description of each session. Through a series of steps these one-sentence descriptions become detailed session plans. Along the way there is much trial and error. As with many acts of creation, designing lifeskills training programmes can be a messy business. However, hopefully order will emerge out of chaos. Leaders need the confidence and persistence to work through the inevitable problems that arise. Mustabatory fantasies about designing the perfect training programme are very much to be discouraged.

When designing training lifeskills programmes, you make trade-offs and compromises all the time. Questions you may ask yourself include: 'Given limited time, how can it best be divided between the skills I want to train?', 'What is a good balance between didactic and facilitative input?', 'What is a good balance between working with either the whole group or breaking down into pairs or sub-groups?', 'How can I best incorporate structured learning activities?' and 'How can I make allowance for individual needs within the context of a group approach?' Rarely are the answers to these questions straightforward. Try not to get discouraged if your programme does not fall neatly into place at your first design attempt.

Example: outline for a training programme in assertion skills

Let us take as an example outlining eight weekly two-hour sessions plus a follow-up session after three months for a training group in assertion skills to be run in a college counselling centre. There is one leader. The mixed-sex group comprises eight participants who have either volunteered themselves or been referred by counsellors. All participants are in the 18–22 age range.

The overall goal of the training group is to help participants to become more assertive. The leader operationalizes being assertive into broad thinking and action skills areas.

The broad *thinking* skills goals targeted for the group are:

- attributing cause accurately;

- choosing realistic personal rules;

- using coping self-talk;

- realistically predicting gain and loss.

The broad *action* skills goals targeted for the group are:

- using 'I' statements;

- initiating skills;

- requesting changes in behaviour;

- giving and receiving positive feedback.

The leader decides to encourage self-assessment before the first session. During an intake interview, participants are asked to answer an assertion questionnaire in their own time. They are to bring their completed questionnaire to the first session. In addition, during the intake interview, participants are notified that they will be asked to complete the assertion questionnaire again at the group's end. Furthermore, participants will be requested to complete a three-month follow-up questionnaire focused on how well they maintain their skills. Table 4.1 provides an outline overviewing the assertion programme.

Table 4.1 Outline for a lifeskills training group programme on assertion

SESSION	GOALS	ILLUSTRATIVE CONTENT
Pre-group	Screening Assessment Facilitating self-assessment	Intake interview Assertion questionnaire

1.	Getting acquainted
	Enhance motivation
	Increase awareness of what
	   assertion means
		Breaking the ice exercises
		Outline of programme
		Lecturette on non-assertion,
		   aggression and assertion
		Review of questionnaire
		   answers/setting personal
		   goals
		
		Homework
		Monitoring assertive and
		   non-assertive actions

2.	Increase awareness of
	• Influence of thinking on
	   feelings and actions
	• owning responsibility for
	   choosing
	• attributing cause
	   accurately
		Discussion of homework
		Lecturette: ABC framework
		Exercises: being a chooser
		Exercises: attributing cause
		Group discussion
		
		Homework
		Thinking-related exercises
		   and self-observation

3.	Consolidate choosing and
	   attributing skills
	Developing skills of
	   choosing realistic
	   personal rules
		Discussion of homework
		Lecturette/demonstrations
		   on unrealistic rules
		Self-assessment exercise
		Group discussion
		Lecturette/demonstrations
		   on: choosing realistic rules
		Exercises and rehearsal
		
		Homework
		Thinking-feeling-actions log
		Personal rules exercises

4.	Consolidate rules skills
	Increase awareness of
	  sending messages
	Develop initiating skills
	Develop realistic predicting
	  skills
		Discussion of homework
		Lecturette/demonstrations
		  on: sending messages
		    making 'I' statements
		Exercises and rehearsal
		Lecturette/demonstrations
		  on: taking initiatives
		    predicting gain
		    and risk
		Group discussion
		Exercises and rehearsal
		
		Homework
		Practise 'I' statements
		Initiating experiment
		Monitor own and others'
		  initiating behaviours

5.	Consolidate 'I' statement and
	  initiating skills
	Develop behaviour change
	  request action skills
		Discussion of homework
		Lecturette/demonstrations
		  on: behaviour change
		    requests
		Self-assessment
		Group discussion
		Videoed role-plays
		
		Homework
		Monitor own and others'
		  behaviour change
		  requests
		Behaviour change request
		  experiment

6.	Consolidate behaviour
	  change request action
	  skills
	Develop coping self-talk
	  skills
	Develop skills for coping
	  with difficulties and
	  setbacks
		Discussion of homework
		Lecturette/demonstrations
		  on coping self-talk
		Exercises: coping self-talk
		Rehearsing behaviour
		  change requests and
		  self-talk
		Rehearsing facing
		  difficulties
		Group discussion

		Homework Coping self-talk exercise Visualized rehearsal Practise all skills learned to date
7.	Consolidate behaviour change request skills Develop giving and receiving positive feedback skills Perceiving others' strengths	Discussion of homework Lecturette/demonstrations on positive feedback skills Self-assessment Group discussion Rehearsal of positive feedback skills **Homework** Positive feedback experiments Assessment questionnaire including coping with post-group difficulties Practise all skills learned to date
8.	Consolidate trained skills as self-help skills Self-assessment Set goals for future Programme evaluation	Discussion of homework Summarizing of lessons learned by leader and participants Exercise: personal assertion goals Discussion/rehearsals: maintaining skills Lecturette: developing skills Programme evaluation questionnaire Group discussion/ goodbyes
		Post-group homework Rehearse, practise and develop assertion skills

Three-month follow-up	Consolidate trained skills as self-help skills Enhance motivation Mutual support	Progress questionnaire Group discussion Discussion/rehearsals: maintaining and developing assertion skills

The information contained in Table 4.1 is an introductory overview of the structure and content of a lifeskills group. Ultimately leaders require much more information: for example, detailed session outlines and well-developed training materials. Detailed session outlines are not provided for the above assertion group for two main reasons. First, constructing session outlines is reviewed later. Second, readers, who are interested in other lifeskills might be bored with details of individual assertion sessions.

Exercise 6 is designed to give you an introductory opportunity to develop your skills at constructing lifeskills group programmes. You may wish to return to Exercise 6 when you have worked through the book.

Exercise 6 Design a lifeskills training programme

This exercise is probably best done on your own so that it forces you to think through some of the numerous issues involved in designing a lifeskills training pro-gramme. However, the exercise can also be done in either pairs or small groups.

Design a training programme for a lifeskill and a participant group of your choice. Assume that you have eight two-hour weekly sessions plus a three- to six-month follow-up session. You are the only leader. Your group consists of eight participants. Formulate and write out details for the following items:

1.   The overall goal of your group.
2.   The broad thinking and action subskills for your group.
3.   A session-by-session outline of your training programme, using Table 4.1 as a model.

CHAPTER HIGHLIGHTS

In designing lifeskills training programmes, leaders are hypothesis makers.

Each programme represents a series of 'If . . . then . . .' statements relating process and content to desired outcomes.

Lifeskills programmes may be designed: around existing training manuals and packages; in consultation with third parties; on your own; and in consultation with participants in your training groups.

Considerations in designing lifeskills programmes include: goals stated in skills terms; possessing an adequate knowledge base; the group's structural parameters; environmental considerations; management of learning considerations; consolidating trained skills as self-help skills; evaluation; and how much time the leader has.

Designing lifeskills training programmes is a journey from the general to the specific. Drawing up a moderately detailed session-by-session outline is a useful intermediate step.

FIVE

How to Assess and Help Self-Assessment

Please listen carefully and try to hear
What I'm not saying
What I'd like to be able to say
What for survival I need to say
But what I can't say

Anonymous

CHAPTER QUESTIONS

Why is assessment in lifeskills training groups important?

What are some methods of assessing participants' lifeskills?

How can participants assess themselves?

How can group leaders devise their own assessment measures?

How might participants specify personal goals and sub-goals for developing their skills?

INTRODUCTION

Assessing participants' skills is an important process that requires delicate handling throughout all four stages of a lifeskills training group. Although as a leader you may have your own valid reasons for assessing participants' lifeskills, ultimately what counts is that participants acquire the 'take-away' skills of assessing their own lifeskills. Consequently, right from the start, assessment is a means of helping participants to assume more responsibility both for learning lifeskills and for maintaining, developing and using them afterwards. Clumsy assessment can do more harm than good. For instance, it may threaten participants, create excessive dependency on your expertise, and obscure their skills strengths by focusing too much on their skills weaknesses.

A simplistic distinction may be made between a medical and a lifeskills model of assessment. In the medical model, doctors are the experts who collect relevant information about patients to make diagnoses and prognoses that lead to treatment interventions, such as medication, bed rest and surgery. The role of patients is not to play an active part in the diagnostic process but rather to speak when spoken to and follow their doctors' advice. In the lifeskills model, leaders collaborate with participants to identify their strengths and weaknesses so that participants may better understand both how they sustain their current level of functioning and how they can work for change. This model of assessment encourages self-help rather than reliance on external experts. In reality, the two models of assessment overlap. There can be numerous agendas, both overt and hidden, for conducting and participating in lifeskills group assessment. Also, skilled doctors encourage patients to play active roles in understanding and managing their health.

Can assessment be overdone? The answer is most definitely 'yes'. Leaders need to be clear about their purposes for engaging in assessment and the likely impact that their assessment behaviours are going to have on participants. Also, leaders conducting either group or individual assessments need to be sensitive to when 'enough is enough'. Furthermore, partly to overcome resistances, leaders when assessing require the ability to establish rapport.

PURPOSES OF ASSESSMENT

Training group leaders, participants and third parties may each have their own agendas and purposes for conducting and participating in assessment.

Leader purposes

Leader purposes in conducting assessment procedures include the following. First, assessment may be used for *selection*. Leaders may wish to ascertain whether participants meet the criteria for inclusion or exclusion from their proposed lifeskills groups. Where places are limited, a further purpose of assessment may be the prediction of those most likely to gain from the groups. Second, assessment may be used to *improve programme design*. Initial assessment of skills can provide valuable information for leaders to alter and fine-tune programmes to meet the needs of each participant group rather than assume that the same programme is right for all groups. Third, assessment can *motivate* participants. By breaking skills down, assessment may make their attainment seem more manageable. Assessment may help participants to acknowledge their strengths as well as identify their weaknesses. Furthermore, assessment can provide the information on the basis of which participants can set their personal goals.

A fourth reason why leaders focus on assessment in lifeskills training groups is to *encourage participant self-assessment*. Lifeskills are for life, not just for the duration of a lifeskills group. Consequently, leaders always need to be mindful of ways to encourage transfer and maintenance of skills. An essential ingredient of skill transfer and maintenance is participants' ability to engage in the self-talk of monitoring and, where necessary, changing their behaviours. Fifth, skilled assessment can help leaders to *state working definitions of participants' problems*. Frequently, lifeskills group participants will describe problems in their personal, work or leisure lives, but show little insight into how to manage them. Participants may make remarks like: 'We always seem to end up arguing', 'I just don't know what to do with my time now that I'm unemployed', and 'I'm lonely and wish I had more friends'. Competent training group leaders are able to take these descriptive statements and help participants to arrive at working definitions of their problems. Working definitions identify the skills weaknesses that sustain problems. To take a simple example, the descriptive statement of a problem, 'I am lonely and wish I had more friends', might be broken down into thinking skills weaknesses, such as having unrealistic personal rules about rejection, and action skills weaknesses, such as poor skills at initiating relationships and conversing. A working definition of a problem gives the participant a set of 'handles' with which to open the door for change.

Assessment is also necessary for *monitoring the progress of individuals and the group*. Individual assessment can range from feedback during the initial acquisition and rehearsal of a skill to monitoring success in homework assignments and attempts to transfer skills into daily life. Group assessment can be either getting an overall impression of the individual assessments or systematically assessing all participants in the same way. Assessment can play a critical part in *consolidating participants' self-help skills*. Assessment at the end of a training group focuses on helping participants to transfer, maintain and develop their skills on their own. Participants' skills strengths and weaknesses require reassessing so that the participants may acknowledge progress and identify areas for further work. Additionally, potential barriers to transfer and maintenance of skills, on the part of both participants and their environments, require assessment to develop appropriate coping strategies.

A further purpose of training group assessment may be to *fulfil obligations to third parties*. Leaders may be required to provide assessments to third parties, such as businesses, government agencies and other sponsoring organizations. This information may be used in decisions covering such matters as selection, promotion, salary increase, transfer, and even dismissal. Other instances of providing assessment data to third parties include assisting in: parole decisions for juvenile delinquents; discharge decisions for psychiatric hospital in-patients; and providing marks in educational institutions where a lifeskills programme forms part of a formal curriculum, for instance in a college of further education.

Assessment by leaders may also be used to *evaluate training groups*. Such evaluations can serve many external and longer-term purposes rather than the immediate interests of the group. Evaluation that assesses both processes and outcomes may improve future groups. If this evaluative research is of publishable quality, others may learn from it too. In addition, evaluations can help training group leaders to demonstrate accountability to their paymasters. Demonstrating accountability may engender goodwill, be good publicity, lessen the likelihood of budget cuts and increase the possibility of budget increases.

Participant purposes

Participants may have their own purposes when it comes to assessment. Some of these purposes may accord with those of their leaders, but others may differ. 'Legitimate' purposes that motivate participants to take part in assessment are those destined to help them to achieve the stated goals of their groups. Participants wishing to improve their lifeskills cooperate in assessment for reasons that include: getting selected, better understanding their strengths and weaknesses, setting themselves personal goals, monitoring their progress, and consolidating their self-help skills at the end of groups. In addition, participants sent on training programmes may wish to demonstrate that they have met the expectations of their sponsors.

Sometimes participants may have reasons for engaging in or resisting assessment that diverge considerably from those of their group leaders. Consciously or unconsciously, participants may have their own separate agendas. Below are some examples.

- Annie is a 'delinquent' teenager in a remand home. The staff have nominated her for a training group on controlling aggression and learning to become more assertive and cooperative. Annie resists the notion that she needs these skills and does everything she can to frustrate the leader's efforts at assessment.

- Martin thinks of himself as the golden boy among the up-and-coming young managers in his company. Martin's boss recognizes his strengths, but also thinks he is far too hard on those who work under him. The leader's attempts to get Martin honestly to assess his people skills are hampered by three of Martin's other agendas: his desire to be seen in the best possible light by the leader; his wish to maintain his picture of himself as having superior people skills; and his fear of a negative report being sent back to his boss.

- Martha takes part in a human relations training course as part of the general education programme at her college of further education. Martha is not interested in improving the way she relates, but she is very motivated to attain a good mark. Consequently, in the assessment exercises on the course she plays a game of trying to provide the answers that are likely to obtain her a high mark rather than making a sincere effort to appraise her skills strengths and weaknesses.

Even at the best of times, participants are likely to have resistances and fears when it comes to assessing their lifeskills. Many may be unfamiliar with thinking of themselves as needing lifeskills as contrasted with just doing what comes naturally. Assessment implies the possibility that participants may be inadequate in some ways. These inadequacies may be difficult to admit. Also, identification of weaknesses means that participants may have to leave the 'safe' ways of the present and change their behaviours. Added to this, some participants may be genuinely disadvantaged if they are assessed and found wanting: for instance, those being considered for promotion in business and industry.

Third party purposes

Third parties may also have interests in the assessment of participants' lifeskills. Frequently, people are assessed by others as being ready for or needing to go on training programmes to improve their skills. In business organizations, the suggestion that someone attends a training group is sometimes intended as a reward: for instance, for an employee who is being considered for a supervisory or managerial promotion. Sometimes the suggestion is intended to improve another's performance, without casting any negative aspersions on their abilities. On other occasions, there may be a clear message that the individual sent to attend training is required to perform better in the area in question or otherwise negative consequences will follow. In educational institutions, administrators may recommend teachers for training groups and teachers and parents may recommend students for them. Other instances of third parties assessing people as needing to attend lifeskills training groups include: therapists for their clients; nurses and doctors for their patients; clergymen for people intending to get married or in marital difficulty; career workers for the unemployed; and social workers for people with substance abuse problems.

Leaders need to be sensitive to the interests of people who have recommended participants for their lifeskills training groups. Sometimes third parties can be actively supportive of participants attaining training objectives. In such instances there may be no conflict of interest between assessments conducted for the participants' purposes and the requirements of third parties. Indeed, third parties such as teachers may be asked to provide feedback on how participants are using their skills back in their natural settings. On other occasions, leaders may be in much more difficult positions of being contracted to provide reports to third parties that may not always help participants attain personal goals outside the group.

METHODS OF ASSESSMENT AND SELF-ASSESSMENT

Assessment may be either leader-centred or participant-centred. In leader-centred assessment, the source of power and control is the leader. It is the leader who decides what assessment takes place, when and how. In participant-centred assessment, participants discuss with the leader those methods of assessment that are most likely to be of value to them. Participants then make the final decisions as to which assessment methods are used. The dividing line between leader assessment and encouraging participant self-assessment is not exact. Leaders can establish expectations that are conducive or run counter to participants assuming responsibility for their learning. In practice, the difference may be more concerned with how an assessment method is used than with the method itself. Also, it may be in the best interests of participants to trust leader assessment choices, rather than to get bogged down in discussing them at the expense of time spent developing their skills. Nevertheless, the fundamental point remains: participants will not have their leaders around after the group ends, so both they and their leaders must collaborate to develop their self-assessment skills.

In counselling and psychotherapy, it is important that counsellor and client form a working alliance to attain therapeutic objectives. Similarly, in lifeskills groups, it is important that leader and participants form a working alliance to attain training objectives. Therapeutic working alliances are more likely to occur where the counsellor offers empathic understanding, genuineness and respect to the client. The emotional climate should be task-orientated, yet at the same time relaxed and friendly. The same holds true for training groups. Leaders can introduce the idea of assessment in ways that enlist the interest of participants and make them feel that the findings may be of value to them in attaining their personal goals. On the other hand, leaders may introduce assessment in ways that threaten and distance participants and make them feel that the lifeskills group is a waste of time.

Leaders have to design assessment procedures that are appropriate for their specific training goals. Below, different methods of assessment and of encouraging self-assessment are reviewed.

Interviews

Interviews in lifeskills training groups can be conducted by either leaders or participants. Formal leader assessment interviews tend to take place, if at all, in the preparatory stage of training groups. At other times during their groups, leaders may ask a series of assessment questions that constitute a more informal kind of interviewing. However, this is likely to be done with other group participants present, whereas intake interviews are conducted one-to-one. Leader purposes in intake interviews can include helping potential participants to assess whether the programme is right for them as well as helping them to understand better their strengths and weaknesses in the targeted lifeskills.

AREAS FOR ASSESSMENT

In an intake interview for a lifeskills training group, areas for leader assessment and participant self-assessment may include the following: reasons for wanting to join the lifeskills group, including whether a referral was involved; knowledge and expectations about the training group; motivation for change and ability to handle setbacks; level of functioning in the skills area – behaviour, thinking, feelings and physical reactions in specific situations; the length of time the skills area has been a problem; brief details of its history; perceived strengths both in relation to the targeted skills and in other relevant areas; the degree of interference of the skills weaknesses with the participant's well-being; factors maintaining the skills weaknesses – antecedents and payoffs of problematic behaviours; past coping strategies and their consequences; the nature of the participant's other problems;

support factors for attaining training objectives; environmental barriers to attaining training objectives; and current life stresses and demands.

ASSESSMENT INTERVIEW SKILLS

A few assessment interview skills are briefly mentioned here. Most of these skills may fruitfully be adapted to leading training groups. Readers wanting more detailed discussion of the skills of individual interviewing are referred elsewhere (Brammer, 1985; Cormier & Cormier, 1985; Egan, 1990; Nelson-Jones, 1988b).

- *Physical setting.* Attention should be paid to the environment and seating arrangements. Quiet, privacy, absence of interruption and pleasant decor are all important. Chairs should be of the same height, possibly with a coffee table between them, and placed at a slight angle to avoid the possibility of the interview seeming like a face-to-face interrogation.

- *Empathic understanding.* Leaders need to show that they are interested in the perceptions and personal meanings of participants and value and respect them as unique persons. They require the skills of both understanding and also showing that they have understood what participants try to tell them. This understanding entails creating a safe emotional climate and having good skills at decoding verbal, vocal and body messages. A useful skill is to reflect what the participant has just said and pause to see if they want to continue before asking your next question. By doing this you show that you have heard, check the accuracy of your understanding, give yourself more time to formulate your next question, and help to prevent participants from feeling interrogated.

- *Use of questions.* Various kinds of questions help assessment and self-assessment. Open-ended questions, unlike closed-ended questions, allow participants much choice in how they wish to respond. An example of a closed-ended question is: 'Is your boss good or bad?', whereas an open-ended question might be: 'What do you think about your boss?' Open-ended questions can be helpful at the start of interviews to encourage participants to tell their stories in their own words. They can be useful later to help participants share personal meanings without putting words into their mouths.

When conducting thorough assessments, leaders require detailed information. Specify questions help participants to work on their problems by enabling them to understand them more specifically and clearly. Specify questions include: 'Can you give a specific example?', 'How did you and the other person actually behave?', 'What were your thoughts in the situation?' Leaders often need to clarify that theirs and participants' understanding of words and phrases correspond. For example, participants who say that they feel low might be asked: 'When you say you feel low, what do you mean?'

Reality-testing questions can also help to clarify skills strengths and weaknesses. Examples of such questions are: 'You say that you have no friends;

where is the evidence?' or 'You say that you are poor at public speaking; where is the evidence that you are poor and is there any evidence that you may have some strengths as well in the area?' An advantage of such questions is that they encourage participants to confront themselves with the evidence rather than having the confrontations coming from the leader. Leader confrontation may be more threatening and less useful in helping participants to perceive the evidence accurately.

- *Use of experiential information.* Leaders may learn much about participants' skills strengths and weaknesses through observing body and voice messages. Skilled interviewers 'listen with the third ear' and learn to trust their inner experiencing of the client. Sometimes the voice and body messages that may be indicative of skills strengths and weaknesses are sent clearly. For example, people may or may not: take care over their physical appearance; look as though they are on drugs; attend the interview on time; maintain a reasonable level of eye contact; talk about their feelings in ways that show they feel them too; and so on. On other occasions, the cues that the participant is anxious, economizing on the truth, confused or something else may be much more subtle. Leaders may choose to stay within the participant's frame of reference and just reflect the messages they receive and possibly ask for clarification. Alternatively, leaders may go further and gently or more forcibly confront participants not only with how they experience their behaviours but also with their possible significance for their lifeskills difficulties.

- *Use of role-play.* Especially where relationship skills are involved, valuable information may be provided by leaders performing assessment role-plays with participants. Lifeskills entail sending voice and body as well as verbal messages. Leaders are limited in their ability to assess if they restrict themselves to verbal descriptions of behaviour. At its simplest an assessment role-play might entail asking a participant to imagine you are someone with whom they experience difficulty. Then they are instructed to speak to you with the voice and body as well as with the verbal messages that they would use in real life. Elaborations of this can include more effort in setting the scene and coaching you in how to respond. You may also mirror their behaviour or reverse roles to help them to assess how they communicate. Participants may need encouragement to overcome their anxiety about engaging in role-play. You can explain to them that you are more likely to be able to help them if you observe how they actually behave rather than just hear their descriptions. You understand that they may feel uncomfortable at first, but this should pass.

- *Summarizing.* Summaries may be used at various stages of the assessment interview. They may perform bridging functions between the different sections of the developing session. Summaries can also be very useful at the end of assessment interviews when they can: give the session closure; ensure that leaders have accurately understood participants; provide feedback to participants on skills strengths and weaknesses; and check with participants that they have accurately understood the content of the session. Participants should always be asked for their reactions to leader end-of-session summaries and also whether or not they wish to add anything. Sometimes it is a good idea to have participants summarize the gist of the session in their own words to check how much they have really understood. If relevant, it is important at the end of an assessment interview to communicate whether or not the participants have been admitted to the group. Also, you should check whether or not they understand the group's administrative details.

Exercise 7 Self-assessment and assessment of a specific lifeskill

Part A Self-assessment
Select a specific lifeskill that you wish to improve. Write out an analysis of your strengths and weaknesses for this lifeskill. Cover each of the areas for assessment mentioned in the text, starting with 'motivation for change and ability to handle setbacks'.

Part B Conducting an assessment interview
Acting as a training group leader, conduct an interview with a partner in which together you assess a specific lifeskill that he or she wishes to improve. Pay attention to the areas of assessment mentioned in the text. Select a suitable physical setting for your interview and try to use the following skills:

Empathic understanding
Good use of questions (open-ended, specify, reality testing)
Use of experiential information
Use of role-play
Summarizing

Afterwards discuss with your partner and then reverse roles so that your partner acts as the training group leader interviewing you about a specific lifeskill that you wish to improve.

PEER INTERVIEWS

Peer interviews in which participants help each other to assess lifeskills can be interspersed throughout training groups. For example, participants can be asked to pair off and to spend ten minutes each way, with one acting as interviewer and the other as interviewee. Interview tasks can include: initial assessment of a skills area, monitoring progress and homework, and end-of-lifeskills-group assessment. During a group, the leader cannot afford to spend much time with any single participant in comparison to the others. Consequently, one of the most effective ways of encouraging assessment and self-assessment is to make time for brief participant interviews. Helping others often helps participants with their own self-assessment. Furthermore, participant interviews get everybody in the group involved. A variation of interviewing in pairs is to have threes in which the third participant acts as either an observer who later makes comments or as a coach for the interviewer.

Group interaction

Participants can learn much about their lifeskills through interacting in groups as well as in pairs. A skilled leader facilitates participants learning from each other. Some of these leader skills are presented in the next chapter. Ways in which group interaction helps participants to assess their lifeskills include: discussing the purposes of assessment; discussing problems of mutual concern; obtaining feedback from others; learning from others' experiences inside and outside the group; and observing how others behave. If the numbers in a training group are large, assessment through group interaction may be encouraged by sub-grouping. Sometimes audio- or video-recording and playback of group interactions provides participants with valuable self-assessment information.

Observation in natural settings

Assessment information can be obtained about participants through observations made on them in their natural environments. Often, participants are recommended for lifeskills training groups on the basis of observations by others: for instance, managers by senior managers, workers by bosses, patients by doctors, teachers by administrators, pupils by teachers, and clients by counsellors. Sometimes, either verbal or written reports will be sent to leaders explaining the referral. Referral information may be useful in helping leaders to assess both participants' lifeskills and their degree of environmental support. However, referral information requires cautious treatment, since it may be heavily influenced by referees' personal needs and biases.

Observational assessment information about behaviour in natural settings can come from many sources and be collected either systematically or otherwise. Teachers, parents, spouses, friends, bosses, and colleagues can all be sources of such information. However, such people may require instruction in what to look for. Additionally, leaders may spend time observing participants in their natural settings and seeing how they exhibit lifeskills strengths and weaknesses. For instance, leaders may observe in action either managers poor at conducting meetings or people poor at making requests in shops. Collecting information from natural or 'home' settings may take place before, at the start of, during, at the end of and after training groups. Such information may be especially useful in assessing the extent to which there is transfer of lifeskills to everyday life.

BEHAVIOUR RATING FORMS

Systematic collection of observational information involves the use of behaviour rating forms. The simplest way of recording behaviours is quantitative – namely, counting the number of behaviours in each category that occur in a given period of time. Table 5.1 is an example of a behaviour rating form that might be used to assess conversation skills, say talking to a few friends or how family members

Table 5.1 Behaviour rating form for verbal conversational skills

Initiates topic	
Maintains conversation	
Reveals personal information	
Asks for personal information	
Gives opinion	
Asks opinion	
Listens	
Agrees	
Disagrees	
Shows aggression	
Shows support	
Shows appreciation	
Uses humour	

interact at dinner. If this form is being used to collect initial or 'baseline' data, the subjects should be asked to behave as closely as possible to normal.

The conversational skills behaviour rating form contained in Table 5.1 may be filled out quantitatively by marking each time the subject engages in a category of behaviour. A qualitative dimension may be built into the assessment by putting a minus sign (−) for each inappropriate behaviour and a plus sign (+) for each appropriate behaviour. Filling in the form might be made even more qualitative by using a 5-point scale of appropriateness ranging from 1, very inappropriate, to 5, very appropriate, for each behaviour. If the rater wishes to assess more than one person's behaviour, each of them can be assigned a column with their name at the top. Behaviour rating forms can focus on voice and body as well as verbal messages. Because there are many issues connected with what actually is a unit of behaviour and what each category measures, leaders have to think carefully before using such rating scales. Also, untrained raters may require training. If correctly used, behaviour rating forms filled out in natural settings can provide a useful record of both initial baseline behaviour and of transfer of training and change over time.

Observational behaviour ratings may be made on how participants handle situations simulated from their natural settings. For example, managers can be set tasks such as either counselling underperforming workers or taking part in group discussions on marketing initiatives (Gratton, 1985). Behaviour rating forms may also be used during lifeskills training groups. For example, in a programme on conversational skills, the group can be divided into a 'goldfish' format with an inner and outer circle. The inner circle can be instructed to converse with each other. Participants in the outer circle rate the behaviours of one or more of their peers in the inner circle.

SOCIOMETRIC MEASURES

Moreno developed the sociometric method to establish patterns of feelings of acceptance and rejection and of like and dislike among members of groups (Moreno, 1934). Sociometric ratings can be made in participants' natural settings to ascertain how they behave and are perceived to behave. For example, a leader running a team-building course for a group of workers in a company may assess such matters as: patterns of like and dislike, patterns of respect and disrespect, and frequency of contact in the group. Teachers who run lifeskills programmes to develop pupils' making-friends skills may trace the patterns of interactions within a class group by gathering information about who the children consider to be their friends, to whom they feel they can disclose personal information, and who they would invite to activities such as birthday parties.

Sociometric data may be collected by means of interview schedules, question-naires, or direct observation. A simple way of collecting sociometric information is the use of circles. For instance, a classroom group of children might be given a rating form with a series of four circles of increasing size, each having the same mid-point. They could be asked to put the name of their best friend or friends in the inner circle, their good friends in the next circle, their acquaintances in the next circle and the names of those people whom they dislike in the outer circle. Sociometric data are also often presented by allocating a numbered circle to each member of a group and then drawing lines with arrows between the circles indicating contact and either liking (a straight line) or dislike (a broken line). Sometimes, when depicting patterns of family interaction, females are depicted as circles and males as squares.

Participants may have mixed feelings about being observed in their natural settings. Some may welcome it as a means of improving their lifeskills. Others may see it as an invasion of privacy that interferes with the building of trust with their leaders. Furthermore, collecting information in 'home' settings may threaten participants. For instance, evidence of unpopularity may cause pain. In addition, some participants may fear that assessment information collected in 'home' settings, for instance at work, may be used against rather than for them. Leaders need to be sensitive to participants' feelings regarding both whether and how they collect this information. Furthermore, leaders need to be good at giving what may be unwelcome feedback.

Participant self-observation and monitoring

At every stage of a training group, participants can collect their own self-observation data. Self-observation and monitoring takes place both inside and outside scheduled group sessions. Participant self-observation has many purposes for both leaders and participants, including: initial assessment of skills strengths and weaknesses; establishing a baseline against which to measure change; testing accuracy of perceptions regarding behaviour; monitoring progress; monitoring homework assignments; collecting data on the consequences of trying out changed behaviours; providing information on transfer of skills to real life settings; and contributing to end-of-group assessment of strengths and weaknesses.

DIARIES AND JOURNALS

With the growth of cognitive-behavioural approaches to training, participants are increasingly being encouraged to monitor not only their actions, but also their thoughts and feelings. Keeping a diary or journal is one way of monitoring and recording observations in a lifeskills area. Special attention may be paid to writing up critical incidents where skills may have been used well or poorly. The learnings from different experiences can be recorded for future reference. Although diaries and journals may be useful, some participants find this approach too unstructured and too easy to ignore. A further drawback is that the collection of information may be insufficiently systematic. Nevertheless, occasions may occur where the freedom allowed by choosing what one writes in a diary or personal journal has much to recommend it. Also, participants have different learning styles and some may work hard and profitably on this method of self-assessment.

THINKING, FEELING AND BEHAVIOUR LOGS

Based on the work of cognitive psychologists and psychiatrists like Albert Ellis (1962, 1980, 1989) and Aaron Beck (Beck & Greenberg, 1974; Beck & Emery, 1985), there has been a trend towards self-observation and monitoring using an ABC format. In the ABC format:

A = The activating event or stimulus.
B = The individual's beliefs, thoughts and visual images about the activating event.
C = The individual's feeling and behaviours as a consequence of the activating event; C may be extended to include the consequences provided by others for the individual's behaviours.

What cognitive therapists try to do by means of the ABC format is to go beyond description of behaviour to show clients how their thoughts, feelings and behaviours are interrelated. The idea is that how individuals feel and behave at C is heavily influenced by how they think at B about A, the activating event. Table 5.2 shows entries for one day in a thinking, feeling and behaviour monitoring log for a man

Table 5.2 Example of thinking, feeling and behaviour log in the ABC format

A (THE ACTIVATING EVENT, STARTING WITH DATE, TIME AND PLACE)	B (BELIEFS AND THOUGHTS)	C (CONSEQUENCES, FEELINGS, BEHAVIOURS, OTHERS' REACTIONS)
July 14, 8 a.m., home. Wife comes to breakfast in curlers.	Why can't she make more effort to please me?	Resentment, made sarcastic comment, stormed out of house.
July 14, 1.15 a.m., work. My secretary is late back from her lunch break.	She is ripping the company off and does not respect me.	Very angry and tense, made no comment, gave her extra task, tension between us.
July 14, 7.45 p.m., home. Read son's average report.	I'm paying for him to go to a private school, he should work harder.	Got mad, told son to pull his socks up or else, son withdrew to his room.

entering a managing-anger lifeskills group. Often such a log would be kept for one or two weeks.

The following guidelines may help you to use thinking, feeling and behaviour logs.

1. Always supply the log yourself. Do not expect participants to make up their own logs. They may not do so in the first place and, even if they do, they may get them wrong.

2. Keep your logs simple and in line with participants' capacities to understand and complete them.

3. Provide participants with a rationale for why it is important to fill in the log. You need to motivate them to do so. You can say something like: 'Filling the log in conscientiously will help both of us to understand your difficulties and thus make better decisions about how to handle them.'

4. Give clear instructions on how to fill in the log and make sure that participants are capable of following them.

5. Reward participants for filling in their logs by showing an interest in their answers and praising them. This guideline is based on the basic behavioural principle that actions that are rewarded are more likely to be repeated.

6. Encourage participants to use logs as a way of building up their self-assessment skills. Try to get them to take an active role in analysing the significance of the findings. Get them to share their assessment of what the logs communicate to them about their pattern of thinking, feeling and behaving.

7. Do not expect participants to change their behaviour on the basis of self-observation alone. They are likely to need assistance, work and practice to build up their skills strengths.

AUDIOVISUAL FEEDBACK

Participants may learn much by observing how they actually behave in various lifeskills areas. For example, a couple who join a managing-conflict lifeskills group can be videoed after being given the instruction: 'Show us how you behave when you have a good fight at home. Do not hold back and be polite – try to make it as real as possible.' Another example is that of employees sent on public speaking courses who can be videoed speaking before an audience. In each of the above instances, participants can be shown the playback and asked to evaluate what are their skills strengths and weaknesses.

Audiovisual feedback can also be used during the lifeskills programme to encourage participant self-assessment. A couple who are learning managing-conflict skills can be asked to show how they might use their new skills in a difficult area for them. At the playback, they might be asked to identify which of their own and their partner's behaviours they thought were helpful or harmful. Sometimes participants may fill in a 'yes' or 'no' checklist when they watch the playback (Saskatchewan Newstart, 1973). For instance, items on a checklist for someone learning public speaking skills might include 'I talked direct to the audience', 'I gave a clear introduction', 'I avoided a large number of uhm's' and 'My voice could easily be heard'.

PSYCHOLOGICAL TESTS AND LIFESKILLS INVENTORIES

Numerous psychological tests and skills inventories are available from which leaders may choose. Anastasi writes: 'A psychological test is essentially an objective and standardized measure of a sample of behavior' (Anastasi, 1988, p. 23). 'Objective' means that the test has been constructed to measure and score the behaviour under consideration in as objective a way as possible, thus minimizing the chances of using invalid samples of behaviour and of subjectivity in marking. 'Standardized' means that the test will be administered in a standard way and scored so that an individual's score can be compared with the scores of a group of similar people. Traditionally, psychological tests have been developed to gather information in the following areas: mental ability; aptitudes; achievement; personality; and interests and values. Sometimes psychological tests are designed to be self-administered rather than administered by a professional person, for example Holland's Self Directed Search (Holland, 1987).

Although they overlap, a distinction is made here between psychological tests and skills inventories. Skills inventories are self-report measures designed to elicit participants' perceptions of their behaviours and cognitions in different skills areas, for example assertion. Clearly, leaders have to choose skills inventories that meet their assessment purposes for any lifeskills group that they run.

Who can use psychological tests and lifeskills inventories?

Leaders need to be competent in the three major aspects of using tests and skills inventories: selection, administration and scoring, and interpreting results. Test publishers and distributors may apply user qualification criteria before making tests and inventories available. In any event, there is an ethical obligation for lifeskills group leaders to be trained and competent in the use of any skills inventory that they select.

Sources of information about tests and skills inventories

Leaders may find information on tests and measures in the following places.

SOURCEBOOKS

A very important source of information is the series of Mental Measurements Yearbooks compiled by the Buros Institute of Mental Measurement at the University of Nebraska. The introduction to the most recent yearbook states: '*The Ninth Mental Measurements Yearbook*, like the eight earlier yearbooks in the series, is designed to assist test users in education, psychology, and industry to choose more judiciously from the many tests available' (Mitchell, 1985, p. XIII). The yearbooks are composed of test reviews during a specified period; thus each yearbook supplements rather than supplants previous yearbooks. The Buros Institute has also compiled *Tests in Print 111* (Mitchell, 1983), which is an index to tests, test reviews and the literature on specific tests.

Test Critiques (Vols 1–6) is another series of test review books (Keyser & Sweetland, 1984–1987). From Vol. 3 on, each volume has a cumulative subject index incorporating the tests reviewed in all editions to date. A further valuable source of information is *Tests* (Sweetland & Keyser, 1986). The introduction to the second edition states: '*Tests*, a reference guide containing information on thousands of assessment instruments, is designed especially for psychologists, educators and human resource personnel who search for tests to satisfy assessment needs' (Sweetland & Keyser, 1986, p. IX). Readers are advised to look at the most current editions of each of the above sourcebooks.

PUBLISHERS' CATALOGUES

Publishers' and distributors' test catalogues provide another source of information on which tests are available. A comprehensive directory and index of North American test publishers, with their addresses, is provided at the end of the latest Mental Measurements Yearbook. Anastasi provides a listing of the names and addresses of some of the larger American publishers and distributors of psychological tests (Anastasi, 1988).

Important test publishers and distributors outside North America include: the National Foundation for Educational Research – Nelson (Darville House, 2 Oxford Road East, Windsor, Berkshire SL4 1DF, UK); the Australian Council for Educational Research (P.O. Box 210, Hawthorn, Victoria 3122, Australia); Harcourt Brace Jovanovich, Australia (Locked Bag 16, Marrickville, New South Wales 2204, Australia); and the New Zealand Council for Educational Research (Education House, 178–182 Willis Street, Wellington, New Zealand). Quite apart from publishing and distributing local instruments, the above organizations are often distribution agents for North American test publishers.

RESEARCH ARTICLES AND BOOKS

Research articles evaluating training in specific lifeskills areas can be a good source of information about tests and skills inventories. Also, books that summarize research and practice in different skills areas can provide leaders with helpful ideas on assessment measures. Additionally, leaders may keep abreast of developments in testing by reading measurement journals such as *Educational and Psychological Measurement, Measurement and Evaluation in Guidance*, the *Journal of Personality Assessment* and the *Journal of Applied Measurement*.

Assessing psychological tests and skills inventories

Leaders always need to evaluate the information provided in the manual of any test that they consider using. *Standards for Educational and Psychological Testing* is a comprehensive guide to the evaluation of psychological tests (American Psychological Association, 1985). Additionally, leaders are well advised to look at the individual items of, if not actually complete, any assessment instrument that they seriously review. The following are some important considerations in reviewing a psychological test or lifeskills inventory manual.

- *Rationale.* Review the constructor's purpose in devising the instrument. Also, look for the date when the instrument and its manual were first published and for any subsequent revisions.

- *Who can take the instrument?* Carefully examine the population for which the instrument is intended.

- *Administration details.* Administration details include: difficulty of administration from the leader's viewpoint; whether any special training or professional qualifications are needed; the time that the instrument takes to complete;

whether it is for group or individual administration; the format or formats in which the instrument is available; whether there are practice items; whether the administration instructions are clear, including allowable variations in administration and their likely consequences; and whether the instrument is machine- or hand-scored and the ease with which scoring can be performed.

- *Reliability.* Reliability refers to the consistency of an instrument. Different ways of assessing reliability include: the same instrument taken at two different times, test–retest reliability; two different forms of the same instrument, alternative forms reliability; and measuring internal consistency on comparable halves of a test from a single administration, split-half reliability. Usually reliability is expressed in terms of correlation coefficients indicating the extent to which two measures are related, with test–retest and internal consistency coefficients possibly being most common. High reliability is not in itself a measure of high validity.

- *Validity.* Validity, a central concept in measurement, means how well an instrument measures what it sets out to measure. The three main kinds of validity are predictive, content and construct. Predictive or criterion-orientated validity refers to the soundness with which predictions can be made on the basis of a test score against some future criterion, such as the future performance of a task. Content validity refers to how well the instrument samples the behaviours that it seeks to measure. Construct validity involves setting up a number of hypotheses about the test variable as a construct or concept and then examining the evidence relative to these hypotheses (Professional Affairs Board, 1980). When assessing the validity of a measure, leaders need to be clear about their own purposes, since the kinds of validity that are important for them relate to their purposes.

- *Item analysis and scale development.* Test items can be analysed qualitatively, in terms of their content and form, and quantitatively, in terms of their statistical properties, such as item difficulty and item validity. Some manuals provide details of how the items for a test were selected and analysed. Furthermore, many tests add the scores on groups of individual items to form scales. A manual may provide details on the rationale, statistical and otherwise, for the selection of items to form a test's scales.

- *Norms.* Psychological tests are generally interpreted with reference to norms. These norms illustrate the performance on the test of the population or populations for which the test was intended. Norms enable the test score of an individual to be related to the distribution of scores of a suitably large and relevant reference group.

- *Interpretation.* The intentions of the psychological test or skills inventory constructor for interpreting results should be clearly indicated. Information should be provided on common interpretive errors and on any other special factors that might affect interpretation.

Choosing psychological tests and skills inventories

Since there is a multiplicity of group leader, participant and third party assessment purposes and also a wide variety of lifeskills areas, generalizations about choosing psychological tests and skills inventories need to be made and treated with caution. An instrument may be useful for training purposes if it fulfils some of the following criteria. First, there is a considerable amount of evidence about just what lifeskill it measures. At best, most psychological tests and skills inventories are self-report measures rather than objective measures of observable behaviours. Second, the instrument lends itself to being used for self-assessment and not just for leader assessment. Third, using the instrument fits into the lifeskills learning process rather than disrupts it. Such disruptions may be either practical, in terms of time and inconvenience, or emotional, in terms of generating resistances, or both. Leaders should avoid saturation testing, involving the 'buckshot' use of a comprehensive battery of tests and skills inventories. They should beware of 'testing for testing's sake'. Instead, leaders should aim for precision testing, only using an instrument or instruments appropriate to the specific needs and states of readiness of the particular participants in a given group.

A further issue in selecting psychological tests and lifeskills inventories is the extent of participant involvement in their choice. If participants do not see the relevance of instruments, they either may refuse to complete them or complete them in invalid ways. Some leaders consider that participant completion of any assessment measures should be voluntary (Priestley *et al.*, 1978). However, the voluntary versus compulsory participation issue is not so simple where participants are being sent on training programmes at the expense of their employers. It may be more important for participants to be helped by leaders to see the relevance to improving their lifeskills of any psychological test or skills inventory that they are asked to take than for them to have a say in the selection of these instruments. Participants have a right to know the purposes for which the information is being collected and the degree of confidentiality that they can expect.

Administering psychological tests and lifeskills inventories

Stress has already been laid on the importance of leaders forming a working alliance with participants with regard to any assessment procedures used in a training group. This rapport should help participants to take the procedures seriously. Psychological tests and lifeskills inventories need to be administered and scored in a standard way or else they lose their statistical meaning. Leaders can contribute to ensuring standardization before, during and after the testing process. Before the session, they can ensure that the test materials are suitably prepared and that they themselves are fully versed in how to administer them. In addition, they can see that the testing conditions are as adequate as possible. During the session, they can follow any psychological test or lifeskills inventory manual precisely. Additionally, if it is a group administration, leaders can make periodic visual checks to ensure that the participants are completing each instrument properly. After the session, leaders can see that the scoring instructions are followed as intended. Needless to say, the safe transit and storage of participants' responses to instruments is vital.

Interpreting psychological tests and lifeskills inventories

Many lifeskills inventories do not require scoring by third parties; rather, participants can score and evaluate their own answers. Participants can assess the meaning of their answers either on their own or in conjunction with their group leaders and other participants. Sometimes the leaders may need to score and feed back the findings of instruments. Although each participant may be given information in written form, leaders may have to discuss the meaning of findings in the group. Here it is important that leaders do not over-interpret the significance of the data, but discuss them as clearly and objectively as possible. Participants should be allowed to share their reactions to the findings. The information provided by psychological tests and lifeskills inventories may threaten participants. Despite the validity of instruments, it is still possible for participants to distort findings to meet their psychological needs. Consequently, to minimize this risk, leaders need to provide a safe emotional climate for the discussion of findings.

Some problems in using psychological tests and lifeskills inventories

Below are just a few of the many considerations that leaders need to bear in mind about using tests and lifeskills inventories. Some respondents may respond in set ways. The concept of *response sets* implies that some people have tendencies to answer items in fixed ways that do not truly represent their behaviour and perceptions. For instance, certain participants may have an acquiescence response set, tending to answer 'yes' to questions. *Faking* implies conscious misrepresentation. Faking is especially likely to take place where participants have external reasons for doing well or badly, for instance obtaining or not obtaining a promotion. Some participants may let their need for *social desirability* or to be seen by the leader in an approved light interfere with the accuracy of their responses. *Test anxiety* may distort some people's test scores. Psychological tests and lifeskills inventories can threaten participants. Test anxiety may debilitate rather than facilitate their performance. Leaders who are good at establishing rapport with participants may lessen test anxiety.

Resistances to taking psychological tests and lifeskills inventories may stem from fears about *invasion of privacy*. Anastasi observes that protection of privacy involves two key elements: relevance and informed consent (Anastasi, 1988). Relevance means that the information that participants are asked to reveal must be relevant to the stated purposes of assessment. Informed consent refers to agreement by participants, after being adequately briefed about the nature and purposes of the assessment procedures, to take part in completing them. An obvious and extremely serious invasion of privacy is when a leader breaks a verbal or written contract involving not divulging test findings. *Test and lifeskills inventory bias* may be introduced, albeit unknowingly, into developing, selecting, administering and reporting the results of instruments. Reasons for bias may include sexism, racism, ageism and insensitivity to socio-economic and cultural differences. For instance, although this is increasingly unlikely, tests and inventories may still use sexist language.

Exercise 8 Using psychological tests and lifeskills inventories

Write out your answers to the following questions.

1. Finding out about tests and inventories
Think of a specific lifeskill around which you might build a training group. Assuming that you are so inclined, what are some of the psychological tests and lifeskills inventories that you might consider as part of your assessment procedures? To answer this question you are encouraged to look up some of the sources of test information mentioned in the text.

2. Assessing your skills strengths and weaknesses
Make up a worksheet similar to the following. Use the worksheet to assess your skills strengths and weaknesses in each of the three major aspects of using tests and inventories as a lifeskills group leader.

USE OF TESTS AND INVENTORIES	SKILLS STRENGTHS	SKILLS WEAKNESSES
Selection		
Administration		
Interpretation		

3. Problems associated with using tests and inventories
What are some of the main problems that might be associated with using psychological tests and lifeskills inventories in any future lifeskills training groups that you may choose to offer?

DEVISE ASSESSMENT MEASURES

The earlier discussions on behaviour rating forms and on thinking, feeling and behaviour logs assumed that, as a leader, you might want to devise your own assessment measures. You cannot always assume that existing psychological tests and lifeskills inventories are suitable for your purposes. For example, you may want something simpler, shorter, more focused on a specific set of skills, more tailored to the language ability and to the age range of the groups with whom you work, and cheaper and more available than assessment measures already on the market. The following are some formats that you can use for developing your own assessment measures.

Sentence completion

You can ask participants to complete sentences that elicit information about how they think, feel and act. Let us take the example of unemployed teenagers who join a lifeskills group in job-seeking skills. Sample sentences that these teenagers might be asked to complete include:

My biggest problem in getting a job is ....

My other problems in getting a job are ....

The skills that I have to offer an employer are ....

The sorts of things that I want out of a job are ....

When I go for a job interview, I feel ....

When I go for a job interview, I think ....

When I go for a job interview, I act ....

An advantage of the sentence completion method is that it taps into participants' personal meanings with open-ended rather than closed-ended sentences. Furthermore, your ability to develop sentences focused on feeling, thinking and action allows you a high degree of flexibility in what you focus on. Sentence completion may seem simple and naïve, but then in lifeskills training groups simple is often smart, and leader naïvety may be shown up in trying to be too sophisticated.

Pose problem situations

Leaders can assess participants current skills levels by asking how they might behave in specific problem situations relevant to the focus of a lifeskills programme. You may seek responses to the problems in either open-ended or closed-ended ways. In an open-ended format, you may describe a scene and ask a question to find out how participants either currently behave or would like to behave. For example, an assessment problem in a making contact skills programme for university students might be as follows.

> 'You are five minutes early for class and a man/girl that you have been interested in for the past few weeks, but never spoken to, comes and sits next to you. How would you behave (like to behave)————?'

Nelson *et al.* (1985) used a similar question in their research on ways of assessing social inadequacy. They developed the following criteria as indicative of socially skilled performance: (1) person must introduce himself/herself; (2) person must make 'small talk' before specific invitation is made; (3) a specific invitation is made; and (4) specific information must be given concerning the invitation (where, when, what etc.). As a leader, you may go beyond setting problems, to devising criteria whereby you assess whether participants show skills strengths or weaknesses in their responses.

With the closed-ended format, you set a problem with alternative answers as in a multiple choice test. Let us take an example from a lifeskills programme focused on teaching 10–11-year-olds assertion and social problem-solving skills.

'You are standing in line in the school canteen waiting to be served lunch when another student roughly your own size pushes in front of you; tick the answer below that most represents how you would most likely behave.'

—I would push him/her back hard and tell him/her to get the hell out of my way.

—I would pretend that I had not noticed and do nothing.

—I would firmly say that I was in line first and would he/she please go to the end of the line.

In the above example, each of the answers represents a different kind of behaviour: namely, aggressive, non-assertive and assertive. Consequently, participants' answers categorize them in terms of this particular question.

Checklists

Checklists can focus on virtually any aspect of a lifeskill that you want. Many psychological tests are checklists in which respondents are asked to check behaviours that, unknown to them, the test constructor has grouped into various categories for scoring purposes. You can devise your own checklists to suit your assessment purposes. Below is a simple checklist that a leader running an overcoming-shyness lifeskills group has devised to help participants to identify specific categories of people with whom they feel shy.

What people are associated with any feelings of shyness that you may have? Please tick those categories of people with whom you feel shy.

Mother ——————————   Same sex ——————————

Father ——————————   Opposite sex ——————————

Aunts ——————————   Children ——————————

Uncles ———————	Friends ———————
Grandparents ———————	Neighbours ———————
Boyfriend/Girlfriend ———	Marital partner ———
Mother-in-law ———————	Unmarried partner ———
Father-in-law ———————	Strangers ———————
Authorities by virtue of knowledge ———————	People of higher status ———————
Authorities by virtue of role ———————	People of lower status ———————

Checklists can provide more information if they have boxes in which people can tick frequency. For instance, a question on a checklist for a stress management programme might be: 'I worry about my physical fitness', with participants having the option of placing a tick in one of three boxes: often, sometimes, never.

Card sorts

Card sorts are another way of collecting assessment and self-assessment information. Instead of using a paper-and-pencil questionnaire format, the items are printed on to individual cards which the participant then sorts into piles. For instance, in a developing-leisure-skills lifeskills group, a large list of different leisure activities might be placed on different cards. Participants could be asked to sort these cards into piles in various ways: for example, whether they currently engage in the activities often, sometimes, or never, or whether they like, dislike or are indifferent to the activities.

Rankings

Rankings provide another source of evaluative information. Rankings can be helpful in providing positive and negative information: what a participant likes and wants or dislikes and does not want. For example, in a job search lifeskills group, participants might be given a list of 12 characteristics of jobs, such as wages above a certain figure, brief travel time to work, and opportunity to meet people, and asked to rank them from 1 to 12 in terms of importance in choosing a job. Other uses of rankings are for finding out which of their problems participants consider most important to work on, and sociometric rankings in which participants rank which of the other group members they like, might want to spend time with and so on.

Rating scales

Rating scales provide another way of obtaining evaluative information, either quantitative or qualitative, concerning various items. For example, in an initial assessment as part of a supervisory skills training programme, a leader could request that participants complete a questionnaire with the following instructions.

> The questionnaire below lists a number of super-
> visory skills in five broad areas. Using the
> following scale, rate how satisfied you are with
> your specific skills in each of the five areas:
>
> 3   Much need for improvement
>
> 2   Moderate need for improvement
>
> 1   Slight need for improvement
>
> 0   No need for improvement
>
> Put a question mark (?) rather than a rating by
> any skill whose meaning is not clear to you at
> this stage of the training programme.

Another format for a rating scale is to ask participants to circle which of the numbers is nearest to where they think they are for individual items. For example, the following are two items on an initial assessment measure for a managing-test-anxiety programme.

> When you take a college test, circle the number
> that best describes you.
>
> Anxious   3 2 1 0 1 2 3 Relaxed
>
> Organized 3 2 1 0 1 2 3 Disorganized

Perhaps enough has been said to show you that there are many ways in which you can devise your own measures for assessing participants' lifeskills strengths and weaknesses and helping them to assess themselves. You may already know other ways. Later, when faced with a real life assessment challenge, you may become creative in finding different ways, for instance devising a game or some form of group task. Exercise 9 is designed to build up your skills and confidence at devising your own assessment measures.

Exercise 9   Devise your own assessment and participant self-assessment measures

Think of a specific lifeskill around which you might wish to build a training group – this may be the same lifeskill that you selected for Exercise 8. You may need to refer back to the text to answer the following questions, each of which may help you to assess and participants to assess themselves with regard to the lifeskill you have chosen.

1. Design a behaviour rating form to measure observable behaviours.

2. Design a thinking, feeling and behaviour log for participants to monitor themselves.

3. Formulate at least three sentences for participants to complete.

4. Pose two problem situations, one of which has an open-ended format and the other a closed-ended format.

5. Design a checklist to assess some aspect of the lifeskill.

6. Design a card sort having at least 15 items that participants might sort into at least three categories.

7. Design a question asking participants to rank at least eight items.

8. Design a rating scale to go at the front for participants to use in rating each item in a questionnaire.

9. Design a questionnaire made up of at least five pairs of adjectives. Ask participants to circle one of the following numbers between each pair of adjectives: 3,2,1,0,1,2,3.

10. Summarize which of the following ways of assessment and of helping participants assess themselves that you might want to use for:

    (a) initial assessment of the lifeskill either before or at the start of your training group

    (b) monitoring the lifeskill during the training group

    (c) end-of-training-group assessment of the lifeskill.

ENCOURAGE PARTICIPANTS TO SET PERSONAL GOALS

Having worked with participants to collect assessment information, how do leaders then use it to help them to improve their effectiveness? A major theme of this chapter is the importance of building participant personal responsibility by developing their skills at self-assessment. However, self-assessment is not an end in itself; rather, it is the stepping-stone to setting personal goals. In Chapters 3 and 4, mention was made of the need for leaders to clarify and state goals and sub-goals for their lifeskills programmes. Similarly, it can be helpful for participants to have overall goals that they wish to attain by the end of a programme as well as sub-goals that involve acquisition of the specific skills that will enable them to attain their overall goals.

State overall goals

Participants may set overall personal goals at any stage of a lifeskills training group as indicated in the following incomplete sentences.

'By the end of this group, my goal(s) is to be able to ....'

'By the end of the month, my goal(s) is to be able to..'

'By the end of this session, my goal(s) is to be able to..'

'By the end of this homework assignment, my goal(s) is to be able to..................'

'In the three months after the lifeskills group has ended, my goal(s) is to............'

Participants may require help in stating their overall goals. Considerations for good statements of overall goals include the following.

- *Realism*. Participants' goals are realistic when they adequately acknowledge the constraints of their emotional resources and personal skills. These constraints should be neither overestimated nor underestimated. Goals should reflect realistic and potentially attainable standards.

- *Specificity*. Participants should state their goals specifically. Ideally, goals should be stated so that participants can easily measure the success of their attempts to attain them. For instance, 'I want to make more friends' is not as good as 'I want to have a minimum of four new friends by the end of the group'.

- *A time frame*. Participants should state the time frame in which they want to accomplish each goal. Vague statements of intention are insufficient.

Leaders should encourage participants to keep written records of their personal goals. These goal statements may be placed in prominent positions at home or at work to act as reminders and motivators. At the end of the stipulated time frame, written statements of goals provide a yardstick for participants to measure how well they have done. A more formal approach to written statements of goals is that they constitute all or part of learning contracts that participants make with either themselves or their leaders (Wehrenberg, 1988).

State sub-goals

At the start of a lifeskills programme, participants may have insufficient insight into their skills weaknesses to be able to state sub-goals well. For instance, a participant on a public speaking programme may have as an overall goal: 'By the end of the programme I want to be able to address my fellow sales representatives in a calm and relaxed way, and make all my points clearly and cogently.' This participant is still likely only to have a vague idea of the specific thinking and action skills needed to attain this overall goal. As the programme develops, the participant is likely to have the required knowledge to state his or her specific sub-goals. The following is a format that leaders can use for helping participants to state goals and sub-goals.

By the end of...(stipulate period), my goal is to be able to .... (stipulate overall goal).

To attain my goal(s), the specific *thinking* skills that I need to develop are: (state specific thinking skills in 1,2,3 fashion).

To attain my goal(s), the specific *action* skills I need to develop are: (state specific action skills in 1,2,3 fashion).

CHAPTER HIGHLIGHTS

Assessment and self-assessment of lifeskills can take place at each of the four stages of a lifeskills training group: preparatory, initial, working and ending.

Training group leaders should always help participants to acquire the 'take-away' skills of assessing their own lifeskills.

Leaders, participants and third parties may each have their own agendas for conducting and participating in lifeskills assessment. Sometimes there are conflicts of interest between these agendas.

Methods of assessment and of self-assessment include: interviews, group inter-action, observation in natural settings, participant self-observation and monitoring, psychological tests and lifeskills inventories, and leader-devised assessment measures.

Leaders require skills of choosing and devising assessment measures that are tailor-made to the needs of specific lifeskills training groups. 'Buckshot' approaches to assessment are to be avoided.

Assessment and self-assessment measures that leaders can devise include: behavi-our rating forms; thinking, feeling and behaviour logs; sentence completion questions; posing problem situations; checklists; card sorts; ranking questions; and questions using rating scales.

Lifeskills assessment and self-assessment is not an end in itself: rather it should help participants to clarify and state personal goals and sub-goals.

Three important considerations in participants effectively stating personal goals are: realism, specificity and a time frame.

SIX

How to Facilitate Training Groups

I pay the schoolmaster, but 'tis the schoolboys that educate my son.

Ralph Waldo Emerson

CHAPTER QUESTIONS

Why do training group leaders require good facilitation skills?

What are the main ways in which group leaders send messages?

What either similar or different facilitation skills might a leader use in each of a training group's initial, working and ending stages?

What thinking skills weaknesses might interfere with how well training group leaders use facilitation skills?

INTRODUCTION

Below are some examples of where leaders can use and have used facilitation skills to help attain lifeskills training group goals.

- In an employment skills group for young prisoners, helping participants to assess their employment and communication skills.

- In a job club group for the handicapped, both supporting participants and also helping them to support each other as they seek employment (Azrin & Philip, 1979).

- In a problem-solving skills group for shy adolescents, helping participants to verbalize how they would apply the skills to a range of interpersonal problems (Christoff *et al.*, 1985).

- In a pain management group, assisting participants to share their experiences in using cognitive-behavioural skills to make the most of their lives despite their pain (Turner & Clancy, 1988).

- In a parent effectiveness training group, getting parents to be open about their weaknesses and misgivings about how they relate to their children (Gordon, 1970).

- In a relationship skills programme for college students, helping participants to overcome their anxieties about participating in role-plays in front of the group.

- In a psychological skills group for adult children of alcoholics, helping participants to talk about growing up in a 'chemically dependent' family and, where necessary, assisting them in confronting and diminishing denial (Downing & Walker, 1987).

- In management training workshops on a range of topics, such as interpersonal communication and making speeches, helping managers to participate actively (Zelko, 1986).

Though there is overlap, group leaders differ in how they use facilitation skills in training as contrasted with counselling groups. Training group leaders require both the skills of facilitating interactional groups and the additional skills of facilitating focused learning.

PURPOSES OF FACILITATION

Friends show their love in times of trouble, not in happiness.
Euripides

Some insight into the role of facilitation in lifeskills training groups may be gained from Yalom's research into therapeutic factors in group psychotherapy (Yalom, 1985; Bloch & Crouch, 1985). Therapeutic factors are factors that patients regard as being most salient to their improvement. Yalom acknowledges that a number of studies by himself and others have differed in their rank orderings of the value of the therapeutic factors. Yalom's 12 therapeutic factors are as follows: (1) altruism – thinking of and helping others; (2) group cohesiveness – a sense of belonging to the group, feeling accepted by the group and finding the group and its members attractive; (3) universality – learning that others have the same thoughts and problems too; (4) interpersonal learning (input) – learning how I come across to others and why; (5) interpersonal learning (output) – the opportunity to be more trustful and to work on how I relate to others; (6) guidance – either the group leader or group members making suggestions or giving advice to me; (7) catharsis – being able to ventilate and to learn how to express my feelings; (8) identification – finding role models in the behaviour of either the group leader or other group members; (9) family re-enactment – being in a simulated family that helps me to understand the influences on me of my original family; (10) self-understanding – learning about how, through the influences of my childhood and development, I distort my perceptions of myself and of others; (11) instillation of hope – seeing other group members improve and solve their problems; and (12) existential factors – learning to acknowledge more fully the existential parameters of death, freedom, responsibility and isolation and to make the most of my life.

Though training groups have the added agenda of a specific skills focus, many of Yalom's therapeutic factors are highly relevant to why training group leaders require good facilitation skills. Training group leaders use facilitation skills not just to work with individuals, but also to create a climate in which participants help each other. A willingness to work on real rather than surface issues may come about through the climate of cohesiveness, safety, trust and acceptance that leaders are able to foster in groups. Leaders seek to create norms or rules conducive to the group's work: for instance, honesty, openness and willingness to assume personal responsibility for changing skills weaknesses. Much of the learning in lifeskills training groups takes place between participants. Universality, instillation of hope and identification may come from other participants' disclosures. Interpersonal learning and self-understanding come from sharing and feedback within the group as well as from the advice and suggestions of the other participants. In addition, altruism is more likely to be experienced if leaders are skilled at releasing the group's healing potential.

A further set of reasons why good facilitation skills are important for leaders is that they help to build their influence base. Leading lifeskills groups may be viewed as a social influence process in which trainers use their facilitative and didactic skills to help participants to develop targeted behaviours (Strong, 1968, 1978; Corrigan *et al.*, 1980; Brehm & Smith, 1986). A distinction can be made between possessing power, being able to force participants to do something whether they like it or not, and having influence, being able to affect participants' feelings, thoughts and actions without having control over them (Steiner, 1981). At best, most training group leaders possess influence. Good facilitation skills are likely to help participants to feel understood and, thus, may enhance participants' perceptions of their leaders as expert, trustworthy and attractive. These perceptions enhance the influence base of leaders when facilitating both group discussion and didactic learning.

Facilitation skills in different stages of lifeskills training groups

Mention has already been made of the use of facilitation skills, such as empathy, in the *preparatory stage* when conducting intake interviews and initial assessments.

Preparing participants well for entering a training group may also help leaders to attain some of their later purposes when they use facilitation skills. Some leaders encourage inter-member interaction by asking participants to commit themselves to group contracts stressing such skills as self-disclosure, honesty, and listening to others. Also, leaders may ask participants to watch pre-group training videos in which these interpersonal skills are demonstrated.

In the *initial stage* of a lifeskills training group, leaders use facilitation skills to help participants to get to know one another and manage their anxieties about being in the group. Especially if attendance is involuntary, leaders require facilitation skills to help participants to verbalize and explore their resistances to being in or working in the group. If the participants in the group have characteristics different either from their leaders or from each other – for instance, culture, race, sex, status, age – the leader may use facilitation skills to help members to work through any initial sense of isolation they may have from perceiving themselves as different (Moracco, 1981). A further use of facilitation skills is in helping participants to assess their skills strengths and weaknesses and set personal goals.

Facilitation skills in the *working stage* of a training group are used to foster both individual and interpersonal learning. Some participants may require help in overcoming self-consciousness about participating in structured activities before others, for instance role-plays. Facilitation skills are useful for debriefing participants after coaching and rehearsal sessions as well as for getting participants to offer feedback. Also, leaders need good facilitation skills to help participants to describe their outside-group and homework experiences in using the skills. Leaders who demonstrate and use facilitation skills can help participants to support each other as they experience the inevitable setbacks and difficulties of developing their skills. In addition, good facilitation skills may help participants to share and express pleasure in each other's successes.

In the *ending stage* of a training group, leaders can use facilitation skills for a number of purposes. Participants can be assisted in assessing their end of programme skills strengths and weaknesses and in helping others to do likewise. Leaders can help participants to set personal goals and develop programme for consolidating and maintaining their trained skills as post-group self-help skills. Leaders can assist participants to acknowledge and deal with feelings about the group's end. In addition, leaders can help participants to set up networks of peer support on either a buddy or a support group basis.

GROUP LEADERS AS SENDERS OF MESSAGES

Whether they are being didactic or facilitative, training group leaders are always sending and receiving messages. Sending and receiving messages are interlinked. People who receive others' messages poorly lack a good information base for sending appropriate messages. However, even people who receive others' messages well can still possess poor sender skills.

There are five main ways that humans send messages (Nelson-Jones, 1990). In varying degrees, each of these ways is relevant to the leader role.

- *Verbal messages*. Messages expressed in words; for example, what you say in response to participants or what you say about yourself.

- *Voice messages*. Messages relating to how you talk; for example, quickly or slowly, loudly or quietly, with or without emphasis, high-pitched or with a deep voice.

- *Body messages*. Sometimes called body language or non-verbal communication; messages that you send with your face, with other parts of your body and by how you dress and are groomed.

- *Touch messages*. Special kinds of body messages involving physical contact with another. Sometimes touch can be indirect; for example, a group leader may rest an arm on the back of someone's chair rather than touch them directly.

- *Action messages*. Messages that are what you *do* as contrasted with what you *say* or how you say it; for example, do you start and end your training sessions on time?

Whatever training interventions they use at any given moment, skilled training group leaders make appropriate choices in each of these five message areas. Genuineness becomes an important issue when leaders can send messages in so many different ways. Rogers was a prime advocate of the importance of genuineness in working with groups as well as in other personal and helping relationships (Raskin & Rogers, 1989; Rogers, 1957, 1961, 1969, 1970, 1980). Are the messages that you send as a leader congruent or do you seem confused and insincere because you send mixed messages? You always require awareness of not only what but also how you communicate. Also, do your actions match your words?

INITIAL-STAGE FACILITATION SKILLS

Some facilitation skills for starting lifeskills training groups are now discussed. Although they overlap, the leader skills mentioned here focus more on facilitating group discussion than on supporting structured learning experiences.

Arrange seating

Leaders who are serious about the value of group interaction do not arrange the seating in rows with the trainer up front. This 'jug and mug' seating arrangement can lead to most comments being directed to and from leaders. Counselling and psychotherapy groups use a circular seating pattern with each chair being evenly spaced from the others. There is a clear message in this democratic seating arrangement about the value of group interaction. However, circular seating arrangements may also send messages that the group leader is not going to emphasize teaching. A horseshoe seating pattern has many advantages for training groups. A horseshoe allows the leader to operate both as a facilitator and teacher without having to keep rearranging the furniture. However, where appropriate, the leader can still use other seating patterns, for instance either a circle or pairs.

Open the group

Rogers used to start his encounter groups in an extremely unstructured way. He would make comments like: 'Here we are. We can make of this group experience exactly what we wish' or 'I'm a little uneasy, but I feel somewhat reassured when I look around at you and realize we're all in the same boat. Where do we start?' (Rogers, 1970, pp. 46–47). Rogers' opening remarks are too unstructured for lifeskills training groups. Leaders would lose credibility by opening groups in this way. Participants might rightly think 'If he/she doesn't know where to start, why should I be here?'

You need to tailor your opening remarks to the goals of your group. You have the twin goals of setting a safe emotional and also a task-orientated climate. Further structuring may take place throughout the life of groups, both by means of specific statements intended for that purpose and by your voice, body and action messages. In addition, climate setting takes place by the way that you instruct and respond to participants. The following areas can be included in your opening remarks.

- Calling the session to order.

- Introducing yourself.

- Welcoming participants.

- Communicating the time limits both of individual sessions and of the life of the group.

- Stating your purposes for the group.

- Clarifying your own role.

- Indicating participants' roles.

- Encouraging active participation and personal responsibility for skills development.

- Communicating an agenda for the remainder of the first session.

Your voice and body messages are also important accompaniments to your opening remarks. Your voice messages need to show commitment to the task. Even if you do not feel particularly confident, try not to appear diffident and uninvolved. Speak with a clear and firm voice and at a comfortable speed for your listeners. Speak directly to your audience in 'you–me' language and try to join with each one of them by looking in their direction. Under no circumstances read your opening remarks. Below is an example of a possible opening statement.

> Hello, I would like to start the session now. As you know I'm (state name). I have talked with each of you individually but this is the first time we are meeting as a group. We plan to meet every Tuesday from 4 to 6 p.m. for the next ten weeks. The group's purpose is to help you to develop (identify focus) skills. My role is both as a trainer and as someone who enables you to learn from one another. In this group you help yourself and each other by participating actively and by working hard to attain yours and the group's goals. The remainder of this session will be spent as follows: first, introducing ourselves; second, outlining the work of the group; third, clarifying personal goals; and fourth, setting a homework task of monitoring your behaviour.

Decide about getting-acquainted exercises

Many training group leaders use getting-acquainted exercises to speed up the self-disclosure and trust-building process between participants. There seems much less risk in using such exercises in lifeskills groups than in counselling or psychotherapy groups, where they may lead to pseudo-authenticity. Some leading writers on encounter and therapeutic groups do not favour using such exercises (Rogers, 1970; Yalom, 1985). Even in lifeskills training groups, getting-acquainted exercises can be gimmicky and demeaning to participants (Whitaker, 1985). However, well-chosen getting-acquainted exercises can short-cut the acquaintance process in ways that, unlike in therapy groups, do not impede the group's task.

Below are some ways in which leaders can approach the task of getting acquainted. Leaders always have to take into account the practical realities of any groups with whom they work – for instance, group size and participants' age range – in choosing getting-acquainted exercises. Sometimes the participants of a training group will have had prior contact: for instance, being classmates or workmates. Even in such instances, leaders should not assume that participants know each other well: they may be acquaintances relating in ritualistic ways.

- *Introduce oneself.* Participants can be asked to introduce and say a few words about themselves. A variation of this is that participants start by saying their name and then repeat the names of all those who have introduced themselves already before saying something about themselves (Corey *et al.*, 1988a). Sometimes the leader may ask participants to cover specific topics in their statements: for instance, 'What I want to get out of coming to this lifeskills group?' or 'How does it feel right now joining this lifeskills group?' The order of participants introducing themselves can be either when they choose to speak up or by starting with one person and then going round the group in a set order. Especially when groups are large, name tags often help in learning names.

- *Brief introductory speech.* A variation of introducing oneself is to get participants to stand up in front of the group for a set period of time, say for either 90 seconds or two minutes, and introduce themselves. You can allow them the last 15–30 seconds for answering questions. This method lends itself to programmes where public speaking skills form the major or one of the main skills being taught.

- *Use a ball or cushion.* Here the participant to whom the ball is thrown thanks by name the person who has thrown the ball, says his or her own name, self-discloses while holding the ball, and then throws the ball to another person and so on. For some groups and individuals there may be at least three advantages to this approach: the element of playing a game lessens anxiety; participants have something to do with their hands when it is their turn to speak; and the uncertainty of not knowing who will be next keeps participants awake. As with all introducing-oneself exercises, leaders can ask participants to cover specific topics: for example, I have asked undergraduates to describe their cultural background and to identify specific difficulties they have faced in cross-cultural communication. There can also be risks in using a ball or cushion: for example, some adult groups may consider it childish and some school groups may take it as an excuse either to break a window or to throw the ball hard at the breasts of an attractive classmate.

- *Introduce a partner.* Another getting-acquainted exercise is to divide the group into pairs. Partner A self-discloses to partner B, who listens and may ask a few questions. After a set time period, say two or three minutes, the partners reverse roles. This pairs work is followed by introducing your partner in a plenary session. There are a number of drawbacks to this method. First, participants are not speaking for themselves when they get introduced to the group. Second, participants may forget salient information about the people that they introduce. However, the partner being talked about may be given the opportunity to add missing information. Third, especially if their introductions come at the end, participants may be so busy remembering information to disclose that they do not listen properly to all the other introductions. A possible advantage of this method is that some participants may find it easier to break the ice by talking to the group about someone else rather than directly about themselves.

- *Use triads and small groups.* Participants can be divided into threes or into small groups. These groupings can be instructed to introduce themselves to each other during a set time period. Either alternatively or in addition, the sub-groups can be asked to discuss a self-referent topic pertinent to the work of the group: for example, my difficulties in either being assertive or managing stress. Where appropriate, sub-grouping can be followed by either putting participants into different sub-groups or holding a whole-group sharing and discussion session.

- *Self-assessment exercises.* Prior to the initial session participants may have been asked to fill out a self-assessment questionnaire with regard to the lifeskill(s) targeted by the group. Participants can share their responses to the questionnaire either in pairs or in sub-groups. Even if they have not filled out a questionnaire, participants can be divided into pairs or sub-groups and asked to share their assessments of their strengths and weaknesses in the targeted lifeskills area(s). Such self-assessment exercises can be followed by whole-group sharing and discussion sessions.

- *Circulate with personal information visible.* Participants can be asked to fill out either an index card or a yellow 'post-it' sheet with information about themselves. For instance, in the top left-hand corner they put how they like to be called; in the top right-hand corner they put a couple of pieces of biographical information – for example, age, place of residence, birthplace, marital status; in the bottom left-hand corner they put three adjectives to describe themselves; and in the bottom right-hand corner they put three hobbies. The information requested can vary with the purposes of the group. Participants then pin or stick their information on their fronts. They are then asked to circulate and hold brief conversations with as many new people as they can within a set time period. Some participants like this exercise because it allows them to meet whoever they want and more closely resembles real life, where people relate to individuals rather than to whole groups. Furthermore, moving around sometimes helps to energize participants.

- *Form a continuum.* Another getting-acquainted exercise is to set participants the task of forming a continuum on some basis: for example, supervisors or managers can be asked to sort themselves into a line based on how long they have worked for a company, how tall they are or the darkness of their hair. Such tasks, without creating much threat, get participants interacting with each other.

- *Use movies and videos.* Movies and videos can be used to facilitate self-disclosure and sharing of experiences. For example, Downing and Walker state how they used the movie *My Father's Son: The Legacy of Alcoholism* (Rogers, 1984) as an 'ice-breaker' in the first session of their psycho-educational programme for adult children of alcoholics (Downing & Walker, 1987).

A few closing points about using getting-acquainted exercises. First, leaders can use more than one. Second, many of the later learning experiences of lifeskills groups, for instance role-plays with other participants, have an element of getting acquainted in them. Third, leaders may bring about a greater sense of group cohesion if they participate actively by introducing themselves in some of the exercises than if they sit on the touchline in an 'expert' capacity. Fourth, the getting-acquainted exercises can be used to make the existential point that participants are always choosers and, thus, need to take responsibility for the outcomes of their choices: for example, when introducing themselves participants choose what to conceal and what to reveal.

Exercise 10 is designed to get you thinking about the advantages and disadvantages of using getting-acquainted exercises when leading lifeskills groups. In addition, where possible, the exercise encourages you to experience the different approaches.

Exercise 10 Use getting-acquainted exercises

1. Make up a worksheet with three columns headed: EXERCISE, ADVANT-
    AGES, and DISADVANTAGES. Discuss the advantages and disadvant-
    ages of using each of the following getting-acquainted exercises in the
    initial session of a lifeskills training group.

    Introduce oneself

    Brief introductory speech

    Use a ball or cushion

    Introduce a partner

    Use triads and small groups

    Self-assessment exercises

    Circulate with personal information visible

    Form a continuum

    Use movies and videos.

2. If you are in a group practicum, try out as many of the above getting-
    acquainted exercises as you have time and interest available so that you
    can get the feel of them. You may wish to defer discussing the advantages
    and disadvantages of the getting-acquainted exercises until you have had
    the opportunity to experience them first-hand.

Encourage participation

When leading groups it is vital that you do not dominate, but encourage participants to make it their group as well. There is a Chinese proverb 'You have a great oak tree, but beneath it nothing grows.' Even though in lifeskills training groups your task is to be more didactic than in counselling groups, you still want to convey clear messages to participants that their contributions are welcome. The previous section focused on getting-acquainted exercises that foster later interaction. Below are some further skills that you can use, both in the initial and subsequent stages of training groups, to encourage participation.

- *Opening statements.* You can include in your opening statement comments that indicate that participation in the group is desirable. For instance, the earlier example of an opening statement included the comment: 'My role is both as a trainer and as someone who enables you to learn from one another'.

- *Encourage self-referent talk.* You encourage participants to own and talk about their thoughts, feelings and actions by means of 'I' statements'. Where appropriate, you encourage them to give concrete examples of their experiences. You discourage them when they intellectualize and generalize. Even early on, but using tact, you encourage participants to own rather than to distance themselves from their problems and skills weaknesses.

- *Encourage talking to each other.* Ways by which you may encourage participants to interact with each other and not just with you include: asking them to do this and using body messages, for instance an arm gesture or turning your gaze in the direction of the group.

- *Make linking statements.* You can find ways of relating what one participant has to say to what other participants have said: for example, in an overcoming shyness group for adolescents, 'Mandy has just said something that many of you have also been saying one way or another, that it can be very scary meeting people for the first time'.

- *Invite participation.* You can give invitations to participate to the whole group: for example, 'Does anyone else have anything they would like to share about what Richard has been saying?' Alternatively, you may give an invitation to a specific member who may have trouble contributing without your encouragement: for example, 'Di, I've been watching your expression as Richard has been talking and wonder whether you would like to say something'.

- *Give permission to discuss differences.* If you consider that members of the group might feel 'out of it' because of age, race, culture, sex, socio-economic status, rank or other differences, you can make comments that show you are sensitive to this possibility. Such comments may act as permissions to air feelings of difference as well as indicate that difference does not have connotations of inferiority as far as you are concerned.

- *Give permission to discuss fears.* Both participants and leaders are inevitably going to have anxieties about starting a new group. Leaders can acknowledge that this will be the case, disclose their own anxieties, and encourage participants to do likewise. For instance, in lifeskills training groups participants may have fears about starting off further behind in the skills than others, making mistakes, being slower learners, and admitting difficulties in public. Leaders who, early on in training groups, facilitate a sense of acceptance of others and of universality make an invaluable contribution to group participation and cohesiveness.

- *Offer support.* You always support genuine attempts to participate by showing good attending behaviours, for instance slight forward trunk lean, gaze, and head nods (Ivey & Authier, 1978; Egan, 1990). You choose whether to add verbal encouragement, for instance by a reflective response, or to leave it to the group to respond. If necessary, you support participants in coping with negative reactions from others.

- *Foster group rules conducive to participation.* Any group develops implicit and explicit rules or norms that constitute the 'do's and dont's' about how participants should behave. As leaders, you can influence the development of norms which are helpful rather than harmful to participating. Whitaker distinguishes between groups that find either restrictive or enabling solutions to the tasks and problems they face (Whitaker, 1985). As leaders you have to decide whether to let the group work through problems with minimum assistance from you or whether to take a more active role in bringing about enabling rather than restrictive solutions. For example, if the group is just focusing on the problems of one participant, do you intervene? If you sense that fears of confidentiality are an issue in the group, do you either leave it to the group to do something about it or make sure the issue is discussed and, if possible, worked through satisfactorily? If you want a group rule about openness, do you wait for this to happen or do you actively try to influence the process by saying that this is what is best for the group and then reward participants who take risks? Training group leaders are likely to be more active than counselling group leaders in openly influencing group rules. The briefer length and more structured nature of lifeskills training groups pressures leaders to intervene rather than to observe the group constructing its own norms at its own pace.

- *Role-model.* You use 'I' statements yourself and are direct and open with the group. You help participants to feel that you are involved in the group as a person and not just as a technical expert.

Assist self-assessment and stating personal goals

Training group leaders tend to be active in encouraging participants to engage in an ongoing process of assessing their skills strengths and weaknesses. Related to this, participants are encouraged to define and redefine their personal goals in the targeted skills areas. Mention has already been made of intake interviews and getting-acquainted self-assessment exercises, with or without prior questionnaires. In the initial stage of a group, training group leaders may actively establish self-assessment and goal-setting agendas rather than wait for agendas to emerge as in group counselling. Leaders then facilitate the ensuing sharing and discussion. As the group develops, participants should achieve a clearer understanding of how they sustain their skills weaknesses. Nevertheless, even in the group's initial stage, participants can start gaining more insight into their behaviour and into what specifically they want to get out of the group.

The skills mentioned in the previous chapter for individual assessment interviews are also relevant for assessment and goal-setting discussions in groups. For instance, leaders may use questions that encourage participants to be more specific both about their experiences and about what they want to achieve. Sometimes leaders may choose to work on breaking down the problems of one participant as a way of demonstrating to other participants how to break their problems down into component parts. Leaders can also help participants to develop the skills of setting goals that are realistic, specific and have a time frame.

Some leaders encourage participants to go beyond self-assessment and goal setting by making learning contracts (Wehrenberg, 1988). Corey and Corey write: 'Basically a contract is a statement by the group member concerning what he or she is willing to do during a group session or outside of the group meeting' (Corey & Corey, 1982, p. 110). Mention has already been made of contracts that set out appropriate behaviours for participating in lifeskills groups. The contracts envisaged here are specific to individual participants. These personal contracts outline actions to be undertaken and behaviours to be changed. Their time frame may be a session, a between-session break or a longer period. Such contracts aim to encourage participants to assume responsibility for their learning by committing themselves to specific behaviours.

Handle resistances

There are numerous reasons why people participate in lifeskills training groups. Some may be sent by third parties, for instance their managers, or attend because they are institutionalized, for instance juvenile delinquents. There may be varying degrees of involuntariness in training groups. How can leaders attempt to cope with participants' resistances and, at the very least, try to prevent them from interfering with the motivation of the rest of the group? Leaders need to avoid pressurizing or selling reluctant participants on the group's value. Pressure like this risks heightening rather than diminishing their resistances. Below are some suggestions for dealing with involuntary or reluctant participants.

- *Conduct intake interviews.* Personal meetings between leaders and participants prior to training groups can perform a number of functions in lessening resistances: building rapport, diminishing anxiety, clarifying the group's purposes and exploring 'whether there might be anything in it for me'.

- *Give permission to verbalize reservations.* Training group leaders can show sensitivity to participants' feelings about not wishing to be in groups by encouraging them to verbalize their reservations. Leaders may facilitate a sharing and discussion of reservations and correct any inaccurate fantasies about being in the group; for example, 'my defences will be stripped away' or 'they are collecting information to use against me'. Resistant participants who see that leaders have bothered to understand their positions may feel less hostile to the group because of this. Leaders can also self-disclose with 'I' statements about how participants' resistances affect them. Reluctant participants may appreciate this genuineness.

- *Facilitate assuming personal responsibility.* After participants have had a chance to air their reservations, leaders can attempt to help them to move on. There are various techniques for doing this. You can encourage questions about the purpose of the group and what participants might expect to get out of it. You can confront participants with their current existential predicaments of not particularly wanting to be in the group, but having to be there and ask 'How can you best make this situation work for you?' You can encourage participants to clarify and formulate personal goals. With some groups, you may choose to go further and adopt the approach that Glasser has used in his reality therapy groups with juvenile delinquents. Glasser confronts participants with the fact that much of their behaviour to date has not been particularly helpful for them, that they have basic needs for love and worth, and that together they can work to help to meet their basic needs more successfully (Glasser, 1965, 1984a, 1984b). This 'tough love' approach has much to recommend it so long as leaders convey to participants genuine concern and commitment.

- *Control damage.* Sometimes the best that leaders can do is to try to limit the damaging effects that resistant participants may have on the rest of the group. You can acknowledge their reluctance to participate and ask them at least to give the group a try. You can request that they do not interfere with the work of other participants. You can also encourage other participants to speak up and give the same message. If you face continuous disruption, for the sake of the whole group you may have to exclude certain participants from future sessions. Exclusion is not always an easy option where, as in a school, all pupils may be expected to attend all classes.

Further facilitation skills

All of the facilitation skills that you use in working with individuals are helpful for performing the lifeskills group leader role. However, you need to adapt your use of individual helping skills. Also, you always have to weigh carefully whether you should allow space for participants to respond to each other rather than respond yourself.

- *Empathic understanding.* Though you may choose to respond empathically to individual members, there are at least five ways in which empathic responding may be different in group than in individual work. First, you may wish to respond empathically to an interaction between two or more members. One way to do this is to clarify what each has said. Another way is to summarize themes in the interaction. Second, you may respond to the group as a whole. For example, you may reflect anxiety at participating in self-assessment and in meeting a group of strangers. Third, you may respond to the unspoken needs of members who are not participating overtly and/or who may feel particularly vulnerable. Fourth, you may try to release the helping and healing capacity of the group by encouraging members to respond empathically to each other. Fifth, you may identify empathic responding as a useful self-help skill and encourage members to use it not only inside but also outside the group.

- *Use of questions.* As well as questions addressed to individuals, some of your questions may be addressed to the group. Such questions include: 'Hannah has raised the issue of confidentiality. What does the group think?', 'Do Joanne's experiences trigger off any thoughts and feelings in others of you?', and 'It seems to me that David would like some feedback or help from the group. Is anyone willing to provide this?'

- *Facilitative confronting.* Confrontations are challenges either to individuals or to the group as a whole that invite them to assess some aspect of their functioning. Often confrontations are focused on highlighting inconsistencies, for instance between either what participants say and how they say it or what they say and what they do. An example of the latter inconsistency is agreeing to come to sessions on time and then coming late. Sometimes confrontations aim to challenge possible distortions of reality: for example, 'You say you have no friends; where is the evidence for this perception?' (Beck & Emery, 1985; Nelson-Jones, 1990). Sometimes you may choose to confront the whole group, for instance when they use the restrictive solution of focusing excessively on one participant's concerns as a way of avoiding dealing with their own anxieties.

  How you confront is important along with what you confront. You may soften your confrontation if you begin with a reflective response that shows you have heard and understood a speaker's message. Then build on this with your confronting response. This way you are more likely to keep the speaker's ears open to what comes from your viewpoint. Only confront as strongly as is necessary to achieve your goal. Heavy and insensitive confrontations create resistances. Also, try not to overdo confrontations. Nobody likes being persistently challenged. You can help participants to move forward with skilled use of confronting responses. However, you can block and threaten participants as well as harm your relationship with them if you confront too often and too clumsily.

- *Self-disclosing.* An issue in lifeskills training groups is how much of a participant a leader should become. Leader self-disclosure can be for good or ill. At best, leader self-disclosure can contribute to an honest person-to-person working climate. Training group leaders always send messages about themselves. If leaders send congruent messages they are perceived as authentic or genuine. However, if leaders say they are committed to the group, but do not indicate this with voice and body messages, lack of commitment may be the overall impression left with participants. Also, if leaders say that they want a spontaneous and relaxed atmosphere yet appear tense and uptight, their incongruent messages interfere with attaining their stated goal.

Disclosing personal experiences, showing involvement and using humour are three important aspects of self-disclosure (McCarthy, 1982). Many leaders run lifeskills training groups in skills areas where they have had problems themselves. Disclosing your experiences may help participants to feel that you understand their experiences: for example, coping with unemployment, coping with career as well as family, and overcoming substance abuse. So long as they are brief, to the point and not overwhelming, such disclosures may engender feelings of universality, cohesiveness and identification. On the other hand, leaders who keep talking about their experiences risk switching the focus of their group from the participants to themselves.

Self-involving disclosures are spontaneous and direct reactions to what participants say or do. There is a here-and-now quality about such reactions. Examples of self-involving disclosures are: 'That's great', 'I'm happy too', and 'I'm sorry that he/she reacted that way'. Sometimes self-involving disclosures are confrontations: for example 'You seem to think of yourself as a weak person, but I do not experience you that way' and 'I really have to make an effort to keep listening when you start repeating yourself'. Even negative self-involving disclosures can be constructive if they represent invitations to look at specific behaviours.

Humour provides a good vehicle for revealing your humanity and loosening up the emotional climate of groups. Humour can release the potential for fun in the group. Terence Rattigan, in his play about a schoolmaster, *The Browning Version*, had the central character observe that boys learn much more from humour than earnestness. Probably this observation holds true for training group participants. Humour need not necessarily block the exploration of deeper issues. Given the right relaxed atmosphere, participants may be more able and willing to expose themselves and to work for change.

- *Summarizing.* In general, when facilitating training groups, it is undesirable to provide lengthy summaries of what individuals have said. Such summaries may block the processes of group interaction and learning. However, sometimes when leaders work with individual participants in front of the group, this rule may not apply. Leaders' summaries focused on individuals may then stimulate other participants to think differently about their problems.

Summaries focused on the group may take place at the beginning of, during and at the end of sessions. At the start of a session, leaders can summarize the main lessons from the previous session. During a session, leaders can summarize the main lessons, feelings, themes and emerging directions in the group. At the end of a session, leaders can summarize the session's main lessons. After summarizing, leaders can ask how accurate they have been and if participants have any further comments. A variation on the leader doing the summarizing is to ask participants to summarize either instead of or with the help of leaders.

Table 6.1 is an evaluation questionnaire for assessing your use of initial-stage facilitation skills when leading training groups. Many of these facilitation skills are highly relevant for leading other kinds of groups.

Table 6.1 An evaluation questionnaire for initial-stage facilitation skills

This questionnaire has three purposes: (1) to guide you in preparing to use facilitation skills in the initial stage of training groups; (2) to assess your use of these skills; and (3) to allow others to assess your skills. You may answer the questionnaire by placing a tick for 'yes' or a cross for 'no' in the blank space by each item, or by responding to the items in your head, or by responding verbally in a learning or supervisory setting.

.... I arranged the seating appropriately

.... I formulated and made a good opening statement

.... Where appropriate, I used getting-acquainted exercises well

.... I encouraged participation in the group

.... I encouraged participants to self-disclose relevant information

.... I encouraged participants to address each other

.... I gave permission to discuss fears about being in the group

.... I gave permission to discuss feelings of being different

.... Where appropriate, I supported individual participants

.... I fostered group rules conducive to participating in the group

.... I encouraged participant self-assessment in the targeted skills area(s)

.... I encouraged participants to formulate and state personal goals

.... I helped the group to work through resistances to participation

.... I demonstrated empathic understanding

.... I used questions well

.... I used facilitative confronting well

.... Where appropriate, I disclosed personal information

.... Where appropriate, I expressed feelings

.... Where appropriate, I used humour

.... I used good summarizing skills

Exercise 11 provides somes practice at facilitating the early stages of a lifeskills training group. The first part of the exercise is designed to give you practice at formulating and making opening statements. The second part of the exercise focuses on facilitating group interaction. Like many of the subsequent leader skills exercises, this exercise may be done either on your own or with others as part of a group leadership course or practicum.

Exercise 11 Develop initial-stage facilitation skills

Part A Formulate and make opening statements

1. What are the important considerations for formulating an opening statement for the first session of a lifeskills training group?

2. Choose a lifeskills training group that you might want to run. Draft an opening statement for it. Speak your opening statement into a cassette recorder as though you were making it to the group. Play back your statement and modify both your content and delivery as necessary. If you are in a group leadership skills practicum, you may deliver your opening statement either in a sub-group or before the whole group.

Part B Facilitate group discussion

This part of the exercise is best done in groups of six to eight. Each person acts as leader and facilitates a 30–45-minute group discussion in a lifeskills area both of their choice and also of relevance to the rest of the group. The facilitator's task is to help participants to share their experiences, assess their skills strengths and weaknesses and formulate at least one personal goal. The skills to be used by facilitators include the following:

- formulating and making an opening statement

- encouraging participation

- assisting self-assessment and setting personal goals

- handling resistances

- where appropriate, empathic understanding, use of questions, facilitative confronting and self-disclosing

- an end-of-session summary.

At the end of each session, there is a brief feedback period focused on how well the leader has used facilitation skills. To allow participants to be fresh and to avoid 'halo' effects of moving from one skills area to another, the sessions may need to be spread over a period of days or weeks.

There are many possible variations on Exercise 11. These variations include: using smaller groups, say one facilitator and three members; using co-facilitators; and using the 'fishbowl' format, in which the inner circle or horseshoe are participants in the facilitation exercise and the outer circle or horseshoe are observers. These observers may be invited to provide feedback at the end of the session, possibly based on Table 6.1, and, on other occasions, may act as the inner group. Video-recording and playback may add to the exercise's value.

WORKING-STAGE FACILITATION SKILLS

Most of the initial-stage facilitation skills are highly relevant to the working stage of lifeskills training groups. In the working stage the training group leader requires both good facilitation and good didactic skills to be maximally effective. Elsewhere, I have suggested that the working stage of most counselling groups centres on two main modes of interactive work: first, working in the 'here and now' – developing the skills of intimacy; and second, working in the 'there and now' – developing the skills of managing problems (Nelson-Jones, 1988b).

Lifeskills training groups, with their limited focus, tend to have a less intense focus on intimacy than counselling or psychotherapy groups. Nevertheless, in training groups a reasonable degree of inter-participant intimacy is important to achieve such therapeutic factors as group cohesiveness, interpersonal learning (input), interpersonal learning (output), universality and catharsis. In addition, leaders who facilitate participants helping others to manage their problems better help to achieve such therapeutic factors as altruism and guidance. However, facilitation in training groups has additional functions beyond those of counselling and psychotherapy groups. Training group leaders facilitate task-orientated learning. The didactic role of leaders necessitates using facilitation skills in such areas as: running structured learning experiences; reviewing homework and use of skills outside the group; and encouraging participants' ongoing self-assessments of their skills strengths and weaknesses. In reality, no clear distinction exists between facilitation skills being used for didactic purposes and group interactive purposes. Facilitating group interaction can greatly assist the didactic process. The present section focuses mainly on the facilitation of group discussion.

Leaders need to be mindful that facilitating discussion in training groups may require more focus than in counselling or psychotherapy groups. To what extent does discussion support or impede attaining training goals? Discussion in the working stage of a lifeskills group can help participants to integrate their learning experiences inside and outside the group. Experiential learning requires not just participation in structured experiences, but also the opportunity to give personal meaning to these experiences and share these meanings with others. Furthermore, discussions involving self-disclosure and feedback are crucial ways in which participants learn from one another. A fatal assumption for training group leaders is that they are the only source of significant input. However, leaders always have to make choices about the balance between discussion and structured experiences. In addition, even when permitting discussion, leaders need to make choices concerning whether or not participants' self-disclosures are relevant to attaining group goals and, if not, whether and how to intervene.

Facilitate self-disclosure

A major reason for using facilitation skills in the initial stage of training groups is to build trust between participants and also between participants and their leaders. During the working stage, even more than in the initial stage, leaders endeavour to get participants to drop their social masks and defences. Much learning in lifeskills training groups takes place in public. Consequently, in addition to their private anxieties, participants have the additional anxieties of being expected to expose and work on their skills strengths and weaknesses in front of others.

Below are some of the rules or norms relevant to participants' self-disclosure that a leader may try to establish in lifeskills training groups.

- 'We're all here to learn.'

- 'Each of us is worthy of respect and acceptance as a human being.'

- 'We will help ourselves more if we take responsibility for our learning and honestly admit our skills weaknesses and strengths.'

- 'We will help each other more if we share our difficulties and successes.'

- 'It's okay to talk about feelings and personal meanings as well as about thoughts and actions.'

- 'When discussing our experiences, we try to use "I" statements and to be specific.'

- 'It's okay to make and admit mistakes. Significant learning involves setbacks and mistakes.'

- 'It's okay to take risks in revealing myself in this group.'

- 'To get the most out of our skills group we need to collaborate rather than to compete with each other.'

- 'Each of us has a right to "air time" in the group.'

- 'Each of us tries to make our participation in discussions relevant to the group's purposes.'

- 'We respect each other's right to confidentiality.'

How do leaders encourage rules conducive to constructive self-disclosure? Almost all of the initial-stage skills of encouraging participation are also relevant to encouraging self-disclosure. These encouraging-participation skills include: encouraging self-referent talk, linking statements, invitations to participate, giving permission to discuss fears, supporting, fostering norms conducive to participation, and intervening to prevent restrictive solutions to problems about participation. In addition, leaders who offer good facilitation skills of empathic understanding, use of questions and facilitative confronting, and who model self-disclosure, create a climate conducive to honesty and openness.

Training group leaders can openly stress the value of participants' disclosures. Leaders can mention some of the ground rules mentioned above and ask participants their opinions about them. Furthermore, leaders may use and withhold rewards to foster constructive self-disclosure. For example, leaders may say something like 'I appreciate your openness' or 'I admire your courage' when participants are honest with the group about an embarrassing skills weakness or experience. On the other hand, leaders may query disclosures that are focused on other people rather than being self-referent, for example 'I'm wondering what the relevance of that is to you?' Furthermore, if a participant starts monopolizing and the group seems to be either doing little about it or possibly colluding in it, leaders can intervene to broaden participation. Possible statements in such circumstances include: 'Is there anyone else who would like to share an experience?' or 'Is there anyone else who would like to tell the group how they assess their skills?'

Facilitate open mutual feedback

In any group, rules develop about what participants notice and what they do not notice. Also, in any group rules develop about participants giving feedback. Participants learn about themselves from feedback in such areas as: how they come across to others, habits that annoy or please, and how they confuse through not communicating clearly. In addition, participants can give each other feedback about how they perform in the targeted skills, for instance when they speak in public or when they assert themselves. A further important lesson from receiving feedback is that participants may find that they possess the strength to take it. Critical comments, however aggressively given, do not mean the end of the world. Someone else defining their behaviour in a certain way does not mean that they automatically have to define themselves in that way. Instead, participants can assess the comments and try to sort out what is of value. Also, leaders can help participants to develop the communication skills of acknowledging and responding to feedback.

Ivey and his colleagues have identified a skill they call *direct mutual communication* (Higgins *et al.*, 1970; Ivey & Authier, 1978). When using this skill, two people in an interaction try to share how they experience interacting with each other. Egan calls this skill 'you – me' talk (Egan, 1977). Egan distinguishes between three types of immediacy in helping: *self-involving statements* – 'present-tense, personal responses' (p. 224) to another; *relationship immediacy* – your ability to discuss 'where you stand in your overall relationship' (p. 225); and *here-and-now immediacy* – your ability to discuss 'what is happening between you in the here and now of any given transaction' (Egan, 1990, p. 226). Egan's three types of immediacy are applicable to how participants relate in training groups. Here the term *open mutual feedback* is preferred to immediacy. Open mutual feedback can refer to feedback about either an overall relationship, or any interaction in it, or any behaviour in it. In lifeskills training groups, much participant feedback focuses on performance in the targeted skills rather than on relationships.

Open mutual feedback between participants is a complex skill containing a number of different components. These components include participants tuning in to their own thoughts and feelings as well as understanding and showing sensitivity to another's thoughts and feelings. Leaders can help participants to develop the skills of *giving* feedback. It is one thing to give feedback, but another to have it listened to. In general, feedback is more likely to be effective if the speaker: (1) frames it as an 'I' statement starting with 'I feel . . .' or 'I think . . .' rather than as a 'You' statement starting with 'You are . . .'; (2) is specific and clear; and (3) invites discussion rather than being dogmatic.

Leaders can also help participants to develop skills of *receiving* feedback. Some participants may be unrealistically threatened by feedback and need to think more calmly about it. Such participants can give themselves statements like 'I do not need everyone's approval', 'I do not have to be perfect', 'People who give me feedback may be trying to help me', and 'I do not have to accept everything that is said about me. Instead I can evaluate it to see if I can learn something useful from it'.

In addition, participants can develop the action skills of *responding to* feedback and, where appropriate, inviting it. Responding to feedback skills includes reflecting it to make sure that you have understood it and asking for more specific information. Inviting feedback skills includes statements like: 'I wonder how I'm coming over to other people in the group?' and 'How did you assess my skills after this role-play?' Also, leaders may provide feedback to participants on how they block feedback: for example, by getting angry, not paying attention, dismissing it out of hand, belittling the sender, or changing the subject.

Exercise 12 is designed to give you the experiences of (a) trying to facilitate open mutual feedback in others, (b) giving feedback, and (c) receiving and responding to feedback.

Exercise 12 Facilitate open mutual feedback

This exercise may be done in groups of three to six. With numbers larger than six, it may be best to subdivide the group. Video-recording and playback may add to the value of this exercise.

1. Person A acts as facilitator, person B is the recipient of feedback and the remaining participants of the group provide feedback.

2. Person A explains the concept of open mutual feedback to the group, who are seated in a circle. Person A then invites group participants to give person B feedback about either their thoughts and feelings about him/her or their assessments of his/her strengths and weaknesses in a previously agreed upon lifeskills area. Each other participant gives person B feedback. During the feedback, person B is allowed to ask for greater specificity if he/she does not understand the feedback. Only at the end of everybody's feedback is person B allowed to comment on his/her reactions to both the feedback and how constructively it was given. The session ends with person A debriefing both person B and the remainder of the group on what it felt like to receive and give face-to-face feedback.

3. The exercise continues with a new person A and person B until each participant has had a chance to be both the facilitator and the receiver of feedback.

4. At the end, in light of their experience of doing the whole exercise, the group discusses the role in lifeskills training groups of leaders facilitating the giving and receiving of feedback by participants.

Facilitate helping each other to manage problems

As with counselling and psychotherapy groups, in training groups participants often share outside problems with the group. However, this sharing tends to be in areas relevant to the group's objectives. Sharing of problems involving targeted lifeskills may intensify as participants try out new behaviours. Often such sharing takes place either before or after homework focused on transfer of skills outside.

When participants bring in their outside problems for discussion, this is a form of sharing with the whole group and not just with leaders. Participants may gain both from helping and being helped by their peers. Participants can often obtain more insight into their own problems if they help others to break down and understand how they sustain their problems. Furthermore, just as two heads may be better than one, many heads may be better than two. Consequently, group leaders as trainers often help participants to develop the skills of helping each other. Below are a few skills of facilitating this kind of discussion:

- *Facilitate inter-participant empathy.* Leaders may intervene in ways that encourage participants to be sensitive to and accurately listen to what others think and feel as they share problems with the group. Leaders can identify and encourage skills of not just accurately understanding information, but also of showing speakers that you understand and care.

- *Facilitate participants' self-disclosing.* One way that participants can help each other to manage problems is to share their experiences and struggles with others with similar problems. Leaders may need to intervene to help participants to make disclosures relevant to another's problems. Sometimes participants can help each other much more by the disclosing skills of sharing problems than by the listening skills of empathic responding and questions. Frequently, the combination of disclosing and listening is desirable.

- *Facilitate participants making working definitions of each other's and their own problems.* Leaders can help participants to acknowledge and help each other acknowledge the importance of assuming responsibility for their skills weaknesses in sustaining problems. Leaders can help participants to break down and help each other break down problems in such a way that thinking and action skills weaknesses sustaining problems are clearly identified.

- *Facilitate participants helping each other to set goals and develop action plans.* Leaders can help participants to understand the importance of translating insight into action. While keeping responsibility for outside actions clearly with individuals, leaders may encourage participants to discuss their goals in the group and how they plan to achieve them. Furthermore, leaders can help participants to understand the steps of managing and solving problems (D'Zurilla & Goldfried, 1971; Egan, 1990; Nelson-Jones, 1989).

- *Encourage the formation of constructive group rules and behaviours.* Leaders need to influence the development of rules that help participants to work together on managing outside-group problems. Pressures for conformity, excessive dependency on group decisions, and intellectualizing about rather than working on problems, are all rules to be discouraged. Avoiding restrictive rules can mainly be achieved by encouraging constructive ones.

- *Make links.* Leaders can help participants to make connections between others' problems and their own. They help participants to acknowledge that problems are a part of living, and also to realize that they can develop managing-problems skills not only alone, but also by observing and helping each other to work.

The purpose of Exercise 13 is to raise your awareness of the need for training group leaders to assist participants in helping each other to manage problems. Leaders who successfully release their group's helping potential foster cohesiveness.

Exercise 13 Facilitate helping each other to manage problems

This exercise may be done in groups of three to six. With numbers above six, it may be best to subdivide the group. Video-recording and playback may add to the value of this exercise.

1. The group is seated in a circle. Participants agree upon who is to be facilitator and who is to share a problem with the group. This problem should be in a lifeskills area of interest and relevance to most, if not all, participants.

2. The facilitator starts the group by saying that the group has 20 minutes to help the problem sharer to manage it better. The problem is then shared and the facilitator works with participants to assist them to help the sharer. Towards the end of the 20 minutes the facilitator summarizes where the group appears to have arrived at in its helping. Then he/she asks first the problem sharer and then the other participants for their reactions to the summary. The group finishes promptly after 20 minutes. Then there follows time for sharing and discussion focused on (a) feedback from the problem sharer regarding comments experienced as helpful or harmful to his/her managing the problem, (b) comments from the facilitator on issues in facilitating participant helping, and (c) comments from participants on any aspect of the session.

3. The 20-minute sessions are repeated until each participant has had the opportunity to be both facilitator and problem sharer.

Set limits on discussion

Lifeskills training groups are working as well as talking groups. If anything, their task-orientated agendas take precedence over their relationship-orientated agendas. Because training groups mix discussion, presentation and structured activities, leaders often have to set limits on the *amount* of discussion that they facilitate. Sometimes leaders may allocate a set amount of time for discussion either in the whole group or in sub-groups or pairs. For instance, leaders may allocate set amounts of time for discussing homework, getting reactions to lecturettes and reviewing skills at the end of a session. On other occasions, leaders may allocate time for discussion based on the quality of the discussion, the amount of energy invested in it, and on what else requires attention. Leaders may also check with participants their views on the mix in a session between discussion, presentation and structured activities.

Training group leaders may also have to set limits on the *type* of discussion they facilitate. For instance, leaders in pain management groups may allow participants some time to ventilate their negative feelings about being in pain, but then invite them to move on to look at ways of making the most of their lives despite their pain. Participants already know a lot about their pain. If this type of discussion were to go on week after week, leaders would risk colluding in participants getting stuck in unproductive self-pity rather than helping them to develop skills and coping strategies to manage pain better. In the working stage of effective lifeskills training groups, there should be a shift from descriptive discussion of difficulties to discussions in which participants show greater insight into the skills weaknesses that sustain them. Also, there should be an increase in participants' abilities to help each other.

ENDING-STAGE FACILITATION SKILLS

Leaders use facilitation skills differently at the end of lifeskills training groups, as contrasted with counselling and psychotherapy groups. Gazda observes that the group counsellor's responsibility at what he calls the 'termination' stage is '. . . to reinforce the growth made by group members and to make sure that all group counselees have had the opportunity to work out their differences with the counselor and other group members before leaving' (Gazda, 1989, p 82). Training group leaders tend to avoid words like 'growth', considering them insufficiently specific. In ending training groups, leaders are much more focused on reinforcing the specific self-help skills targeted as goals for the programme than on sorting out unfinished relationship issues. The major agendas of the ending stage of training groups are consolidating participants' specific skills and facilitating their transfer, maintenance and development outside.

Group leader skills in ending and evaluating lifeskills groups are covered more thoroughly elsewhere. Suffice it for now to indicate that all the facilitation skills mentioned for the working stage also apply to the ending stage. However, there are differences in emphasis in how these skills are used in the two stages. For example, there may be a shift from facilitating self-disclosure about current problems in using the targeted skills to facilitating disclosure about anxieties about using the skills in future without group support. Open mutual feedback will probably be focused on end-of-group assessments of each other's skills as well as on personal farewells. Also, when leaders facilitate participants helping each other, the agenda may be the problem of how best to maintain and develop individuals' skills after the group ends. Leaders can help participants to look at issues of re-entry into their 'home' environments and how to get the support for their skills development. Furthermore, leaders can facilitate participants discussing whether and how best to support each other after the group ends.

TEN 'MUSTS' THAT INTERFERE WITH GROUP FACILITATION

Group facilitation, be it either of counselling and psychotherapy or of lifeskills training groups, requires leaders to possess good inner game, or thinking, skills, as well as good outer game, or observable action, skills. Group facilitators can be severely hampered by thinking skills weaknesses, sometimes colloquially referred to as 'stinkin' thinkin''. Here the focus is on unrealistic rules or what Ellis terms irrational beliefs (ibs) as contrasted with rational beliefs (rbs) (Ellis, 1980, 1989). The unrealistic 'musts', 'oughts' and 'shoulds' that leaders may bring to facilitation are important not only in their own right, but also because they can adversely influence other leader thinking skills, for example coping self-talk and perceiving.

Ideally, group facilitators possess what Gallwey terms relaxed concentration (Gallwey, 1974). They are alert and relaxed at the same time. However, facilitating a training group may be fraught with anxieties. For instance, leaders may feel very much on display and under pressure to get participants involved. Furthermore, because of their previous experiences, leaders may inadequately comprehend how to facilitate training groups. For example, former teachers may overemphasize teaching, former preachers overemphasize preaching and former encounter group facilitators overemphasize participants encountering each other. Consequently, for both emotional and prior learning reasons, leaders may sabotage their effectiveness as facilitators through how they think.

The following are ten unrealistic rules or irrational 'musts' that may interfere with leaders offering good training group facilitation skills. Such unrealistic personal rules are self-oppressing rather than self-supporting (Nelson-Jones, 1989). These inner pressurizers are the very stuff upon which uptight and inflexible facilitation is built.

1. *I must be the sole source of wisdom in the group*. Leaders who set themselves up as universal experts grossly overvalue their own contribution and also grossly undervalue the contribution that participants can make to each other's skills development.

2. *I must be in control of the group at all times*. The structured focus of lifeskills training groups means that the initial contract has implicit in it a greater degree of leader control than is generally found in counselling and therapy groups. However, this initial contract should not be taken as an excuse for leaders to monopolize and dominate groups. Even if leaders wanted to, they cannot control all the different interactions that transpire. However, there are many other reasons why such a high degree of leader control is undesirable: for instance, infantilizing participants and eroding their motivation and energy.

3. *I must be aware of everything that goes on in the group*. Unlike in individual

work, where helpers can possess a high degree of awareness concerning their clients, such a level of awareness is impossible in groupwork. Skilled leaders are relaxed, yet alert enough to catch most of the significant messages sent in the group. However, skilled leaders also accept their limitations. They realize that, because of the size of the group and their own fallibility, they mass miss some important messages. However, such messages may still be picked up by other participants or later by the leaders themselves.

4. *I must be liked all of the time by all participants.* The demand for approval is one of the classic Ellis 'mustabatory' beliefs (Ellis, 1980, 1989). This belief can lead to a superficial niceness rather than a willingness to be authentic and genuine. Further negative outcomes stemming from this belief may be a heightened self-awareness that takes energy away from true awareness of others, a need to perceive others in ways that sustain possibly unrealistic aspects of your self-picture, and a heightened sensitivity to signs of aggression and rejection. Such a universal demand for approval needs to be disputed and reformulated. A possible reformulation is: 'Though I might prefer to have participants' approval all the time, I certainly do not need it. What is important is that I do my job competently and remain sensitive to how others perceive my behaviour, without being controlled by them.'

5. *I must always maintain a professional façade.* Leaders are at risk of conveying a spurious expertise that may mask underlying insecurities and doubts about their competence. Participants can be highly sensitive to cues that a less than competent group leader is engaging in impression management. Even competent leaders may seem more competent if they can be authentic, spontaneous and honest about their limitations and mistakes. Participants like group leaders to be human as well as competent (Rogers, 1970). Leaders can help participants to feel that they are in a negative 'social exchange' if, unlike themselves, participants are the only fallible people in the group (Homans, 1961).

6. *I must pressurize participants to self-disclose.* Carl Rogers writes of his experience in facilitating encounter groups: 'From my experience I know that if I attempt to push a group to a deeper level it is not, in the long run, going to work' (Rogers, 1970, p. 48). Inexperienced training group leaders may want quick results. They may expect deep and meaningful disclosures before a climate of trust has been established. Pressing too hard too soon can create resistances to disclosure. Alternatively, it can lead to pseudo-disclosure where participants feel that they have to catalogue their sins and skills weaknesses. Sound leader facilitation skills can help participants to drop their social masks so that they disclose and work on more fundamental issues in their lives. Groups tend to

vary in their willingness to and the pace at which they are prepared to disclose. Clumsy leader pressure to disclose, possibly coupled with gimmicky games and exercises, may well do more harm than good.

7. *I must ensure that great attention is paid to relationship issues between participants.* This unrealistic rule has been included as a caveat to those at risk of not fully making the transition from facilitating counselling and psychotherapy groups to facilitating training groups. There are limits to which leaders can allow participants to discuss relationship issues without jeopardizing the overall task of developing specific lifeskills. Sometimes leaders can use relationship problems between participants as here-and-now examples of their strengths and weaknesses in the targeted skills areas. However, leaders must beware of letting the group lose momentum by lengthy discussions of participants' feelings about one another, especially if unrelated to the skills focus of the group.

8. *I must always have an explanation or interpretation for everything.* Rogers mistrusted facilitators who frequently gave interpretations of the motives and causes behind group members' behaviours. He objected to labelling people with comments like 'You certainly have a lot of latent hostility' (Rogers, 1970, p. 67). Even if such interpretations were accurate, he felt that such comments might arouse defensiveness and unnecessary feelings of hurt. For two important reasons lifeskills group leaders do not need to have explanations for everything. First, when facilitating, leaders should keep quiet much of the time and let the group do the work. Second, as Rogers rightly observed, interpretations and explanations may not always be helpful. However, sometimes leader explanations may be helpful: for example, to throw light on how participants sustain skills weaknesses.

9. *Facilitating a training group must be all work and no play.* Just because some of the content of lifeskills training group may be serious does not mean that the group needs to be conducted in an atmosphere of self-negation and pain. All work and no play makes for dullness. Often pain, tragedy and laughter are not far apart. Participants who can use humour constructively have a great asset with which to confront difficulties. Skilled leaders do not take themselves too seriously, but know when to be serious. In addition, groups where it is okay to reveal happy as well as sad feelings are much more likely to be human and welcoming places than those where participants and leaders must wear mandatory long faces. Life is too short always to be serious. Lifeskills groups can and often should be fun!

10. *I must always get the balance between presentation, structured activities and group discussions right.* Such a 'must' erroneously assumes that there is a single correct balance between didactic input and group

discussion. Furthermore, this 'must' erroneously assumes that leaders should carry all the responsibility for the decision about balance and not involve participants in it. Inevitably leaders are going to make on-the-spot decisions about balance, depending on their assessments of the relevant variables at the time. Such variables include their session objectives, how long the presentations and structured activities take to do properly, whether group discussion at that stage is likely to enhance skill development, and whether or not the group needs the opportunity for the emotional release of participating in discussion.

The above section makes the point that facilitating a lifeskills training group is not only what you do, but also how rationally you think about what you do. How much at risk are you of harming your outer game of facilitating a training group because of weaknesses in your inner game of how you think about it?

CHAPTER HIGHLIGHTS

Training group leaders use facilitation skills both for facilitating group discussion and for facilitating structured learning experiences.

Whether they are being didactic or facilitative, training group leaders always send and receive messages.

Leaders send messages in five main ways: verbal, voice, body, touch, and action. It is important that leaders send congruent or consistent messages.

Initial-stage facilitation skills include: arranging suitable seating; making opening statements; using getting-acquainted exercises; encouraging participation; assisting self-assessment and stating personal goals; handling resistances; and further facilitation skills such as empathic understanding, use of questions, facilitative confronting, self-disclosing and summarizing.

Working-stage facilitation skills relevant to group discussion include: facilitating self-disclosure, facilitating open mutual feedback, and facilitating participants helping each other to manage problems. In addition, leaders may need to set limits on the amount and type of discussion.

Ending-stage facilitation skills include those for the working stage modified for the different concerns that participants have when lifeskills training groups are about to terminate.

Training group leaders require good inner game or thinking skills as well as good outer game or action skills to perform both their didactic and facilitative functions.

Leaders may possess unrealistic rules or irrational 'musts' that interfere with the relaxed concentration required for effective facilitation of lifeskills groups. Ten of these interfering 'musts' are identified and discussed.

SEVEN

How to Speak in Public

All the great speakers were bad speakers at first.
Ralph Waldo Emerson

CHAPTER QUESTIONS

How do training group leaders give effective presentations?

What are some of the dimensions of speech anxiety?

How can leaders use good thinking skills to manage speech anxiety?

What are some considerations in preparing systematic content for lifeskills presentations?

What are some of the main audiovisual aids that leaders use?

What are good delivery skills?

When giving presentations, what voice and body messages should leaders employ?

INTRODUCTION

Previous chapters focused on assessing participants and facilitating training groups. The next three chapters specifically focus on training group leaders in their didactic role. Leaders work with each of the three training modes: 'tell', 'show' and 'do'.

The corresponding learning modes are learning from hearing, observing and doing. Table 7.1 depicts training and learning modes for lifeskills groups. The notion of consolidation has been incorporated into Table 7.1 to highlight the importance of leaders focusing throughout groups on issues of transfer, maintenance and development of skills for when they end.

Table 7.1 Modes of training and learning

TRAINING MODE	LEARNING MODE
Assess	Learning from self-evaluating and self-monitoring
Facilitate	Learning from interacting in the group
Tell	Learning from hearing
Show	Learning from observing demonstrations
Do	Learning from doing structured activities and homework tasks
Consolidate	Learning from developing self-help skills in all the above modes

This chapter reviews public speaking skills, 'tell', or learning by *hearing*. Chapter 8 covers demonstrating lifeskills, 'show', or learning by *observing*. Chapter 9 is on managing structured activities skills, 'do', or learning by *doing*. With varying degrees of success, many academic presentations emphasize learning by hearing. However, training people to integrate applied lifeskills into their repertoires is generally more effective if it adds learning by observing and by doing. Figure 7.1 schematically represents interrelationships between learning by hearing, observing and doing. During lifeskills groups these three training and learning modes influence each other. For example, when initially presenting a lifeskill, 'tell' may be accompanied by 'show' and then 'do'. As participants practise a skill, 'do' may be interspersed with 'show' and 'tell'.

Frequently leaders, even those basing programme on training manuals, present information. Below are examples of leaders with varying degrees of public speaking, 'tell', or enhancing-learning-by-hearing skills.

- Angela gives a presentation on saying 'no' to unreasonable requests. Though Angela has prepared thoroughly, she handles her anxiety by reading her talk. Consequently, she fails to make contact with her audience.

- Rajiv gives a talk on identifying leisure interests. He has failed to structure his talk clearly. He further confuses his audience by using long and rambling sentences.

- Gillian introduces the topic of how to reduce parent–child conflict. She has thoroughly researched her talk. She then translates her notes into an interesting script with short and easily comprehensible sentences. She delivers her talk with good voice and body messages.

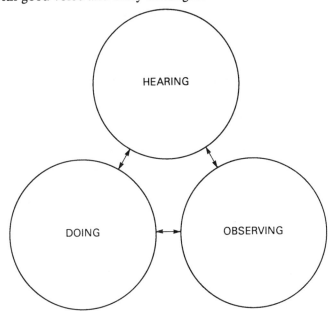

Figure 7.1 *Representation of interrelationships between learning by hearing observing and doing*

There is no magic about public speaking skills. If you have observed polished speakers, you can be certain that they have worked hard to acquire their polish. They have learned to avoid inflicting on audiences what *New York Times* columnist Bill Safire describes as MEGO (My Eyes Glaze Over) (Valenti, 1982). Where appropriate, they use their hold over their audience's attention to influence them. Polished speakers may also have learned to avoid inflicting MATO (My Anxiety Takes Over) on themselves and their audiences. Thus polished speakers possess the inner and outer game skills of effective public speaking.

In all lifeskills training sessions, there is a tension between the need for didactic and facilitative interventions. A balance is required, depending on the objectives of a particular session. The use of formal presentations can be overdone at the expense of learning by doing and group participation. Consequently, most often, leaders give lecturettes of 5, 10 or 15 minutes rather than longer talks. Though these lecturettes often include skills demonstrations, here the focus is on public speaking skills.

SPEECH ANXIETY

Speech anxiety or 'stage fright' is a very real affliction for many aspiring training group leaders. Even famous actors, such as the late Laurence Olivier, suffer stage fright. Some anxiety prior to and during a performance can facilitate rather than debilitate (Alpert & Haber, 1960). However, too much or the wrong sort of anxiety interferes with competent task performance. Meichenbaum and his colleagues suggest that there are two general types of people suffering from speech anxiety: those for whom speech anxiety is part of a shy response across a number of interpersonal situations and those for whom speech anxiety is only a problem in public speaking situations (Meichenbaum *et al.*, 1971). Group leaders suffering from speech anxiety may fall into either category.

What is speech anxiety?

Though not exhaustive, below are some considerations for defining speech anxiety and for assessing how much you suffer from it.

- *Feelings*. Feelings associated with speech anxiety include: tension, insecurity, bashfulness, embarrassment, confusion, fear, vulnerability and inadequacy.

- *Physical reactions*. Physical reactions associated with speech anxiety include: feeling faint, nausea, blushing, perspiring, shaking, pounding heart, shallow breathing, butterflies in stomach, mind going blank, mouth going dry.

- *Thoughts*. Negative self-talk and unrealistic personal rules are two thinking skills weaknesses contributing to speech anxiety.
  (a) Negative self-talk is inner speech that is more negative than a realistic appraisal of the objective evidence warrants. Some of this negative self-talk involves negative and catastrophic predictions. Negative self-talk statements include the following: 'I'm no good'; 'I'm going to make a mess of it'; 'I can't cope with my speech anxiety'; 'I lack the skills to hold my audience'; 'My audience will think I'm incompetent'; 'My audience is not interested in what I have to say'; and 'My audience will think less of me because I am nervous'.
  (b) Unrealistic personal rules cause speakers to put counterproductive pressures on themselves. Such rules, which may be at or just below awareness, include the following: I *must* be a good public speaker immediately; I *must* make the perfect speech every time; I *must* have my audience's total attention and approval; I *must* be the absolute master/mistress of my subject matter; and I *must* be in control at all times.

- *Verbal, voice, body and action messages*. Illustrative verbal, voice, body and action messages associated with speech anxiety include the following:
  (a) Verbal messages: being neutral and not stating your own opinions; being too ready to agree; too many 'uhms' and 'ers'; and using confused and rambling sentences.
  (b) Voice messages: speaking quietly; speaking too quickly; stammering; and loudness that masks insecurity.
  (c) Body messages: poor gaze and eye contact, for example reading your talk; smiling too much; tight body posture; scratching your face; and shuffling papers.

(d) Action messages: avoiding public speaking situations; only doing individual rather than group helping; speaking for as short a time as possible; avoiding time for discussion; leaving the speaker's position as soon as possible; and muddled use of audiovisual aids.

- *Defensive roles*. Some people handle public speaking anxiety by wearing either social or professional masks. These masks may be viewed as defensive roles to the extent that they contain hidden agendas not directly relevant to the tasks at hand. Examples of defensive roles include: pretending to be more of an expert than you are; acting more helpless and vulnerable than necessary; playing the clown; playing the cynic; playing the flirt; monopolizing; and being aggressive.

- *Anxiety-evoking people*. You may experience speech anxiety more with some categories of people than with others. Such people may include the following: strangers, authorities by virtue of their knowledge, authorities by virtue of their role, colleagues, the opposite sex, older people, children, resistant people, and reluctant people forced to attend.

- *Anxiety-evoking situations*. Situations associated with speech anxiety include the following: participating in discussion groups; leading discussion groups; situations involving formal assessment; a lifeskills talk before 5 to 9 people; a lifeskills talk before 10 to 20 people; a lifeskills talk before 21 to 50 people; a lifeskills talk before more than 50 people; answering questions after a lifeskills talk; having your lifeskills talk audio-recorded; having your lifeskills talk video-recorded; and going for an interview.

This section has developed some of the dimensions of speech anxiety. Some people may suffer from speech anxiety, but deny or dilute its extent. Awareness of a problem and breaking it down into component parts is a first step in coping with it. Exercise 14 (on the next page) is designed to raise your awareness of how you may suffer from speech anxiety.

MANAGE SPEECH-ANXIOUS THINKING

How can lifeskills group leaders suffering from speech anxiety develop the skills of preventing MATO (My Anxiety Takes Over)? You may help to combat speech anxiety by learning, rehearsing and practising the skills of putting your talks together and delivering them in interesting ways. These composition and delivery skills are covered later. Here the focus is on learning to support rather than oppress yourself by how you think about speaking in public. Below are nine broad areas of thinking skills, albeit overlapping, in which you may have either weaknesses or strengths or, most likely, both (Nelson-Jones, 1989).

Exercise 14 Assess your speech anxiety

Make a worksheet like the one below. For each of the dimensions fill in your assessment of how, if at all, you exhibit anxiety when you speak in public.

Feelings
Physical reactions
Negative self-talk
Unrealistic personal rules
Verbal messages
Voice messages
Body messages
Action messages
Defensive roles

1. What kinds of people that you are likely to come across either evoke or might evoke anxiety when you speak in public?

2. What kinds of public speaking situations that you are likely to face either are or might be anxiety-evoking for you?

3. Summarize how anxious you are when you speak in public and in what ways you experience and show your anxiety.

4. What are the consequences of any speech anxiety that you possess for your effectiveness as a training group leader?

- Own responsibility for being a chooser

- Be in touch with your underlying feelings.

- Use self-talk constructively.

- Have goals that you articulate clearly

- Choose realistic personal rules.

- Choose to perceive yourself and others accurately.

- Accurately attribute cause.

- Make realistic predictions.

and that reflect your values.

- Use visualizing to best effect.

Each of these thinking skills is now reviewed in turn. The object is both to help those of you with speech anxiety to identify the skills weaknesses that maintain your anxiety and also to suggest some ways of thinking more effectively.

Own responsibility for being a chooser

Some speech-anxious people may possess insufficient awareness that they are always choosers in their lives (Frankl, 1959; May & Yalom, 1989). For example, they may drift along in varying states of awareness that speech anxiety is a problem for them without ever trying to do much about it. Many people fail adequately to realize their responsibility for making the thinking, feeling and action choices that help them to best realize their potential. They may possess illusions of assuming responsibility for their lives and yet not have the knowledge, skills and discipline to do this effectively. People not thinking about speech anxiety in terms of its component skills possess a major stumbling block to working on their problems.

Be in touch with your underlying feelings

Being insufficiently in touch with your own feelings and valuing process may contribute to public speaking difficulties in a number of ways. First, you may deny or dilute the extent to which you feel anxious about speaking in public. Insufficient awareness of the problem may impede taking corrective action. Second, you may lack a sufficient sense of your own identity. Because of this you feel very exposed when giving public presentations. You may fear people perceiving no substance under your surface. Third, you may overly focus on feelings of insecurity and anxiety and insufficiently focus on feelings of strength and competence. You are only in touch with part of your range of feelings. Fourth, you may place a value on the importance of perfectionist achievement in public speaking situations that is a 'hand-me-down' of someone else's values. Rogers has used the term 'conditions of worth' to describe valuing yourself on the basis of another's beliefs rather than on your own feelings and thoughts (Rogers, 1959; Raskin & Rogers, 1989).

Some people badly out of touch with their valuing process require counselling and psychotherapy. Self-help approaches include developing your skills of inner listening and focusing on aspects of your thinking in ways described below. Developing inner listening skills starts with acknowledging the importance of awareness of feelings (Gendlin, 1981). Feelings often appear first as feeling fragments rather than as full-blown emotions. You need to be able to identify and label these feeling fragments to be able to assess their significance. Sometimes you may need to clear a temporal and emotional space so as to spend quiet time focusing on your true feelings.

Use self-talk constructively

Coping self-talk is another thinking skill for managing public speaking anxiety (Fremouw & Zittler, 1978; Meichenbaum, 1983, 1985, 1986; Meichenbaum & Deffenbacher, 1988; Meichenbaum *et al.*, 1971). The idea is to replace anxious and task-irrelevant negative self-talk with more constructive self-statements. Kendall and Hollon have developed an Anxious Self-Statements Questionnaire (ASSQ) (Kendall & Hollon, 1989). Anxious self-talk items include the following: 'I can't take it'; 'I can't cope'; 'I can't do anything right'; 'Don't let me be crazy'; 'I wish I could escape'; 'Can I make it?'; and 'I feel totally confused'.

Coping self-talk involves replacing anxious and negative self-talk statements with helpful ones. In coping self-talk, calming and coaching statements tend to be interspersed.

- *Calming self-talk.* Two important areas of calming self-talk are as follows:
  (a) Tell yourself to stay calm. Sample self-statements include: 'Keep calm', 'Relax' and 'Take it easy'. In addition, you can instruct yourself to 'Take a deep breath' or 'Breathe slowly and regularly'.
  (b) Tell yourself you can cope. Sample self-statements include: 'I can handle this talk' and 'My anxiety is a signal for me to use my coping skills'.

- *Coaching self-talk.* Coaching self-talk can help you cope with speech anxiety in the following ways:
  (a) Specify your goals. For example, 'I will give a talk lasting five minutes and speak at a comfortable rate for me and my audience'.
  (b) Break tasks down. Think through the specific steps and tasks required for attaining goals. For example, 'I need to maintain good eye contact with my audience'.
  (c) Concentrate on the task at hand. You instruct yourself like pilots talking themselves through to difficult landings. A small but important tip is that self-instruction is easier if your external speech rate is not fast.

You may use coping self-talk before, during and after public speaking situations.

Possible coping self-talk statements *before* a stressful lifeskills talk situation include:

'I know I will feel less anxious if I am properly prepared.'

'No negative self-talk. Just think rationally.'

'Calm down. What is it I have to do?'

Possible coping self-talk statements *during* a stressful lifeskills talk situation include:

'Relax. The audience is not expecting perfection so I don't need to expect it either.'

'Stay calm. Take my time. Just aim for a steady performance.'

'Hang in there. I'm using my coping skills and I'm doing okay.'

Possible coping self-talk statements for *after* a stressful lifeskills talk situation include:

'My fears were not justified by how I felt once I got started.'

'Each time I cope it seems to get easier.'

'I'm proud of the way that I'm learning to manage my fears.'

Acquiring and using coping self-talk involves much work and practice. Those speech anxiety situations in which leaders need their coping self-talk skills most are often the same situations where they are least likely to use them. Speech-anxious leaders need to identify the coping self-talk statements that work best for them. Then they need to rehearse and practise these statements both in real life situations and in their imaginations. Imaginal rehearsal in which you talk yourself through public speaking situations as you visualize them has many advantages. You are not restricted to requiring a live audience. You can anticipate and work through difficulties and setbacks. You can choose your rehearsal times and rehearse regularly.

Choose realistic personal rules

As mentioned in Chapter 2, your personal rules are the 'do's' and 'don'ts' by which you lead your life. Each of you has an inner rule book that guides your living. If your rules are self-supporting, they can motivate and help you to attain realistic goals. However, if your rules are self-oppressing, they leave you open to a triple dose of self-disparagement. John has a rule that he must be a good public speaker immediately. However, his first lifeskills talk does not go particularly well, so this activates his first dose of self-disparagement. His second dose of self-disparagement is because he then becomes anxious and depressed about his overall public speaking. His third dose of self-disparagement comes about because now he starts devaluing not just his public speaking ability but his whole worth as a person.

Ellis has coined the term 'mustabation' to refer to rigid personal rules characterized by 'musts', 'oughts' and 'shoulds' (Ellis, 1980, 1989). He has a simple ABC framework for showing how people's thinking affects their feelings and behaviour (Ellis, 1962).

A   The activating event.
B   Your beliefs about the activating event.
C   The emotional and behavioural consequences.

Ellis regards the emotional and behavioural consequences to be determined by your beliefs relating to the activating event rather than by the activating event itself. Here the term personal rules is preferred to beliefs. Let us place the example of John into the ABC framework.

A   John's first lifeskills talk does not go particularly well.
B   John has the personal rule that I must be a good public speaker immediately.
C   John's emotional consequences include anxiety and depression. Behavioural consequences for John may include either giving up trying or trying too hard next time.

Inappropriate feelings and actions may each be signals that you possess one or more inappropriate personal rules. For example, if your speech anxiety is persistent and uncomfortable, you may oppress yourself through inappropriate personal rules. In addition, if you become aware that you behave inappropriately when giving a talk, for instance speaking too much or being too gushing, again look at the realism of your rules. Earlier, when defining speech anxiety, five unrealistic personal rules that may contribute to speech anxiety were suggested: I *must* be a good public speaker immediately; I *must* make the perfect speech every time; I *must* have the audience's total attention and approval; I *must* be the absolute master/mistress of my subject matter; and I *must* be in control at all times.

Once you become aware that your underlying self-talk contains one or more unrealistic personal rules, what can you do about it? Disputing and reformulating these self-oppressing rules are two skills that can help you to move towards self-supporting rules. Ellis (1980, 1989) considers the technique of disputing to be the most typical and often-used method of rational-emotive therapy (RET). Disputing involves logically challenging the false assumptions that you may hold about yourself, others and the world.

Wendy is a training group leader who has the personal rule: 'I must give the perfect talk every time.' Questions that Wendy might ask herself to dispute her self-oppressing rule include the following.

'What evidence exists for the truth of my personal rule?'

'What is the worst that might happen if I give a less than perfect talk?'

'Do I demand the same standards of other people who give lifeskills talks as I demand of myself?'

'In what ways does giving a less than perfect lifeskills talk make me worthless as a person?'

'What are the costs and consequences to me and others of my demand that I must always give a perfect talk?'

'To what extent does my wanting always to give the perfect lifeskills talk represent my past learning history rather than the reality of my present situation and wishes?'

You may need to dispute the same self-oppressing rules again and again. This is because such rules have become well-established habits. Ellis strongly emphasizes that people need to work hard to change. He regards most of his clients as 'natural resisters who find it exceptionally easy to block themselves from changing and find it unusually hard to resist their resistances' (Ellis, 1987, pp. 370–371).

Reformulating involves substituting self-supporting for self-oppressing characteristics in specific personal rules. Some of the main characteristics of self-supporting personal rules include:

- *Expressing preferences rather than demands.* Though you would prefer to give a competent talk, it is not absolutely necessary for your survival.

- *A coping emphasis.* Focusing on managing or coping with your speech anxiety rather than being perfectionist about mastering it altogether.

- *Being based on your own valuing process.* Your public speaking rules are not just rigid internalizations of others' rules.

- *Flexibility.* Where appropriate, your rules are amenable to change.

- *Absence of self-rating.* Your rules lead to a functional rating of your specific speaking skills according to whether they help you to attain realistic objectives. Your rules do not lead to rating your whole personhood.

Below are some possible self-supporting reformulations for the earlier examples of John and Wendy.

John

- *Self-oppressing personal rule.* 'I *must* be a good public speaker immediately.'

- *Self-supporting personal rule.* 'Though I would prefer to be good immediately, this may not be realistic. I have to work and practise at developing my public speaking skills. Setbacks are part of the learning process.'

Wendy

- *Self-oppressing personal rule.* 'I *must* give the perfect talk every time.'

- *Self-supporting personal rule.* 'Though my preference is always to give a polished talk, I may not always do so. If I give a less than perfect talk it is something with which I can cope, not a catastrophe, and I may learn something from it.'

The outcome of identifying, disputing and reformulating self-oppressing personal rules is that you should have less speech anxiety and perform better.

Choose to perceive yourself and others accurately

People with speech anxiety may misperceive their speaking abilities both by negative self-labelling and by misperceiving others' reactions to their efforts. Here the ABC framework requires alteration to become:

A   The activating event.
B   Your perceptions.
C   The emotional and behavioural consequences.

The consequences for you of A are influenced by your perceptions of A at B. These consequences do not automatically follow from A. You have a choice of how you perceive at B.

PERCEIVE YOURSELF ACCURATELY

Negative self-labels are unrealistically negative perceptions either about yourself as a person or about your specific abilities, in this case public speaking. You may perceive your speaking skills as deficient, incompetent, weak, pathetic, boring, inferior and inadequate, to mention some labels. At best such labels are overgeneralizations, since public speaking involves many subskills in each of which you may have different strengths and weaknesses. In addition, you may put yourself down by unthinkingly labelling your specific speaking skills in negative terms. While you may have weaknesses, you may also have strengths or areas that you can develop into strengths. Why keep focusing on your negatives? Instead, engage in what Ivey and his colleagues call 'positive asset search' to identify your strengths (Ivey *et al.*, 1987). When assessing both negative and positive characteristics, try to distinguish fact from inference and make your inferences reflect the facts as closely as possible. In this way you are likely to arrive at a more balanced, and possibly less negative, set of perceptions concerning your public speaking abilities.

PERCEIVE OTHERS ACCURATELY

If you are speech-anxious, the way you perceive situations may sustain your discomfort. Often people remain unaware that they jump to perceptual conclusions rather than saying to themselves 'Stop ... think ... what are my perceptual choices?' Beck observes that people frequently have *automatic* thoughts and perceptions that influence their emotions (Beck, 1976; Beck & Weishaar, 1989). Either they are not fully conscious of these thoughts and images or it does not occur to them that they warrant special attention. Beck collaborates with his patients in the scientific or detective work of identifying these self-oppressing perceptions or 'what you tell yourself' (Beck *et al.*, 1979; Beck & Emery, 1985; Beck, 1988). These perceptions are related to unrealistic personal rules. For example, if speakers have a rule, 'I must have my audience's total attention and approval', this is likely to sensitize them to look for signs of rejection. Here is an example in the ABC framework for Max, who gives a lifeskills presentation.

A   Audience members Sally and Chris have a brief word during Max's talk.

B   Max perceives: 'Sally and Chris are bored with my talk.'

C   Max gets anxious and hurries through the rest of his presentation.

However, there were many other perceptions that Max might have had at B. These alternative perceptions include:

'Sally and Chris often talk to each other no matter what is going on.'

'Sally was telling Chris not to sit so close to her.'

'Sally and Chris were passing complimentary remarks about my talk.'

'Sally was making a remark to Chris about someone else in the group.'

'Chris was asking Sally for some paper so that he could take notes.'

If, like Max, you are prone to jumping to negative perceptual conclusions when speaking in public, how can you combat this? First, become aware of your tendency. Second, monitor your thinking in public speaking situations and practise making the connections between upsetting perceptions and upsetting feelings. Third, question your perceptions by logical analysis. This process involves engaging in the following kinds of self-talk:

'Stop ... think ... what are my perceptual choices?'

'Are my perceptions based on fact or inference?'

'If my perceptions are based on inference, are there other ways of perceiving the situation that are more closely related to the factual evidence?'

'If necessary, what further information do I need to collect?'

'What is the perception that I choose because it represents the best fit in relation to the factual evidence?'

Let us assume that Max reviewed with his lifeskills group supervisor why he started rushing his talk. The supervisor asked Max to assess the evidence for his 'Sally and Chris are bored with my talk' perception. On doing this he discovered that there were *no facts* to support this conclusion and that it was an inference on his part. Max then generated the alternative perceptions listed above. He decided that 'Sally and Chris often talk to each other no matter what is going on' was the best-fit perception. This perception did not involve Max in putting himself down unnecessarily.

Accurately attribute cause

Attributions are the explanations, interpretations, or reasons that people give themselves for what happens. You may make attributions both about your public speaking anxiety and about the causes of your success or failure in specific speaking situations. There are a number of possible misattributions or faulty explanations for speech anxiety that may weaken your motivation for change. Such explanations are often partial truths: the mistake is to treat them as whole truths. Below are some possible misattributions concerning speech anxiety.

- *It's my genes.* This is the view that people are anxious by nature rather than by nurture. However, a considerable part of speech anxiety represents learned behaviour that is sustained by thinking and action skills weaknesses.

- *It's my unfortunate past.* Many people, with or without professional help, have learned to overcome skills weaknesses caused by their unfortunate pasts.

- *It's all their fault.* Every time a talk of yours does not go down well, you blame the audience. You get anxious because you do not get the feedback you want, yet are unable to examine your behaviour.

- *It's all my fault.* You blame yourself for everything that goes wrong when you give a talk. You may engage in black-and-white thinking whereby everything is either all right or all wrong. You may fail to take into account that there are many situational and audience considerations related to the success of a talk.

- *I've tried before.* You may have tried to overcome your speech anxiety before and been unsuccessful. However, this failure need not be your guide to the future. For instance, this time you may try harder, understand your speech anxiety better and possess better skills at managing it, know more about your subject, and possess better delivery skills.

- *My anxiety is the cause of my poor public speaking.* Some people get anxious in speaking situations because they are not properly prepared. Consequently their anxiety is a result of inadequate behaviour and not antecedent to it.

The above may be attributions not only of how you acquired speech anxiety but also of how you maintain it. Like unrealistic personal rules, such misattributions of cause require disputation by logical analysis and reformulation. Below are some possible reformulations of the above misattributions.

'Though like many people I experience anxiety when talking before groups of people, my speech anxiety has largely been learned.'

'Though others may have contributed to my speech anxiety, I currently sustain my speech anxiety through skills weaknesses that I can learn to overcome.'

'Though others' behaviours may sometimes contribute to my talks not being a success, I also need to examine the ways in which my own behaviour may have contributed.'

'I am only responsible for my own behaviour in public speaking situations rather than accepting total responsibility for what happens.'

'Though I've tried before, circumstances are different now. With more understanding of how I sustain my speech anxiety, I can develop new and better skills to overcome it.'

'My speech anxiety may be the consequence of inadequate preparation. If so, I need to prepare my lifeskills talks more thoroughly.'

Make realistic predictions

Predictions are thoughts and images about the probability of future events. When thinking of giving lifeskills talks, training group leaders need to view the future realistically. They must avoid the twin dangers of over-optimism and undue pessimism. Leaders can set themselves up for disappointment by being overly optimistic and ignoring the realistic difficulties in giving training presentations. Adequate preparation geared to she needs of specific audiences is essential. Leaders who think they can survive on charm will frequently be disillusioned.

Possibly, more aspiring training group leaders fall prey to undue pessimism than to unjustified optimism. They may fill their heads with catastrophic predictions about their own inadequate presentation skills, their audience's reactions, and their inability to cope with this feedback. Challenging negative predictions with logical analysis and working through the worst possibility are two skills for combating undue pessimism.

CHALLENGE NEGATIVE PREDICTIONS WITH LOGICAL ANALYSIS

People can only make inferences about their futures, since their futures have yet to happen. However, these inferences can possess varying degrees of relatednesses to existing facts. You can dispute your negative predictions about giving talks with logical analysis and reformulate them into more realistic predictions.

WORK THROUGH THE WORST POSSIBILITY

You can visualize the worst that could happen when you give a talk, assess how realistic this is, and think through whether and how you would cope (Emery, 1982). You may discover that not only is the worst possibility highly unlikely, but also, even if it occurred, you have various personal and environmental resources to cope with it.

Have goals that you articulate clearly and that reflect your values

Training group leaders who suffer from varying degrees of debilitating speech anxiety should clearly make managing speech anxiety a goal. Leaders may also contribute to their lack of confidence by setting their public speaking goals too high. Such goals may reflect internalizations of others' rules rather than their own valuing processes. Frequently, beginning leaders contribute to their anxiety by attempting too much in a given time period. Then they get anxious about not finishing what they set out to do. This anxiety may contribute to muddled and rushed presentations that in turn generate further anxiety. In brief, goals for both yourself as a public speaker and for each lifeskills talk need to be realistic and manageable.

Use visualizing to best effect

Visualizing has already been mentioned with regard to using coping self-talk as you imaginally rehearse upcoming speaking situations. In addition, mention has been made of the skill of confronting unduly negative predictions by visualizing coping with the worst possibility. Another use of visualizing is repeatedly to imagine yourself behaving competently in upcoming speaking situations (Lazarus, 1977). Getting a clear mental picture of yourself performing competently may help you to do so.

Visualizing may also be used to relax yourself mentally before talks and as part of speech anxiety systematic desensitization procedures (Paul & Shannon, 1966; Paul, 1968; Wolpe, 1982; Zemore, 1975). Visual relaxation can be used either independently or in conjunction with muscular relaxation (Jacobson, 1938). Each of you probably has one or more scenes where you feel relaxed. Before giving a talk, sit in a comfortable chair or lie down and imagine a favourite scene. The following is an example of a visual relaxation scene.

> I'm lying on an uncrowded beach on a pleasant,
> sunny day enjoying the sensations of warmth on
> my body. There is a gentle breeze. I can hear
> the peaceful noise of the sea lapping against
> the shore near by. I haven't a care in the world
> and enjoy my feelings of peace, calm, relaxation
> and well-being.

Detailed descriptions of systematic desensitization are to be found elsewhere (for example, Goldfried & Davison, 1976; Wolpe, 1982). Briefly, it consists of three elements: (1) training in muscular relaxation; (2) the construction of one or more heirarchies of progressively more anxiety-evoking scenes – here around the theme of public speaking; and (3) presentation of the scenes to a person's imagination when relaxed. Originally, the idea was that people should feel no anxiety with a presented scene before moving on to the next one. An alternative approach is to view systematic desensitization as training in self-control. People are encouraged to 'relax away' tensions as they build up (Goldfried, 1971; Goldfried & Davison, 1976). Self-desensitization, in which you go through the procedure without professional help, is a further variation of systematic desensitization.

Exercise 15 aims to develop your use of thinking skills to manage speech anxiety.

Exercise 15 Use thinking skills to manage speech anxiety

Part A Use coping self-talk

1. Identify and list anxiety-evoking and negative self-talk statements that contribute to your speech anxiety. One way to do this is to run through your mind in slow motion a public speaking situation in which you have participated and get in touch with what you were saying to yourself.

2. Identify a specific public speaking situation that you find stressful, if possible in relation to being a training group leader. Write out at least three coping self-talk statements for each of:
    (a) before
    (b) during, and
    (c) after the situation.
    It may help if you write these statements on an index card for practice and use in emergency purposes.

3. Rehearse and practise using your coping self-talk to help you to manage speech anxiety. Even where you have access to actual public speaking situations, rehearse and practise your coping self-talk as you imagine the situations in advance.

Part B Choose realistic personal rules

1. Select a past or future public speaking situation, preferably as a training group leader, that you wish to work on.
   A (the event) Describe the situation that contributed to or may contribute to your upset.
   B (your personal rules) Looking out for 'musts, oughts, shoulds, have to's, got to's', list any demands you made or might make of yourself, others or the situation.
   C (the consequences) Describe how you felt and acted or might feel and act. Indicate which of your feelings and actions you consider to be inappropriate.

2. Dispute each of the demands you made or might make in the situation.

3. Reformulate one or more of your self-oppressing personal rules in the situation into a self-supporting rule(s).

4. What do you consider the effects of your new self-supporting rule(s) might have been or might be on your feelings and actions in and about the public speaking situation?

Part C Choose how you perceive

1. Generating different perceptions
   For each of the following public speaking scenarios, generate at least three different perceptions.
   (a) At the start of your lifeskills talk everyone in the group is not present.
   (b) Halfway through your lifeskills talk someone gets up and leaves.
   (c) You get feedback from one participant that your lifeskills talk was not good.

2. Perceiving a specific speech-anxiety situation differently
   (a) Choose a situation in which you have experienced speech anxiety.
   (b) Make up a worksheet with the following format.

SITUATION	UPSETTING PERCEPTIONS	DIFFERENT PERCEPTIONS

(c) Write down the situation and, in the upsetting-perception(s) column, any perceptions associated with your speech anxiety in that situation. Assess the realism of your upsetting perception(s) by logical analysis.

(d) In the different-perceptions column, write down as many different perceptions of the situation as you can generate. Then evaluate and choose which has the best fit for explaining the situation.

(e) Assess the ways in which the emotional and behavioural consequences of your best-fit perception(s) would have been different from those of your original perceptions(s).

Part D Develop thinking skills to combat speech anxiety

1. Assessment
    If you suffer from any level of debilitating speech anxiety, assess the contribution to this of any skills weaknesses that you may have in each of the following thinking skills areas.

THINKING SKILLS AREA	YOUR ASSESSMENT
Own responsibility for choices	
Be in touch with feelings	
Use coping self-talk	
Choose realistic personal rules	
Perceive accurately	
Attribute cause accurately	
Make realistic predictions	
Set realistic goals	
Use visualizing skills	

Summarize and prioritize the key thinking skills that you need to develop to help you to manage your speech anxiety better.

2.   Change
(a) Make out a plan to develop your thinking skills in each of the areas that you have targeted as in need of change. Your plan should include specific and realistic goals and state a time frame for changing each thinking skills weakness.
(b) Implement your plan and evaluate the consequences of any changes in your thinking on your speech-related feelings and behaviours.

PREPARE SYSTEMATIC CONTENT

Speaking well is thinking clearly.
Speaking exceptionally well is thinking exceptionally clearly.

Jack Valenti

The previous section specifically focused on avoiding MATO (My Anxiety Takes Over). The next two sections focus on putting your message together and conveying it to your audience, hopefully in a way that avoids their getting MEGO (My Eyes Glaze Over). Thorough preparation can also help training group leaders to speak with confidence. In addition, such preparation is a necessity for a professional approach to imparting lifeskills information.

Leader presentations in lifeskills training groups are influence attempts designed to impart information relevant to building participants' skills. With their applied focus, lifeskills presentations differ from academic lectures in many ways. Lifeskills talks are most often fairly brief introductions to a skill. Demonstration of the skill is often incorporated into talks. A structured activity to encourage participation may also be included. Talks are usually followed by coaching, rehearsal and practice. In short, lifeskills talks are part of skill-building sequences rather than ends in themselves. Below are some of the component skills of preparing systematic content for your talks.

Set clear goals

Lifeskills group leaders require clear goals for each talk they give. Considerations in goal setting include the following.

- *Be clear regarding the skill or subskill to be communicated.* Some lifeskills talks get off to a poor start and never recover because leaders have inadequately thought through precisely what to convey. Muddled thinking leads to muddled speaking. Furthermore, some leaders have difficulty distinguishing between a descriptive discussion of a skill and a systematic 'how-to' presentation of it.

Clearly stating the specific behaviour or behaviours targeted greatly enhances the development of a systematic presentation. For instance, a goal like 'Learning to use assertion skills to develop self-esteem' is too vague and general. The specific assertive behaviour targeted needs to be clarified: for instance, 'Learning to identify, dispute and reformulate unrealistic personal rules that make it difficult for you to say no'. Even this is probably far too ambitious a goal for a lifeskills talk. It may be best approached in three separate talks: identification, disputation and reformulation.

- *Set a realistic time limit.* Many considerations influence the time allocated to a talk. These considerations include: how much time is needed to give a proper introduction of a skill; the balance between talking and doing; and the attention span of the audience.

- *Have manageable objectives.* As already mentioned, many aspiring lifeskills trainers try to do too much too quickly and succeed in doing nothing well.

- *Be sensitive to sequencing.* All lifeskills talks take place within the context of overall programmes and of individual sessions. The topic for each talk needs to take into account how well it fits into the sequence of skills being developed over the group's life. Furthermore, the goals of talks must take into account what precedes and follows in individual sessions.

- *Be sensitive to your audience.* Bernstein advises public speakers to think like listeners when preparing talks (Bernstein, 1988). The goals of lifskills talks must take into account how well the audience relates to the learning sequence. For example, the learning sequence may be too advanced or too elementary.

Develop a systematic outline

The need for lifeskills talks to have a clear structure is strongly emphasized. Effective training is systematic rather than piecemeal. A clear structure introduces the skill in a logical and easily comprehensible sequence. This acts as a protection against both speaker and audience confusion. A leader giving a presentation on the use of coping self-talk to manage anger might develop the following outline.

OUTLINE OF COPING SELF-TALK PRESENTATION
Goals of talk
Introductory definition of self-talk
  ABC framework
  What you say to yourself at B
  Negative self-talk and anger
  What is negative self-talk?
  Examples of negative self-talk
  Consequences of negative self-talk
  Becoming aware of negative self-talk

Coping self-talk and anger
Changing what you say to yourself at B
Coping as contrasted with mastery
Dimensions of coping self-talk
    Calming self-talk
    Coaching self-talk
Coping self-talk in anger situations
    Before the situation
    During the situation
    After the situation
Developing the skill of coping self-talk
    Coaching, rehearsal and practice in the group
    Doing homework
Summary and conclusions

In the above example, the training group leader would have the choice of whether to give the content of the above outline in a single presentation or in a series of smaller presentations interspersed with structured activities and discussion. In addition, skilled leaders always look for ways to introduce demonstrations into presentations.

Use language effectively

With effective lifeskills talks, speakers make it easy for listeners to receive them 'loud and clear'. However, many factors can introduce 'static' or 'noise' into communication. Speakers may not have good skills at sending clear messages. They may heavily encode them so that they require extensive decoding by listeners. Listeners may not have good skills at decoding messages. In addition, they may have their own agendas and unfinished business as they listen. Also, there may be contextual considerations, for instance external noise, that interfere with communication.

With so many potential difficulties in having your messages received accurately, it is essential that you do not add to them by poor use of language. Below are some considerations in using language effectively.

- *Take the intelligence level and background of your audience into account.* Just as good professional writers always write with specific audiences in mind, so skilled training group leaders prepare their talks. Lifeskills training groups are not just for the educated. There can be enormous differences in educational level, socio-economic status and other factors both between various participant groups and within the same group.

- *Use straightforward and unambiguous language.* In general, where a simple word will suffice, avoid using a more complex one. Beware of psychobabble and jargon. In listening-skills lifeskills groups, even words like empathy may not communicate clearly. Instead of empathy you may use terms like reflective responding, active listening or listening with understanding.

- *Use words economically.* Shakespeare wrote in *Hamlet* 'Brevity is the soul of wit'. Mark Twain observed: 'As to the Adjective; when in doubt, strike it out.' Too many words can block clear communication of meaning. Furthermore, being long-winded can take valuable time away from other elements in the skills-learning sequence, for instance coaching and practice.

- *Avoid long sentences.* Bernstein observes that the language of speech is different from written language. Sentence length is one of the main areas of difference. Bernstein writes: 'Spoken English moves in a simple straight line – a sequence of short sentences' (Bernstein, 1988, p. 75). An important reason for using short sentences is that they add to audience comprehension. Referring to written language, the American Press Institute (API) reports that sentences of: as many as 8 words will be understood by 100 per cent of readers; as many as 15 words, by 90 per cent; as many as 19 words, by 80 per cent; and as many as 28 words, by 50 per cent (Goddard, 1989). With some groups of participants, short sentences may be a necessity. Remember that 50 per cent of the population are below the average intelligence level! The remaining 50 per cent may not be functioning too intelligently either in their areas of lifeskills weaknesses.

- *Address your audience directly.* Prepare your content as though you are about to have a conversation with your audience. They are not just a sea of faces out there, but individual people with whom you will have a dialogue. Think of them as 'you' and prepare as though 'I' am about to talk with 'you'.

Be practical and focused on participants' needs

Skilled leaders enlist their audience's interest and motivation so that they can acquire something of 'take-away' value for outside the group. Lifeskills talks focus on the mechanics of how to perform a skill or subskill. They are the verbal equivalent of a skills manual. They are not academic discourses. Leaders should aim to present skills so that participants understand them well enough to be able to instruct themselves in them on their own. Skills of giving practical 'how-to' presentations include: breaking tasks down step by step; relating content to participants' own experiences; using good examples and case studies; giving clear demonstrations; and indicating the self-talk that participants might use when confronted with the need to use the skill in their daily lives.

Pay attention to beginnings and endings

The suggestion that you pay attention to beginnings and endings is not meant to devalue the middles of presentations. However, unlike middles, where leaders always focus on imparting information, there are special considerations for beginnings and endings.

BEGINNINGS

When you begin a talk you wish to do at least three things: (1) create a relationship with the audience or, if you already have a relationship, nurture it; (2) stimulate their interest and attention; and (3) communicate the goals of your talk. Below are some suggestions for how to open talks. These methods may be used either on their own or in combination.

- *Make some linking comments.* These linking comments may put your talk in the context of what has gone before in your work with participants.

- *State your goals and give the outline of your talk.* Participants may appreciate knowing the structure of your talk from the start. Providing a clear outline can also indicate to participants that you know your material and have taken the time and trouble to prepare it properly.

- *Indicate why the topic is important.* Participants are likely to be more motivated by leaders who genuinely communicate that their message is important than by those who do not. However, there is a danger of alienating participants by overselling.

- *Give an example.* Giving an example is akin to telling a story that illustrates the point of your talk. You may give more than one example.

- *Tell a joke.* You need to ensure not only that your joke is relevant, but also that it will be picked up accurately by your audience. To tell a joke properly you need to have the requisite skills. This is unlike one British aristocrat of whom it was said 'a joke in his mouth is no laughing matter' (Valenti, 1982).

- *Ask a question.* You can ask a question that relates the content of your talk to participants' own lives.

- *Do a brief exercise.* An introductory exercise should be designed to illustrate a major point in your talk. For instance, at the beginning of a presentation on coping self-talk you can invite the audience to close their eyes for 30 seconds and think of nothing. Most participants will become very aware that they were engaging in inner speech rather than thinking of nothing.

Often the introduction to your talk is best left to the end of your preparation. By then you know what follows.

ENDINGS

The ending of lifeskills talks is often the start of practical work. There is much to be said for ending with a concise summary of the main points of your talk. Such summaries echo the advice often given to trainee teachers: 'Tell them what you are going to say, say it, and then tell them what you have said'. If you wish participants to consolidate the lessons from your talk by either reading a hand-out or by completing homework exercises, you may distribute these now. Many lifeskills talks end with time for questions and discussion. You may wish to end your talk this way too, before moving on to coaching, rehearsing and practising.

Prepare a systematic script or set of notes

There are three main ways of giving verbal presentations: without notes, with notes, and from prepared scripts. The term script is used in preference to text to indicate that there are differences in writing for written and for verbal presentation. Giving a lifeskills talk without notes is not for beginners. Experienced training group leaders may be able to carry in their heads the structure and content of their talks. Also, unlike many beginners, experienced leaders are unlikely to be afflicted by debilitating anxiety interfering with recall. Nevertheless, at some stage, these leaders had to make the effort to develop systematic talks. This effort involved making either a good set of notes or a prepared script.

Giving talks from full scripts consumes much preparation time. However, word-processors save time. When it comes to editing and making corrections, word-processors offer much greater flexibility than writing. Leaders and aspiring leaders have to consider whether their talks merit the time taken to prepare scripts. Instances of such an investment being desirable include when leaders: require the discipline of developing scripts to master material; are very nervous; and are likely to repeat the talk on many occasions. If you prepare scripts, it is easier to deliver them double-spaced and with obvious gaps between paragraphs. Some scripts are written in the right two-thirds of pages with the left third being reserved for comments on delivery (Bernstein, 1988). Many leaders avoid prepared scripts, since they are tempted to read them. Reading scripts blocks good audience contact.

Most training group leaders give talks from notes of varying degrees of completeness. For some leaders their outline, either on a sheet of paper or on a series of note cards, is all that they require to cue them. Other leaders require fuller material.

USE AUDIOVISUAL AIDS

Often, skilled training group leaders use audiovisual aids to reinforce spoken words. Accessing participants through their eyes as well as their ears can greatly assist in holding attention and interest. Just putting up the outlines of talks on whiteboards can make it easier for participants to assimilate their messages. Below are some audiovisual methods for accompanying and illustrating talks.

Whiteboard

Whiteboards are essential items in any training facility. The availability of whiteboards can introduce flexibility into your presentations. In addition, you can work together with audiences as you put material up on whiteboards. However, a disadvantage is that you must turn your back on your audience as you write. Also, you need to wipe off existing material if you wish to fill whiteboards more than once. Whiteboards are preferable to blackboards, since audiences receive cleaner images and leaders do not get chalky hands.

Overhead projector

Along with whiteboards, overhead projectors are perhaps the other most essential visual aid. Advantages of overhead projectors include being able to: make up transparencies in advance; use photocopies of existing printed material; move a piece of paper down over transparencies so that you progressively introduce material; add to or make up transparencies during your talks; switch the projectors on or off as you wish; and superimpose images over existing images. In addition, when using overhead projectors, leaders need not turn their backs on audiences since they can point out items of interest on transparencies with pens or pencils.

Leaders require some basic skills both in making up transparencies and in using overhead projectors. Making-up-transparency skills include: not putting too much information on a single transparency; setting the information out clearly; writing it neatly and sufficiently large; and making it more interesting by using different colours. Using overhead projector skills include: being able to turn it on and off; getting it in focus; and placing transparencies on it so that they are in the right position and with the right side up.

Flipcharts

Flipcharts have the big advantage of being able to show many prepared sheets in succession. Sheets can be thrown over the back of the easel as talks progress. The fact that the sheets may already be prepared does not preclude leaders from either adding to existing sheets or interspersing new sheets. A disadvantage of flipcharts is that the sheets are more cumbersome than overhead projector transparencies. Allied to flipcharts is the use of posters hung on walls to illustrate points. A merging of flipcharts and posters can be achieved by putting up individual flipchart sheets as posters as a presentation progresses.

Slides

Probably many more leaders use whiteboards and overhead projectors than slides. However, you can give polished presentations using well-prepared slides. On the other hand, as you know from viewing friends' travel slides, presentations built around slides can be very boring. The technology and repeated visual images can get in the way of the message. Flexibility and spontaneity can be lost. In addition, rooms may need to be darkened. Also, slide projectors may not function properly. Possibly you require more skills for using slide projectors moderately well than for using the overhead projectors well. If you possess or are prepared to learn the requisite skills, then seriously consider using slides.

Film

Films may be shown as part of presentations. However, films have many disadvantages. Unless you keep a film library, films have to be hired. In addition, they require projectors and possibly projectionists. Another disadvantage is that they require darkened rooms. The advantages of film over videotape are greater clarity and larger images. However, it is a rare training session in which films are shown in which the technology does not become intrusive.

Videotape

Videotapes can be extremely useful for demonstrating skills. In large lifeskills groups, the drawback of a smallish video screen can be overcome by the use of two or three monitors. Videos do not require as darkened a room as films. Another advantage of videos is that most leaders are accustomed to using them. Furthermore, leaders can push the start, stop or pause buttons as necessary. If you make your own videos, strive for as professional a result as possible. Some institutions, such as universities, have audiovisual centres where you can get advice and help in recording videos. If you have large budgets, you may hire outside video firms to produce training material (Miles, 1988).

Photographs and cartoons

Leaders may choose to integrate photographs and cartoons into presentations. For instance, in training groups on non-verbal communication, photographs may be worth the proverbial thousand words. In my thinking skills groups, I use cartoons of Mr and Ms Self-Oppression and Mr and Ms Self-Support, displayed with dialogue balloons coming out of their heads for various thinking skills weaknesses and strengths (Nelson-Jones, 1989).

Training manuals and hand-outs

Leaders can help participants to consolidate their learning either by referring them to the relevant sections in a training manual or by providing them with hand-outs. Always provide written instructions for any inside- or outside-class assignments.

Audiocassettes

Audiocassettes can be useful for demonstrating skills. Sometimes audiocassettes may be preferable to videotapes. For example, in teaching public speaking skills, audiocassettes may be preferable for illustrating voice message skills and videotapes preferable for illustrating body message skills. Audiocassettes are also useful when demonstrating thinking skills, since there are no distracting visual images. When making up audiocassettes, be sure to use a high-quality recording system so that your playback is of a professional standard. Poor-quality recordings introduce static into communicating your messages. Bernstein observes: 'Audio aids work best when short, telling and relevant. They work worst when the audience has to work hard at listening and when they take too long' (Bernstein, 1988, p. 134).

Exercise 16 Prepare a systematic lifeskills talk and integrate audiovisual aids

Part A Set goals and develop a systematic lifeskills talk outline

Think of a lifeskills talk that you might wish to give either now or in future.

1. Set yourself clear goals for your talk. Take the following considerations into account:

   • clarity regarding the skill or subskill to be communicated

   • a realistic time limit

   • manageable objectives

   • sensitivity to sequencing

   • sensitivity to your audience

2. Write out a systematic outline for your talk using the example in the text as a guide.

Part B Prepare a systematic script and set of notes

Either for the lifeskill you outlined in Part A or for another lifeskill:

1. Write out a fully prepared script for a 10 to 15 minute presentation making sure to:

   • set clear goals

   • use language effectively

   • be practical and focused on participants' needs

   • pay attention to beginnings and endings

   • develop your content logically and systematically

2. Translate your fully prepared script into as many note cards as you need to be able to remember the main message that you wish to convey.

Part C Integrate audiovisual aids into your talk

1. For the lifeskills talk for which you wrote out a systematic prepared script and developed a set of notes, consider which of the following audiovisual aids would be appropriate at the different stages of your talk.

   • Whiteboard

- Overheard projector
- Flipcharts
- Slides
- Film
- Videotape
- Photographs and cartoons
- Training manuals and hand-outs
- Audiocassettes

2. Develop appropriate audiovisual material to accompany your lifeskills talk.
3. Incorporate into the notes for your talk instructions for when you intend using audiovisual material. What effect is the inclusion of audiovisual material going to have on the length of your talk? Still try to observe the 15-minute time limit suggested in Part B.

DEVELOP DELIVERY SKILLS

I do not much dislike the matter, but
The manner of his speech.

William Shakespeare, *Antony and Cleopatra*

It ain't what you say, but the way that you say it.

Anonymous

Think of your school teachers. How many of them either were or are skilled at getting their messages across? How many stimulated and held your interest? Apart from the adequacy of their content, what distinguished effective from ineffective performers? Training group leaders can have great intellects, excellent content, and be largely in control of their nerves, yet still leave audiences with a bad dose of glazed-over eyes (MEGO). The missing ingredient is that they lack delivery skills. Presenting a lifeskills talk necessitates giving a performance. You cannot just be your usual conversational self. Instead, put over your material in such a way that you build rapport with your audience and hold their interest. An analogy is that of giving a stage performance. Good actors and actresses pay great attention to the skills of delivering their lines. Assuming that you have a coherent talk, you now need to put it across. Training group leaders require awareness that preparing a talk does not stop at preparing its content, but incorporates putting time and energy into preparing its delivery. In particular, polished delivery entails sending effective voice and body messages.

Send effective voice messages

Developing voice awareness is the first step in learning to use your voice as a delivery tool. Voice awareness entails breaking down voice communication into its principal component skills. You then possess a framework for assessing your own and others' strengths and weaknesses in these skills areas. Once you develop voice awareness you can make better voice message choices for polishing your training presentations. Below are some of the components of sending effective voice messages. These voice message components form the acronym VAPER: volume, articulation, pitch, emphasis and rate.

VOLUME

Volume refers to loudness or quietness. You need to speak at a volume that can be comfortably heard by all participants. Most lifeskills training groups are small enough for leaders to be easily heard with only moderate voice projection. However, if necessary, use a microphone and amplification. Speaking either too softly or too loudly are common mistakes. Perhaps more beginning leaders speak too softly than too loudly. Some leaders have the bad habit of fading, beginning either a sentence or their whole talk with adequate loudness and then letting their voices trail away.

ARTICULATION

Leaders may speak with adequate loudness, but still be unintelligible. They must enunciate words clearly. Articulation or enunciation refers to the distinctness and clarity of continuous speech. Fischer writes: 'A speaker is said to articulate correctly when his sounds and words are clearly made and easily understood, without their being overly precise' (Fischer, 1972, p. 47). Mumbling and slurring words are examples of poor articulation. Some leaders with regional or overseas accents may have to work on their pronunciation so that they articulate words clearly. Leaders possessing excessively nasal, gutteral or throaty voices that interfere with articulation might consider consulting speech therapists.

PITCH

Pitch refers to the highness or lowness of voices. Voices can range from high-pitched and shrill to low-pitched and deep. In general, women's voices are higher pitched than men's. Also, when people are anxious, their voices may be higher pitched than when they feel calmer. Kruger (1970) observes that an optimum pitch range includes all the levels at which a pleasing voice can be produced without strain and that most good speakers vary their pitch within a range of at least an octave or two. Errors of pitch include being either too high-pitched or too low-pitched, with perhaps being too high-pitched being the more common error (Bernstein, 1988). A further error is using too narrow a range of pitch.

EMPHASIS

Monotonous speakers use too little emphasis. Melodramatic speakers use too much emphasis. By emphasizing certain words you add variety, clarity and rhythm to talks. The following sentence from John Kennedy's 1961 Inaugural Address as President of the United States would have been much less effective without his emphasizing the italic words: 'And so, my fellow Americans – ask *not* what your country can do for *you* – ask what *you* can do for your country' (Valenti, 1982). By emphasizing certain words or phrases, you highlight your main points. In addition, by using emphasis you convey interest and commitment to your audience.

RATE

Speech rate or pace is often measured by words per minute. Kruger suggests that a rate of between 140 to 180 words per minute is appropriate for average explanatory material that is neither too easy nor too difficult for average adult audiences (Kruger, 1970). Speech rate depends both on how quickly words are spoken and on the frequency and duration of pauses between them. Many nervous people speak too quickly. Especially when beginning talks, it can be a good strategy to slow your speech rate down. Speaking more slowly may help you to control your nerves and, thus, appear less nervous. A slower speech rate both gives you more time to think of what to say next and also, within a given time period, enables you to refer to your notes less often.

Pauses are a form of vocal punctuation. Great actors and actresses are adept at using pauses to create clarity and emphasis in their speeches. They make pauses for effect and not just to breathe. John Kennedy used pauses to great effect in his 1961 Inaugural Address. Here is the sentence quoted above with dashes indicating pauses: 'And so, my fellow Americans – ask not what your country can do for you – ask what you can do for your country.'

In lifeskills talks pauses can be used to give participants time to grasp your meaning, to relate what you say to their own experience and to take notes. Pauses should be free of extraneous sounds, such as 'uh' and 'er' (Fischer, 1972). Other pause errors include having either too many or too few and having them either too long or too short. A further error is that of pausing in the wrong places.

Exercise 17 focuses on the voice message dimension of delivery skills.

Exercise 17 Delivery skills: be aware of your voice and send effective voice messages

Part A Be aware of your voice

This exercise is best done with a cassette recorder. You may record and play back the exercise in segments that have most meaning for your learning. Take the following sentence from John Kennedy's inaugural address: 'And so, my fellow Americans, ask not what your country can do for you, ask what you can do for your country.' Imagine that you need to communicate this sentence to a lifeskills training group of eight participants.

- VOLUME. First speak the sentence loudly, then speak it quietly, then try to arrive at a comfortable volume.

- ARTICULATION. First speak the sentence with poor articulation, then speak it with excessively precise articulation, then try to arrive at a comfortable, yet clear, level of articulation.

- PITCH. First speak the sentence in a high-pitched voice, then speak it in a low-pitched voice, then try to arrive at a pleasing pitch.

- EMPHASIS. Speak the sentence emphasizing the 'incorrect' bold words: 'And so, my fellow **Americans**, ask not what your **country** can do for you, ask what you can do for your **country**.' Then repeat the sentence emphasizing the 'correct' bold words: 'And so, my fellow Americans, ask **not** what your country can do for **you**, ask what **you** can do for your country.'

- RATE. First speak the sentence quickly and without pausing, then speak it slowly with many and frequent pauses, then try to arrive at a way of speaking it that is effective in terms of speech rate and pauses.

- VAPER – VOLUME, ARTICULATION, PITCH, EMPHASIS AND RATE. Practise speaking the sentence until you consider that you have put all the VAPER voice message components together satisfactorily.

Part B Send effective voice messages

In Exercise 16 you wrote out a fully prepared script for a 10- to 15-minute presentation and then put it on note cards.

1. Go through the introductory section of your talk and put dashes where you want to pause and underline words and phrases that you wish to emphasize. Practise delivering the introductory section of your talk into a cassette recorder until you are satisfied with your volume, articulation, pitch, emphasis and rate.

2. Repeat the above for the middle and ending sections of your talk.

3. Deliver your whole talk from your prepared script into a cassette recorder until you are satisfied with your volume, articulation, pitch, emphasis and rate.

4. Deliver the introductory section of your talk from notes into a cassette recorder emphasizing effective voice messages. Critically evaluate your performance and, where necessary, alter it.

5. Repeat the above for the middle and ending sections of your talk.

6. Deliver your whole talk from notes into a cassette recorder until you are satisfied with your volume, articulation, pitch, emphasis and rate.

Send effective body messages

Presenting a lifeskills talk is a performance. Leaders need to learn to make their body messages work for rather than against their overall messages. Leaders may send ineffective body messages both unconsciously and consciously. Nervous speakers may remain unaware or only partially aware of how they betray their lack of confidence through such mannerisms as: inadequate eye contact; scratching their faces or heads; trembling arms or legs; excessive smiling; pacing up and down; and wooden and inappropriate gestures.

Training group leaders can prepare and rehearse their body messages. Leaders require awareness of the power of body messages. By identifying subskills, leaders can gain greater control over body messages. The acronym GAME is used below to help you to memorize some key body message components. GAME is shorthand for: gestures and facial expressions, appearance, movement and posture, and eye contact.

GESTURE AND FACIAL EXPRESSION

Gestures are movements of parts of the body with the purpose of aiding in the expression of ideas and feelings. There are three main types of gestures (Fischer, 1972). First, there are *emphatic* gestures, such as pointing the finger, designed to make it clear that what is being said is important. Second, there are *descriptive* gestures, for instance stretching your arms out when you say that marital partners are poles apart, designed to help to illustrate your points. Third, there are *symbolic* gestures to which a commonly understood meaning has been ascribed: for instance, shaking the head in negation or the thumbs-up sign to indicate success or approval. Some rules for using gesturing include: having a purpose; being appropriate to the accompanying words; making gestures clearly; using gestures with and in moderation; and being sensitive to cultural and regional differences (Argyle, 1986; Ekman *et al.*, 1984).

Your facial expressions can also help to illustrate ideas and feelings. Good facial expressions are congruent with speech. You can choose to control your facial expressions in the interests of your overall effectiveness. For example, if nervous when starting a talk, give your audience a pleasant smile rather than a deep frown.

APPEARANCE

Appearance consists of a number of considerations, including: how you dress; your hairstyle; and how well washed and groomed you are. When meeting groups for the first time, your appearance can either help you to establish rapport or alienate some or all participants. For example, leaders' appearances may indicate either that they are rebels or conformers. The warmth of their subsequent receptions depends on the groups with whom they work. While needing to be true to themselves, leaders also require sensitivity to the effect of their appearance on others. Leaders should avoid drawing unnecessary attention to their appearance, for instance by pulling at a cuff or picking lint off their clothes.

MOVEMENT AND POSTURE

Some speakers move and stand in relaxed and comfortable ways, others in tense and rigid ways. Leaders' movements and postures can speak volumes about their relationships with themselves and their audiences. Do they rush around seemingly bound up in their own agendas or are they relaxed and accessible to their audience? Good speakers use movement to achieve their purposes. Poor speakers may use many distracting movements, such as pacing up and down or swaying from side to side. Good speakers use posture to show confidence and competence. Poor speakers may use their posture in ways that communicate sloppiness and anxiety.

EYE CONTACT

The importance of establishing relationships and keeping in touch with audiences by using good eye contact cannot be overemphasized. Whether through nervousness, lack of experience, or both, novice leaders frequently make poor contact with audiences because they rarely look at them. Possibly, there is no quicker way to glaze over your audience's eyes (MEGO) than reading your talks eyes down. Look at the members of your audience as though you converse with them. Help each member of your audience to feel that you communicate directly with him or her. This kind of eye contact not only draws them into your talk, but also enables you to assess reactions. Do not look at the floor. Do not look at the ceiling. Do not look through your audience. Do not look only at one side of your audience or at just a few people. Make eye contact with all of them. Even if reading from a prepared script, develop the technique of looking down, memorizing a passage and then looking up and delivering it direct to the audience.

Exercise 18 focuses on developing your skills of making eye contact and sending body messages when giving lifeskills talks.

Exercise 18 Delivery skills: make good eye contact and send effective body messages

Part A Make good eye contact

Preferably video-record yourself as you do this exercise. Failing that, do it in front of a mirror. Practise giving a lifeskills talk to eight people. They sit in a horseshoe and you stand up front.

1. Deliver the above instructions for this part of the exercise to your audience. Look down and read each sentence before looking up and delivering it out loud as you maintain eye contact with your audience. Evaluate your performance and try again if you are dissatisfied with it.

2. Memorize all four sentences of the above instructions and deliver them out loud to your audience as you maintain good eye contact with them. Repeat your delivery until you are satisfied that you have learned how to make good eye contact with your audience.

Part B Send effective body messages

Preferably video-record yourself as you do this exercise. Failing that, stand in front of a mirror. You are giving your lifeskills talk to eight people. They sit in a horseshoe. You stand up front.

1. Prepare the introductory section of the talk that you composed in Exercise 16, paying particular attention to how to integrate body messages, such as gestures, facial expressions, movement and eye contact, into your talk. Rehearse giving the introductory section of your talk until you are satisfied with your performance.

2. Repeat the above for each of the middle and ending sections of your talk.

3. Deliver your whole talk, paying particular attention to sending effective body messages.

Put verbal messages, audiovisual aids, and voice and body messages together

The preceding sections have focused on managing speech anxiety, preparing systematic content, using audiovisual aids and developing good voice and body message delivery skills. Table 7.2 is a public speaking skills evaluation questionnaire for use before and after talks.

Table 7.2 Public speaking skills evaluation questionnaire

This public speaking skills questionnaire has three uses: (1) as a guide to preparing lifeskills presentations; (2) as a self-evaluation measure for after presentations; and (3) as a means for others to provide feedback to speakers. Answer each item by putting either a tick or a cross or 'yes' or 'no' in the blank space.

Manage-speech-anxiety skills (other than good preparation)

.... I used coping self-talk

.... I challenged unrealistic personal rules

.... I accurately perceived my speaking strengths

.... I accurately perceived my audience's reactions

.... I accurately attributed cause for my speech anxiety

.... I realistically predicted the consequences of my talk

.... I set realistic goals for how well I might do

.... I used visualized rehearsal and practice

.... I used relaxation skills (such as breath management)

Prepare-systematic-content skills

.... I set clear and realistic goals

.... I planned my talk with my audience in mind

.... I developed a systematic outline

.... I used language effectively

.... I was practical and focused on participants' needs

.... I had the right amount of material for the time available

.... I prepared a systematic script/set of notes

.... I introduced my talk well

.... I ended my talk emphasizing my main points

.... I conveyed self-instructions for implementing the skill(s)

.... I used humour appropriately

Use-audiovisual-aids skills

.... I reviewed how best to use audiovisual aids

.... I used good audiovisual material

.... I rehearsed integrating audiovisual material into my talk

.... I took my audience through my audiovisual material well

Send-effective-voice-message skills

.... I was easy to hear

.... I articulated words clearly

.... I spoke fluently

.... I spoke at a pleasing level of pitch

.... I emphasized key words and points

.... I communicated enthusiasm with my voice

.... I spoke at a comfortable rate

.... I used pauses effectively

.... I rehearsed my voice as well as my verbal messages

Send-effective-body-message skills

.... I spoke directly to my audience and made eye contact with them

.... I made good use of gestures

.... I avoided distracting mannerisms

.... My facial expressions were appropriate

.... My dress and grooming were appropriate

.... I appeared relaxed

.... My posture was good

.... I rehearsed my body messages as well as my voice and
verbal messages

Further skills

.... I incorporated demonstration into my talk

.... I encouraged learning by doing (for example, with a structured activity)

.... I allowed time for and invited questions

.... I answered questions well

The need for thorough preparation has been either implicit or explicit throughout these discussions. The time has now come for you to give your lifeskills talk, integrating effective verbal messages, audiovisual aids, and voice and body messages. Exercise 19 asks you to rehearse giving your talk and then, if possible, to deliver it to a live audience.

Exercise 19 Make an effective lifeskills presentation: put verbal messages, audiovisual aids, and voice and body messages together

If possible, video-record and play back this exercise. Failing that, use a mirror and audiocassette recorder.

1.   Rehearse and practise

Rehearse and practise delivering parts of the presentation and then the whole of the presentation for which you wrote out the content in Exercise 16. Work on giving a performance that successfully integrates verbal messages, visual aids, and voice and body messages.

2.   Make a live presentation

Where possible, make your lifeskills presentation to a live audience. Afterwards, hold a discussion and feedback session with the audience, focusing on your public speaking skills strengths and weaknesses, possibly using the evaluation questionnaire in Table 7.2. Assess this feedback and, where necessary, set goals for change.

CHAPTER HIGHLIGHTS

Frequently, training group leaders make short presentations as part of skills-learning sequences.

Successful leaders work hard to develop and maintain their public speaking skills. They are aware of the necessity to prepare thoroughly both content and delivery.

Speech anxiety can either facilitate, or interfere with, or both facilitate and interfere with, effective speaking.

Thinking skills for managing speech anxiety include: own responsibility for being a chooser; be in touch with your underlying feelings; use coping self-talk; choose realistic personal rules; choose to perceive yourself and others accurately; accurately attribute cause; make realistic predictions; have goals that you articulate clearly and that reflect your values; and use visualizing to best effect.

Skilled training group leaders prepare systematic content for their presentations. They use either prepared scripts or a good set of notes.

Skills of preparing systematic content include: set clear goals, use language effectively, be practical and focused on the needs of participants, and pay attention to beginnings and endings.

Leaders can use a range of audiovisual aids to help convey their messages. Such aids include: whiteboards, overhead projectors, flipcharts, slides, films, videotapes, photographs and cartoons, training manuals and hand-outs, and audiocassettes.

Effective delivery skills include being aware of and sending good voice and body messages.

The components of effective vocal messages form the acronym VAPER: volume, articulation, pitch, emphasis and rate.

The components of effective body messages form the acronym GAME: gesture and facial expression, appearance, movement and posture, and eye contact.

Skilled group leaders manage their speech anxiety and put together their verbal messages, audiovisual aids, and voice and body messages into well-prepared and coherent presentations.

EIGHT

How to Demonstrate Lifeskills

A picture is worth a thousand words.
Chinese proverb

CHAPTER QUESTIONS

What is observational learning?

What are the main methods of demonstrating lifeskills?

What demonstrator characteristics should training group leaders consider?

What demonstration characteristics should leaders consider?

How can leaders increase the attention of observers?

How can leaders demonstrate thinking skills?

How can leaders demonstrate action skills?

How can leaders demonstrate action skills with accompanying self-talk?

INTRODUCTION

Chapter 7 focused on public speaking skills or 'tell'. This chapter focuses on demonstration skills or 'show'. Chapter 9 focuses on structured activity skills or 'do'. In teaching applied skills, 'show' provides an important bridge between 'tell' and 'do'. Observational learning is another term for showing people what to do. Below are examples in lifeskills training groups of observational learning from demonstrations.

- Parents of conduct-problem children, aged three to eight, observing videotape programmes demonstrating parenting skills (Webster-Stratton *et al.*, 1988).

- Chronically aggressive adolescents observing several examples of expert use of social skills, e.g. starting a conversation or dealing with an accusation, as part of an aggression-replacement training programme (Glick & Goldstein, 1987).

- Institutionalized juvenile delinquents observing models handling situations such as, at a job interview, dealing with the fact that they have a criminal record, or how to cope with negative peer influence, for instance not going along with the crowd and stealing a car (Sarason, 1976).

- Unassertive adults being asked to observe in their imaginations models behaving assertively in a range of situations (Kazdin, 1976).

- Trainee helpers being assisted to develop interview microskills by means of observing demonstration videotapes, for example how to demonstrate attention with your body messages (Ivey Authier, 1978).

- Existing job club members being played taped commentaries of former job-seekers who were successful in obtaining employment (Azrin *et al.*, 1975).

- Young people participating in 'work shadowing' programmes in which they follow a worker around for a period of time, observing the various tasks and components of his or her role (Herr & Watts, 1988).

- Children highly fearful of dentists observing videotapes of two children practising controlled breathing and visualizing techniques to cope with their fears (Klingman *et al.*, 1984).

- Impulsive hyperactive children being asked to observe models instructing themselves out loud as they approached various tasks (Meichenbaum, 1977; Meichenbaum & Goodman, 1971).

Training group leaders can use demonstration skills for imparting virtually every lifeskill. The inclusion of demonstration when teaching a skill or subskill should be normal rather than exceptional. Beginners in leading training groups may insufficiently acknowledge the power of good demonstrations. Frequently, they replicate methods of academic teaching rather than make the switch to methods of applied skills training.

WHAT IS OBSERVATIONAL LEARNING?

Defining terms

Many terms are used to describe elements of learning from observation, including: imitating, copying, mimicking, following the example of, identifying with, modelling, showing, and demonstrating. Modelling is perhaps the most commonly used of these terms in the psychology literature (for example, Bandura 1969, 1977). Perry and Fukuhara define modelling as '. . . the process of observational learning in which the behavior of an individual or group – the model – acts as a stimulus for similar thoughts, attitudes, or behaviors on the part of another individual who observes the model's performance' (Perry & Fukuhara, 1986, p. 66). In acquiring and maintaining day-to-day behaviours, modelling is frequently both unintentional and also observed by people who are not fully conscious of its possible implications for their later behaviour. For example, children copy some of their parents' vices as well as some of their virtues. This copying takes place without parents ever consciously engaging in vice education programmes or children being aware that they are acquiring some negative behaviour patterns.

In real life, much modelling is unintentional. However, in lifeskills training groups leaders consciously promote observational learning of desired skills and subskills. Demonstrating is used here in preference to modelling. Unlike modelling, demonstrating is a word commonly used outside psychological circles. Leaders may intentionally either demonstrate or arrange for others to demonstrate skills. Both model and demonstrator describe the person demonstrating.

Goals for observational learning

Observational learning can be used in lifeskills groups to: initiate new skills strengths; develop existing skills strengths; disinhibit existing skills strengths; and inhibit and weaken existing skills weaknesses. Observational learning is applicable to training participants in all lifeskills. Within this broad mandate, the goals of observational learning can be viewed in the following categories.

- *Thinking skills.* A demonstration focused on thinking skills might identify upsetting perceptions in a situation, assess their appropriateness through logical analysis and generate and evaluate different perceptions to see if there are more accurate perceptions (Beck, 1976; Nelson-Jones, 1989). The demonstrated thinking skills need not be related to any immediate observable actions.

- *Action skills.* Action skills demonstrations focus on observable behaviours. An example of an action skills demonstration is where the demonstrator shows – focusing on verbal, voice and body messages – how to handle aggressive criticism.

- *Action skills with accompanying self-talk.* Here the demonstration focuses on both action skills and their accompanying self-instructions. Examples of teaching self-talk to guide behaviour include training impulsive children to self-instruct their way through tasks (Meichenbaum, 1977; Meichenbaum & Goodman, 1971) and training test-anxious students in the self-verbalizations and principles for completing anagrams (Sarason, 1973).

The above three goals – thinking skills, action skills, action skills with accompanying self-talk – may each be demonstrated in different parts of either the same session or an overall programme. For example, in an anger management training group, demonstrations can: reframe provocations (thinking skill), express anger by using 'I' statements (action skill), and show appropriate behaviours in a specific anger-evoking situation with accompanying self-instructions (action skills with accompanying self-talk).

Leaders and participants as role models

Apart from demonstrating or arranging for demonstrations of specific lifeskills, there are two other important aspects of observational learning in training groups: leaders as role models and participants as role models.

LEADERS AS ROLE MODELS

The importance of group leaders as role models is frequently stressed (for example, Bloch & Crouch, 1985; Corey, 1990; Corey *et al.*, 1988a, Yalom, 1985). Training group leaders cannot *not* demonstrate behaviour. Even when you are not consciously demonstrating a specific lifeskill, your behaviour is always under the microscope and capable of influencing participants for good or ill. If leaders demonstrate commitment to programme goals, participants are more likely to do so too. Leaders who arrive at sessions on time encourage participants to do the same. Leaders who listen well and show respect may unobtrusively help participants to improve their skills in these areas. Leaders who are able to express feelings, be relaxed, show humour and reveal appropriate personal information demonstrate these skills to participants. Leaders offering constructive feedback model this skill. Also, leaders set emotional climates in training groups as much by demonstration as by exhortation.

PARTICIPANTS AS ROLE MODELS

Leaders can work to help participants to demonstrate desirable behaviours for each other. These behaviours fall into at least three main interrelated categories: behaviours conducive to the group process; behaviours illustrating how to learn skills; and behaviours demonstrating various levels of performance of targeted skills.

By using group facilitation skills, leaders can assist participants in becoming role models for each other in the process factors conducive to successful group therapy (Bloch & Crouch, 1985; Yalom, 1985). For example, other participants can demonstrate such therapeutic factors as the level of acceptance necessary for developing group cohesiveness, self-understanding, altruism, universality, being more trustful, and providing feedback on how people come across to them.

Leaders can help participants to develop skills of being good lifeskills learners. These learning skills include: own responsibility for learning, adhere to any learning contract, set personal goals, admit mistakes, take acceptable risks, fully participate in structured activities, work through setbacks and complete homework assignments. The more that leaders can help participants to develop these learning skills, the more opportunity there is for other participants to demonstrate them to each other.

A third way in which leaders can help participants to become role models is to create good emotional climates for observational learning when participants acquire, rehearse, practise and talk about targeted skills. This observational learning takes place in many ways. The leader may work on coaching, rehearsal and feedback with an individual participant in front of the group. Participants may be broken into sub-groups and then observe each other as they work on their skills. Furthermore, participants can discuss in either pairs or larger units how they have progressed in using the skills outside of the group. In addition, former training group participants can be invited back to give testimonials about their success in using targeted skills.

CONSIDERATIONS IN DEMONSTRATING LIFESKILLS

Who demonstrates?

Options for who demonstrates include the following. These demonstrator options may be used singly or in combination.

- *Leaders*. In their initial presentations of skills or subskills, leaders may systematically include formal demonstration by themselves. Also, during training groups, less formal leader demonstrations are almost inevitable.

- *Leader's aides*. Training group leaders may be assisted by one or more aides who provide specific demonstrations. These demonstrations are sometimes performed together with leaders.

- *Participants*. Participants may be demonstrators both for other participants and for themselves. Leaders may ask individual participants to take part in live or pre-recorded demonstrations. In addition, participants may be asked to demonstrate skills for themselves. These self-demonstrations may be in their imaginations (Kazdin, 1976) or in 'self-as-model' edited video-recordings of their own performances (Cormier & Cormier, 1985; Hosford *et al.*, 1976; Hosford & Johnson, 1983).

- *Third parties*. Numerous categories of people from outside the group may be used as demonstrators. Such people include: actors or acting students who role-play scenes; participants from previous groups; associates of the leaders who volunteer their services; and those who take part in demonstration films and videotapes recorded elsewhere.

- *Puppets and cartoon characters.* Puppets may be used as demonstrators, especially with children. For example, a survey found that 21 per cent of all paediatric hospitals in the United States use puppet show presentations to prepare children for hospitalization and surgery (Peterson & Ridley-Johnson, 1980). Cartoon characters can also be used to present lifeskills. For instance, dialogue balloons can be used to demonstrate thinking skills.

Demonstrator characteristics

This section particularly applies to characteristics of third party demonstrators. Demonstrator characteristics are important in that they influence how much observers attend, retain and are motivated. Characteristics to consider in selecting demonstrators include the following:

- *Similarity to observers.* In general, the greater the similarity between demonstrators and observers, the greater the effect of demonstration on subsequent behaviours (Kazdin, 1976; Perry & Fukuhara, 1986). Demonstrators who are similar with respect to characteristics such as age, sex, socio-economic status, ethnic grouping, race and other attributes are more likely to be identified with and imitated than dissimilar demonstrators.

- *Prestige.* The examples from demonstrators prestigious to observers may be followed more than examples from those not so prestigious. A caution is that observers may find it hard to identify with demonstrators who are so prestigious that they are unable to relate to their behaviours (Perry & Fukuhara, 1986).

- *Competence level.* The competence level of demonstrators relates to the issue of coping versus mastery. Kazdin suggests that there is an advantage in demonstrators showing behaviours similar to those of observers but then overcoming problems (Kazdin, 1976). Demonstrators who are seen to develop coping skills when dealing with problems may be more powerful influencers than those showing mastery or expert performance throughout.

- *Warmth and personal attractiveness.* Bandura observes of everyday life: 'Attention to models is also channeled by their interpersonal attraction' (Bandura, 1977, p. 24). Models without engaging characteristics are either ignored or rejected. Observer attraction to demonstrators influences the outcomes of lifeskills demonstrations. For example, warmth and a nurturing nature may enhance demonstration effects (Perry & Fukuhara, 1986).

Methods of demonstration

Training group leaders have many options with regard to how to present demonstrations. These options are not mutually exclusive. Demonstrations can take place in the following ways, which are summarized in Table 8.1.

Table 8.1   Methods of demonstrating lifeskills

METHODS OF DEMONSTRATING LIFESKILLS	SKILLS AREAS		
	THINKING SKILLS	ACTION SKILLS	ACTION SKILLS WITH SELF-TALK
Written demonstration	✓	Difficult	Difficult
Pre-recorded demonstration	✓	✓	✓
Live demonstration	✓	✓	✓
Visualized demonstration	Less suitable	✓	✓

WRITTEN

Much demonstration takes place through the printed page. Written demonstrations are possible for thinking skills, for instance either changing negative into coping self-talk or reformulating unrealistic into realistic personal rules. Written demonstrations can be supplemented by visual images such as cartoons. Written demonstrations can be easily stored and retrieved by participants. Another advantage is that written demonstrations can be introductory examples for subsequent written or live skills development exercises.

LIVE

Live demonstrations have the advantage of here-and-now communication. Observers can receive verbal, voice, body and action messages as they actually happen. Models can be trained and rehearsed, so the input of the demonstrations is carefully controlled. However, live demonstrations also allow the possibility of spontaneity: for example, in front of groups, leaders can work with participants on current problems. Live demonstrations have the advantage that the demonstrator can interact with the audience and, if appropriate, show different or simpler ways to enact skills. However, live demonstrations have disadvantages too. Sometimes live demonstrations do not go according to plan: unlike with pre-recorded demonstrations, you cannot edit out mistakes. Also, depending on the size of the audience, it may be difficult to hear or see demonstrators. Furthermore, in settings such as schools where leaders may have discipline problems, unruly observers may interfere with the concentration of both demonstrators and interested observers (Nelson-Jones, 1986).

PRE-RECORDED

Pre-recorded demonstrations use films, videotapes and audiocassettes. Demonstrators may be group leaders, participants or third parties. Pre-recorded demonstrations have some advantages. If you make the material yourself, you can carefully control input and edit out mistakes. Though demonstrators may be initially nervous in front of cameras or cassette players, unlike with live performances they have the opportunity to repeat demonstrations marred by anxiety. The process of making pre-recorded demonstrations allows for successive attempts to rewrite scripts and improve role-plays. Successful demonstration tapes and cassettes can be stored for future use. Also, if you have access to funds for purchasing or renting films, videocassettes and audiocassettes, you may use professionally made products and be spared the work of developing your own materials. In addition, pre-recorded demonstrations can be either made or purchased in multiple copies. Consequently, participants may view or listen to copies either during training groups or when revising afterwards. Another advantage of pre-recorded material is that leaders can press the pause or rewind buttons to emphasize points.

Training group leaders also have to consider the disadvantages of pre-recorded demonstrations. Demonstrations may not be tailor-made to training requirements. Considerable time and expense may need to go into developing and recording material. Pre-recorded material requires good equipment both when being made and when being shown to observers. Good-quality equipment may not be readily available. In addition, training tapes and films may get worn out with age and repeated use. Leaders who use pre-recorded material may lose some of their flexibility in adjusting demonstrations to the level of attention and needs of their audience. For example, the recorded units may be longer or shorter than required. Furthermore, using playback equipment and possibly having to darken rooms may obstruct the smooth flow of learning sequences.

VISUALIZED

In the psychological literature, visualized demonstration is called covert modelling (Cautela, 1976; Cormier & Cormier, 1985; Kazdin, 1976). Here leaders request that participants visualize the demonstration scenes that they describe. Depending on the instructions, participants either visualize themselves or third parties demonstrating the skills. Visualized demonstration has the advantage of flexibility. Different situations can be readily presented to participants' imaginations, depending on their collective and individual needs and learning rates. Leaders have the choice of suggesting demonstrations either live or in pre-recorded form. In addition, whether the initial suggestions were either live or pre-recorded, participants can instruct themselves when rehearsing at home.

Visualized rehearsal may be used after live and pre-recorded demonstrations. In such instances, the timing of visualized rehearsal may be either immediately after the demonstration to help with memorizing skills or as a homework assignment to help with performing the skills.

Visualized demonstration has disadvantages. It is only appropriate for participants who have the capacity for visualizing scenes adequately. However, since scenes are never actually demonstrated, even for good visualizers there may be important slippages between what leaders describe and what they visualize. For example, in being asked to visualize assertion demonstrations, participants may miss important body messages depicted in live or pre-recorded demonstrations.

Characteristics of the demonstration

What are some of the other factors in setting up effective demonstrations for lifeskills training groups? Leaders still have numerous choices beyond selecting methods of demonstration.

SINGLE OR MULTIPLE

Generally it is much easier if there is just one demonstrator or pair of demonstrators for each skills sequence. Single demonstrators economize on leader time and effort. Also, it may be easier to control the verbal, voice, body and action messages of single demonstrators. However, strong reasons exist for using multiple demonstrators if practical. Kazdin observes of covert modelling: 'Generally, clients who have imagined several models show greater behavior change ... In view of the evidence from both overt (filmed) and covert modeling, the practicing counselor or therapist should employ different models over the course of therapy' (Kazdin, 1976, p. 484). Bandura has developed a participant modelling approach, consisting of demonstration followed by assisted performance of the demonstrated skill. In his approach, desired behaviours 'are repeatedly modeled, preferably by different models' (Bandura, 1976, p. 248).

Some of the reasons why multiple demonstrators may be preferable to single demonstrators are as follows. In group approaches there are likely to be people with a range of characteristics. Multiple demonstrators increase the possibility of different participants identifying with demonstrators. In addition, in the outside world, there is often a range of ways of dealing with situations. Multiple demonstrators are more likely to reflect the possible differences in implementing skills. This variability may increase the flexibility with which participants learn and perform skills. Furthermore, for performing feared tasks such as asking someone for a date, multiple demonstrators have the advantage of showing that a range of people can learn to overcome their fears and act appropriately. A risk in using multiple demonstrators is that little observational learning may occur if they are too inconsistent in their behaviours (Perry & Fukuhara, 1986).

SCRIPTED OR UNSCRIPTED

Whether or not to use prepared scripts is an issue for both live and pre-recorded demonstrations. The main advantage of prepared scripts is that they lend themselves to systematic presentation of skills. Also, demonstrators can receive coaching feedback and practise to develop a polished performance. However, in training groups there is also a role for unscripted demonstrations. For example, in anger management groups, leaders may get participants to show how they behaved in particular situations and then demonstrate alternative behaviours. Some advantages of spontaneous demonstrations are that they are tailor-made to participants' problems and that they provide here-and-now feedback. In summary, for initial skills presentations, scripted demonstrations may be preferable to unscripted. However, for showing skills for application in individual participants' daily lives, unscripted demonstrations may be preferable.

POSITIVE AND/OR NEGATIVE

An issue in the demonstration literature is whether negative demonstrations should be provided as well as positive demonstrations (for example, Newman & Fuqua, 1988). Put more simply, should demonstrations be provided of 'don'ts' as well as of 'do's'? Ivey and Authier, when developing microcounselling training videotapes, consider that observing ineffective models makes it possible to identify the behaviours that constitute skills weaknesses. They write: 'Viewing these negative behaviors, then, makes it possible to develop positive models representing an antithesis' (Ivey & Authier, 1978, p. 309). Sometimes, great humour can be injected into lifeskills training by showing negative models; for instance, think of someone like John Cleese making outrageous mistakes.

Among reasons for only showing demonstrations of positive behaviours are the following. Demonstrating negative behaviours before showing positive ones takes additional time that may not be justified by results. Showing negative as well as positive behaviours may confuse rather than clarify the information that leaders want demonstrated. Furthermore, sometimes negative demonstrations may worsen rather than improve participants' skills. For example, if a demonstrator overcoming a phobia showed an increase rather than a decrease in anxiety, the demonstration could backfire (Perry & Fukuhara, 1986). To be of any help to phobic observers, the demonstrator should then show the skills of overcoming heightened anxiety.

No simple answer exists to the issue of whether to include negative demonstrations along with – and generally before – positive ones. Lifeskills training covers a huge variety of skills and populations. Leaders must use their judgement in individual instances. If in doubt, when initially introducing skills it is probably best to leave out negative demonstrations. Participants will probably have plenty of opportunity to observe negative models as they and their peers work in the group.

GRADUATED

Some skills may be either so complex, difficult or anxiety-arousing that leaders decide to present them by means of a series of demonstrations. For example, with a skill like speaking in public the various verbal, voice and body component subskills of effective public speaking may each be demonstrated and focused on separately prior to being reconstructed as a single overall skill. Graduated demonstration may be used in lifeskills programmes to help participants to overcome specific phobias. For example, people who are afraid of snakes may view models interacting with snakes in progressively threatening scenes (Bandura, 1976). Graduated demonstration may also be used for the specific problems that participants bring into lifeskills training groups. For example, a young man with difficulty standing up to his father may observe the leader demonstrating the handling of a low-level confrontation before later observing a more difficult confrontation.

REWARD FOR PERFORMANCE OF SKILL

Research into demonstrations shows that observers who see demonstrators rewarded for a particular behaviour are more likely to perform that behaviour than if it is not rewarded (Kazdin, 1976). However, direct rewards have an even greater motivating effect in maintaining behaviour over a period of time than do indirect or vicarious rewards (Bandura, 1977). An example is an observer demonstrating the assertion skill of returning a defective purchase to a shop. Having the demonstrator rewarded for the assertive behaviour by the salesperson admitting the error and offering either a replacement or a refund is more likely to motivate than if the assertive behaviour does not achieve the desired results. However, still more motivating is the observer's assertion being directly rewarded in real life.

Even if not externally rewarded, demonstrators can still reward themselves for performing desired behaviours. If, in the earlier example, the demonstrator was unsuccessful in getting the purchase changed, he or she could say to himself or herself 'Well done' for having performed the targeted assertive behaviours. Likewise, in real life, even if they are unsuccessful in achieving desired outcomes, participants can still reward themselves for using their skills.

RATIONALE

Training group leaders require care in how they introduce demonstrations. Observers can be given a rationale for the importance of learning from demonstration. For example, as part of the introduction for his demonstration programme for juvenile delinquents, Sarason stated: 'Having people watch others doing things and then discussing what has been done is a very important way and a very useful way to learn' (Sarason, 1976, p. 58). For his covert modelling or visualized demonstration treatment, Kazdin stressed how people, by rehearsing situations in their imaginations, can alter their behaviours in real life situations (Kazdin, 1976).

INSTRUCTIONS

Leaders need to pay attention to what commentaries they provide for their demonstrations. Observers' attention to demonstrations may be increased by initial instructions both telling them what to look out for and also informing them that they will later be required to perform the demonstrated behaviours (Perry & Fukuhara, 1986). Participant motivation may be further enhanced by making connections between the behaviour to be demonstrated and its importance for their lives.

During pre-recorded demonstrations, voice-overs can tell participants what specifically to observe. During live and pre-recorded presentations, breaks can be interspersed in which instructional comments are made on what observers either will see or have seen or both. At the end of a demonstration, a summary of its main points can be provided. Furthermore, participants can be given written as well as spoken instructions about the content of demonstrations. These written instructions can be in hand-outs or sections of training manuals.

OBSERVER SUMMARIES

Observers can be encouraged to summarize the main points of demonstrations. Research studies indicate that observers who actively summarize the salient points of demonstrators' behaviours are better able to learn and remember this information (Bandura *et al.*, 1966; Perry & Fukuhara, 1986). After a lifeskills demonstration, leaders may break the group down into pairs or other sub-groups to allow each participant to have the opportunity to summarize.

TIMING OF OBSERVERS' PERFORMANCE OF DEMONSTRATED SKILLS

The timing of observers' performance of demonstrated skills can range from at the same time as the demonstration to not at all. An example of simultaneous performance is that of children highly fearful of dentists being asked to practise controlled breathing as they watch a film of a child model demonstrating the skill (Klingman *et al.*, 1984). Sometimes, as for instance in Bandura's participant modelling approach, demonstration and performance of skills are intermingled in progressively more difficult steps (Bandura, 1976). Within a single session, a skill is demonstrated and the observer is then assisted by the demonstrator to enact it, and this is followed by further demonstration and enactment of a slightly more difficult skill, and so on. To date, participant modelling appears to have been an approach used largely with individuals. However, depending on the skills involved, participant modelling might fruitfully be adapted to groups.

Most often, when demonstrations from part of initial skills presentations, enactment by participants follows shortly afterwards. Though lifeskills can be acquired from demonstrations alone, they are more likely to be learned if demonstrations are followed by coaching, rehearsal, feedback and practice (Bandura, 1976, 1977; Perry & Fukuhara, 1986).

Ways to enhance observer attention

Bandura writes: 'People cannot learn much by observation unless they attend to, and perceive accurately, the significant features of the modeled behavior' (Bandura, 1977, p. 24). How can leaders enhance observers' attention? At risk of repetition, below are some suggestions.

- *Pay attention to demonstrator characteristics.* Demonstrator characteristics have already been reviewed.

- *Match demonstrations to observers' states of readiness.* Take into account the intellectual levels and attention spans of observers. For example, Sarason approaches the problem of holding juvenile delinquents' attention by incorporating physical movement and a break for soft drinks into his modelling programme (Sarason, 1976). For all age levels, do not give lengthy and boring introductions to demonstrations and then expect wide-awake observers. Use appropriate language when making up scripts. Be prepared to use graduated demonstration for skills that are complex or threaten.

- *Orientate observers.* Let observers know how, by watching demonstrations, they can help themselves to achieve their goals. Without engaging in false selling, convey enthusiasm for observational learning. Make sure that participants know what to look out for in demonstrations. Let participants know that next it will be their turn to use the demonstrated skills.

- *Reduce debilitating anxiety.* Anxiety can interfere with participants' abilities to attend and observe. Kazdin states that research on live and filmed demonstrations suggests that training people to be relaxed facilitates observational learning (Kazdin, 1976). Relaxing participants may be especially appropriate for his covert modelling approach, which relies on participants visualizing scenes. However, Perry and Fukuhara concluded that the role of relaxation across a broad range of modelling treatment programmes has yet to be fully evaluated. Relaxation may prove helpful for unusually anxious observers (Perry & Fukuhara, 1986). Other ways in which leaders can reduce participants' anxiety are by developing rapport with them and by fostering a group norm that, in subsequent enactments of demonstrated skills, mistakes are okay.

- *Reduce extraneous distractions.* Mention has already been made of dealing with within-group distractions caused by the different agendas of audience members. In addition, participants' attention can be badly disrupted by extraneous distractions. Such distractions include corridor noise and people coming into the room when demonstrations are in progress. Placing a sign on the door that says that a training group is in progress and that requests no interruptions and silence outside may be better than doing nothing.

DEMONSTRATE THINKING SKILLS

Training group leaders subscribing to the cognitive-behavioural theoretical position are faced with the need to demonstrate not only action skills, or overt behaviours, but also thinking skills, or covert behaviours. Thinking skills are lifeskills in themselves and are also relevant to all specific lifeskill areas, such as relationships, leisure, work, and health. For example, the capacity to identify, dispute and reformulate irrational beliefs or unrealistic personal rules is both a thinking skill in its own right and a skill that can be applied to all areas in which such beliefs or rules occur (Ellis, 1989; Nelson-Jones, 1989). Consequently, group leaders have the option of either teaching one or more thinking skills as such or teaching relevant thinking skills together with action skills for use in specific areas: for example, managing stress, job interviewing, or handling relationship conflicts.

Thinking is an inner process mostly involving self-talk. Therefore, thinking skills lend themselves more readily to written and audiocassette demonstrations than action skills. The visual images provided by videotape or films are not required for thinking skills. Furthermore, visual images may interfere with demonstrating thought processes. Thinking skills can also be demonstrated live. Live demonstrations can be either when skills are initially presented or later as leaders endeavour to change participants' thinking both by repetition and by working with material brought into the group.

Written demonstration

Written demonstrations of thinking skills may come from published sources. However, here the focus is on building skills of developing your own demonstration materials. If you are a skilled cartoonist, you may draw dialogue balloons to illustrate points. Probably, most of you do not have this talent and have to rely on the written word alone.

Written demonstrations often form part of instructional manuals or hand-outs. Leaders require clear goals for what they wish to achieve in each learning unit. Furthermore, they need to explain clearly the skill or subskill being demonstrated so that participants know what to look for, both when introduced to the skill and also when later rehearsing and practising it.

Below is an example of an instructional hand-out for the thinking skill of coping self-talk. Meichenbaum and others have trained many different groups of people in coping self-talk. The lifeskills they have targeted include: managing anger, managing stress, being creative, curbing impulsiveness, managing pain, and controlling weight (Meichenbaum, 1977, 1983, 1985; Meichenbaum & Deffenbacher, 1988). The example of coping self-talk provided here is for a lifeskills programme to train adolescents, college students and others in the skills of managing shyness (Nelson-Jones, 1990).

COPING SELF-TALK SKILLS HAND-OUT

Coping self-talk is a useful thinking skill for managing feelings of shyness. The idea is that during your waking hours you continuously engage in an internal dialogue, or perform self-talk. The goals of coping self-talk are to calm your anxieties and to help you to deal effectively with the task at hand. Thus coping self-talk contains two major elements: calming self-talk and coaching self-talk. Coping self-talk is about coping or 'doing as well as I can' rather than about mastery or 'being perfect' and 'having no anxiety'. Coping is a much more realistic goal than mastery.

Coping self-talk involves replacing negative self-talk statements with helpful ones. Let us take the example of Anne and Mary going to a party. Note how Anne's self-talk oppresses her, while Mary's self-talk supports her.

> *Anne*: 'I know that I am going to find this party difficult. Everybody is looking at me. I feel unattractive. I don't want to make a mistake. I'm feeling tense and, when this happens, I know it will only get worse.'

> *Mary*: 'I enjoy parties and meeting new people. Although I get a little anxious with strangers, I know I can overcome it. I have developed some good party skills and these usually work. All I have to do is my best.'

Calming and coaching statements tend to be interspersed in coping self-talk.

Two important aspects of *calming* self-talk are as follows.

- *Tell yourself to stay calm*. Simple self-statements include 'keep calm,' 'relax' and 'take it easy'. In addition, you can instruct yourself to 'take a deep breath' or 'breathe slowly and regularly'.

- *Tell yourself you can cope*. Sample self-statements include 'I can handle this situation' or 'My anxiety is a signal for me to use my coping skills'.

Coaching self-talk can help you to cope with shyness in the following ways.

- *Specify your goals*. An example could be 'I will go up and talk to a minimum of three new people at the party.'

- *Break tasks down*. Think through the steps needed to attain your goal.

- *Concentrate on the task at hand*. You instruct yourself, as pilots do when they talk themselves through difficult landings.

You may use coping self-talk before, during and after stressful social situations – for example, going to a party full of strangers or out with a new date.

Examples of possible coping self-talk statements *before* a stressful social situation include the following:

'This anxiety is a sign for me to use my coping skills.'

'Calm down. Develop a plan to manage the situation.'

'I know if I use my coping skills I can manage.'

Examples of possible coping self-talk statements *during* a stressful social situation include the following:

'Take my time. Breathe slowly and regularly.'

'Relax. I can manage if I just take one step at a time.'

'I don't have to be liked by everyone. All I can do is the best I can.'

Examples of possible coping self-talk statements *after* a stressful social situation include the following:

'Each time I cope it seems to get easier.'

'I'm proud of the way I'm learning to manage my fears.'

'I've shown myself that I can do it now.'

A few comments about the above written demonstration. First, written demonstration can be used in conjunction with other kinds of demonstration, for example audiocassette or live. In lifeskills training groups, written demonstration should rarely, if ever, be used alone. Second, both negative and positive demonstrations, namely Anne and Mary's self-talk, were provided prior to breaking down the skills of coping self-talk and giving examples of specific coping self-statements. Anne and Mary's statements were intended as attention getters to help participants to see the relevance of coping self-talk to their own lives. Third, the above demonstration of coping self-talk for shy people lends itself to being followed up with an exercise, either in the group or as homework, to consolidate the skills being taught. For example, participants can be instructed to identify any negative self-talk contributing to their shyness and socially incompetent behaviours. Then, they could be asked to identify a specific social situation that they find stressful and to write out at least three coping self-talk statements for before, during and after the situation. In addition, participants could be encouraged to use coping self-talk skills to manage shyness both inside and outside the group. Fourth, written demonstrations like the above can be easily stored and retrieved for revision and reuse purposes.

Audiocassette demonstration

Self-help audiocassettes are often used in conjunction with psychological counselling (Yamauchi, 1987). For both individual and group use, audiocassette demonstrations of thinking skills have the advantage over written demonstrations that participants can hear how demonstrators think. People talk to themselves when they think. Audiocassette demonstrations much more closely replicate this self-verbalizing process than written demonstrations. In addition, if they do not require copyright permission, audiocassette demonstrations are relatively inexpensive to reproduce. Accordingly, participants might receive copies for homework and revision purposes. Participants are likely to require much work and practice to change established partterns of thinking (Ellis, 1987, 1989). Consequently, a demonstration mode lending itself to repeated listenings has much to recommend it.

The initial audiocassette-recorded demonstration of a thinking skill is best done either by leaders or third parties. It is unreasonable to expect participants to demonstrate skills that they may not understand. However, leaders can encourage participants later in the learning process to make up their own demonstration cassettes. At the conclusion of lifeskills training groups, participants have to listen to their own self-talk without leaders. If participants are encouraged to use themselves as demonstrators of targeted thinking skills during groups, they may be more likely to maintain these skills afterwards. Participants probably require repeated listenings to their demonstrations for the thinking skills to become part of their everyday repertoires.

Here the focus is on building skills of developing your own demonstration audiocassettes rather than encouraging you to use commercial ones. You may still decide to use other people's voices rather than your own. Audiocassettes provide the opportunity to pick up feelings from voice inflections. Consequently, audiocassettes may bring scripts much more to life than the printed page. However, even after playback, participants may not memorize details of audio-recorded presentations. In such cases you can also provide written scripts.

Below are two examples of scripts for audio-recorded demonstrations. The instructions, left out in these examples, can either be given live, put on the cassette, provided as a hand-out or a mixture of these. For instance, leaders may stop their demonstration cassettes to highlight points and make comments. Leaders may also rewind and play again key sections of demonstrations.

The first thinking skill demonstrated is that of not jumping to unwarranted perceptual conclusions. The target audience is an adult lifeskills group on managing anger and conflict. The component subskills of not jumping to unwarranted perceptual conclusions include: tuning into upsetting feelings, logically analysing their appropriateness, generating and evaluating different perceptions and then selecting the 'best-fit' perception. Mark is angry when his girlfriend, Jan, is half an hour late for a special meal he has cooked. However, rather than sulk, Mark decides to use the thinking skill of challenging his initial perception and seeing if there is a more accurate perception. The script for Mark demonstrating this thinking skill is as follows.

> 'I'm feeling mad because Jan has not arrived on time. Stop and think. What are my perceptual choices? Let's see if I am jumping to unwarranted conclusions. At the moment I'm thinking that Jan has deliberately put me down. What is the evidence for that perception? When I stop to think, I know that Jan is very reliable and would not want to hurt me deliberately. She has never missed a special occasion before. Are there any other possible explanations? Let me think of a few. One possibility is that we did not make our arrangements clearly enough – I remember now that I had to rush off immediately after I gave the invitation. Another possibility is that something has happened to Jan on the way over, for instance a flat tyre. Still another possibility is that Jan was forced to work late and then got caught in the traffic. A further explanation is that Jan may have stopped off to collect something

for me. Another explanation for my anger is that I am still too insecure in our relationship and am threatened by her lateness. This last perception seems to have the ring of truth about it. Consequently, when Jan comes I won't make a fuss over her lateness. I'm sure there is some good reason for it.'

The second audiocassette demonstration script focuses on the thinking skill of identifying, disputing and reformulating an unrealistic personal rule. The target audience is an adult group of executives and professional people attending a stress management workshop. The script focuses on Marge, a highly successful accountant, challenging her personal rule that life must be all work and no play.

'I haven't been eating or sleeping properly recently. Also, I'm feeling depressed and tense. I have to force myself to get through the day. Why do I keep pushing myself so hard? I seem to have this underlying personal rule that my life *must* be all work and no play. Let's try disputing this rule. Do I expect other people to sacrifice everything for their careers? Definitely not. I seem to have a double standard in which I'm harder on myself than on other people. Do I need the extra money and status that comes from working this hard? I want a good standard of living and for people to recognize my competence. However, I would still earn enough money even if I were to ease off a bit. Also, what I think of myself is more important than needing recognition from others all the time. I know I'm competent. Is the rule about all work and no play helping or harming me? The rule helped me when I was studying for my accountancy exams and getting started. I have just kept going at the same frantic pace ever since. My body and low feelings are telling me to watch my stress level. Also, I'm concerned that, in my early thirties and single, I'm having virtually no social life. There are also a lot of recreational activities I would like; for instance, I used to be a good tennis player. It would be fun to play again.

'Let's try reformulating that personal rule about all work and no play into a rule that might work better for me at this stage of my life. Here's a try: "I want to earn good money and be respected for my competence as an accountant.

> However, I am likely to be a more successful
> person – and not necessarily a less successful
> accountant – if I lead a more balanced life and
> treat my social and recreational activities as
> though they are as important as my work." This
> new personal rule represents a drastic change
> from my current way of thinking. I will need to
> work hard to keep it in mind and also to change
> my behaviour in line with it.'

If possible, use highly sensitive recording equipment when you make up your audiocassettes. Aim for a professional standard of recording. Most home audio-cassette recorders will not achieve the required level of clarity. Audiocassette recorders are on the market that eliminate virtually all motor noise and background hiss. You greatly lessen the effectiveness of audiocassette demonstrations if participants have to struggle with poor-quality recordings. Also, be prepared to rehearse and retake your efforts if inadequate. Notable performers like Phil Collins and Marti Webb go to these lengths when recording; perhaps you might too.

Live demonstration

In live demonstrations of thinking skills, the demonstrators may be either training group leaders or third parties. Third parties require careful coaching in how to present thinking skills. Many leaders may also have to work hard at preparing and delivering competent live demonstrations. However, if leaders are experienced in teaching about and demonstrating specific thinking skills, they may dispense with scripts and either make up demonstrations on the spot or demonstrate material used before. Competent impromptu demonstrations may come over as more real than those memorized from prepared scripts.

Whether intended or unintended, live demonstrations of good and poor thinking skills happen much of the time in training groups. The group's focus does not have to be on thinking skills. When participants talk about virtually any subject they demonstrate for each other thinking skills strengths and weaknesses. In groups focused on thinking skills both leaders and participants can reinforce initial skills demonstrations with follow-up demonstrations. For example, participants may further demonstrate skills as they rehearse and practise them together. Also, leaders may use material generated in the group to illustrate effective thinking skills.

Exercise 20 aims to raise your awareness of and build your skills in demonstrating thinking skills. Readers wanting ideas for thinking skills on which they might focus are referred to the section on managing speech anxiety in Chapter 7 and also to Nelson-Jones (1989).

Exercise 20 Demonstrate a thinking skill

Work through the following sequence.

Part A Write out a demonstration
Either as part of a lifeskills training group targeted on a specific thinking skill or as part of a group taking both a thinking- and an action-focused approach to a specific skill, for example overcoming shyness or assertion, write out an instructional hand-out for a thinking skill or subskill that covers the following points:

- Your goal or goals for the learning unit.

- The audience for your learning unit.

- Clear instructions that identify for the audience the key points of the skill or subskill you aim to teach.

- One or more demonstrations of the targeted thinking skill or subskill.

- Some questions that enable your audience to practise the demonstrated skills either in the group and/or as homework.

Afterwards, indicate how you might incorporate written demonstrations into your overall presentation of your chosen thinking skill or subskill. For instance, would you plan to provide verbal as well as written instruction and demonstration?

Part B Audio-record a demonstration
Either for the thinking skill you worked on in Part A or for another thinking skill or subskill, make a demonstration audiocassette.

- Clearly state your goal or goals for a learning unit in which a specific thinking skill or subskill will be demonstrated.

- Identify your audience.

- Develop a script that demonstrates, using the first person singular, the use of your targeted thinking skill or subskill.

- Rehearse your script using either your own or other people's voices.

- When you are ready, make an audiocassette recording of your script.

- Play back your cassette, and modify it as many times as is necessary to attain a polished performance.

- Evaluate the likely effect of your final demonstration cassette in helping participants to acquire your targeted thinking skill or subskill.

Think through how you might incorporate audiocassette demonstrations into your overall presentation of your chosen thinking skill or subskill. For instance, would you either provide all your instructions up front or stop the cassette to highlight points and provide commentary?

Part C Demonstrate live
Either for the thinking skill or subskill for which you prepared a script in Part B of this exercise or for another thinking skill or subskill, rehearse and give a live demonstration. If relevant, do not take part in the live demonstration, but coach and rehearse a third party to do it. Indicate how you might provide instructions for your live demonstration.

Assess what are the main advantages and disadvantages for lifeskills training groups of live over written and audio-recorded thinking skill demonstrations.

DEMONSTRATE ACTION SKILLS

Action skills differ from thinking skills in that they are outer game skills that act on the environment rather than inner skills involving inner game thought processes. Action skills involve sending observable verbal, voice, body and action messages. Another relevant distinction is that demonstrations of action skills frequently show two people interacting, for example boss and worker, rather than the thinking or action skills of only one person. Consequently, with two-person demonstrations, leaders use confederates to play either or both roles. Methods of demonstrating action skills include audiocassette, videotape, live and using visualization.

Audiocassette demonstration
Audiocassettes are not recommended if training group leaders wish to include a focus on body messages in skills demonstrations. However, if the main focus is on showing verbal and voice messages, audiocassette demonstrations of action skills may be appropriate. A focus on body messages can still be incorporated in different demonstrations. For example, in lifeskills groups on public speaking skills, demonstrating verbal and voice messages may come before showing the accompanying body messages.

Below is an example of a script for a brief audiocassette demonstration in which a teenager, Diana, returns a defective compact disc to a shop and requests that it be replaced. Within the overall goal of helping teenage participants to become more assertive, the leader wishes to demonstrate the following verbal and voice messages. The verbal message sub-goals are using 'I' statements, giving specific feedback, making clear requests and reflecting resistances. The voice message sub-goals are speaking with good volume, firmly, at a moderate rate and in a relaxed manner.

Diana goes into the shop and up to the salesperson who served her yesterday.

Diana: Hello.
Salesperson: Hello. What can I do for you?
Diana: Yesterday I bought this Prince compact disc and here is the receipt. When I got home I found that the disc was scratched. I request that the store replaces it.
Salesperson: It's almost impossible for there to be anything wrong with CDs.
Diana: You feel that there is rarely anything wrong with CDs, but unfortunately I have found something wrong with this one.
Salesperson: Okay, you may be right in this instance. I'll change it. I know we still have others in stock. This time I will check it more carefully.
Diana: That's great. Thanks a lot.

In the above example, the leader might role-play the salesperson, and a teenage contact of the leader might role-play Diana. Alternatively, the leader might coach people for both roles. Though only verbal messages have been provided in the above script, it is essential that the demonstrators are coached in appropriate voice messages. An assertive verbal message can be countermanded if it is given with either unassertive or aggressive voice messages (Alberti & Emmons, 1986). As with thinking skills, leaders making action skills demonstration cassettes must expect to polish initial efforts. On hearing the above example, the teenage audience may ask 'What happens if the salesperson persists in saying no?' The leader could either anticipate this question by placing a further demonstration on the cassette showing some skills of coping with this contingency or discuss the situation and possibly give a live demonstration in the group.

Videotape demonstration

Both film and videotape demonstrations of action skills have the great advantage over audiocassette demonstrations that participants observe body messages. Many lifeskills training films and videotapes are already on the market; for example, the British Association for Counselling has a film library. Since the making of demonstration films necessitates more resources than most group leaders readily have available, here the focus is on making training videotapes. When making training videotapes, leaders have to specify body message sub-goals as well as verbal and voice sub-goals. For instance, in the previous example of Diana returning a compact disc to a shop, if the leader were to make a videotape he or she might also get Diana to demonstrate the body messages of adequate eye contact, correct posture and good use of gesture.

In making training videos you have the choice of whether or not to do it on your own. If you decide to bring in outside resources, these may range from a professional videotape-making company to a central audiovisual unit in your institution or organization to a technician in your department. As with audiocassette recording, use the best available videotape recording equipment and be prepared to retake scenes. If you make the videotape on your own, you may be restricted to one camera angle and not have the facility for editing. Also, your energies may be diverted into working the equipment rather than concentrating on the quality of demonstration. With more resources, both human and technical, you can do a better job. However, the trade-off for a higher quality product may be unjustified time and expense.

In making training videotapes, group leaders act as 'movie' directors and, as such, require many of their skills. Once scripts have been developed, leaders need to coach demonstrators in how to act them. During the rehearsal process and shooting of scenes, leaders may decide to rewrite parts of the script and also to emphasize targeted skills differently. Much trial and error goes into making polished demonstration videotapes.

Making demonstration videotapes may seem a daunting task to many training group leaders. You have to concentrate on technical, teaching and acting dimensions of videotapes. However, you are encouraged to persist. For many lifeskills, videotape demonstrations add the vital visual dimension over audiocassette demonstrations. Even though your efforts may fall short of Steven Spielberg, they are likely to be much better than no demonstration videotapes at all.

Live demonstration

Training group leaders may arrange for live demonstrations of action skills. Leaders may give these demonstrations themselves, either on their own or with other demonstrators. Alternatively, both roles in a dialogue may be enacted by others. If you only want to show a particular lifeskill once, you save time by demonstrating it live as contrasted with pre-recording your demonstration. However, if on subsequent occasions you wish to repeat your live demonstration, you are faced with the extra time and trouble of working up further polished presentations. In addition, unless live demonstrations are taped, participants have no copies to watch on their own. Needless to say, repeating live demonstrations is easier if you are the only demonstrator than if others are involved too.

Some limitations of live demonstrations in initial action skills presentations have been mentioned above. However, subsequently, live demonstrations can be extremely useful when rehearsing and practising skills. For example, after initial presentations, leaders often demonstrate as they coach participants in targeted skills. In addition, leaders can demonstrate relevant coping skills when participants bring problems from their outside lives into groups. Pre-recorded demonstrations do not have this flexibility.

Live demonstration can also be useful for leaders using Bandura's 'participant modelling' approach. This approach has been used in particular to train those suffering from phobias (Bandura, 1976; Jeffrey, 1976). For example, participants may watch demonstrators perform progressively more threatening tasks in relation to feared objects such as snakes. After each demonstration, participants are given both guidance and ample opportunities to perform the demonstrated behaviours under favourable conditions. Examples of favourable conditions include joint performance of subtasks with leaders and performing subtasks under protective conditions, for instance touching snakes while wearing gloves.

Visualized demonstration

Visualized demonstrations or 'covert modelling' are not used to demonstrate action skills in lifeskills training groups nearly as frequently as videotaped or live demonstrations. Nevertheless, visualized demonstration is a useful leader skill. For example, it may be difficult to portray on pre-recorded videotapes the range of scenes relevant to participants' problems. In addition, unlike in live demonstrations, all participants are actively involved as they imagine either demonstrators or themselves enacting suggested behaviours. Scenes in visualized demonstrations can be standard as well as individual (Cormier & Cormier, 1985). Furthermore, visualized demonstrations in training groups are good precursors to visualized rehearsal and practice outside the group.

In general, people visualize best when relaxed (Kazdin, 1976). Leaders may get participants to visualize neutral scenes as a way of checking that they understand how to visualize. For example, participants may be asked to visualize someone eating dinner with them at home.

Three guidelines for developing visualized demonstrations are as follows.

- *Set the scene.* Describe the situation in which targeted lifeskills are to be enacted in sufficient detail for it to be easy for participants to visualize it.

- *Describe the action skill(s).* Describe how the person enacts the targeted behaviours in the situation. The person visualized may be either a third party or a participant. Remember to describe clearly verbal, voice and body as well as action messages. In brief, give full descriptions of any action skills that you demonstrate.

- *Depict favourable consequences of using the action skill(s).* Get participants to visualize the demonstrator's behaviour being rewarded (Kazdin, 1976).

Below is an example of a visualized demonstration in a parent effectiveness training class. The targeted behaviours are active listening, sending an 'I message' and requesting a behaviour change.

- *Set the scene.* Picture a family consisting of father, mother and two nine-year-old twin girls sitting at their dining-room table. The meal has just started. Mum asks Dad about how his day has gone and Dad starts to reply. Before he has had a chance to finish, one of the girls, Betty, interrupts and asks if he will take her to her dancing lesson tomorrow. Dad, who has had a hard day at work, feels himself tense up at the interruption.

- *Describe the action skill(s).* After the interruption, Dad turns to Betty, catches her eye and says in a warm, but firm voice: 'Sweetie, I know that it is important for you to get to your dancing lesson. However, I haven't finished answering

Mum's question yet. Please let me finish and then we can talk about your concern.' At no stage does Dad raise his voice or give his daughter an angry look. Rather, he calmly asserts his right for respect when he talks.

- *Depict favourable consequences for using the action skill(s).* Betty says in a relaxed voice and without sulking: 'I'm sorry Dad. I'll wait.' Betty does not feel put down by Dad's response. Dad feels good that he has set a limit on her interrupting.

Training group leaders can develop different visualized demonstrations around targeted skills. These visualizations may be graduated by threat or difficulty. In addition, leaders can get participants to visualize a variety of people coping with the scenes. Visualized demonstration has the further flexibility that leaders can get participants to visualize themselves enacting appropriate behaviours in problematic scenes taken from their own lives.

Exercise 21 provides you with the opportunity to try out different ways of demonstrating action skills.

Exercise 21 Demonstrate an action skill

Work through those parts of the following sequence that you find useful for your circumstances.

Part A Audio-record a demonstration
Select a lifeskills training group to whom you might want to demonstrate the verbal and voice dimensions of a specific action skill or subskill. If possible, your demonstration should involve dialogue between two people. Depending on whether or not you participate in the demonstration, you will need one or two other demonstrators. Perform the following tasks:

- Within the context of your overall goal, set clear verbal and voice message sub-goals for your demonstration audiocassette.

- Develop a relatively brief script that demonstrates the verbal skills you want to convey – in the margin indicate appropriate voice messages.

- Coach and rehearse your demonstrator(s) in the verbal and voice aspects of your demonstration.

- Make up at least one pilot audiocassette and then, if necessary, keep altering and re-recording your audiocassette until you are satisfied with it.

Indicate how you might incorporate instructions in your demonstration audio-cassette so that participants know what to look for: for instance, will you pre-record your instructions?

Part B Video-record a demonstration
Use the instructions for Part A to make up a videotape focused on the body message as well as the verbal and voice message dimensions of an action skill or subskill.

Part C Demonstrate live
Either for the action skill or subskill you worked on in Part B or for another action skill or subskill, rehearse and give a live demonstration. If relevant, do not take part in the live demonstration, but coach and rehearse third parties to do it.

Part D Use visualized demonstration
Select a lifeskills training group to whom you might want to demonstrate the verbal, voice and body message dimensions of a specific action skill or subskill by means of visualized demonstration. Perform the following steps:

- Develop a visualized demonstration containing at least two people – the demonstration should contain these elements:
  (a) set the scene
  (b) describe the appropriate action skill
  (c) depict favourable consequences for using the action skill.

- Make up at least one pilot audiocassette and then, if necessary, keep altering and re-recording your cassette until you are satisfied with it.

- Find another person and ask them to visualize your scene as you describe it live to them – afterwards get feedback regarding how realistic they found your demonstration to be.

Indicate how you might incorporate instructions in your visualized demonstration. For instance, would you provide instructions when your audience has their eyes open or shut?

Think through how you might use visualized demonstration in any lifeskills group you either lead now or might lead in future.

DEMONSTRATE ACTION SKILLS WITH ACCOMPANYING SELF-TALK

Training group leaders may often want to demonstrate action skills with the self-talk that accompanies them. Ultimately, participants have to instruct themselves through action skills sequences. There is much to be said for building relevant self-talk into demonstrations. Perhaps lifeskills demonstrations will increasingly be viewed as deficient if they do not contain both action skills and accompanying self-talk. Arranging for demonstrations that show both action skills and self-talk can present an interesting challenge to training group leader ingenuity.

Demonstrating self-talk along with action skills may be done in written form, live, pre-recorded on either audiocassette or videotape, or in conjunction with visualized demonstration. Here, to avoid repetition, each of these methods is not dealt with in turn. Rather, some ways of building self-talk into action skills demonstrations are reviewed.

- *Think aloud.* Here demonstrators pause every now and then and verbalize relevant self-instructions out loud. Think aloud is less intrusive in individual demonstrations than in demonstrations where two or more persons are involved. For example, the thought processes of a demonstrator who looks at an exam paper for the first time can be shown in such a way that the relationship between thinking skills and action skills seems comfortable. However, in a dialogue demonstration, for instance with partners attempting to manage a conflict, it may seem artificial if each demonstrator thinks aloud before responding. In live demonstrations, think aloud is the only way of showing both action skills and self-instructions. In audiocassette and videotape demonstrations, think aloud segments may be interspersed before each action skill segment.

- *Voice-overs.* With demonstration videotapes and films, voice-overs of the demonstrator's self-talk may be edited in. Voice-overs are less disruptive to the flow of the demonstration than alternating between self-talk and action. However, voice-overs have some disadvantages. A technical disadvantage is that the process of recording voice-overs may be beyond the available resources of many leaders. Another problem is that, where demonstrations include much dialogue, finding appropriate openings for voice-overs may be difficult. A possible educational disadvantage is that voice-overs may confuse observers who are trying to learn self-talk and action skills. Participants may find it easier to concentrate first on self-talk and then on the relevant action skill rather than focusing on both simultaneously.

- *Sub-titles.* Sub-titles normally reflect visual images. However, in demonstrating self-talk, sub-titles demonstrate relevant inner rather than outer talk. There are two advantages of sub-titles over voice-overs. First, in demonstrations involving dialogue they do not provide added, and possibly distracting, sound. Second, sub-titles can be left on the screen longer than verbal messages. This extra time may make it easier for participants to assimilate the self-talk being shown.

- *'Thinks' balloons.* 'Thinks' balloons are often found in comic strips. Relevant self-talk can be placed in balloons attached to demonstrators' heads. 'Thinks' balloons are for written, film and videotape demonstrations. They require much technical competence to superimpose on moving images. In such circumstances 'thinks' balloons are probably best left to expert animators.

Below is an example of an action skills plus self-talk demonstration in an examination skills group. The demonstrator, Julie, has the characteristics of an exam-anxious student. She tries to cope with anxiety and stay task-relevant when looking at an exam paper for the first time. Imagine that this is a videotape demonstration. The *self-talk* sub-goals for the demonstration are the use of: calming statements ('Calm down'); focusing statements ('Think, what is it I have to do?'); self-reward statements ('I'm coping well so far'); specific task-orientated instructions ('I need to read the exam paper instructions carefully . . .'); and statements that combat unrealistic personal rules ('All I have to do is as best I can'). The *action skills* sub-goals are anxiety reduction skills, for example breathing slowly and regularly, and exam-taking skills, for example reading the test's instructions carefully. Julie's action skills plus self-talk demonstration are based on the work of Meichenbaum and his colleagues (for example, Meichenbaum & Goodman, 1971). Julie intersperses think aloud self-talk with performing action skills.

> 'Okay, I'm feeling pretty uptight. My anxiety is a signal for me to use my coping skills. Calm down. Breathe slowly and regularly (Julie breathes slowly and regularly). Think, what is it I have to do? I need to read the exam instructions carefully and look out for how the marks are distributed and how many questions I have to answer (Julie reads the instructions carefully). Then I must survey all the questions (Julie surveys the questions). I'm coping well so far. Keep taking it easy. Next I must plan how to spend my time – in which order to do the questions and how much time to allocate to each question. Let's pick an easy question first. Remember to leave time for checking my answers at the end of the exam (Julie drafts a plan). I don't have to answer the questions perfectly – all I have to do is as best I can. I know I can keep calm and use my time sensibly. Now let's see what is really wanted in the first question I've chosen to answer (Julie starts working on the first question).'

All too often leaders, when demonstrating action skills, forget that participants then have to instruct themselves in learning sequences outside the group. For example, leaders of stress management groups may demonstrate the talk that accompanies muscular relaxation in either leader-centred or participant-centred ways. With leader-centred talk, it becomes obvious that leaders give instructions from outside: for example, 'Now close your eyes and get yourself comfortable'. With participant-centred talk, leaders demonstrate the instructions as though participants were instructing themselves: for example, 'Now I close my eyes and get myself comfortable'. Demonstrating participant-centred rather than leader-centred talk is a small but important difference when a goal of the stress management programme is to train participants to use relaxation skills on their own.

Exercise 22 gives you the opportunity to demonstrate an action skill(s) with accompanying self-talk.

Exercise 22 Demonstrate an action skill with accompanying self-talk

Select a lifeskills group to whom you might want to demonstrate an action skill or subskill with accompanying self-talk. Assume that this is an individual demonstration in which the demonstrator talks himself/herself through an action skills sequence that does not involve other people. Perform the following tasks:

- Within the context of your overall goal set clear action skill(s) and self-talk sub-goals for your demonstration.

- State the characteristics of your demonstrator.

- Develop an action skill(s) plus self-talk demonstration along the lines of the example in the text.

- If possible, make up a pilot videotape of your action skill(s) plus self-talk demonstration and then, if necessary, keep altering and re-recording your videotape until you are satisfied with it.

CHAPTER HIGHLIGHTS

Demonstrations should be the rule rather than the exception in training group skills presentations.

Observational learning can be used in training groups to: initiate skills strengths; develop skills strengths; disinhibit skills strengths; and inhibit and weaken skills weakness.

Three important areas for observational learning are thinking skills, action skills, and action skills with accompanying self-talk.

Demonstrators of lifeskills include training group leaders, leaders' aides, participants and third parties.

Demonstrator characteristics that influence learning are: similarity to observers, prestige, competence level, and personal attractiveness.

Methods of demonstration include written, live, pre-recorded and visualized.

Demonstration characteristics include: single or multiple, scripted or unscripted, positive and/or negative, graduated, demonstrator reward, rationale, instructions, observer summaries, and timing of observers performing the skill.

Methods by which leaders can increase observers' attention include orientating them to the relevance of demonstrations, telling them in advance what to look out for, and trying to reduce debilitating anxiety.

Thinking skills can be demonstrated either in writing, by audiocassettes, or live. Visual images are unnecessary for demonstrating thinking skills.

The verbal and voice message components of action skills can be demonstrated by audiocassette. However, visual images are necessary for demonstrating body messages.

In making training videotapes, group leaders act as movie directors and require many of their skills: for instance, coaching demonstrators, developing and altering scripts and retaking scenes.

Live demonstration of action skills may be particularly useful in coaching participants after the initial presentation of a skill and in showing participants coping skills for their outside group problems.

Visualized demonstration, getting participants to imagine themselves or a third party performing action skills competently, is a useful skill in the group leader's repertoire.

Three guidelines for developing visualized demonstrations are: set the scene; describe the appropriate action skill; and depict favourable consequences for using the action skill.

Participants have to instruct themselves through action skills sequences once training groups end. Where possible, relevant self-talk should be built into demonstrations.

Self-talk may be provided to accompany action skills demonstrations by think aloud, voice-overs, sub-titles and 'thinks' balloons.

NINE

How to Manage Structured Activities

What we have to learn to do, we learn by doing.

Aristotle

CHAPTER QUESTIONS

What are structured activities?

What facilitation skills are relevant to managing structured activities?

How do leaders coach participants after initial skills presentations?

What methods exist for rehearsing behaviours?

What leader skills are necessary for preparing, directing and processing action role-plays?

What kinds of feedback can participants receive?

What might leaders consider in designing exercises and behaviour change experiments?

What are ways of enhancing participants' motivation for completing between-session homework tasks?

INTRODUCTION

Learning by doing is essential to lifeskills training groups. Learning by hearing and by observing get clarified and consolidated by learning by doing. Training group leaders require good skills of promoting and managing learning by doing. You do not learn to drive a car without driving. Likewise, participants acquiring and strengthening specific lifeskills need relevant activities that help them to improve and integrate the skills into their daily lives.

Below are some examples of learning by doing in training groups. Note that in some of the examples learning by doing focuses on thinking skills as well as on action skills.

- Adolescent job seekers being trained in persuasion skills role-play job interview situations with others in their classes (Wild & Kerr, 1984).

- Management trainees play a training board game *Stop Sexual Harassment* whose purpose is to clarify some of the concepts and issues regarding sexism, sexual harassment and sexual politics in the workplace (Wehrenberg, 1985).

- Couples in a Knowledge Increases Sexual Satisfaction (KISS) group do four exercises to improve sexual communication: namely initiating and refusing sexual activities, increasing their sexual vocabulary, giving instantaneous sexual feedback, and sharing sexual preferences and fantasies (Cooper & Stoltenberg, 1987).

- A divorced women's group imagines and then confronts and challenges irrational beliefs about divorce in eight belief areas in which they report discomforting thoughts: children, finances, daily hassles, parents and in-laws, former husband, failure of marriage, rejection, and relationships with others (Graf *et al.*, 1986).

- Patients with chronic low back pain attend weekly lifeskills sessions focused both on progressive muscular relaxation and on identifying maladaptive thoughts connected with negative emotions related to pain and replacing them with more adaptive thoughts (Turner & Clancy, 1988).

- Trainee helpers, to develop their cross-cultural awareness and skills, participate in scripted role-plays in which they are interviewed by people from Arab cultures (Merta *et al.*, 1988).

The above are just some examples of structured activities in lifeskills training groups. Especially during the working stage, sessions are incomplete if they do not contain learning by doing.

As with demonstration skills, structured activities can focus on thinking skills, action skills and action skills plus self-talk. Sometimes the structured activities are integrated with the learning sequence containing the initial demonstration. For example, coaching, rehearsal and feedback take place immediately after a skill demonstration. On other occasions, structured activities are less planned as leaders help participants to develop and apply skills to outside-group situations.

WHAT ARE STRUCTURED ACTIVITIES?

I hear I forget
I see I remember
I do I understand
Chinese Proverb

No helping or training group is entirely unstructured. Even person-centred encounter groups operate within frameworks. However, there are degrees of structure both within and across groups. Learning activities that are consciously chosen in advance by leaders constitute an important way in which structure is built into training groups. As leaders you do not leave participants' skills development to chance. Instead you intentionally set up and manage activities that allow participants to understand, rehearse and practise targeted skills.

The following are some of the main structured activities, albeit overlapping, used by training group leaders:

- *Self-monitoring forms.* Participants may be encouraged to monitor their out-of-session behaviours. These behaviours may be feelings, thoughts and actions as well as their consequences for self and others. Such self-monitoring is used not only to collect initial assessment data, but also to help participants to evaluate their progress throughout a group's life. Self-monitoring forms require both adequate introduction and also adequate processing once data are collected.

- *Coached performance.* Coaching consists of providing instructions, tips, hints and rules for enacting skills. Before participants rehearse skills, they are likely to require coaching in specific 'how-to' points. Learning by hearing and observing are usually insufficient to enable skills to be performed properly. Consequently, after demonstrating, leaders take participants through coached performances of skills.

- *Behaviour rehearsal.* Behaviour rehearsal can be either covert, such as with thinking skills, or overt, such as with action skills, or both, for instance with action skills plus self-talk. Behaviour rehearsals can be scripted or ad-libbed.

- *Role-play.* There is no clear dividing line between behaviour rehearsal and role-play. Role-plays can be used to consolidate initial presentation and demonstration of skills. Another use of role-plays is in assessing participants' outside behaviours and in developing skills to manage external problem situations.

- *Feedback.* Leaders can systematically arrange for participants to obtain feedback on their skills strengths and weaknesses. Feedback may come from other participants and from audiocassettes and videotapes as well as from leaders.

- *Exercises.* Exercises are activities specially designed to give participants practice in developing and performing targeted skills. For example, in listening skills groups, participants may do exercises on identifying speakers' internal frames of reference and on making reflective responses. Exercises may be written as well as action-orientated. Written exercises are especially common for thinking skills: examples are Ellis's rational-emotive self-help forms focused on identifying and disputing irrational beliefs (Ellis, 1989) and my series of Thinksheets (Nelson-Jones, 1989). Exercises, broadly defined, include activities like games, feedback, and task assignments.

- *Games.* Depending on the extent to which they involve play, exercises may be called games. Sometimes lifeskills board games are commercially produced (Wehrenberg, 1985). On other occasions, leaders develop their own games. For instance, in relationship skills groups, an exercise about sending 'I' messages is turned into a game by having senders toss a ball along with an 'I' message to their receivers. Try speeding this up and it becomes even more of a game!

- *Task assignments.* Groups or sub-groups can be given specific tasks and instructed to come up with solutions. Alternatively, sub-groups can be given sub-tasks in overall tasks. For example, in training groups on team building, participants are given a problem to solve. They are then asked to evaluate the processes of trust building and decision making that occur in their group when solving the problem (Johnson & Johnson, 1987).

- *Critical incidents.* Training groups can be given brief scenarios for situations relevant to the targeted skills. Then participants are invited to think through what are the relevant issues and skills. Hopson and Scally give the example of a teenage girl going to a disco, arriving home two hours later than agreed, and finding her father waiting up for her (Hopson & Scally, 1981). The group's attention can be directed to answering such questions as what each protagonist in the scene may think and feel, what thoughts and behaviours each needs to avoid, and what skills each could use to attain his or her goals.

- *Case studies.* Case studies tend to be more detailed and longer-term descriptions of problem situations than critical incidents. Case studies are frequently used at business schools for training managerial and supervisory skills. However, the use of case studies need not be restricted to business. For instance, case studies can be introduced into parent education or couples education groups. A case study for a parent education group might be based on a videotape that invites participants to look at helpful and harmful communication patterns in a specific family.

- *Computer-assisted learning.* Increasingly, training group leaders are likely to explore computer learning. Computers have already been used in such areas as helping secondary school students to explore career options (Johnson, 1985) and simulating job interviews to improve the decision-making skills of employers (Ganger, 1989).

- *Behaviour change plans.* Structured activities for obtaining targeted lifeskills goals can be performed outside as well as inside groups. An important leader function is the design of outside-group structured activities. Such activities enhance the transfer and maintenance of skills and their integration into participants' daily routines. Participants can be encouraged to develop plans to change their behaviour and achieve their goals. Behaviour-change plans can be worked on both within and outside lifeskills sessions. Plans should be realistic, clearly stipulate the goals, outline how they are to be achieved, and state a time frame. Plans are a notable feature both of Glasser's reality therapy groups (Glasser, 1965, 1984b) and of cognitive-behavioural self-management programmes (Kanfer & Gaelick, 1986).

- *Behaviour change experiments.* In conducting experiments participants make behaviour change hypotheses, implement them, and then evaluate the consequences for themselves and others of their changed behaviours (Beck & Emery, 1985; Nelson-Jones, 1990). Even though the implementation of experiments is performed as homework, their design and some of the subsequent evaluation take place inside groups.

- *Homework tasks.* As well as experiments, a range of other structured activities can be designed and set as between-session homework tasks. Outside practice is important for extending the learning opportunities provided by groups. Filling out self-monitoring forms, behaviour rehearsal and practice, exercises, games, working through case studies and critical incidents are all structured activities to set as homework tasks in one session and process in the next.

FACILITATE STRUCTURED ACTIVITIES

Training group leaders require good skills at facilitating structured activities as well as good skills at facilitating group interaction. Even at the best of times participants enter groups with varying levels of commitment and motivation. Much learning in training groups is public. Consequently, in addition to any anxieties that they have about developing specific skills, participants may have further anxieties about developing them in public. Many participants feel exposed, vulnerable, clumsy and awkward when performing structured activities. They may get frustrated at their comparatively slow rate of learning. The skills on which participants work may be in sensitive areas. In addition, some structured activities may seem strange to them, for instance role-plays. Group leaders cannot assume that participants will automatically cooperate in structured activities. They may resist such activities for many reasons, including: lack of a trusting group atmosphere, not seeing the point of particular exercises, shyness, trying to one-up the leader, and not wishing to work if others do not work too.

How can training group leaders enhance participants' motivation and commitment to learning from structured activities? Below are some suggestions. First, leaders can create a safe and trusting emotional climate in which participants are prepared to take risks. Such risks may entail disclosing problems, admitting mistakes and volunteering to work in front of the group. All the facilitation skills mentioned in Chapter 6 are relevant to building safe emotional climates. In addition, by competently presenting and demonstrating lifeskills, leaders enhance their credibility and trustworthiness.

Second, leaders may allow performance fears to be aired and explored. Leaders may show sensitivity to participants being uneasy about having to work in public. Leaders may make comments like 'It's okay to feel uneasy about engaging in activities in front of the group' and 'It's okay to make mistakes when learning any new skill'. Participants can be invited to share any fears or anxieties they may have about learning by doing in public or about participating in specific activities. Such invitations to air performance fears may be by way of comments made to the whole group or, alternatively, by means of a 'round' in which each participant is invited to speak (Jacobs *et al.*, 1988). In addition, leaders can reassure participants that they will not be coerced into divulging private material or into doing any exercise with which they persistently feel uncomfortable. Leaders should ensure that all participants have equal opportunity to work on their skills and problems in the group. Certain participants may be less resistant to working if they know that their turn will inevitably come.

Third, leaders can ensure that the reasons for doing each structured activity are clear. Participants are more likely to perform structured activities if they see connections between the activities and targeted skills. Leaders should clarify reasons for structured activities whose purposes are unclear. Sometimes it is good to check with groups which activities work best for them. Later in a group's life such checking may have more meaning than earlier: participants by then have experienced a range of structured activities.

Fourth, leaders can enhance participants' motivation and commitment by helping them to process their experiences with structured activities. Working participants are defined as those who do behaviour rehearsals, role-plays or other structured activities in front of groups. Working participants may have thoughts and feelings both about the structured activities and about the material that they present. Leaders who conduct structured learning activities should not be cold and impersonal. Often, structured activities provide opportunities for valuable emotional and cognitive insights. Leaders can help participants to share and work through these insights. Nevertheless, the problem of how to balance individual work with the group's needs is always present. Time spent helping working participants to access significant thoughts and feelings may help others too. Leaders can use working participants' contributions as springboards for encouraging others to work.

Fifth, leaders can encourage involvement in structured activities by facilitating feedback. Peer feedback can be very valuable to working participants. Leaders may create a group norm that 'It is okay to give and receive constructive feedback. We are all here to learn'. Leaders may give permission to the group to provide feedback: for example, 'Does anyone have any comments that they would like to make about how Gerry handled that situation?' Invitations to the group may be by way of 'rounds' in which each participant is given the opportunity to provide feedback. Leaders may refrain from giving their feedback until the group has had its opportunity. In addition, leaders may notice participants reacting to a specific activity and give them an 'opener' to speak: for example, 'Judy, I noticed you reacting pretty strongly when Brian did his role-play about standing up to his boss; is there anything that you would like to share with the group?'

Sixth, leaders can encourage involvement in structured activities by using different formats. Just as structured activities may be done in pairs, threes or other small groups as well as in the overall group, so leaders can allow some of the processing of activities to be done in sub-groups. Training group leaders are managers of learning. They do not have to do everything themselves. Rather, they need to create learning environments and opportunities. By sub-grouping, they facilitate participants sharing personal meanings and giving and receiving feedback. In a given time period, more people have the opportunity to be working participants and offer feedback in sub-groups than in full groups.

COACH PARTICIPANTS IN SKILLS

Here coached performance refers to coaching taking place immediately after an initial skills presentation and demonstration. Then participants require 'how-to' coaching in the skill. Learning from hearing and observing must be translated into learning from doing. Also, unless leaders as coaches observe participants performing skills, they cannot know whether they have properly grasped them.

Some coaching considerations

Below are some of the considerations that group leaders need to take into account when coaching participants to perform lifeskills that have just been presented and demonstrated.

- *Consider who coaches.* Different ways of approaching the task of coaching include the following. First, a training manual may be the coach. Participants may be referred to written coaching manuals that give specific instructions and illustrations of how to enact skills. Second, the training group leader coaches. This is the most common model in lifeskills training. Third, leaders' aides may coach. Even if done in small groups, coaching ultimately should look at how individual participants perform skills. Small-group and individual attention is labour intensive. Consequently, leaders' aides may be valuable additional coaches. Fourth, other participants may coach. All participants have just heard and seen the skills of initial presentation and demonstration. Learning may be enhanced if they become coaches. Participants may coach either in front of leaders and the full group or in pairs or sub-groups where leaders may be absent. Self-coaching is a fifth method of coaching. Working participants can be encouraged to instruct themselves through the performance of a skill. Last, there are various possible mixtures of the above coaching methods: the mixture may contain self-coaching as well as coaching from others.

- *Consider the balance between facilitative and didactic coaching.* In *didactic* coaching an external source, probably the leader, gives a series of explicit instructions to learners on how to perform skills. The leader's comments take the form: 'First, you do this. Then you do that. Then you do that' and so on. The leader is the expert taking beginners through sequences of performance choices.

  In *facilitative* coaching, leaders have two important objectives: first, to draw out and build upon learners' existing knowledge and skills; and second, to help them to acquire the skills of self-coaching, not just for now but for after the group. Leaders' initial comments may take more the form: 'Now that you have had the initial presentation and demonstration of the skill, what has it told you about how to do it?', 'Where are your strengths and weaknesses?' and 'Assume that I am the other person in the situation; now you show me how to use the skill just presented'.

  When coaching, training group leaders need to be both facilitative and didactic. For example, leaders might start with trying to build on the existing knowledge and skills of learners, but then intersperse didactic prompts when learners get stuck. On the one hand, it can be wasteful of everybody's time to rely solely on drawing out participants' learning potential. On the other hand, coaching without using facilitative skills lessens the likelihood of targeted skills being owned and integrated into participants' daily routines. Also, didactic coaching alone can create counterproductive resistances.

- *Give clear instructions.* Chapters 7 and 8 have emphasized clear goals for each lifeskills learning sequence. These goals and sub-goals may be in the areas of thinking skills, action skills, or action skills plus self-talk. When participants are coached through 'how-to' performances of targeted skills, goals and sub-goals need to be translated into clear and precise instructions.

- *Break tasks down.* Leaders have to consider whether to break skills and subskills down further when initially getting participants to perform them. Leaders, when coaching participants after initial presentations and demonstrations, may still decide to break skills down further. Leaders need to consider how much participants can assimilate in each learning trial. For example, with a teenager wishing to return a CD to a shop, one trial might focus on verbal messages, another on voice messages, another on body messages, and another on putting it all together.

- *Use graded steps.* Cumulative learning is built into well-designed lifeskills programmes. When coaching participants in specific areas, leaders may decide to break the learning trials down to include successively more difficult steps. Participants may be asked to volunteer areas in which they find it either easier or more difficult to apply the targeted skills.

- *Use demonstration skills.* Demonstrations can be a vital part of coaching. For example, where participants make assertive requests in weak voices, leaders may mirror existing voice messages and then demonstrate more appropriate voice messages.

- *Use feedback and reward skills.* Feedback and reward skills are covered in much more detail later in the chapter.

- *Decide on scripted or unscripted performance.* There are advantages to leaders using prepared scripts when initially coaching participants to perform skills. As with theatre or film scripts, prepared scripts can contain directions about voice and body messages. Participants asked to generate how they should behave may not highlight the points being taught. Coaching participants using prepared scripts can be a useful stepping-stone to coaching participants when they use their own material. Participants need not always memorize scripts. However, they should memorize the main rules, concepts and points illustrated in scripts.

- *Use checking skills.* Skilled leaders not only try to convey the main points in which they coach participants before and during performances, but at the end they also check whether participants have fully understood what they performed. For example, at the end of coaching trials, leaders can ask working participants to summarize the main learning points.

- *Decide on number of trials.* How many coaching trials do participants require before they perform a skill or subskill competently? Coaching for initial skills acquisition overlaps with behaviour rehearsal and practice. With or without graded steps, participants may require many attempts before they perform skills well within, let alone outside, their training groups.

- *Consider individual or group coaching.* To what extent and in what ways can leaders coach more than one participant at a time? Some lifeskills, for instance progressive muscular relaxation (Jacobson, 1938), lend themselves to group coaching. Inevitably, much coaching is with individual participants in front of groups. However, leaders can break down groups into sub-groups and coach within them. Also, participants can be asked to make up videocassettes and audiocassettes to play back in groups or sub-groups for coaching purposes.

- *Consider visual and written prompts.* Prompts are interventions that direct participants' attention to required behaviours (Karoly & Harris, 1986). Apart from verbal instructions from leaders and participants, other prompts include: cue cards, posters, hand-outs, and training manuals.

- *Consider fading.* Fading means the gradual removal of external sources of instruction and prompting. Participants require coaching to the point, and sometimes beyond the point, where they can perform skills competently on their own. Coaching should emphasize ways in which participants can help themselves, for instance clear self-instructions. Self-directed behaviour rehearsals and practice can help participants to build up skills so that leaders can withdraw external sources of instruction and prompting.

Exercise 23 aims to give you practice at coaching another person or persons to perform a lifeskill competently.

Exercise 23 Coach a lifeskill

1. Imagine that you have just given a verbal presentation followed by a demonstration of a specific skill or subskill to a lifeskills training group of your choice. You are now about to coach participants in how to perform the skill. How might you take each of the following considerations into account?

   - The balance between facilitative and didactic coaching.
   - Who coaches.
   - Give clear instructions.
   - Break tasks down.
   - Use graded steps.
   - Use demonstration skills.
   - Use feedback and reward skills.
   - Scripted or unscripted performance.
   - Use checking skills.
   - Number of trials.
   - Individual or group coaching.
   - Visual and written prompts.
   - Fading.

2. If possible, work with another person or persons. Give them a verbal presentation that includes demonstration of a specific lifeskill or subskill. Do not attempt too much. Afterwards, coach them to the point where, within the limits of this exercise, they competently perform the skill.
3. Repeat the second part of the exercise until you have coached another

person or persons in (a) an action skill, (b) a thinking skill, and (c) an action skill plus self-talk.

CONDUCT BEHAVIOUR REHEARSALS AND ROLE-PLAYS

Learning by doing generally requires repeated performances of targeted skills. Behaviour rehearsals may be of thinking skills, action skills and action skills plus self-talk. Behaviour rehearsals may involve enacting specific skills and subskills as part of presentation, demonstration, coached performance and rehearsal training and learning sequences. Behaviour rehearsals may take place either immediately after initial coached performance of skills or later as participants apply targeted skills to material that they bring to groups. Rehearsals may be either coached or self-instructed.

Below are some examples of training group behaviour rehearsals and role-plays:

- Helping culturally disadvantaged secondary school students to develop skills for entry into the post-secondary world by means of mock interviews with prospective employers followed by videotaped feedback (Hamilton, 1984).

- Students in a secondary school group on 'Planning your future' role-play talking over vocational choice ideas with their parents.

- Participants in a 'Coping with depression' class spend two sessions each on learning and rehearsing how to (a) relax, (b) increase pleasant activities, (c) change aspects of their thinking, and (d) improve social skills and increase positive social interactions (Brown & Lewinsohn, 1984).

- Participants develop using the telephone skills by being divided into groups of three – caller, listener and observer – and then being asked to play each role. The role-plays are of conversations of not more than two minutes on prearranged topics such as ringing a company about a job or asking for a date (Priestley *et al.*, 1978).

- Participants in an anger management group visualize personal anger scenes, experience their anger, and then rehearse using cognitive and relaxation coping skills to manage it (Deffenbacher *et al.*, 1987).

Methods of behaviour rehearsal

The terms behaviour rehearsal and role-play are often used interchangeably (for example, Goldfried & Davison, 1976). However, it is a simplification to equate behaviour rehearsal with role-play. The one does not necessarily imply the other. Different methods of rehearsing behaviours include the following. First, there is *live rehearsal*. Take sports personalities like golfers or tennis players. When they wish to rehearse their shots they go out and practise, either on their own or with others. Similarly, many lifeskills can be rehearsed live, with or without assistance either from others or from response aids (for instance gloves, for those afraid of snakes or furry animals).

Certain behaviours can be rehearsed live inside training groups. For example, participants in a making friends group can rehearse basic conversational skills, such as self-disclosure, within as well as outside their group. Also, the skills of progressive muscular relaxation can be rehearsed both inside and outside stress or anger management lifeskills groups without the need for role-plays. However, when progressive muscular relaxation is rehearsed as part of a coping response to specific stressors or anger provocations, elements of role-play may be introduced.

Live rehearsal can assist practice either inside or outside of some training groups. For example, a within-group adaptation of Bandura's participant modelling approach would use assisted rehearsal and practice as participants have repeated trials in graded steps with stimuli such as snakes (Bandura, 1976; Jeffrey, 1976). In other training groups, such as for agoraphobics, assisted rehearsal might take place outside of the central group meeting place as leader or leader's aides take participants, either on their own or with others, out into anxiety-evoking settings.

Action role-plays provide a second method of rehearsing behaviours. In action role-plays, participants rehearse observable behaviours in simulated or pretend situations. For instance, in the examples provided at the start of this section, training group members rehearse interview skills, discuss vocational choices with parents, and try out telephone skills in mock settings. Throughout a group's duration, action role-plays can be used to assess skills weaknesses as well as to develop and rehearse skills strengths.

A third method for rehearsing behaviours is *mental rehearsal*. In mental rehearsal, participants rehearse and practise specific thinking skills: for example, either identifying and reformulating unrealistic personal rules or identifying upsetting perceptions and finding better ones. Mental rehearsal may be private or public. Private mental rehearsal involves repeatedly practising a thinking skill on your own. Such private rehearsal may entail writing down your thought processes. Public mental rehearsal can be by thinking aloud in the group or sharing written answers to self-help thinksheets.

Visualized rehearsal is a fourth method of rehearsal. Visualized rehearsal, otherwise known as imaginal or covert rehearsal, is a form of mental rehearsal involving pictorial images. The pictorial images in visualized rehearsal are usually of actual rather than role-played scenes. As such, visualized rehearsals are often stepping-stones to transferring skills rehearsed in action role-plays into live situations. After action role-plays you imagine yourself actually coping with an interview, talking to your parents about your vocational choices or asking someone out on the telephone. You can also imagine yourself using appropriate calming and coaching self-talk. In training groups, visualized rehearsal is a common form of homework task.

A fifth method of behaviour rehearsal is *action role-play with accompanying self-talk*. In a mixed action and thinking skills behaviour rehearsal, leaders may ask participants to rehearse and verbalize relevant thinking before proceeding with action role-plays. For example, before Andy role-plays asking a female classmate to have a coffee with him, the leader rehearses Andy in calming and coaching self-talk. Unknown to Andy, during the role-play, the confederate has been asked to indicate mild surprise as well as pleasure at being asked. When this happens, the leader calls for a pause in the role-play and asks Andy to verbalize appropriate self-talk. The role-play ends with Andy succeeding in getting his coffee date. Then the leader asks Aaron to verbalize appropriate self-talk that acknowledges that he has attained his goal. The leader may also rehearse Andy in a scene where his coffee date request is politely turned down and then ask him to verbalize coping self-talk.

Stage-manage role-plays

Role-plays may be performed in front of whole groups, or groups may be subdivided, for instance into triads of working participants, confederates and coaches. This section assumes that the leader 'stage-manages' or 'directs' the role-play with the whole group present. Some leader skills for role-plays are preparing participants, selecting scenes and situations, directing, and processing.

PREPARE PARTICIPANTS

The following skills are relevant to preparing participants to take part in role-plays.

- *Provide a rationale.* When using role-plays for the first time in training groups it is advisable to tell participants how this method may help them to attain personal goals. Here is a rationale for the use of behaviour rehearsal role-plays in a university making-contact skills group.

> 'You have just had a presentation and seen a demonstration of skills that you might use in asking someone for a date. Also, you have seen me coaching Andy as he asked a classmate out for a coffee. Many of you have said that you don't act in these situations as well as you want. Seeing other people enact the skills is okay, but you are unlikely to change your behaviour unless you rehearse and practise using the skills. This group can provide a sheltered environment for you to take risks and try out new behaviours before you have to do it for real. I realize that this may feel awkward at first, but there is no substitute for learning by doing. Also, all of you are in the same boat. How do you feel about doing some role-plays like the one I did with Andy?'

The above rationale attempts to enlist motivation and overcome resistances to role-playing in a number of ways, including: showing enough respect for participants to explain why you want them to role-play; helping participants to see the relevance of role-play to attaining personal goals; showing them you understand feelings of discomfort; letting them know that everybody is in the same boat; and allowing them to air reservations.

- *Ensure that participants know targeted behaviours.* If your goals were clear for your presentation and demonstration, most participants should have a good idea of what is expected of them when their turn comes to role-play. Also, if you have coached one of the participants in front of the group, this further demonstration and your coaching comments should reinforce how to behave. Nevertheless, you may still need to keep reminding participants of what are the main learning points in their role-plays. One way to do this is to ask each participant, prior to playing the lead in a role-play, to summarize what is wanted. You may confuse participants if you have more than two or three learning points for any role-play.

- *Warm participants up.* In psychodrama, leaders commonly use warm-up techniques to induce spontaneity prior to enacting dramas (Moreno, 1959). Training group role-plays are briefer, more focused on developing specific skills and less emotionally charged than psychodrama enactments. Neverthe-less, some writers recommend using warm-up exercises prior to role-plays (for example, Goldfried & Davison, 1976; Wilkinson & Canter, 1982). Warm-up exercises in these circumstances should always be brief. Physical movement exercises are sometimes used to loosen participants up. Examples of physical movement exercises are: running on the spot, flapping your arms like birds' wings; holding your hands together with fingers down; or keeping your legs together and hopping round the room like a kangaroo. Warm-up exercises can be related to later role-plays and possibly defuse some anxiety attached to them. For instance, in a dating skills group, participants can pair off as Romeo and Juliet and each be instructed to take turns at asking for a date in the most lovesick way imaginable. A major risk of such exercises is that they may be perceived as false rather than amusing. Consequently, I only raise the possibility of using warm-up exercises prior to behaviour rehearsal role-plays. You must exercise your judgement about their use.

SELECT SCENES AND SITUATIONS

The following are three possibilities for selecting scenes for role-plays. First, leaders can take participants through *prepared scripts*. Earlier it was mentioned that prepared scripts had advantages in initially coaching participants to perform skills. With prepared scripts leaders can ensure relevance and also that learning points are highlighted. However, prepared scripts may lack the flexibility required in real life.

Second, leaders can use *prepared scenarios* and possibly also role descriptions, but leave participants to improvise dialogue. Prepared scenarios are more flexible than prepared scripts, yet leaders can still ensure relevance. As with prepared scripts, prepared scenarios allow leaders to introduce less complex and less anxiety-evoking rehearsals prior to more awkward ones. Below is an example of a prepared scenario which 'sets the scene' in a university making-contact skills group.

> You sit on your own at a table in the student cafeteria when a male/female in one of your classes whom you find attractive asks if he/she can sit at your table.

A behaviour rehearsal for this scenario might be broken down into four distinct sections: how to introduce yourself, how to converse, how to discriminate cues of interest, and how to request further contact. For each section, either verbally or by giving the actors written role descriptions, leaders can instruct participants how to behave.

Third, leaders can work with *problem situations* that participants bring into groups. If anything, there is a development in training groups from role-plays in which leaders prepare much content in advance to more spontaneous role-plays. Especially as groups develop, behaviour rehearsal role-plays focus on how best to handle problem situations in participants' outside lives. A major advantage of such role-plays is that they help participants to integrate targeted skills into their daily routines. In some groups, participants are asked to keep diaries in which they record problem situations to discuss in the group. Training group leaders must act as gatekeepers regarding the relevance of, complexity of, and amount of time spent on problem situation role-plays. For example, it is generally better to work with situations that have relevance for a number of participants rather than for only one. Also, if possible, work with simple and less anxiety-evoking situations before moving to more difficult ones.

DIRECT

Here, if anything, the focus is on how training group leaders go about directing behaviour rehearsal role-plays for problem situations outside the group. Such role-plays owe much to Moreno's psychodrama approach (Blatner, 1989; Greenberg, 1975; Moreno, 1934, 1959). The following parts are played in role-plays.

- *The director.* The director is usually the group leader who stage-manages the role-play and ensures that it is used as a relevant learning experience.

- *The working participant.* The working participant or protagonist is the person who either volunteers or is selected to role-play a problem situation.

- *The cast.* The cast or *alter egos* are other participants who play roles in the situation described by the working participant. For instance, they may play boss, spouse, brothers and sisters or even the family dog.

- *The audience.* The audience are all those members of the lifeskills training group not in the role-play.

- *The candid camera.* The candid camera is an optional extra that makes it possible to show videotaped feedback of role-plays.

Training group leaders require director skills in the following, albeit sometimes overlapping, elements of role-plays:

- *Select working participants.* If leaders leave it for volunteers to emerge from groups, some people may never volunteer. Training groups require a norm that all participants act in role-plays. Within this framework, the following are options for selecting working participants. Leaders may do role-plays in early sessions with volunteers, but ensure that later everybody has their turn. Alternatively, leaders can ask the group to share problems and then pick a participant with an appropriate problem to illustrate the session's learning points. Where possible, leaders choose problems that have relevance to most participants. Another approach is to work with participants who seem either stronger or weaker in the targeted skills: stronger participants as models for their peers, weaker participants to help them catch up. Still another approach is to work with participants who have pressing concerns. Throughout this selection process, leaders require facilitative skills to deal with anxieties and resistances about role-playing.

- *Set the scene.* Once working participants have been selected, leaders then work with them to set the scene. Leaders elicit information about the physical setting of proposed scenes, what other characters are involved and how they behave. This information lays the basis for, within reason, altering the furniture in the room to establish a 'stage' of, for instance, a family living room or a boss's office. In addition, leaders assemble the cast either from volunteers or by request.

- *Assess current behaviours.* Usually the extra time spent conducting assessment role-plays in which working participants demonstrate how they currently behave in problem situations is time well spent. Assessment role-plays can include reviewing participants' thoughts as well as actions. Training group leader, working participant, cast and audience can each assess the working participant's skills strengths and weaknesses. Also, assessment role-plays give the cast more information for understanding their parts in role-plays.

- *Formulate changed behaviours.* Leaders assist working participants to formulate changed behaviours. For example, leaders may ask: 'How would you like to behave differently in the situation to the way you did?' or 'What are your goals in the situation and what skills would better enable you to attain them?' Leaders attempt to facilitate self-assessment prior to making suggestions. Together, leaders and participants formulate changed ways of behaving that use targeted lifeskills and yet feel 'comfortable'. Leaders try to integrate the targeted skills into participants' existing interpersonal styles rather than impose something alien to them. In addition, leaders and working participants may identify self-oppressing patterns of thinking and reformulate them into self-supporting thoughts. Leaders use many coaching skills, including demonstration, during this formulating changed behaviours process.

- *Try out and rehearse changed behaviours.* Once working participants are reasonably clear about their new roles, trial enactments or rehearsals take place. Care should be taken not to try too much or anything too difficult too soon. Leaders may allow role-plays to run their course. Alternatively, leaders may intervene at one or more points along the way, both to check thinking processes and to coach. For the most part, this coaching focuses on how best to implement the specific behaviours targeted in the group session. In addition, leaders may coach members of the cast in their roles. Video feedback may be used as part of coaching both during and after role-plays.

Behaviour rehearsal role-plays are dry runs of how to behave in specific situations. A number of rehearsals may be needed to shape and strengthen a working participant's skills. Some of these rehearsals may involve the cast behaving in different ways. For example, a working participant asking for a pay rise might get it easily in one rehearsal, have to struggle to overcome a boss's reservations in a second rehearsal, and be refused in a third rehearsal.

Role reversal, mirroring and the double technique are three psychodrama techniques that leaders may use (Blatner, 1989; Moreno, 1959). In role reversal, leaders get working participants to play the other person in interactions. The role reversal technique, which forces participants some way into others' frames of reference, is particularly useful for skills like negotiation and managing conflict. In mirroring, another participant is instructed to represent the verbal, voice and body messages of the working participant. Working participants see themselves 'as in a mirror' as others experience them. In the double technique, another participant is placed either behind or beside the working participant as a double of himself or herself. The role of doubles is to verbalize what working participants may really think and feel but not say.

PROCESS

Processing role-plays can be important learning experiences for both working participants and groups. Processing involves spending time dealing with emotions and thoughts generated by role-plays, discussing lessons learned from them, facilitating feedback and making plans to transfer rehearsed skills outside. Generally, leaders process the feelings and reactions of the working participant first, the cast second, and the audience last.

Leaders can ask working participants processing questions like: 'How were you feeling in that role-play?', 'How do you think that rehearsal went?', 'What have you learned from that role-play that you can apply outside?' and 'What difficulties do you anticipate in implementing your changed behaviour and how can you overcome them?' Processing questions for the group include: 'Does anybody have anything they would like to feed back to . . . (state working participant's name)?' and 'What have you learned from that role-play that is useful for you?' After processing the previous rehearsal, group leaders may move on to the next rehearsal either with the same or another working participant.

Exercise 24 gives you practice at stage-managing behaviour rehearsal role-plays. Also, the exercise highlights some of the issues entailed in incorporating role-plays into training groups.

Exercise 24 Rehearse behaviour by means of role-play

This exercise should be performed either in a group of about five to eight persons or, failing that, with at least two others.

1. Discuss the advantages and disadvantages of leaders incorporating each of the following methods of behaviour rehearsal into lifeskills training groups:
   - live rehearsal
   - action role-plays
   - mental rehearsal
   - visualized rehearsal
   - action role-plays with accompanying self-talk

2. In a specific lifeskill area of your choice, implement a behaviour rehearsal role-play for a problem situation presented by a working participant. Go through each of the following steps.
   - Prepare participants:
   (a) provide a rationale
   (b) ensure that participants know the targeted behaviours
   (c) warm participants up (optional)
   - Direct the role-play:
   (a) select working participant
   (b) select role-play situation
   (c) set the scene
   (d) assess current behaviours
   (e) formulate changed behaviours
   (f) try out and rehearse changed behaviours
   - Process the role-play:
   (a) with working participant
   (b) with cast
   (c) with audience

Each person in the group should have the opportunity to be both the director and the working participant. At the end of the exercise discuss and process what you have learned for leading lifeskills training groups.

PROVIDE AND ENCOURAGE CONSTRUCTIVE FEEDBACK

'How did I do?' and 'How am I doing?' are questions that most learners ask of themselves and others. Participants require knowledge of the results and consequences of their attempts to develop specific lifeskills. Feedback can let them know if they are on the right track or whether and in what ways they need to alter behaviour. Coaching by leaders involves feedback. However, leaders are not alone in providing feedback. Furthermore, there are many considerations concerning how leaders best go about providing feedback and helping others to provide feedback. Feedback can retard as well as enhance skills development.

Sources of feedback

Effective lifeskills group leaders manage feedback to participants rather than always provide feedback themselves. The following are some of the sources of feedback available to participants and to group leaders. First, there is *self-feedback*. Throughout lifeskills groups, leaders should encourage participants to develop the skills of giving themselves feedback. Leaders should assist participants to develop self-help skills of looking not only at how they behave, but also at their behaviour's consequences for self and others.

Second, there is *leader feedback*. Leader feedback is essential because of their special knowledge of skills targeted by groups. A third source is *feedback from other participants*. Providing feedback can be a valuable learning process for both givers and receivers. Working participants can gain useful information about how their behaviour is perceived. Participants giving feedback are forced to discriminate between what constitutes effective behaviour in targeted skills. Fourth, *audiovisual feedback* can be used when assessing existing skills and developing new skills. The candid camera is especially useful for helping participants to observe their body messages.

A fifth source is *feedback from outside group aides*. Training group leaders can enlist the assistance of others. For example, in conjunction with a making-friends group for primary school children, leaders can train teachers and parents in how to provide support and constructive feedback. Sixth, participants may receive *feedback from third parties*. Participants inevitably receive much feedback from people with whom they daily interact. Sometimes leaders actively encourage participants to seek such feedback. For example, in shyness or assertion groups, participants speaking with quiet voices can be asked to check how friends and relatives perceive their speech. Seventh, participants may receive *feedback from computers*. As part of some training groups, for instance career exploration groups, computers analyse data given by participants and provide feedback.

Dimensions of feedback

As managers of feedback, lifeskills group leaders need to bear the following feedback dimensions in mind (Egan, 1990; Gazda, 1989; Hopson & Scally, 1981; National Training Laboratory, 1967; Osipow *et al.*, 1984). Some of these feedback dimensions are located in the receiver, some in the sender and some in the process of giving feedback.

SELF OR EXTERNAL FEEDBACK

Mention has already been made of the importance of leaders encouraging participants to assess not only their behaviours, but also the consequences of their behaviours. As a guideline, after each structured activity, working participants should be the first to comment on what they have learnt and their reactions. In addition, after other participants and the leader have given feedback, working participants should be given the further opportunity to comment on how they perceive the feedback.

AUDIOVISUAL FEEDBACK

Audiocassette feedback is especially helpful when groups focus on verbal and voice messages. Videotape feedback is especially useful when leaders focus on body messages. Audiovisual feedback lends itself to self-assessment by participants. Audiovisual feedback provides facts rather than perceptions and inferences. Playing and discussing audiovisual feedback of role-plays can provide valuable learning for everyone.

Audiovisual feedback also has potential disadvantages. Training group leaders may get distracted by the technology of making video-recordings. Furthermore, leaders require access to suitable equipment. Leaders may slow the learning process down by giving too much recorded feedback. Other participants may find this feedback boring. In addition, some participants may feel threatened by having to perform in front of audiocassette recorders or video cameras.

BEHAVIOURAL OR EMOTIONAL FEEDBACK

A distinction exists between behavioural feedback, 'how you behave', and emotional feedback, 'I feel such and such about you or the way you have behaved' (Bloch & Crouch, 1985). Psychotherapy groups and experiential encounter groups contain much emotional feedback. In lifeskills training groups, behavioural feedback is emphasized. Not only should leaders both give and encourage behavioural feedback; they should also limit the amount of emotional feedback. Where possible, emotional feedback should be preceded by behavioural feedback, 'when your behaviour contains the following element(s), I feel such and such'.

SPECIFIC OR NON-SPECIFIC FEEDBACK

Imagine a behaviour rehearsal on how to ask someone for a date. Afterwards the leader says to the working participant: 'I don't think you did that very well' and leaves it at that. The leader did not provide specific feedback on how to improve, but instead gave negative feedback leading nowhere. Even worse would have been leader feedback that negatively rated the participant's personhood: for example, 'I don't think you did that very well. It illustrates how weak you are'. Feedback should always be specific and concentrate on targeted behaviours. After a dating skills role-play, an example of specific feedback to the working participant, Lewis, would be: 'Lewis, when you asked Rachel for a date, I thought you did not make much eye contact with her and you spoke in a very quiet voice.' If the behaviour rehearsal had been videotaped, the leader could say to the working participant: 'During the playback, I want you to notice how well you made eye contact with Rachel and how loudly you spoke to her.' Here, the leader cues the participant on what specifically to look for during the video feedback. When giving specific feedback, try not to cover more than two or three points at any one time. Recipients suffer from and get confused by feedback overload.

CONFIRMATORY, CORRECTIVE, AND MOTIVATING FEEDBACK

Feedback can be confirmatory, corrective and motivating (Egan, 1990, Gilbert, 1978). Confirmatory feedback lets participants know which specific behaviours they develop along the right lines. Corrective feedback lets participants know which specific behaviours require altering and in what ways. Much feedback is both confirmatory and corrective: for example, 'Lewis, when you asked Rachel for a date you made good eye contact (confirmatory feedback). However, I thought you spoke in too quiet a voice (corrective feedback).' Motivating feedback points out the consequences of good and poor use of skills and includes suggestions for improving performance: 'Lewis, the consequence of your speaking in a quiet voice was that you seemed diffident about wanting to be with Rachel; if you spoke louder, she might take more notice (motivating feedback)'.

Related to the dimensions of confirmatory, corrective and motivating feedback are the dimensions of constructive or destructive feedback and of positive or negative feedback. Confirmatory feedback, so long as it is accurate, is likely to be both positive and constructive. However, corrective and even motivating feedback may be given in ways that are unnecessarily negative and destructive. A number of ways exist whereby leaders can detoxify feedback. First, leaders can work to establish trusting emotional climates in groups. The timing and strength of their feedback reflect the degree of trust. Second, leaders can always give participants the opportunity to share their reactions to corrective and motivating feedback. Third, where possible, confirmatory or positive feedback can precede corrective feedback. Fourth, as far as possible, corrective feedback can be stated in the positive. An example of corrective feedback stated in the negative is: 'Lewis, your voice was too quiet when you asked Rachel for a date.' A more positive statement of the same corrective feedback might be: 'Lewis, I think your voice should be louder when you ask Rachel for a date.' Here corrective feedback takes on a characteristic of motivating feedback in that it suggests how to improve performance. Giving feedback in groups requires tact, not least since it is usually both given and received in public.

'I' MESSAGE OR 'YOU' MESSAGE FEEDBACK

Another way of detoxifying corrective and motivating feedback is to use 'I' messages rather than 'You' messages. Givers of feedback should always take responsibility and locate its source clearly in themselves. Locating the source of feedback in senders reduces the chance of it being received defensively. For example, the message: 'Lewis, I think your voice should be louder when you ask Rachel for a date' is gentler and a more open invitation for discussion than: 'Lewis, your voice should be louder when you ask Rachel for a date.' The sender acknowledges that feedback reflects his or her perception. A further point is that 'I' message feedback should always be given directly to the individual for whom it is intended.

VERBAL OR DEMONSTRATED FEEDBACK

Feedback may be given largely by means of words. However, feedback may often be communicated even more clearly and received even more accurately if verbal description is accompanied by demonstration: for instance, by videotapes or audiocassettes. Feedback can also be demonstrated without audiovisual aids. For instance, in the previous example either the leader or another participant could mirror Lewis's voice messages when asking Rachel for a date. In addition, they could show Lewis more appropriate behaviours.

FEEDBACK OR CONFRONTATION

How can feedback be distinguished from confrontation? Much feedback is either in line with or reasonably close to participants' existing perceptions. Such feedback does not provide any major challenge or threat to their self-pictures. Confrontation is a category of feedback where participants' self-pictures are challenged. In training groups, confrontations may focus either on inconsistencies, for instance between words and actions, on distortions of reality, for instance selecting out inconvenient feedback, or on not owning responsibility for the consequences of one's behaviour. How, as well as what, leaders confront is important. Given the right trusting atmosphere, constructive confrontations have their place in groups. However, where possible help speakers to confront themselves: for example, by asking them to search for evidence to back their statements. Also, use a minimum amount of 'muscle'. Although sometimes necessary, strong confrontations are generally to be avoided. Strong confrontations can create resistances. Also, always be mindful of the effects of confronting on observing participants.

FEEDBACK OR REWARD

As well as specific feedback concerning how participants perform behaviours, leaders may provide social rewards or reinforcers. Leader praise and encouragement are important sources of reward. Leaders can use reward to encourage desired group rules: for example, by saying 'good' or 'well done' when participants volunteer for behaviour rehearsals. In addition, leaders can use reward when participants achieve targeted behaviours either inside or outside of groups. Rewards can be non-verbal as well as verbal. Applause, head nods, smiles and pats on the back are all examples of non-verbal rewards. In addition, forms of reward like money, soft drinks, candy, and exchangeable tokens are used in lifeskills training groups. Such rewards should be appropriate to the participants in question. Also, leaders need to beware of participants only performing targeted behaviours under conditions of external reward rather than self-reward.

Feedback needs to take into account the social and cultural milieu of participants. Leaders coming from different backgrounds to some or all of their participants require sensitivity to these differences. Leaders may require awareness of differing rules governing feedback in other cultures and social groupings. Participants can be encouraged to relate how feedback is handled in their own cultures.

FEEDBACK TRAINING

Since much feedback in groups takes place between participants, leaders may train participants in the basic skills of constructive feedback. Feedback skills include: sending 'I' messages, commenting on specific behaviours, and allowing receivers to react to feedback. Feedback training can be by brief instruction, initial and ongoing demonstrations, commenting on participants' feedback, and encouraging participants to comment on the feedback that they receive.

USE EXERCISES

Lifeskills training groups tend to contain many structured exercises. Most exercises are specifically designed to help participants to develop targeted skills. Especially when working with children, leaders may choose to use exercises involving play. Whether designed for children or adults, exercises involving play are called games.

Exercises and games can be used in initial, working and ending stages of groups. In Chapter 6, many breaking-the-ice exercises were mentioned for use in initial sessions of lifeskills groups. Such breaking-the-ice exercises set emotional climates for skills learning rather than develop specific targeted skills. Warm-up exercises used during the working stage of a group perform a similar function. Most exercises during the working stage of lifeskills groups focus on developing targeted skills. For example, leaders using skills manuals get participants to perform relevant exercises as they work through the manual.

Kinds of exercises

Exercises may focus on developing action skills, thinking skills and action skills plus self-talk. The following are six different kinds of structured activity that fall into the broad category of exercises:

- *Action exercises.* Action exercises involve physical movement; for example, role-playing. Lifeskills training groups lay heavy emphasis on action exercises.

- *Written exercises.* Though the instructions for most exercises are written, written exercises require participants to write out their answers. Written exercises are often used for self-monitoring and assessment and to develop thinking skills.

- *Discussion exercises.* Discussion exercises require the group to discuss specific topics: for example, in a group for dual-career couples, discussing sex-roles for males and females.

- *Task exercises.* Task exercises require the group to achieve or plan to achieve specific tasks.

- *Feedback exercises.* Feedback exercises enable participants to receive comments or audiovisual feedback on how they are performing in the targeted skills areas.

- *Games.* Games are structured exercises involving play.

Design considerations

There are two main sources of exercises and games; either using other people's or making up your own. For this book I made up my own exercises. Using the relationship skills area as an example, existing sources of exercises include those in Egan (1977), Johnson (1986), Nelson-Jones (1990) and Pfeiffer and Jones (1969–1985).

Other people's material may not be entirely appropriate for all or part of your training group. If so, you may need to construct some exercises. You are encouraged not only to use existing material, but also to tap your creativity and design some exercises for any training group that you run. The following are considerations in designing exercises and games.

- *Set clear, specific and relevant goals.* Participants should know the targeted skills that they are expected to work on by means of the exercise. Where possible, these skills should already have been presented and demonstrated.

- *Emphasize take-away skills.* Training groups are about developing skills for daily living. Vague exercises unrelated to the development of specific take-away skills are to be avoided. Many trainee lifeskills leaders have difficulty putting sufficient practical emphasis into their exercises.

- *Make written instructions available.* If instructions for the exercise are only given verbally, there is a greater chance of slippage between instructions and performance of the exercise than if the instructions are also written down.

- *Demonstrate the exercise.* As well as written instructions, the leader often needs to demonstrate the exercise to ensure that participants know precisely what is expected. Since exercises are frequently performed in sub-groups, leaders cannot always be present to correct misunderstandings.

- *Build in participation.* When designing exercises for training groups, try to build in roles for most, if not all, participants. If necessary, break the group down into sub-groups.

- *Coach and provide feedback.* Pay attention to how participants obtain coaching and feedback on how they perform the exercise.

- *Process the experience*. Participants should be given the opportunity to process with the group leader their experiences and what they have learned from the exercise.

- *Pilot the exercise*. If possible, pilot your exercise to see if it works. If necessary, refine the exercise or even discard it and try again.

Exercise 25 is intended to help you become less dependent on others' exercises, by giving you the opportunity to design one of your own.

Exercise 25 Design an exercise or game

This exercise can be done on your own, in pairs or in a small group. Pick a specific skill in a lifeskills training area of your choice that you wish to impart through learning by doing. If possible, familiarize yourself with the existing exercises and games in the area. Design and write out a hand-out for an exercise or game that helps a group of six to eight participants achieve your learning objectives. Take the following considerations into account as you design your exercise:

- Set clear, specific and relevant goals.

- Emphasize take-away skills.

- Make written instructions available.

- Demonstrate the exercise.

- Build in participation.

- Coach and provide feedback.

- Process the experience.

- Pilot the exercise.

DESIGN BEHAVIOUR CHANGE EXPERIMENTS

A major concern for all effective leaders is how best to help participants to transfer learned skills to outside groups. Behaviour change experiments provide an excellent way to do this. Participants in conjunction with their leaders develop hypotheses about the consequences of using learned skills outside of groups. Participants then implement their changed behaviours and evaluate their consequences. Whereas exercises can be done either inside or outside of groups, experiments always provide a direct bridge to developing outside skills. Most training group leaders set homework. Participants are asked to perform exercises and other tasks between sessions. Often, participants are given a general instruction to try using their new skills outside the group and monitor how they get on. Behaviour change experiments provide a way of tightening up this general instruction into a more specific instruction.

Steps in behaviour change experiments

Experiments focus on the use of targeted skills in specific situations. There are six main steps in designing, conducting and evaluating behaviour change experiments:

1. *Assess.* Existing behaviours in the problem situation are identified and assessed with special reference to targeted skills.
2. *Formulate changed behaviours.* Participants and leader work out how to behave differently in the situation using targeted skills.
3. *Make an 'If . . . then . . .' statement.* The 'If . . .' part of the statement relates to rehearsing, practising and then using your specified changed behaviours. The 'then' part of the statement indicates the specific consequences that you predict will follow from the changes in your behaviour.
4. *Rehearse and practise.* Participants need to rehearse and practise their changed behaviours to give themselves a reasonable chance of implementing them properly.
5. *Try out changed behaviours.* Participants try out their changed behaviours in actual problem situations.
6. *Evaluate.* Initially, participants should evaluate their changed behaviours on their own. This evaluation should focus on such questions as 'How well did I perform the changed behaviours?', 'What were the positive and negative consequences for using the targeted skills for myself and for others?' 'Have my predictions been confirmed or disconfirmed?', and 'Do I want to use my changed behaviours, either without or with modification, in future?' Later on leaders can help participants to process in the group what they have learnt from their experiments.

Below is an example of a behaviour change experiment taken from Nelson-Jones (1990, pp. 165–166).

What happens when I am more open about sharing my feelings in a relationship?

1. EXPRESSING POSITIVE FEELINGS

PART A: ASSESSMENT

1. Think of a relationship that you think you could improve if you shared more of your positive feelings towards the other person.

---

2. For an appropriate period, say three days, monitor how you send positive and negative messages to the other person.

_____

_____

_____

3. List all the positive feelings that are left unspoken in your relationship.

_____

_____

PART B: MAKE AN 'IF . . . THEN . . .' STATEMENT
Make an 'If . . . then . . .' statement along the lines of 'If I express these positive feelings (specify), then these consequences (specify) are likely to follow'.

_____

_____

PART C: TRY OUT AND EVALUATE YOUR CHANGED BEHAVIOUR
Try out your changed behaviour. Assess its positive and negative consequences for yourself and the other person. Have your predictions been confirmed or disconfirmed? Has this experiment taught you something about the power of expressing positive feelings rather than leaving them unsaid? If so, what?

_____

_____

_____

2. EXPRESSING NEGATIVE FEELINGS
If appropriate, carry out the above experiment, but this time focus on expressing a negative rather than a positive feeling. Follow the guidelines for expressing feelings about another person.

_____

_____

_____

Exercise 26 encourages you to find out about the use of behaviour change experiments in training groups by conducting an experiment on yourself. You are then asked to act as group leader and help another person to design an experiment to change their behaviour.

Exercise 26 Design, conduct and evaluate behaviour change experiments

Part A
Select a specific lifeskill on which you wish to work. Conduct and write up an experiment in which you change your behaviour. Make sure to adequately cover each of the following six steps:

1. Assess.

2. Formulate changed behaviours.
3. Make an 'If . . . then . . .' statement.
4. Rehearse and practise.
5. Try out changed behaviours.
6. Evaluate.

Part B

This part of the exercise should be done in pairs. Partner A acts as training group leader and helps partner B, the participant, to design and rehearse a behaviour change experiment for a particular lifeskill. Together the partners go through steps 1–4 of the six steps for behaviour change experiments. After discussing what they have done together, partners reverse roles.

EMPHASIZE HOMEWORK

Training group leaders plan for participants to perform structured activities between sessions. Such homework activities include: self-monitoring, behaviour rehearsals, exercises, experiments and more general practice of targeted skills. There are two main reasons why leaders set homework. First, homework can speed up the learning process. Second, homework helps to transfer learned skills to outside life. In their initial programme presentations, leaders can let participants know why they attach great importance to participants completing homework tasks. Some leaders make a commitment to completing all homework tasks a clause in formal group contracts.

Participants are more likely to complete homework tasks if the following conditions apply. First, the task *requirements are clear*. To avoid misunderstandings, participants should receive hand-outs of homework assignments and of any worksheets that they are expected to complete. Second, the homework *tasks are relevant*. The tasks are not only seen by leaders as relevant but also perceived by participants as relevant. Third, the homework tasks *consolidate earlier learning*. The homework builds on what has been learnt earlier by hearing, observing and doing within the previous session or sessions. Fourth, the homework tasks are of an *appropriate difficulty level*. The tasks take into account participants' levels of readiness. Where appropriate, graded steps are used. Fifth, a *realistic amount* of homework is set. Leaders can work out with participants what is a realistic amount of between-session homework. Sixth, leaders conduct *progress reviews*. At the start of the next session, leaders review how participants have fared in their homework. Such reviews have numerous functions: reward, feedback, coaching, support, targeting difficulties, and collecting information with which to plan future sessions. Seventh leaders encourage *constructive group norms* regarding homework. Such norms include: the expectation that all participants do all of the homework, open discussion of successes and failures, and encouraging effort rather than ridiculing mistakes.

Numerous reasons exist why participants fail to do homework. For instance, in a school or college setting, an ungraded lifeskills group may have to compete for homework time with graded academic subjects. Sometimes participants attend training groups compulsorily rather than voluntarily. Also, homework may entail risks in trying new behaviours outside of the group. As a group leader, you have to acknowledge and deal with any such difficulties and resistances as best you can.

CHAPTER HIGHLIGHTS

Learning by doing is essential to lifeskills training groups. Leaders structure activities to help participants to develop targeted skills.

Structured activities include: self-monitoring forms, coached performance, behaviour rehearsal, role-play, feedback, exercises, games, task assignments, critical incidents, case studies, computer-assisted learning, behaviour change plans, behaviour change experiments and homework.

Training group leaders require good skills at facilitating structured activities. Such facilitation skills include: creating a safe and trusting emotional climate, allowing performance fears to be aired and explored, helping participants to process significant experiences and facilitating peer feedback.

After the initial presentation and demonstration of any skill, leaders coach participants through a performance of it. Coaching skills include: facilitate self-coaching, provide clear instructions, break tasks down, use graded steps, demonstrate, and check participants' understanding of the skill.

Behaviour rehearsals may take place either immediately after the initial coached performance of a skill or as participants bring problem situations from their lives into the group.

Methods of behaviour rehearsal include: live, action role-play, mental, visualized, and action role-play with accompanying self-talk.

Leader skills for action role-plays include: prepare participants, select scenes and situations, direct and process.

Preparing participants' skills include: provide a rationale, ensure that participants know the targeted behaviours, and warm up participants.

Role-plays may be based on prepared scripts, prepared scenarios, or on problem situations in participants' lives.

Directing role-play skills includes: select working participants, set the scene, assess current behaviours, formulate changed behaviours, and try out and rehearse changed behaviours.

Processing entails: facilitate participants dealing with thoughts and feelings generated by role-plays, discuss learning, give and receive feedback, and make plans to transfer rehearsed skills outside of the group.

Training group leaders are managers of feedback rather than always providing feedback themselves.

Dimensions of feedback include: self or external; audiovisual; behavioural or emotional; specific or non-specific; confirmatory, corrective and motivating; 'I' message or 'You' message; verbal or demonstrated; confrontation; reward; sociocultural considerations; and training in feedback skills.

Training group leaders may either use other people's or make up their own exercises.

Considerations in designing exercises include: set clear, specific and relevant goals; emphasize take-away skills; make written instructions available; demonstrate the exercise; build in participation; coach and provide feedback; process the experience; and pilot the exercise.

Behaviour change experiments are an excellent way of helping participants to transfer targeted skills into their daily lives.

Behaviour change experiments contain six steps: (1) assess; (2) formulate changed behaviours; (3) make an 'If . . . then . . .' statement; (4) rehearse and practise; (5) try out changed behaviours in real life; and (6) evaluate.

Training group leaders should emphasize the importance of participants completing structured homework activities between sessions. Leaders must take care to design and introduce homework tasks so that participants are motivated to do them.

TEN
How to Prepare and Lead Sessions

A teacher should have maximal authority and minimal power.

T.S. Szasz

CHAPTER QUESTIONS

What are leader skills for preparing individual sessions?

How might leaders outline sessions?

What are leader skills for managing the initial, working and ending stages of sessions?

What are ways of evaluating individual sessions?

INTRODUCTION

Lifeskills training sessions are microcosms of overall groups. Each session has its preparatory, initial, working and ending stages. Training group leaders are managers of learning. For any given session, the leader's function is to design and implement learning experiences to help the group attain targeted skills. The leader may perform numerous roles: energizer, facilitator, support, public speaker, information giver, demonstrator, coach, role-play director, disciplinarian, timekeeper, assessor, technician, and resource person, among others. Throughout any session, there will always be tension, as well as sometimes harmony, between the leader's didactic and facilitative roles. There is no such thing as the perfect group session. Leaders are constantly making choices between conflicting demands regarding both content and process.

THE PREPARATORY STAGE

Training group leaders who do not thoroughly prepare sessions risk performing poorly in them. Leaders cannot just arrive and rely on their charm, facilitative skills and the group's contribution. Lifeskills training sessions require careful planning and preparation.

Plan sessions

Effective leaders arrive at training group sessions with well-thought-through session or 'game' plans. Such leaders acknowledge that numerous things can go wrong in lifeskills sessions. They try to anticipate problems. The purpose of a session plan is to clarify objectives and to arrange a series of learning experiences to attain them. In this context, a session includes the period of time up to the start of the next session. If working with a co-leader, always try to plan sessions together. Below are some important considerations in planning sessions.

STATE CLEAR, RELEVANT AND MANAGEABLE GOALS

Leaders need to be crystal-clear about specific goals for each session. Vague goals lead to vague session plans. Irrelevant goals waste everyone's time. Goals that are not manageable lead to frustration on the part of both leaders and participants. Often, beginning leaders try to cover too much ground. As a consequence, they may either do a little well and then find that they have insufficient time for the remainder of their material or they may do everything superficially. A good guideline when planning sessions is that a little done thoroughly is much preferable to much done superficially. Quality is preferable to quantity.

ATTEND TO SEQUENCING OF CONTENT ACROSS SESSIONS

Different design objectives and considerations are required for a group's beginning, middle and ending sessions. Sessions are not isolated events. Each session should be designed in relation to what comes before and after. Much of the sequencing of session content comes from the overall or 'master' plan of the lifeskills training group. This overall plan is the programme plan as contrasted with the session plan. Programme plans are designed before the first session, though they may be revised during a group's life. Most often, programme plans contain outlines of individual session plans. An assumption in making programme plans is that learning takes place in an orderly and cumulative sequence. Leaders need to consider carefully the implications of any large deviations from what was outlined for each session in their programme plans.

START FROM WHERE PARTICIPANTS ARE

In planning sessions, leaders may have to deviate from original programme plans in response to the starting points and rates of learning of the group. Furthermore, if there clearly are fast and slow learners in a group, leaders may design their sessions to take these differences into account for instance, either by giving slow learners a chance to learn from fast learners or by grouping slow and fast learners separately for some activities. Leaders should always tailor the language, teaching materials and activities they use to a group's learning level.

CONSULT WITH PARTICIPANTS

At one extreme, training group leaders can be authoritarian and make all decisions about session agendas and processes themselves. At the other extreme, leaders can be, when making decisions, oversolicitous of the wishes of the group and thus abrogate much of their leadership function. Effective leaders are neither tyrants nor wimps. They have clear learning objectives for the group, but nevertheless are willing to consult with participants about both content and process. An added bonus from consulting is that participants may work harder if they have voices in making decisions (Johnson & Johnson, 1987). The group becomes theirs as well as their leader's. Leaders may engage in systematic consultation at the end of sessions to check individuals' perceptions of their progress, their satisfaction with the group, and their ideas about the next session.

EMPHASIZE SELF-REFERENT LEARNING

There is an old saying: 'Nobody loves yourself as much as yourself'. Effective leaders take care to plan sessions so that participants are able to relate content to their own lives. Participants may quickly tune out of sessions either too intellectual or too focused on the needs of others rather than themselves. Participants have personal goals and reasons for being in groups. Though sometimes seemingly ambivalent about their acquisition, participants want specific take-away skills to apply to specific life situations. Leaders who do not build on individuals' healthy interests in improving their lives are likely to elicit boredom, apathy and other resistances.

INVOLVE PARTICIPANTS IN LEARNING PROCESSES

One way of enhancing participants' involvement and motivation for learning is to make session content self-referent. A related way is to get participants involved in the learning process. Effective leaders are skilled at drawing participants into the processes of the group, be they discussions or structured activities. In making session plans, leaders ensure that participants are actively involved in their own learning rather than either being treated as passive objects by 'having stuff thrown at them whether they like it or not' or being infantilized through spoon-feeding.

BALANCE LEARNING BY HEARING, OBSERVING AND DOING

Chapters 7, 8 and 9 have stressed learning by hearing, observing and doing. Leaders need to ensure that all three modes are incorporated into their session plans. Group size permitting, all sessions should have a high 'doing to talking' ratio. Demonstrations should accompany both initial presentations and subsequent learning by doing.

BALANCE FACILITATION WITH DIDACTIC INPUT
When planning sessions, leaders must remember that they are not the sole source of learning in groups. Participants need time to share and discuss reactions to what transpires. Leaders should build in time for discussion and for processing structured activities. Participants rushed through a learning sequence without care for their thoughts and feelings may become resistant. However, too much time spent on discussing and processing can also have negative outcomes: for instance, boredom because the group moves too slowly.

ATTEND TO SEQUENCING AND VARIETY
The distribution of time within a session needs to be such that the main learning points receive most attention. Adequate time should be allowed for each activity. The sequencing of material needs to be logical. For example, presentation and demonstration precede coaching and behaviour rehearsal. Easy or less anxiety-evoking exercises precede more difficult and threatening ones. Variety is another consideration. If learners are passive, the same teaching and learning methods quickly become boring. Sometimes variety can be introduced by breaking learning units down and interspersing presentation and demonstration with rehearsal and practise.

THINK THROUGH HOW TO START
Effective leaders think through how best to start their sessions. The following are some beginning-of-session questions that leaders may pose for themselves: 'How do I link this session with the previous one?' 'How do I let the group know what we are going to do this session?' 'How can I help to create an emotional climate whereby participants are glad to be back in the group?' 'Do I need to help participants to warm up?' 'If homework was set at the end of the last session, how should I go about checking on whether and how it was done?', and 'What do I do about people who missed the last session?' Introducing a session requires careful planning. Participants can sense if you are poorly prepared. Also, you lower your confidence if unable to start a session competently.

THINK THROUGH HOW TO END
Effective leaders do not end sessions in the middle of an activity by looking at their watches and saying: 'Gosh, I'm sorry, I've lost track of the time. We've got to end now.' Ending a session well is a critical part of leading a session well. Leaders can see that the main lessons of the session are summarized either by themselves or group members. Participants can be consulted on how they thought the session went and the agenda for the next session can be discussed. Time needs to be spent to clarify and, possibly, to formulate homework tasks. In short, how you end training sessions requires careful planning.

DESIGN HOMEWORK

Training group leaders should think of each session as including the period prior to the next session. Consequently, plan how participants can best use between-session time to attain their own and the group's goals. Usually, planning a session includes designing relevant homework. Leaders need to ask themselves questions not only about the content of the homework, but also about how best to introduce it. If sufficient time is not set aside for introducing, formulating and clarifying homework, it may be done poorly, if at all.

DECIDE ON BETWEEN-SESSION CONTACT

Apart from contact with a co-leader, between-session contact can be between leader and participants and among participants. Also, leaders may seek between-session contact with third parties. Whether or not leaders encourage between-session contact may influence how they distribute time within a session. For example, leaders available to participants between sessions may consider that they need to spend less time explaining homework than if they were not available. Also, when designing sessions, leaders can consider whether and how much to encourage participants to work with and support each other between sessions. Furthermore, leaders may plan to contact third parties cooperating in the training programme. For instance, leaders may systematically contact teachers helping children to make friends or managers helping supervisors to develop skills. Purposes of such leader contact include monitoring how third parties support participants in their home settings and obtaining feedback on participants' progress.

ANTICIPATE DIFFICULT PARTICIPANTS

Difficult participants can be defined in two ways: participants experiencing difficulties developing the targeted skills and participants whom the leader experiences as difficult. Effective lifeskills group leaders are sensitive to individual differences, rates and styles of learning. Leaders who have observed participants with learning blocks can think in advance whether and how best to approach them. In addition, leaders can prepare strategies for coping with participants who are difficult. For example, if Donald and Fay make a habit of whispering to each other, the leader could go into the next session prepared with some options for handling them appropriately. In addition, if, as is common in schools, disciplinary problems involve many participants, leaders can use the time between sessions to think through what to do and, if necessary, consult colleagues.

PREPARE AUDIOVISUAL MATERIALS AND EQUIPMENT

If leaders are planning to use audiovisual materials, such as videotapes, they need to make sure that the training materials and equipment are available and in good condition. If leaders are going to make their own audiovisual material, this requires even more advance planning. When preparing a session, you have to make sure that even simple aids, like whiteboards and overhead projectors, are available when wanted.

CONSIDER THE AVAILABILITY OF WRITTEN TRAINING MATERIALS

What written material is to be used in conjunction with a session? If the lifeskills group uses a training manual, is this readily available to all participants? Often hand-outs are useful adjuncts to lifeskills training sessions. Hand-outs may contain such items as: session goals, session outlines, main learning points of sessions, homework tasks, and any worksheets required either during sessions or for homework. Participants may either be given or asked to purchase binders for keeping hand-outs. A practical tip is that hand-outs are more likely to end up in binders if they contain pre-punched holes. If participants are being asked to read an article or articles in conjunction with sessions, leaders need to make sure that the articles are available. Also, if participants are referred to library books, leaders should see that they are in the library.

ALLOW FOR FLEXIBILITY

Nothing is absolutely certain in training groups. Each session is different and provides different challenges. All the time leaders make choices concerning what to do, how to do it, what to say, when to be quiet, when to move on, how to divide their attention and so on. In addition, the pace of individual and group learning varies. Different participants have different weaknesses within a skills area and different blocks to developing skills. Also, you cannot predict what pressing problems participants may bring into sessions. Furthermore, if participants feel that you have a stopwatch and are moving them rigidly through your session plan, your rigidity is an invitation for non-cooperation. When designing session plans, leaders need to be conscious of the varying degrees of importance of session items. Thus, if necessary, they know what items to sacrifice.

Make a session outline

Making a session outline is a necessary part of planning a session. A session outline presents the session's structure. Numerous considerations influence the session outline: for instance, targeted skills, group size, and whether it is a training group's beginning, middle or ending session. Below are examples of session outlines for a first and a middle session. The time indicated for each item is a guideline rather than a strait-jacket.

Example 1: First session

The first session of a ten-week two-hour stress management group for 12 adults.

Welcome, outline of session	5 minutes
Warm-up exercise: moving around and introducing self as if at party	10 minutes
Process warm-up exercise	5 minutes
Round: introduce self and say what you want from group	10 minutes

Leader outlines programme	15 minutes
Group discussion of programme and of 'contract'	15 minutes
Lecturette on dimensions of stress	20 minutes
Dyad exercise: participants assess how they experience stress on each dimension	20 minutes
Process exercise in whole group	10 minutes
Summarize; set and discuss homework on self-monitoring and assessment of stress; consult about next session	10 minutes

Example 2: Middle session

The fourth session of an eight-week two-hour session assertion training group for eight college students (four males and four females).

Welcome, brief outline of session	3 minutes
Warm-up in dyads: experiences of assertion and non-assertion in the past week	7 minutes
Process homework	10 minutes
Lecturette/video demonstrations: making assertive requests for behaviour change	20 minutes
In front of group, coached performance, using prepared script and video feedback, of a participant	10 minutes
Triad exercise: role-plays based on prepared scripts	15 minutes
Process exercise in group	5 minutes
Behaviour rehearsal role-plays with video feedback in whole group based on common problem situations	40 minutes
Summarize; discuss, formulate and clarify homework; consult about next session	10 minutes

Formulating a session outline helps leaders to clarify how to approach each session. Leaders still need to prepare material and ensure that needed equipment is available for the different parts of sessions: for instance, for lecturette/demonstrations. Exercise 27 gives you practice at designing session outlines.

Exercise 27 Design session outlines

For a lifeskills training group of your choice:

1. Specify the basic characteristics of the group: for instance, targeted skills, group size, number of sessions, and session length.

2. Specify your goals for the group's first session. Design a session outline to attain your goals. As well as your outline, what additional preparatory work is required to increase the likelihood of success for the group's first session?

3. Specify your goals for a middle session of the group. Design a session outline to attain your goals. As well as your outline, what additional preparatory work is required to increase the likelihood of success for this middle session?

4. Summarize your lessons from this exercise with regard to preparing future training group sessions.

A checklist for preparing training sessions

Leaders have so much to consider when planning lifeskills sessions that it is easy to overlook important things. Consequently, Table 10.1 provides a checklist for preparing training group sessions. Also the checklist can be used for evaluating completed sessions.

Table 10.1 A checklist for preparing a lifeskills training session

---

———— Do I have clear, relevant and manageable goals?
———— Am I paying adequate attention to the sequencing of content across sessions?
———— Am I starting from where participants are?
———— Have I consulted adequately with participants?
———— Am I sufficiently emphasizing self-referent learning?
———— Does the session contain sufficient involvement through participation?
———— Is there a good balance of learning by hearing, observing and doing?
———— Am I adequately balancing facilitation with didactic input?
———— Is the sequencing of items within the session appropriate?
———— Is there sufficient variety within the session?
———— Is the start of the session adequately planned?
———— Is the ending of the session adequately planned?
———— What homework is to be set?
———— What, if any, between-session contact should I be either encouraging for participants or planning for myself?
———— How can I help participants who have specific learning difficulties?
———— What coping strategies can I use with participants who are difficult?
———— What audiovisual material do I require?
———— What written training materials do I require?
———— Am I sufficiently flexible in how I approach the session?
———— Have I designed an adequate session outline?

THE INITIAL STAGE

It is important that sessions get off to good starts. If the opening minutes are a 'downer', this negative atmosphere may be hard to retrieve. There are a number of functions to be performed early in a training session. Leaders require the skills to perform these functions adequately.

Set a positive emotional climate

Below are a few simple guidelines for setting positive emotional climates at the starts of sessions. Effective group leaders strive for businesslike, yet friendly, atmospheres.

1. *Arrive fresh*. Leaders require sufficient energy to interact well with a group of participants over the whole session. If you start the session tired and out of sorts, not only may your own performance suffer, but also you risk demotivating the group.
2. *Arrive a few minutes early*. If you arrive a few minutes early, you can sort out your materials and compose yourself. If you arrive late, you risk sending negative messages about the importance of both punctuality and the group's work.
3. *Welcome participants*. Another advantage of arriving early is that you can welcome participants as they arrive. A pleasant welcome to each participant helps to create a positive emotional climate, reinforces punctuality, and enhances leader attractiveness.
4. *Start punctually*. Starting on time is one of the most effective ways of creating the norm that participants come on time, if not early.
5. *Show commitment when introducing sessions*. Presumably as a group leader you consider the work of the session important. Without being overwhelming, let your commitment to the work of the group show by means of positive verbal, voice and body messages.

Provide a session outline

At the end of the preceding session, you may have discussed with participants the agenda for this session. Nevertheless, it is a good idea at the start of a session to state what are the targeted skills and to provide an outline of how time will be spent. Most participants like to know both where they are going and how the leader intends to help them to get there. Outlining sessions may reduce anxieties and help participants to see how the different items fit together. In addition to leaders' verbal statements, session goals and outlines can be written on a whiteboard or in a hand-out. When outlining sessions, be prepared to answer questions and clarify the group's understanding of them. In some instances, in light of group feedback, you may decide to renegotiate and alter parts of sessions.

Actively involve participants

Early in each session, try to get participants actively involved. Effective leaders strive to avoid participants passively sliding into their shells. For example, participants may be divided into pairs or small groups and asked to review their behaviour in the targeted skills area since the last meeting. Alternatively, the leader may ask each participant in turn what they want from the upcoming session (Corey & Corey, 1982). Here the focus has been on getting participants actively involved by interacting either in the whole group or in dyads or sub-groups. Alternatively, some leaders start sessions with physical warm-up exercises.

Review the previous session

Lifeskills training groups use cumulative learning. Sessions build on what has gone before. Leaders can provide brief reviews of the main lessons of the previous session. Alternatively, leaders can turn the review into a warm-up exercise in which participants pair off and summarize for each other their main lessons from the previous session. Reviewing the previous session is especially useful for those participants unable to attend it. In addition, non-attending participants should receive hand-outs from missed sessions. Furthermore, both leaders and non-participants missing sessions must think through how to make up lost ground.

Review homework

An important starting-session task is to review between-session homework. Gazda observes: 'Homework is much the content of the session itself; therefore those who do not complete the homework cut down on their potential involvement in the group' (Gazda, 1989, p. 435). Leaders need to be alert to whether or not and how well participants do homework. If homework is not being done satisfactorily, leaders should explore reasons for this. Often participants will want to discuss specific difficulties they experience with homework tasks and with practising targeted skills. Some coaching and feedback from both leader and the group may take place immediately. However, sometimes both leader and participants may defer working with outside-group material until later in sessions. For example, specific difficulties in implementing skills may be topics for later behaviour rehearsal role-plays.

Deal with new and unfinished business

Leaders need to be sensitive to new business that participants bring into groups and to unfinished business from previous sessions. Many things may have happened in participants' lives since the last session. Participants may bring new joys, hurts and momentous events into sessions. Participants may come obviously emotionally distraught or happy. In addition, participants may be faced with immediate pressing situations involving use of targeted skills. There are no simple answers on how to deal with new business brought into groups. Probably it is best for leaders to allow major emotions to be aired. Bottling up strong emotions can act as a block to participation and learning. Participants themselves may act as gatekeepers for relevance. For example, they may appreciate the chance to get support during a personal crisis, but be very sensitive about disrupting the group's skills learning. Furthermore, though this is not guaranteed, personal crises can be good material for illustrating and working on targeted skills. Sometimes, both participants and leader may have issues arising from previous sessions that they wish to bring up. Again, it is probably wise to allow such issues to be aired. Both leader and group can then decide how much attention these issues merit.

Exercise 28 is designed to raise your awareness of some issues and leader skills for the initial stage of training sessions.

Exercise 28 Start a training group session

Carry out the following activities.

1. Make up a worksheet by drawing a line down the middle of a page and at the top of the left column writing HARMFUL ACTIVITIES and at the top of the right column writing HELPFUL ACTIVITIES. Think back over any lifeskills training groups in which you have participated either as participant or leader. In the relevant columns list harmful and helpful activities when starting sessions.

2. Discuss the role and importance of each of the following skills in the initial stage of training sessions:

   • Set a positive emotional climate.
   • Provide a session outline.
   • Actively involve participants.
   • Review the previous session.
   • Review homework.
   • Deal with new and unfinished business.

3. If possible, work with colleagues and role-play starting a training group session in the middle of a group's life. After the role-play, discuss the major lessons for when you lead training group sessions in future. If possible, give everyone the chance to be a leader in a different role-play.

THE WORKING STAGE

Spoon feeding in the long run teaches us nothing but the shape of the spoon.

E.M. Forster

There is no clear working stage to lifeskills training sessions. The work of the group takes place in the initial and ending stages as well. Here the working stage is defined as the middle section of the session – say, after the first ten minutes and up to the last ten minutes. The working stage is the large central heart of the session. During this period new material is introduced and previous material worked over. Many leader skills for the working stage have been discussed in previous chapters. Here the focus is on some further working-stage skills.

Maintain a skills focus

Participants join lifeskills groups to acquire and develop specific skills, be they action skills, thinking skills or both. These skills entail learning specific behaviours. Training group leaders as managers of learning need to beware of allowing sessions to lose much, if not all, of their skills focus. Sometimes sessions are not planned with sufficient skills emphasis in the preparatory stage: for instance, leaders are insufficiently specific about targeted skills. In addition, leaders may have wrongly planned the balance between discussion and structured skills development.

Three ways in which leaders may dilute the skills focus of a session are overly focusing on feelings, relationships and problems. In each instance the issue is likely to be one of balance rather than rightness or wrongness. With regard to overly focusing on feelings, take the example of a spouse in a managing-conflict group who comes to a session extremely agitated after a marital fight. One option is for the leader to focus only on feelings: for example, 'Tell us more about how you felt in the situation?' Another option is to focus only on behaviours: for example, 'How did you behave in the situation and how could you have improved on it?' Still another option is to focus on both feelings and behaviours: 'You are extremely upset; what was good and what was possibly not so good about the way you managed your feelings and behaved?' In the last example, the leader's response both reflects a feeling and focuses on feelings in the context of developing skills.

Leaders may overly focus on the relationships within the group. However, in lifeskills sessions, such relationships are important mainly to the extent that they enhance or obstruct the group's learning. If relationship issues within the group can be used to illustrate targeted skills, they may merit attention. Otherwise, leaders should resist turning training group sessions into encounter group sessions. Also, when participants bring problem situations into sessions, leaders may focus too much on the emotions and details of problems rather on the application of targeted skills to problems. Also, solving problems well in groups does not necessarily mean that participants have learned the requisite skills to implement solutions.

Use the group creatively

Many training group leaders, either by choice or by necessity, work in groups of over eight participants. These leaders are faced with trying to design learning experiences that overcome some of the disadvantages of large group size. One way of mitigating or getting around the problem of large group size is to use co-leaders or leaders' aides. However, bringing in extra leaders is not always possible. Another way is to use good audiovisual presentations. You can then use your energy for managing the group. A third way is to be creative in your use of the group. Varying

its format is recommended even for small groups of six to eight.

Leaders can vary the tasks, numbers and seating in their groups. In Chapter 9, suggestions have been made for varying the tasks in which the group engages. Numerical variations include working with the whole group or breaking it down into small groups, quartets, triads, dyads or even singles. Leaders may make decisions on the size of working groups either on their own or in consultation with participants. Leaders can also vary the seating pattern of the group from that of a horseshoe. Seating variations include: circular, be it the whole group or sub-groups; the fishbowl, with inner and outer rings; and having a 'stage' for role-plays in some part of the room with the audience in a semicircle (the stage's location may depend on where a video camera is mounted). In addition, as in some initial-session breaking-the-ice exercises, participants may stand rather than sit.

Actively involve participants

Getting and keeping participants actively involved is a major skill of effective lifeskills group leaders. Participant MEGO (my eyes glaze over) can set in at any stage and not just during leader presentations (Valenti, 1982). It is all too easy for participants' attention spans and motivation to falter during what may be a long working stage of over an hour or more. Already, some suggestions have been made for getting participants involved at a session's start. Also, throughout a session, breaking the group down in various ways can encourage involvement. Furthermore, judicious use of structured activities can provide excellent opportunities for participation. Below are some additional suggestions for how leaders can get and keep participants actively involved.

TUNE IN AND CHECK OUT

Training group leaders as managers of learning should pay close attention to whether items in a session work for participants. Leaders need to be sensitive to how learning experiences are understood and received. For instance, leaders who sense that participants are getting restless with a presentation may either try to be more stimulating or move on to something more active. Leaders also require checking skills. For example, leaders perceiving that participants show little energy for or interest in specific structured activities can check their perceptions with the group. Tuning in and checking skills are also applicable to working with individuals. Leaders require sensitivity to individual differences in learning styles and attention spans. However, leaders can distort the group's work if they pay too much attention to unrepresentative feedback from individuals. Nevertheless, helping individual participants through learning blocks may be good for both individuals and groups.

ASK DRAWING-IN QUESTIONS

Good training group leaders rarely, if ever, allow participants to be passive for long periods of time. Active participation covers thinking as well as doing. Even when giving presentations, leaders try to keep participants' minds active. Leaders can ask questions that have the effect of drawing participants into sessions. Such questions may be either for anyone in the group to answer, or entail going round the group with each person answering, or be addressed to individuals – possibly those who have not participated much to date. The following are examples of drawing-in questions.

'Can anyone give me an example of...?'

'Has anyone had an experience of ....?'

'What are your reactions to...?'

'To what extent and in what ways is he/she taking responsibility for his/ her behaviour?'

'What skills does he/she need to manage the situation better?'

'Does the demonstration trigger off anything which might make any of you behave differently?'

'Does anyone have any specific feedback that they would like to give to .... (mention name) after observing that role-play?'

In all the above instances, if leaders ask questions of the group, their body messages should match their intentions. For example, their eyes should scan the group rather than be fixed on one individual. Any arm movements should show openness to the group, for instance a sweeping gesture, rather than close off options, for instance by pointing at someone.

REWARD HELPFUL INVOLVEMENT

Leaders can literally encourage – give courage to – participants who share experiences, answer questions and take part in activities. Leaders can give both verbal and non-verbal rewards. Examples of verbal rewards for active involvement include: 'Thanks for volunteering for the role-play', 'That's a good example', and 'I appreciate your sharing that with the group'. Sometimes, leaders may choose to reflect participants' answers, to show and check that they have heard them correctly. In addition, leaders can support participants as they take part in activities and exercises, for instance by showing consideration for their thoughts and feelings. Examples of non-verbal rewards for getting actively involved include: head nods, smiles, pats on the back, hugs and so on.

CURTAIL HARMFUL INVOLVEMENT

Participants singly or as a group can disrupt the leader and each other by interrupting, showing off, making a joke of the proceedings, being aggressive, being over-critical, arguing, being irrelevant, being boring, whispering, talking loudly to each other, and throwing paper darts, among other behaviours. Sometimes destructive behaviours are best ignored by the leader. Either the behaviours will drop off of their own accord or other participants will deal with perpetrators.

If the disruptive behaviours persist in interfering with the learning of the remainder of the group, leaders must consider how best to intervene. Leaders must make their interventions appropriate to the behaviours that they want to curtail. For instance, if participants ramble on vaguely, they can be asked to talk about specific behaviours. If participants are causing discipline problems, there are a number of options. Part of the skill of the group leader is to get potentially disruptive elements in the group 'on-side' rather than 'off-side'. Consequently, leaders should use the minimum 'muscle' necessary to achieve the desired results. Sometimes humour can defuse situations of potential conflict. Giving disruptive participants 'the teacher's eye' may be sufficient to curtail their behaviour. Also, leaders can help disruptive participants to explore their resistances. Moving further up the hierarchy of 'muscle', leaders can make behaviour change requests in a firmer voice and, if necessary, repeat them. In addition, leaders and the other participants can point out the effects of the disruptive behaviour on the learning environment. Leaders in some lifeskills groups, if unable to exclude certain participants, may be faced with ongoing disciplinary problems. In such circumstances, they have the difficult task of containing the disruptive elements at the same time as helping those wanting to benefit from the group.

USE MINI-BREAKS

Sometimes the use of mini-breaks can help to keep participants actively involved. When working with juvenile delinquents, Sarason initially estimated that their attention span was 20–30 minutes. Consequently, about midway through a one-hour session, he provided a soft drink for each boy (Sarason, 1976). Having brief breaks and providing coffee, tea and soft drinks may both be conducive to involvement. In addition, opportunity for fresh air and physical movement – not just calls of nature – may help.

Make balancing choices

During a session, training group leaders are faced with numerous choices concerning what is a good balance between conflicting considerations. Some of the considerations that leaders have to balance include the following: being didactic or facilitative; making decisions alone or sharing decisions with the group; presenting and demonstrating versus doing structured activities; how much to work with individuals; whether to work with the whole group or break it down; how much to focus on action skills or on thinking skills; whether to adhere to or deviate from session plans; whether to allow discussion or cut it off; and whether to be serious or humorous.

Constant tensions between conflicting considerations exist in all training groups. Leaders can make some of the above choices in advance. However, what actually happens depends on the choices that they make during sessions. Leaders who decide in advance what their main session goals are, how they want the emotional climate in sessions to be, and what are their own roles, are in stronger positions to make balancing decisions than those unclear about these issues. If leaders think that they have got the balance between some of these considerations wrong, they can often retrieve situations either later in the same session or in subsequent sessions.

Keep the session moving

Training group leaders need to keep sessions moving. Keeping a session moving does not mean pressurizing participants all the time. Rather, assuming that the time distribution has been well planned, leaders can keep the group moving at a comfortable pace to complete the session's various tasks. Providing an outline at the session's start can help to keep it moving. As a result, participants should be clear about the ground to be covered. Also, the outline provides a positive context for the leader's transition statements. Such transition statements are not just cutting off and moving *from* statements, but also opening up and moving *to* statements.

Below are some possible leader transition statements:

'Well, that's the end of my initial presentation of how to generate and evaluate different perceptions in situations that you find difficult. If there are no further questions, I would now like to coach one of you through the steps of this skill in relation to a specific situation in which you feel shy.'

'Does anyone have anything pressing that they would like to add before we move on to .... ?'

'Does Terry have anything to add or does anyone else have anything that they would like to feed back to Terry before we move on to the next role-play?'

'Though this is an interesting discussion, we seem to be getting away from the skills-building purpose of this session. I suggest we curtail the discussion and move on.'

'I seem to be picking up a lot of body messages that we have spent enough time on that activity and should be moving on. Do you agree?'

THE ENDING STAGE

Effective group leaders pay close attention to how they end sessions (Corey & Corey, 1982; Jacobs *et al.*, 1988). Much of the work of lifeskills training groups goes on between sessions. Therefore, leaders have an added reason for ending sessions well: to take full advantage of between-session time

Ending-stage tasks

Quite apart from calling a halt to the proceedings, a number of tasks may be performed in the ending stage of a session. These tasks include the following:

- *Summarize.* The main points of the session can be summarized either by the leader or by participants. Leaders can check that participants know not only

what to do, but also how to instruct themselves when using targeted skills.

- *Correct misunderstandings.* If participants misunderstand some of the session's lessons, the leader may be able to put them right before the session ends. However, leaders must defer major corrective instruction and coaching to the next session.

- *Set and formulate homework.* Sometimes leaders will ask participants to complete prepared homework tasks. On other occasions, leaders may work with participants to design individual behaviour change experiments and other activities. Leaders need to ensure that participants are clear about what is wanted in homework tasks. Also, leaders can help participants to identify and work through blocks to doing homework.

- *Obtain feedback.* Leaders can check with participants their reactions to the session – what seemed to work for them and what did not.

- *Consult.* Leaders can share with participants their ideas for the agenda and activities for the next session. Participants can be asked for their reactions and suggestions.

- *Deal with unfinished business.* With their emphasis on behaviours rather than emotions, training group sessions tend to end with less unfinished business than interactional group sessions. Nevertheless, if there are feelings and hidden agendas that may interfere with the group's work, it is probably best for these to be aired. Leaders can then decide whether these emotions and agendas merit more attention, either now or in future.

- *Arrange for mutual support.* Leaders can raise the issue of participants supporting each other, perhaps on a buddy system, between sessions. For example, participants might phone their buddy at least once to discuss progress.

- *Indicate between-session contact with leader.* Leaders may indicate what, if any, between-session contact they are prepared to have with participants. If participants appear particularly distressed during the session, the leader might have a brief word with them afterwards. Many leaders discourage participants from asking routine questions, for instance concerning homework, between sessions. They expect participants to stay alert and ask such questions during sessions.

Ending-stage skills

During the ending stage of sessions leaders use numerous skills: facilitating, checking, summarizing, and setting homework, among others. Here a few further skills specific to the ending stage are discussed.

END OF TIME

It is a good discipline for both leaders and the group that sessions start and end on time. Ending on time has the following advantages for leaders: providing a firm limit on session content; letting leaders get away gracefully; and cueing participants to raise important issues during the session. Also, participants appreciate it if the contract on session length is kept and they can make arrangements accordingly.

ALLOW TIME FOR ENDING

When designing and managing sessions, leaders need to allow sufficient time to end the session well. Allowing sufficient time for ending means paying attention to time-keeping throughout the session so that there is not a build-up of work by the end. Depending on the length of the whole session and on what the leader aims to achieve in the ending stage, perhaps 5–20 minutes may be set aside for it.

MAKE A TRANSITION STATEMENT

When outlining the lifeskills training programme at the first session, leaders may make it clear to participants that in each session there will be an initial, a working or middle and an ending stage. Nevertheless, when the time comes for the ending stage in each session, leaders still need to make transition statements. Such transition statements shift the focus of the group to the work of the ending stage. The following are examples of leader transition statements.

'I realize that this is an important issue for you and perhaps we can come back to it. However, we have about ten minutes left now. I would like to spend this time to get the group to summarize its main lessons from the session and to clarify homework.'

'We are coming to the end of the session now. The time has come to consolidate learnings, sort out homework and look ahead to the next session.'

ACTIVELY INVOLVE PARTICIPANTS

During the ending stage of sessions, as in earlier stages, leaders can actively involve participants. For example, when summarizing, one format is for the leader to summarize, and another format is for one or more participants to summarize. The listening participants can then be asked to either verify or correct the summaries. Also, leaders can ask questions to be answered by anyone in the group, for example 'Does anyone have any feedback they want to give about the session?' or do rounds in which each participant gets the opportunity to speak, for example, 'I'm now going to give each of you the opportunity to comment on what, if anything, you've learned from today's session'.

STRENGTHEN COMMITMENT TO BETWEEN-SESSION WORK

Leaders can encourage participants to use the time between sessions fruitfully. Homework tasks and using targeted skills outside of the group should be presented in a positive light. The time between sessions is really an extension of the session in which participants get the opportunity to practise, develop and consolidate skills. When devising homework tasks, leaders can check that they have relevance for participants' personal goals. Sometimes leaders may need to help participants to state homework goals specifically, realistically and with a time frame. Leaders may also explore with participants the payoffs for doing between-session homework and changing their behaviour.

Exercise 29 Lead a training group session

1. With regard to either your Exercise 27 middle-session training group outline or to another middle-session outline discuss:

   (a) how you might use each of the following leader skills for the *working* stage of your session
   - maintain a skills focus
   - use the group creatively
   - actively involve participants
   - make balancing choices
   - keep the session moving

   (b) how you might use each of the following leader skills for the *ending* stage of your session
   - end on time
   - allow time for ending
   - make a transition statement
   - actively involve participants
   - strengthen commitment to homework

2. If possible, work with colleagues and role-play leading the whole of a training group session. After the role-play discuss major lessons for when you lead training group sessions in future. If possible, give everyone the chance to be leader in a different role-play (to save time, sessions may have to be co-led).

EVALUATE SESSIONS

Leaders may ask themselves such questions as 'How can I tell if the session worked?' or 'Has the session achieved its objectives?' Leaders can evaluate the effectiveness of a session during it, between sessions and at the start of the next session (Hopson & Scally, 1981; Rose, 1986). Leaders require clarity concerning evaluation criteria. Here are some ways of evaluating if sessions are successful. First, leaders can *observe* from participants' verbal, voice, body and action messages such things as: whether or not they are actively involved in the session; whether or not they understand the session content; their rate of progress in developing targeted skills; and which parts of the session they enjoy and which parts they find boring. Second, leaders can *listen to their own feelings* and use these as a basis for thinking about what is happening or has happened in a session. For instance, a leader may have a feeling of unease about a session and then reflect on why this is the case. Third, leaders can review if *the session outline has been completed satisfactorily*. Assuming a realistic outline, one criterion for a successful session is for leader and participants to consider that they have covered its content adequately. Were all the main learning points and targeted skills communicated?

Verbal feedback provides a fourth way of gauging the success of sessions. Leaders may get informal feedback from casual comments either from participants, colleagues or third parties concerning the success of a session. Such feedback may or may not be representative of what the group thinks. Leaders can also systematically seek verbal feedback, for instance by a round in which all participants can have their say. *Written feedback* offers a fifth way of assessing sessions. Participants can be asked to provide ratings and brief comments at the end of each session. For example, participants could rate on a 7-point scale, ranging from 1 highly dissatisfied to 7 highly satisfied, what they felt about the session. In addition, they could be asked to comment on what they liked and disliked about the session. Also, participants can be asked to rate and comment on the adequacy of their own contributions to sessions. Leaders can also evaluate sessions by means of *videotape feedback*. They can play back videotapes of sessions and assess both their own and participants' behaviours.

Two further ways of assessing the success of sessions are *attendance* and *completion of homework tasks*. If attendance is poor at the next session this may give the leader pause for thought about the adequacy of the previous session. However, beware of paranoia. Numerous reasons exist why participants either do not attend or attend sessions late. Calmly collect evidence before inferring the worst. If participants either fail to complete homework or complete homework tasks poorly, this merits further exploration. Again, calmly collect evidence before assuming the worst. For example, genuine difficulties in their lives may have interfered with homework. Alternatively, when participants attempted the homework, they may have misunderstood what was wanted. Consequently, an accurate attribution of cause might focus on your setting of homework skills in the previous session rather than on the inadequacy of the whole session.

All training group leaders evaluate sessions, albeit with varying degrees of awareness and thoroughness. Between sessions, you are encouraged to reflect on the success and lessons for you and the group from the previous session. Leaders as well as participants should do their homework!

CHAPTER HIGHLIGHTS

Each training group session has its preparatory, initial, working and ending stages. During each stage leaders are managers of learning.

Lifeskills training sessions require careful preparation and outlining to attain clear, relevant and manageable goals. Each session should be planned in the context of what precedes and follows it.

Leader skills for managing a session's initial stage include: set a positive emotional climate, provide an outline, actively involve participants, review the previous session, process homework, and deal with new and unfinished business.

Leader skills for managing a session's working stage include: maintain a skills focus, use the group creatively, actively involve participants, make balancing choices and keep the session moving.

Ending-stage tasks include: summarize, correct misunderstandings of session content, set and formulate homework, obtain feedback, consult, arrange for mutual support, and provide information about between-session contact with leaders.

Leader skills for managing a session's ending stage include: end on time, allow time for ending, make a transition statement, actively involve participants, and strengthen commitment to between-session work.

Ways of evaluating training group sessions include: observing, listening to feelings, completing the session outline, verbal feedback, written feedback, videotape feedback, attendance and completion of homework assignments.

ELEVEN

How to Consolidate Self-Help Skills and End Groups

The final test of leaders is that they leave behind them in others the conviction and the will to carry on.

Walter Lippman (Non-sexist adaptation)

CHAPTER QUESTIONS

What do generalization, transfer, maintenance and development mean in the context of consolidating self-help skills?

What training group leader and participant thinking skills are relevant to consolidating trained skills as self-help skills?

What can leaders do in the preparatory, initial, working and ending stages of training groups to enhance consolidation?

What are different formats for ending training groups?

What are some tasks and agendas for the ending stage of training groups?

INTRODUCTION

A critical issue for all lifeskills group leaders is 'Does my group have any lasting effects?' Kendall emphasizes: 'Training in a skill does not automatically mean that the skill will persist nor that it will appear in contexts meaningfully different from the one in which training took place' (Kendall, 1989, p. 358). The 'train and hope' approach to the transfer and maintenance of treatment gains is not reliable (Goldstein & Keller, 1987; Martin, 1990; Stokes & Osnes, 1989). Leaders require many strategies to increase the chances of participants retaining their skills. As depicted in Figure 11.1, consolidating trained skills as self-help skills for when groups end is at the heart of lifeskills training. Consolidation is the central integrating focus or wheel hub of all leader training skills and participant learning endeavours.

Defining consolidating self-help skills

Generalization, transfer, maintenance and development are four important, albeit somewhat overlapping, terms for understanding what consolidating trained skills as self-help skills means.

- *Generalization.* Skinner observes, 'generalization is not an activity of the organism; it is simply a term which describes the fact that the control acquired by a stimulus is shared by other stimuli with common properties' (Skinner, 1953, p. 132). Regarding lifeskills training groups, generalization refers to the possibility of skills being used in response to non-trained-for situations or stimuli similar to those trained for in groups. Participants are flexible rather than narrow in how they apply targeted skills outside groups.

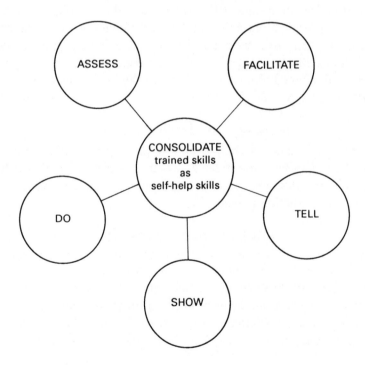

Figure 11.1 *Consolidation of self-help skills as the central integrating focus of training groups*

- *Transfer*. It is wholly insufficient for participants to use targeted skills only in training group settings. Transfer refers to the ability of participants to use trained skills in their daily lives.

- *Maintenance*. Maintenance refers to participants' abilities to keep using trained skills after groups have ended. Maintenance is not always consistent: participants may suffer periods of relapse. However, over time, despite relapses, they still maintain their skills. The opposite of maintenance is going back to baseline or worse.

- *Development*. When groups end, some participants may not only maintain skills, but also develop trained skills to higher levels. These participants are able to shift the balance of weaknesses and strengths in one or more skills areas still further in the direction of strengths.

THINKING SKILLS FOR CONSOLIDATING SELF-HELP SKILLS

Training groups have their endings built into them from their beginnings. Diligent leaders do not leave helping participants to consolidate targeted skills as self-help skills to their group's ending stage. Effective leaders address consolidating self-help skills in the group's preparatory, initial and working stages as well. Leaders wishing to help participants to transfer trained skills into self-help skills must focus not only on relevant action skills, but also on relevant thinking skills (Nelson-Jones, 1989). Furthermore, leaders need to focus on their own thinking skills as well as on those of participants.

Work with leader thinking skills

Group leader thinking skills can help or hinder participants in developing lifeskills as self-help skills. Leaders intent on consolidating participants' self-help skills require the effective thinking skills of attributing cause accurately, possessing realistic rules, and predicting realistically.

ATTRIBUTE CAUSE ACCURATELY

Groups may be too leader-centred. This style of leadership weakens participants' motivation for assuming responsibility for their learning. The causes of training group learning are attributable to participants and leaders together, not just to leaders alone. In addition, leaders need to attribute cause accurately when explaining their own and participants' successes and failures. For example, leaders failing to train for maintenance should not blame participants for skills relapses.

POSSESS REALISTIC RULES

Leaders require realistic rules regarding the processes and outcomes of training groups (Ellis, 1980, 1989). Below are some unrealistic 'mustabatory' rules that interfere with consolidating self-help skills.

- 'I must cure participants.' Cure is a medical rather than a psychological concept. While leaders might prefer it if participants acquired and maintained perfect lifeskills, this is an unrealistic goal. Furthermore, the idea of the leader curing participants contributes to an excessively leader-centred approach to lifeskills training. A more realistic reformulation of the mustabatory rule is: 'My job is, to the best of my ability, to train participants to acquire and maintain targeted lifeskills as self-help skills for when the group ends. Afterwards, participants will still have to work hard to retain their skills.'

- 'I must focus on acquisition training rather than on acquisition and maintenance training.' Here the leader overemphasizes initial acquisition of skills at the expense of realizing that participants must maintain skills themselves. As Stuart observes of marital therapy, 'building skills of maintaining positive therapeutic outcome is fully as important as promoting change in the first place' (Stuart, 1980, p. 367). Stuart's observation provides a more realistic reformulation of the above unrealistic rule.

- 'I must cover a lot of ground.' Leaders can put pressure on themselves to cover too much material both over the group's life and also in individual sessions. A more realistic reformulation is: 'My best approach is to allow sufficient time to teach each skill thoroughly so that participants learn them well enough to apply the skills on their own.'

- 'I must have a standardized programme.' For many reasons, leaders may need to have much of their training programme standardized. Nevertheless, ultimately participants have to use the skills in the specific situations of their own lives. Consequently, transfer and maintenance of skills may be enhanced if leaders provide opportunities to work on individual as well as on group concerns. Individual activities and behaviour change experiments can take place within the context of group approaches. A more realistic reformulation is: 'Lifeskills training groups are composed of individuals with different learning styles, personal goals and life circumstances. Consequently, I need to balance interventions for the whole group with those helpful to specific individuals.'

- 'I must not be criticized.' Leaders need to be open to participants' feedback regarding those aspects of the group that work and do not work for them. Leader defensiveness interferes with participants both acquiring and maintaining skills. A more realistic reformulation is: 'Though some participants' comments may be destructive, probably most feedback is meant constructively. I need to listen carefully to feedback to see how I can improve this and future groups.'

PREDICT REALISTICALLY

Leaders need realism in predicting what can be achieved in training groups, be they either six or twenty sessions. Jacobson, writing of marital therapy, concluded: 'Nevertheless, in retrospect it seemed almost embarrassingly naïve of us to have expected a treatment program lasting six months to have a lasting impact on most couples' (Jacobson, 1989, p. 329). Training group leaders must beware of similar naïvety in themselves and of passing it on to participants. As shown in Chapter 2, most participants enter training groups with long histories of maintaining lifeskills weaknesses in targeted areas. They also have confidence and thinking skills problems that interfere with change. Many participants will require further individual and group interventions to develop their skills. A simple analogy is that of a beginners' group who complete a series of tennis lessons. They have acquired some new skills and must practise to retain them. However, to move beyond the beginner's stage, they must make a commitment to more coaching and practice. Becoming even better requires still more coaching and practice. Quick fixes are rarely the answer in acquiring and maintaining lifeskills.

Work with participants' thinking skills

Though often underemphasized in the maintenance literature (for example, Goldstein & Keller, 1987; Stokes & Osnes, 1989), training to consolidate self-help skills requires paying close attention to participants' thinking skills. The following are some thinking skills that may help participants to maintain and develop targeted lifeskills.

ATTRIBUTING CAUSE ACCURATELY

Throughout training groups, leaders need to emphasize overtly and covertly that participants are personally responsible for making their lives through the quality of their choices. More specifically, participants are personally responsible for making the most of the learning opportunities provided during training groups. Also, participants have responsibility for maintaining and developing their skills when groups end. Potential attributional errors that sustain skills weaknesses require exploration and, if necessary, correction. Such attributional errors include: 'It's my nature', 'It's my unfortunate past', 'It's my bad luck', 'It's my poor environment', 'It's all someone else's fault', and 'It's all my fault'. In addition, leaders need to pay close attention to how participants attribute cause for setbacks. For example, participants should beware of making internal and stable attributions of failure when relapses occur (Kendall, 1989).

POSSESSING REALISTIC RULES

Participants may require assistance in reformulating unrealistic rules about learning lifeskills to more realistic ones. Below are examples of unrealistic rules followed by more realistic reformulations.

Unrealistic rule. 'I must be cured.'
Reformulation. 'While I would prefer to have no problems in future, the best I

can do is to improve my skills during the group and strive to maintain them afterwards.'

Unrealistic rule. 'Change must be easy.'
Reformulation. 'I have not only to develop new and better skills, but also to unlearn bad habits. Consequently, I have to work hard to change during the group and also to persist in working hard afterwards.'

Unrealistic rule. 'During and after the group I must improve all the time.'
Reformulation. 'Learning any new skill involves making mistakes, experiencing periods of uncertainty and encountering setbacks. Ups and downs are inevitable. All I can do is to learn from mistakes and cope with setbacks to the best of my ability.'

Unrealistic rule. 'The leader must teach me.'
Reformulation. 'The leader is a resource person whose job is to assist me to develop self-help skills. I need to work together with the leader during the group and on my own afterwards.'

The above are just a few of the unrealistic rules that participants may have about lifeskills learning. Leaders may identify and reformulate other unrealistic rules that either individuals or groups possess.

SELF-INSTRUCTING

Leaders need to ensure that participants understand the sequences of choices in targeted skills well enough to instruct themselves. For example, when demonstrating skills, leaders can demonstrate self-instructions too. Also, leaders can get participants to summarize these self-instructions either in the group or by making up homework cassettes. Where skills are complex, leaders can instruct participants in the main rules guiding effective enactment, for example communication rules for couples (Stuart, 1980).

COPING SELF-TALK

Use of coping self-talk is highly relevant to maintaining as well as acquiring skills. Coping self-talk can be used when faced with difficult situations in implementing skills, for example public speaking, asserting yourself or making a date. Coping self-talk can also be used by participants to deal with temptations, for instance food, alcohol or drugs. Participants can make both calming and coaching self-talk statements to themselves before, during and after difficult or stressful situations. Furthermore, participants can be helped to talk themselves through setbacks when either learning or implementing skills.

PERCEIVING ACCURATELY

Participants can be helped to perceive their skills strengths and weaknesses accurately. Developing the skills of accurate perception of strengths and weaknesses not only helps participants to improve their skills during groups but also gives them the basis for correcting weaknesses afterwards. Ways in which leaders can help participants to see themselves accurately include: setting self-observation and assessment exercises, facilitating self-assessment, giving feedback and providing the opportunity for others' feedback. Leaders can also work with specific tendencies that participants may have to perceive inaccurately, for example engaging in negative self-labelling or failing to acknowledge progress. In addition, leaders can help participants to perceive others accurately, for instance by encouraging them to provide evidence for questionable perceptions.

PREDICTING REALISTICALLY

Both during and after training groups it is important that participants predict the consequences of their behaviours realistically. Many participants are fearful of change and of taking risks. They may be unduly pessimistic. Leaders can help them to develop the skills of adequately taking potential gains as well as losses into account when reviewing the future. Some participants may be over-optimistic. Here leaders can help them to develop the skills of adequately taking potential losses into account. Also, leaders can help participants to identify and work through specific anxieties about either learning or implementing targeted skills. Furthermore, leaders can assist participants in being realistic in predicting what they can achieve by the group's end and how hard they need to work to retain and develop skills.

GOAL-SETTING SKILLS

By imparting goal-setting skills, leaders can help participants to make their futures both during and after groups. Personal goals in the targeted skills areas need to be specific and realistic and have time frames. Goals can be reviewed in light of experience and feedback.

VISUALIZING

Visualizing may be used by participants both to strengthen desirable and to weaken undesirable behaviours. For example, participants can visually rehearse and practise desired skills. In addition, participants can visualize the negative consequences of behaviours that they wish to eliminate (Cautela, 1967; Lazarus, 1977).

USING SELF-REWARD

Participants can be trained to use self-reward to develop and maintain skills (Kanfer & Gaelick, 1986; Thoresen & Mahoney, 1974). Self-rewards can be external or internal. External rewards include: (1) self-administration of new rewards outside the participant's everyday life, such as a new item of clothing or a special event; and (2) initial denial of some pleasant everyday experience and later administration of it contingent upon some desired action. Internal rewards include self-talk statements like 'That's great', or 'I did well', or 'Terrific . . . I actually did it' that clearly indicate satisfaction with attaining a targeted action.

Positive self-reward programmes require the following component skills.

1. Setting specific goals. Goals may need to be broken down so that

participants reward themselves for attaining graded steps.
2. Self-observation and monitoring of targeted behaviours.
3. Identifying suitable rewards. Kanfer and Gaelick observe that, wherever possible, self-reward should be relevant to the target behaviour. They write: 'the ex-smoker might select the purchase of new perfume or having teeth cleaned and polished, because such rewards emphasize the positive aspects of not smoking in terms of whiter teeth and increased sensitivity to smell' (Kanfer & Gaelick, 1986, p. 324).
4. Developing a behaviour change plan in the form of a contract with clear connections between achieving targeted behaviours and administering self-rewards.
5. Rehearsal and enactment of the behaviour change plan.
6. Review and evaluation of progress.

RELAPSE PREVENTION SKILLS

Once on their own, participants are almost certain to experience relapses and setbacks as they implement targeted skills. Some trainers and therapists build relapse prevention (RP) into treatments (Marlatt, 1980; Marx, 1982). Marx has designed an RP worksheet that asks the respondent to choose an appropriate behaviour to retain (Ivey *et al.*, 1987). Respondents then assess strategies for: anticipating difficult situations in relation to the targeted behaviour; increasing rational thinking to regulate self-defeating thoughts and feelings; implementing action skills, for instance assertion or relaxation, to support self-regulating behaviours; and monitoring and providing rewarding consequences for succeeding with new behaviours. Respondents are also asked to predict the circumstances of the first relapse, including people, places, times, and emotional states. Participants require the skills not only of relapse prevention, but also of dealing with their thoughts and feelings about any relapses that occur. Many relapse prevention strategies are also retrieval skills for getting back on track.

MANAGING-PROBLEMS SKILLS

Participants can fail to retain lifeskills because of problems in the targeted skills areas. In addition, problems in other areas of participants' lives can impact on maintaining targeted skills. For example, Jacobson studied the maintenance of treatment gains after social learning-based marital therapy (Jacobson, 1989). He found that, for couples interviewed after their two-year follow-up assessment, stressful life events were by far the best predictor of relapse.

Elsewhere I described in detail CASIE, a five-step framework for managing problems (Nelson-Jones, 1989). The five steps are:

C   *Confront* your problem.
A   *Assess* and *define* your problem.
S   *Set goals* and *plan*.
I   *Implement* your plan.
E   *Evaluate* the consequences of implementation.

Leaders can teach participants the component skills for each of the five steps. Participants should understand that the framework is not intended as a strait-jacket, but as a tool to be used flexibly. It can be used with varying degrees of formality and rigour, depending on how difficult and important the problem is. For many minor problems, participants may rightly judge that it is not worth the bother of going through the five steps.

Retaining skills and preventing or overcoming relapses relies heavily on participants using effective thinking skills once groups end. Exercise 30 encourages you to examine how you might work with participants' thinking skills to consolidate trained skills as self-help skills.

Exercise 30 Consolidate self-help skills: Work with participants' thinking skills

Make up a worksheet like the one below. With regard to a lifeskills training group of your choice, indicate how you might work with each of the following thinking skills to help participants to consolidate trained skills as self-help skills for when the group ends.

Attributing cause accurately	
Possessing realistic rules	
Self-instructing	
Coping self-talk	
Predicting realistically	
Goal-setting skills	
Visualizing	
Using self-reward	
Relapse prevention skills	
Managing-problems skills	

Summarize the main ways that you might work with participants' thinking skills to facilitate consolidating self-help skills.

This exercise may also be done in a discussion format, either with or without individually completing the worksheet in advance.

ACTION SKILLS FOR CONSOLIDATING SELF-HELP SKILLS

In addition to focusing on thinking, leaders can use other skills to help participants to retain trained skills as self-help skills. These skills often have a thinking component. However, for the sake of simplicity, here they are categorized as action skills.

The preparatory stage

Leaders must be mindful of the need to consolidate self-help skills when designing programmes and preparing groups. Below are some relevant preparatory stage skills.

ALLOW FOR OVERLEARNING

Goldstein and Keller state: 'Overlearning involves the training of a skill beyond what is necessary to produce changes in behavior' (Goldstein & Keller, 1987, p. 116). Participants often require more than one or two trials using a skill to understand and use it properly. Then they may require homework and practice to integrate it into their repertoire of lifeskills. Consequently, when designing programmes, it is important to allow for thoroughness in the number of trials for each specific skill. Programme design strategies for overlearning include: limiting the scope of the overall programme, allowing for repeated skills demonstrations, emphasizing learning by doing, allowing for repeated trials, and ensuring adequate time and supervision for homework and practice.

USE LEADER'S AIDES IN PARTICIPANTS' HOME ENVIRONMENTS

Though not suitable for all groups, sometimes leaders can enlist the help of supportive people in participants' home environments and use them as leader's aides. For instance, a leader running a friendship skills group in a primary school can train teachers to understand, support and reward children as they try using targeted skills in classrooms and playgrounds. Parents might also be enlisted as aides to help their children become more confident and better at using their friendship skills at home. Collaboration between leaders and outside-group supports does not happen automatically. Leaders need to be systematic about: creating roles for leader's aides; contacting them; enlisting support; and, if necessary, training them in how best either to support participants or, at least, how not to do damage.

ADVERTISE REALISTICALLY

Training group leaders can realistically structure the expectations of prospective participants. For example, advertising can indicate that at most a group is a stepping-stone to acquiring and maintaining skills rather than a panacea. In addition, if and when conducting intake interviews, leaders can let potential participants know the limitations as well as the advantages of joining their groups. If it is an introductory group, most lifeskills will only be learned at a basic level. Even then, participants require continuous work and practice to prevent relapses and retain skills.

The initial stage

Structuring realistic expectations and developing participants' self-observation and assessment skills are two action strategies relevant to consolidating self-help skills that leaders can use in the group's initial stage.

STRUCTURE REALISTIC EXPECTATIONS

At the group's start, leaders can consolidate honest advertising and intake interviewing by stating the goals for the group realistically and not promising too much. Leaders can also emphasize the fixed length of the group so that it seems a positive opportunity for participants to make the most of the time. For example, a leader in a managing-anger group might say:

> 'We have ten sessions together. I know that all of you have been angry for much longer than that and are worried enough about the consequences of your anger to join this group. It requires a strong commitment on your part to develop some basic managing-anger skills in ten sessions. During the group you will have to work hard to replace past unhelpful habits with new ways of thinking and acting. However, you should start seeing some positive results for yourselves and others from using your skills. After the group you will need to keep up the hard work to retain both your skills and their benefits.'

DEVELOP PARTICIPANTS' SELF-OBSERVATION AND ASSESSMENT SKILLS

In the initial stage, if not before, leaders need to get participants assessing how they perform targeted skills. Such assessments provide a baseline against which participants can set personal goals and measure progress. Leaders can also help participants to develop skills of self-observation and assessment and emphasize their importance for retaining lifeskills. Self-observation and assessment skills include: making frequency counts and charting; devising and filling out either behaviour logs or thinking, feeling, and behaviour logs; asking for feedback; and openly acknowledging skills strengths and weaknesses.

The working stage

Group leader actions for consolidating self-help skills during the working stage include the following.

USE LEADER'S AIDES IN PARTICIPANTS' HOME ENVIRONMENTS

Leader's aides identified during the preparatory stage need attention during the group's working stage. Aides may require support, training and assistance in how best to help participants. Also, leaders may get useful feedback from their aides on participants' progress.

DEVELOP PARTICIPANTS' SELF-OBSERVATION AND ASSESSMENT SKILLS

Throughout groups, leaders need to maintain the emphasis on participants becoming skilled observers and assessors of their own behaviour. These skills are necessary both for evaluating progress and for designing behaviour change plans.

REMIND THE GROUP ABOUT ITS FINITENESS

During groups, leaders can make statements that remind participants to work now for later benefits. For example, leaders might let participants know when it is their last opportunity in their group to work on a subskill. In addition, leaders may confront certain participants with the desirability of working harder and making more progress before the group ends. For instance, a leader might say: 'What are going to be the consequences for you of maintaining your present level of skills after the group?'

EMPHASIZE REAL-LIFENESS

Paying attention to identical elements in lifeskills groups means that the content of training possesses 'real-lifeness' (Goldstein & Keller, 1987). The content of presentation and demonstrations should be tailored to real life situations faced by participants. Behaviour rehearsal role-plays should resemble as closely as possible the real thing. Working in participants' natural settings, for example in youth clubs, is another way to increase both being and also being perceived to be relevant. In addition, when participants learn skills in home environments, they are more likely to use them there afterwards.

TRAIN DIVERSELY

Stokes and Osnes observe: 'What has been frequently documented is the fact that focused training frequently has focused effects' (Stokes and Osnes, 1989, p. 345). Participants require flexibility when implementing lifeskills on their own. Leaders need to beware of narrow training. Regarding learning by observing, both multiple demonstrators and demonstrating the same skill in different scenes are strategies that enhance generalization and maintenance. Regarding learning by doing, participants can role-play using the same skill in different situations. Also, a single behaviour rehearsal role-play can have more than one trial, each with a different emphasis. For example, in a dating role-play, one trial can be with the date request being successful, another with the date request being questioned and then successful, and another with the date request being turned down.

REHEARSE COPING WITH DIFFICULTIES AND SETBACKS

Relapse prevention is not only a matter of thinking appropriately, but also of possessing appropriate action skills for coping with difficult situations. Action skills can be trained for in behaviour rehearsal role-plays. Participants can be 'prepared for potential setbacks, unsympathetic relatives and friends, and unpredicted pressure through role-play of situations simulating the above conditions' (Rose, 1986, p. 463).

EMPHASIZE HOMEWORK TASKS

Both leaders and participants require a commitment to homework as a bridge between learning and using skills. Homework should be a feature of all between-session periods. In the next session, participants should always have the opportunity to discuss their progress in homework tasks. Homework tasks can be set to give participants the opportunity to practise skills in diverse siuations. In addition, difficulties and setbacks that participants experience can not only be discussed, but can also be the focus of behaviour rehearsal role-plays.

HELP PARTICIPANTS TO USE SUPPORTS

Leaders and participants can work together on identifying people in home environments to support efforts to develop targeted skills. For example, supervisor trainees can seek out senior supervisors or managers to discuss how best to handle difficult situations such as underperforming workers. Students on study skills courses can seek out sympathetic lecturers who may help them to develop specific skills, for instance how to write essays or prepare for tests. Unemployed people can seek out friends and relatives who will not only provide them with emotional support, but may also be a source of job leads. Sometimes peer support is organized within training groups. Participants may adopt a buddy system in which they take an interest in each other's progress, for instance by phone calls. An inverse approach to support is to identify and avoid non-supportive people. If these people are family members, avoiding them may be difficult. However, people can often choose their friendship and membership groups. For example, if juvenile delinquents want to change their ways it can be important for them to change the company that they keep (Sarason, 1976).

USE REWARD STRATEGIES

Various reward strategies can be used by leaders to enhance transfer and maintenance (Goldstein & Keller, 1987; Stokes & Osnes, 1989). For instance, once a skill is initially acquired, leaders can reduce the regularity and frequency with which they reward participants for demonstrating it. In addition, prompts and reminders can be gradually faded. Leader aides can be trained how to provide rewarding consequences for targeted behaviours enacted in participants' home environments. Also, participants can be taught how tactfully to obtain rewarding feedback. For example, they might ask friends or colleagues: 'How is this?' or 'How am I doing?'

BECOME A CONSULTANT

As groups progress, leaders can alter the balance of how they play their roles. In a group's early stages, leaders may be more presenters, demonstrators and coaches. In later stages, they may act more as consultants encouraging participants to work through how to think and act in specific situations. Leaders need to train participants in how to be effective on their own.

Exercise 31 is designed to get readers thinking about how they might act in the preparatory, initial and working stages of training groups to consolidate participants' self-help skills.

Exercise 31 Consolidate self-help skills: Action skills for the preparatory, initial and working stages

With regard to a lifeskills training group of your choice, indicate how you might use each of the following leader skills to help participants to consolidate trained skills as self-help skills for when the group ends.

THE PREPARATORY STAGE
Allow for overlearning
Use leader's aides in participants' home environments
Advertise realistically

THE INITIAL STAGE
Structure realistic expectations
Develop participants' self-observation and assessment skills

THE WORKING STAGE
Use leader's aides in participants' home environments
Develop participants' self-observation and assessment skills
Remind the group of its finiteness
Emphasize real-lifeness
Train diversely
Rehearse coping with difficulties and setbacks
Emphasize homework tasks
Help participants to use supports
Use reward strategies
Become a consultant

Are there any other leader interventions that you might use before the group's ending stage to consolidate self-help skills? If so, please specify.

THE ENDING STAGE

As indicated in the discussion on preparing for ending, in training groups there is no clear division between the ending stage and its preceding stages. The ending stage might start at the conclusion of the penultimate session with a homework assignment focused on self-assessment and post-group plans for retaining and developing targeted skills. The ending stage concludes when all scheduled contact between participants and leaders finishes.

Formats for the ending stage

Some participants may drop out of training groups either because they are dissatisfied or because their life circumstances change. Here, the focus is on ending formats chosen by leaders. The following are possible formats.

- *End when individual goals are attained.* Ending on goal attainment implies open rather than closed training groups. Participants set themselves personal goals. They leave groups when, together with their leaders, they consider that their targeted skills have been attained. Leaders running open groups tend to fill leavers' places from waiting lists. Open groups do not run for ever. Therefore, some participants will be faced with specific cut-off points for developing skills by the time a group ends.

- *End at the last regularly scheduled session.* Many, if not most, training groups meet on a regular basis and terminate at the end of the last scheduled session.

- *Faded ending.* Here the group's ending is gradual. For example, instead of meeting weekly, the group's final two sessions may be at bi-weekly or even monthly intervals.

- *Massed ending.* Massed ending is the opposite to faded ending. The group, which may have been meeting weekly for two hours, ends with an all-day or weekend marathon session.

- *Regular ending plus one or more follow-up group sessions.* The follow-up sessions are not to teach new skills, but to assess participants' post-group progress, motivate them, and help work through difficulties in translating trained skills into home environments.

- *Regular ending plus individual interview(s)/phone call(s) with leaders.* The timing of individual interviews can vary. Some leaders conduct exit interviews to help participants to set personal goals and develop strategies for consolidating self-help skills. These individual interviews may be as brief as 15 to 30 minutes. Other leaders find it more valuable to schedule follow-up interviews three to six months after final group sessions. Leaders can also schedule follow-up phone calls with participants. In addition, leaders can indicate if and under

what circumstances participants can initiate phone calls and interviews with them. Leaders may also contact participants and ask them to complete questionnaires evaluating post-group progress.

- *Different permutations of the above.* For example, massed endings could still be followed either by booster sessions three to six months later or by one or more individual interviews with leaders.

Consolidate self-help skills

The main leader task of the ending stage is to help participants to further consolidate their trained skills as self-help skills. Many skills that leaders use during this stage build on skills used earlier in groups. Below are some ending-stage skills for consolidating self-help skills.

MAKE TRANSITION STATEMENTS

Mention has already been made of reminder statements concerning a group's finiteness to encourage participants to make the most of the group. One or more transition statements that introduce the ending stage can reinforce earlier reminders. The following are possible transition statements to the ending stage.

> 'Our next session is the final session. Maybe we should discuss how we can use the the time we have left, including the time between sessions, to help you retain and build on the skills that you've learned when the group ends.'

> 'Since this is the start of the final session, in this session I want to focus on helping you to integrate the skills that you've learned in the group so that they become part of your daily lives. This integration includes assessing how much you have changed, identifying where you still need to change, and committing yourself to personal goals and to developing skills of dealing with setbacks.'

SUMMARIZE

Approaches to summarizing include the following. During final sessions, the main lessons conveyed throughout groups can be summarized by leaders. Alternatively, participants might summarize the main lessons either in the whole group or in pairs or small groups. Summarizing is more personal if participants summarize the main lessons that they personally found useful. Formulating a personal summary can be a homework assignment prior to final sessions. Participants might also be asked to cassette-record their summaries as reminders for afterwards. In addition, leaders may distribute hand-outs summarizing the main lessons learned by the group. Leaders may use more than one of the above ways of summarizing.

FACILITATE SELF-ASSESSMENT, GOAL SETTING AND PLANNING

During the ending stage, leaders continue to develop participants' skills of self-observation and assessment. Leaders may administer end-of-group self-assessment questionnaires. One option is to administer such questionnaires in final sessions. However, given committed groups, a better option may be to administer questionnaires at penultimate sessions as homework tasks. The advantages of homework completion of questionnaires are that: questionnaires do not use up contact time; participants have more time to think about their answers; participants can assess progress if ending questionnaires are similar to beginning questionnaires; and participants have more time to think through post-group personal goals and develop plans to attain them.

During final sessions, leaders and participants need to review assessments, personal goals and plans to attain them. In addition, leaders can help participants to devise ways of assessing themselves once groups end. For instance, leaders may hand out self-assessment worksheets for evaluating post-group progress.

GIVE AND FACILITATE FEEDBACK

Feedback during final sessions can be useful for helping participants to assess their progress over the group's life. Participants may receive leaders' and groups' perceptions of: their strengths and weaknesses; unhelpful ways of thinking and behaving; hopes for their future; ways to handle specific situations; and the adequacy of their personal goals and plans. Participants should be asked to give constructively critical as well as positive feedback. Constructive feedback gives participants further insights for goal setting and planning. Open acknowledgement from others of positive behaviour changes motivates participants to keep working.

REINFORCE EFFECTIVE THINKING SKILLS

Leaders can use the ending stage to reinforce thinking skills that help participants to retain and develop trained skills. Effective thinking skills include those for: attributing cause accurately, possessing realistic rules, self-instructing, using coping self-talk, goal setting, relapse prevention and managing problems. Before final sessions, leaders should introduce any thinking skills conducive to retaining targeted skills – the final session is almost too late. During final sessions leaders can review the use of already-presented thinking skills, both by way of summaries and also when dealing with participants' personal agendas.

REHEARSE COPING WITH DIFFICULTIES AND SETBACKS

Rehearsing coping with difficulties and setbacks should be part of role-plays during groups, not afterthoughts left to final sessions. Nevertheless, in final sessions, leaders may fruitfully take their groups through some useful strategies for coping with difficulties, setbacks and re-entry problems. Leaders can emphasize that, even though participants can only influence other people, they can have considerable power over their own behaviour. Therefore, when in difficulty, looking at the adequacy of one's own thinking, behaviour and use of targeted skills is the best place to start. Participants can ask themselves such questions as 'What are my goals and how is my behaviour helping me to attain them?' 'What might I be thinking or doing that blocks my effectiveness?' and 'How well am I using the skills that I have learned and how can I improve?' Action strategies for dealing with setbacks vary considerably, depending on the focus of the lifeskills training group.

WORK WITH LEADER'S AIDES IN PARTICIPANTS' HOME ENVIRONMENTS

At the ending stage, leaders may contact their aides. During this contact, leaders may receive assessments of participants' outside-group progress. Leaders may also work with aides to identify ways in which they can support participants once programmes end. Sometimes a three-way meeting between leader, participant and aide is desirable. For example, at the end of a supervisory skills training programme, leader, trainee supervisor and manager could together plan how the trainee supervisor might continue to receive appropriate learning experiences and feedback.

HELP PARTICIPANTS TO USE SUPPORTS

During groups, leaders should help participants to identify and use supports for learning targeted skills. At groups' endings, leaders can help participants to identify and use supports for maintaining and developing targeted skills. These supports may not be the same people who helped them during groups. For instance, some participants might continue the buddy system with partners they had worked with during a group. Alternatively, one or more participants might decide to enter peer self-help groups independent of their training groups.

ARRANGE FOR FOLLOW-UP LEADER–PARTICIPANT CONTACT

Given the high probability of some degree of relapse in using targeted skills, leaders need to think through whether and how they might schedule follow-up contact with participants. Options include: whole-group booster sessions, individual interviews either scheduled or at participants' request, phone calls either scheduled or at participants' request, and follow-up questionnaires. In addition, groups may schedule social reunions during which progress and strategies for coping with difficulties are discussed. However, good attendance at reunions cannot be guaranteed.

PROVIDE INFORMATION ON SKILLS-BUILDING OPPORTUNITIES

Leaders can provide information on resources that participants can use to improve skills. Sometimes, leaders refer participants for counselling help. Referral discussions are best conducted on an individual basis. Suggestions can be made of counsellors and psychotherapists with a cognitive–behavioural orientation, preferably within a humanistic-existential framework. Also, leaders can discuss opportunities for further training groups, courses or workshops, be they run by themselves or others. Leaders can review skills for choosing other lifeskills groups, including what to avoid.

SUGGEST FURTHER READING AND AUDIOVISUAL MATERIAL

If not using training manuals, participants may retain information by receiving session hand-outs and storing them in binders. In the final sessions leaders can give out and go through annotated lists of further reading suggestions. Participants learn in different ways. Some benefit from having their post-group attempts to learn reinforced by self-help reading. In addition, participants can be referred to appropriate self-help cassettes and videos.

Exercise 32 builds on Exercise 31 by encouraging readers to think through ending-stage strategies for consolidating trained skills as self-help skills.

Exercise 32 Consolidate self-help skills in the ending stage

With regard to a lifeskills training group of your choice, indicate how, during the group's ending stage, you might use each of the following leader skills to help participants to consolidate trained skills as self-help skills for when the group finishes.

Make transition statements
Summarize
Facilitate self-assessment, goal setting and planning
Give and facilitate feedback
Reinforce effective thinking skills
Rehearse coping with difficulties and setbacks
Work with leader's aides in participants' home environments
Help participants to use supports
Arrange for follow-up leader–participant contact
Provide information on skills-building opportunities
Suggest further reading and audiovisual material
Other skills not mentioned above

Summarize how as a leader you would aim, during your group's ending stage, to help participants to consolidate trained skills as self-help skills.

Further ending-stage tasks and agendas

Along with the major task of consolidating self-help skills, there are other tasks for the ending stage of training groups. Leaders and the group can choose how much time and emphasis to allocate to each task.

EVALUATE THE GROUP

In the final session, participants may make unstructured comments about the group's degree of success and the reasons for it. Alternatively, leaders can initiate rounds in which each participant has the opportunity to share views. Leaders may also share their thoughts and feelings about the group's processes and outcomes. Another possibility is for participants to fill in end-of-group questionnaires either

before, during, or possibly after final sessions. Training groups being researched may have extra time set aside for post-test evaluation. Also, rigorous researchers schedule follow-up evaluations.

EVALUATE THE LEADER(S)

During training groups, all leaders receive informal feedback and some collect systematic feedback on how participants react to them and perceive their skills. The main focus at the group's end should be on participants' needs. However, leaders can also solicit feedback about themselves. One method is to ask an open-ended question: 'Does anyone have anything they would like to feed back to me about the way I led the group?' Leaders may also encourage each participant to comment about their leadership either in front of the group or by answering end-of-group questionnaires.

DEAL WITH EMOTIONAL BUSINESS

Training groups tend to be less emotionally charged than long-term counselling and psychotherapy groups. Nevertheless, participants may have feelings of sadness, anxiety and possibly abandonment when the time comes to end. Other participants may breathe a sigh of relief. Hopefully, most participants will have a sense of accomplishment. Leaders can facilitate open discussion of feelings about the group ending. Training groups spend much less time and effort than interactional groups on trying to work through unfinished emotional business either between participants or between participants and leaders.

SAY GOODBYE

Leaders should pay close attention to how they close the group's final session. Much earlier good work may be undone through closing the session sloppily. Assuming that the group has worked hard, leaders' verbal, voice and body messages should communicate appreciation of this fact. If leaders have enjoyed working with the group, they can share this feeling. Last impressions as well as first impressions are important. In addition, participants want to say goodbye to each other and, possibly, exchange phone numbers and addresses. Some participants may want to go for an end-of-group drink or meal either immediately after final sessions or at later dates.

END ETHICALLY

A number of important ethical issues exist concerning how leaders terminate training groups. For example, if participants clearly have major unresolved personal issues at a group's end, leaders should offer individual interviews. Another issue is how much support to offer participants after the group. Leader support can be important for participants as they try out their skills. However, too much support can engender dependency. Still another ethical issue is that of being honest about the limitations of groups and not overselling them. As stressed throughout this chapter, participants need to to be prepared for a continuous struggle to retain and develop skills. A further issue is that of confidentiality. Leaders can remind participants of their ethical obligation to keep confidences.

CONCLUDING COMMENTS

Ending stages of lifeskills training groups represent beginnings too. The closure of the ending stage represents a commencement of the need for participants to consolidate trained skills on their own. This consolidation of trained skills as self-help skills is a life-long endeavour. For those participants able to retain some or all of their trained skills, the rewards to themselves and others should justify the effort.

CHAPTER HIGHLIGHTS

Leaders should not just train and hope that their groups will have lasting effects on participants. Instead, in all the group's stages, leaders must use strategies to help participants to consolidate trained skills as self-help skills.

Generalization, transfer, maintenance and development are four important dimensions of consolidating trained skills as self-help skills.

Leader thinking skills relevant to consolidating participants' self-help skills include: attribute cause accurately; possess realistic rules; and predict realistically.

Participant thinking skills relevant to consolidating self-help skills include: attributing cause accurately; possessing realistic rules; self-instructing; coping self-talk; predicting realistically; goal-setting skills; visualizing; using self-reward; relapse prevention skills; and managing-problems skills.

Leader preparatory stage skills for consolidating participants' self-help skills include: allow for overlearning; use leader's aides in participants' home environments; and advertise realistically.

Leader initial-stage skills for consolidating participants' self-help skills include: structure realistic expectations; and develop participants' self-observation and assessment skills.

Leader working-stage skills for consolidating participants' self-help skills include: use leader's aides in participants' home environments; develop participants' self-observation and assessment skills; remind the group of its finiteness; emphasize real-lifeness; train diversely; rehearse coping with difficulties and setbacks; emphasize homework tasks; help participants to use supports; use reward strategies; and become a consultant.

Different formats exist for the ending stage of lifeskills groups. These formats include follow-up contact with the leader in either group sessions or individual interviews.

Leader ending-stage skills for consolidating participants' self-help skills include: make transition statements; summarize; facilitate self-assessment, goal setting and planning; give and facilitate feedback; reinforce effective thinking skills; rehearse coping with difficulties and setbacks; work with leader's aides in participants' home environments; help participants to use supports; arrange for follow-up leader–participant contact; provide information on skills-building opportunities; and suggest further reading and audiovisual material.

Further ending-stage tasks and agendas include: evaluate the group; evaluate the leader; deal with emotional business; say goodbye; and end ethically.

TWELVE

How to Evaluate and Research Training Groups

The whole of science is nothing more than a refinement of everyday thinking.

Albert Einstein

CHAPTER QUESTIONS

What information might leaders collect when evaluating themselves and their training groups?

What evaluative questions might leaders ask of participants?

What are the main variables to consider in researching training groups?

What designs are appropriate for researching training groups?

INTRODUCTION

This chapter on evaluating and researching training groups builds on the earlier discussions regarding designing lifeskills programmes in Chapter 4 and assessment and helping self-assessment in Chapter 5. Effective training group leaders monitor and evaluate throughout their groups. Participants, interested third parties, supervisors and researchers are among others who evaluate training groups. Here, three approaches to end-of-group evaluation are reviewed: leader self-evaluation; participant evaluation; and evaluation by research.

LEADER SELF-EVALUATION

By a group's end, leaders have many sources of information for evaluating themselves. These sources of information include: recollections and impressions (Whitaker, 1985); session notes; journal entries (Corey *et al.*, 1988a); verbal feedback; written feedback; comments made at post-group interviews; feedback from colleagues and interested third parties; video feedback; attendance; and compliance with homework tasks. Leaders need to evaluate their experiences soon after the group ends, or they risk forgetting valuable information.

Leader self-evaluation has numerous purposes. First, it may give leaders opportunities to gain more perspective on their groups. Second, they may get a clearer idea of how successful their groups have been. Third, they may get affirmation that their efforts have made positive differences. Fourth, leaders may identify processes and factors contributing to both positive and negative outcomes. Fifth, leaders may identify skills strengths to maintain and skills weaknesses on which to work. Sixth, they may clarify ideas for leading future groups.

Leader self-evaluation need not be a long and arduous process. Below is a series of questions that leaders can ask themselves to guide self-evaluation.

Leader self-evaluation questions

1. To what extent did the group achieve its overall goal and broad sub-goals? How do I know?
2. To what extent were individual participants satisfied that they had attained their personal goals as a result of the group? How do I know?
3. Were there any additional positive and negative outcomes from running the group?
4. Did I set sufficiently clear and realistic goals for the group?
5. Am I satisfied both with the programme I used and with the way it was designed?
6. Am I satisfied with the group's size and composition?
7. Did I do sufficient groundwork and consult adequately with third parties with an interest in the group?
8. Did I have a sufficiently clear contract with participants?
9. Am I happy with the ways in which I encouraged participants to assess themselves and to set personal goals?
10. Am I satisfied with the way that I opened the group and conducted the initial session?
11. Under what circumstances and how well did I use facilitation skills during the group?
12. How satisfied am I with the written training material I used?
13. What were my public speaking skills strengths and weaknesses?
14. What were my demonstration skills strengths and weaknesses?
15. What were my using-structured-activity skills strengths and weaknesses?

16.   How satisfied am I with how I used and monitored between-session homework?

17.   How satisfied am I with the way I planned individual sessions during the group's working stage?

18.   How satisfied am I with the way I conducted individual sessions during the group's working stage?

19.   What strategies for consolidating trained skills as self-help skills did I use and how effective did they seem?

20.   How well did I end the group?

21.   How satisfied am I with the way I identified and handled ethical issues arising from the group?

22.   Did I have adequate personal and professional support and supervision when leading the group?

23.   What aspects of leading the group did I find rewarding and what aspects less rewarding?

24.   What specifically did I learn about my style and skills for leading training groups?

25.   What are my goals for improving my performance as a training group leader?

26.   Should I continue to lead training groups and, if so, in what lifeskills areas?

When leaders evaluate themselves they need to beware of tendencies to perceptual distortion. Two important perceptual skills are the ability to distinguish between facts and inferences and to make your inferences follow logically from the available facts. Some leaders may be so intent on validating their efforts that they selectively perceive positive feedback and give it too much weight. At the other extreme are leaders who discount successes and dwell excessively on shortcomings. Other perceptual errors that interfere with self-evaluation include: black-and-white thinking, 'the group is either going extremely well or extremely badly'; tunnel vision, focusing on only a portion of the available information in situations rather than taking into account all significant data; and self-rating, going beyond functional ratings of specific characteristics of your group leadership to devaluing yourself as a whole person (Beck, 1976; Beck & Emery, 1985; Beck & Weishaar, 1989; Nelson-Jones, 1989).

PARTICIPANT EVALUATION

Leaders can get participants to evaluate lifeskills training groups in two main ways. First, participants can evaluate what they learned from the group and how helpful it was for attaining personal goals. Second, participants can evaluate group processes and leader skills.

Self-assessment

Participants can be asked to fill in self-assessment forms before or at final sessions and at follow-up sessions. The following are some of the questions that might be asked.

Participant self-assessment questions

1. List each of your goals on joining this training group. How satisfied are you with your progress in attaining each goal?
2. In what specific situations, if any, are you coping better as a result of skills developed in the group?
3. With what specific people are you coping better as a result of skills developed in this group?
4. What kinds of difficulties and setbacks did you encounter when you tried to implement your skills outside the group?
5. What coping strategies did you find helpful when you faced difficulties and setbacks in implementing trained skills outside the group?
6. What kinds of feedback and support have you received from significant people in your life when you tried to implement your skills?
7. What, if any, negative outcomes and consequences have your participation in the group had for you?
8. How actively did you participate in the learning process in the group?
9. How actively did you participate in homework tasks outside the group?
10. What are your goals for maintaining and developing your skills after the group?
11. How do you intend assessing your post-group progress?
12. What difficulties and setbacks do you anticipate in implementing your skills after the group and how do you plan to cope with each?

Evaluation of group

Leaders can also systematically collect participants' perceptions of how skilfully they led groups. An issue here is whether or not to allow the feedback to be anonymous. Gazda (1989) favours anonymous post-treatment questionnaires. Perceptions of group experiences may change over time, so follow-up data may also be of interest. Simple end-of-group questionnaires can consist of four items:

1. A rating of the group on a scale of 1, no good at all, to 7, excellent.
2. 'State as specifically as possible what you consider the strengths of the group to have been.'

3. 'Indicate as specifically as possible what areas of the group are in need of improvement.'
4. 'Make any other comments in the space below.'

Participants can evaluate groups and leaders both in more detail and more systematically than the above brief questionnaire. For example, participants could be asked to rate and provide comments on: usefulness of sessions; effectiveness of each intervention; and dimensions of leadership such as acceptance, warmth, competence, attractiveness, cultural sensitivity, trustworthiness and respect. Readers are referred to the section in Chapter 5 on devising assessment measures for further ideas on ways to design simple evaluation procedures.

EVALUATION BY RESEARCH

The great tragedy of Science – the slaying of a beautiful hypothesis by an ugly fact.

T.H. Huxley

Dictionary definitions of research tend to use adjectives like 'careful' and 'systematic' and nouns like 'study', 'inquiry' and 'investigation'. Research into lifeskills training groups involves systematically studying their processes and outcomes. Training group leaders may conduct research solely for their own benefit. Alternatively, leaders can publish and share research findings with others. Leaders can also invite third parties to conduct research into their groups. The fact that a research literature on training groups already exists gives researchers a base for designing further studies.

Research into lifeskills training groups can be of different degrees of methodological tightness. Training groups do not lend themselves to the kind of almost total environmental control sometimes achievable in the natural sciences. Also, many variables in training groups, for instance leader empathy, do not lend themselves to precise quantification. Consequently, at best training group researchers are limited in the extent to which the content and outcomes of their studies will be reliable and valid. What training group researchers must strive for is the maximum degree of tightness. They always need to be conscious of actual and potential sources of invalidity in their work. Furthermore, training group researchers need to beware of misinterpreting and overinterpreting findings. In addition, they should always view their findings in the context of relevant findings from other studies.

Research variables

Leaders require clear goals for any research they conduct into their groups. Research goals need to be formulated in the group's preparatory stage, or necessary baseline data may not be collected. What can be looked at in training groups? Below are suggestions of variables, albeit sometimes interrelated, that might be explored.

- *Leader variables.* Leader variables include: age, sex, race, culture, socio-economic status, professional training, relevant background and experience, leadership style, theoretical orientation, facilitative skills, didactic skills, emotional well-being, thinking skills, attitudes and values, perceived trustworthiness, perceived attractiveness, perceived competence, non-verbal communication, access to support and supervision, and expectations (Beutler *et al.*, 1986; Rose, 1986; Smith & Glass, 1977).

- *Participant variables.* Participant variables include: age, sex, race, culture, socio-economic status, education, occupation, emotional well-being, attitudes and values, expectations, commitment to the group, self-disclosure, non-verbal communication, thinking skills, group attendance, and homework compliance rates (Garfield, 1986; Rose, 1986).

- *Process variables.* Process variables consist of specific details regarding the content and management of training programmes. Process variables include: group size, pre-group training, type of group, focus of group, number of sessions, frequency of sessions, duration of sessions, use of training manual, balance of discussion and didactic input, verbal presentations, method and use of demonstrations, use of structured activities, use of homework tasks, and post-group contact (Gazda, 1989; Matarazzo & Patterson, 1986).

- *Outcome variables.* The main outcome variables for training groups are participants' performances in targeted skills. Additional outcome variables include premature termination and level of satisfaction. Outcome variables may focus on individual as well as on group change. Methods of assessing outcomes were reviewed in Chapter 3. Assessment methods include: participant self-observation and monitoring; observation in natural settings; psychological tests and lifeskills inventories; and leader-designed measures.

Training group researchers can explore relationships among the above variables. For example, level of satisfaction with groups might be explored in relation to racial and cultural similarity between leaders and participants.

Research designs

Basically, two main groupings of research designs exist for investigating lifeskills training groups: comparison-group designs and single-group designs.

COMPARISON-GROUP DESIGNS

The most common design in the group work literature is that based on a control group and an experimental group. Gazda reports that 70 per cent of the group studies published in 1983–1987 that he reviewed used some form of a control group (Gazda, 1989). In the case of an assertion programme, those undergoing the intervention would form the experimental group, whereas the control group would be a no-treatment condition. Comparison-group designs can be more elaborate. For example, as well as the control group, there could be three experimental groups, each with a different focus. For instance, one assertion group could emphasize group discussion, another demonstration and structured activities, with the third combining group discussion with demonstration and structured activities.

A minimum requirement for comparison-group designs is that of pre-test and post-test administrations of evaluation or assessment measures. By administering pre-tests and post-tests on experimental and control groups, researchers may find that positive changes in targeted skills found in experimental groups above those found in control groups are attributable to experimental interventions. With more than one experimental group, researchers investigate not only whether the experimental interventions make a difference over no treatment, but also which interventions are more effective than others.

Wherever possible, training group researchers should administer follow-up measures. Follow-up data allow researchers to find the extent that trained skills are retained and consolidated as self-help skills. If a training group is designed with a post-group booster session, follow-up data may be collected in conjunction with this session. However, the presence or absence of a booster session also lends itself to research. For example, participants may be more inclined to retain skills if they know there will be a booster session than if there is no booster session. Thus, it is important for training group researchers to discover not only whether or not groups have lasting effects, but also the processes whereby transfer, generalization and development of skills can be enhanced.

Webster-Stratton and her colleagues provide an example of a lifeskills group study using a control group, three treatment conditions and collection of follow-up data (Webster-Stratton, 1989; Webster-Stratton et al., 1988, 1989). Parents of conduct-problem children were randomly assigned to either a waiting list control group or to one of three treatment programmes: (1) video modelling of parenting techniques plus group discussion focused on the videotape vignettes; (2) group discussion of the same topics covered in the videotapes, but without seeing the videotapes; and (3) self-administered watching of the videotapes without group discussion. Research measures were completed at baseline, immediately after treatment, and at a one-year follow-up. These measures included: mothers and fathers answering two checklists on their children's behaviour and also a parenting stress inventory; teachers filling out a questionnaire on the children's behaviour; mothers filling out a daily report on their children's behaviour during the assessment periods; and direct observation of mother–child and father–child interactions in the home. In addition, a consumer satisfaction questionnaire was administered.

Some advantages of comparison-group studies have already been indicated. Such studies are experimental in they allow for intervention hypotheses to be tested against control group performance. Also, they allow for comparisons to be made among various interventions. Disadvantages include the extra time and effort involved in measuring control groups. Most leaders find running lifeskills training groups time-consuming enough as it is. In addition, there are ethical issues entailed in withholding treatment from control groups. Such issues may be mitigated if control groups are waiting groups that receive the same training programmes soon. However, providing training for control groups shortly after experimental groups end limits the collection of comparative follow-up data. Comparison-group designs may also be criticized on the grounds of paying insufficient detail to 'moment-to-moment behavior changes or individual variations in responding' (Thoresen & Mahoney, 1974, p. 34). This criticism is not fully justified since, in comparison-group designs, individual data can be analysed and reported along with group data.

SINGLE-GROUP DESIGNS

Gazda reports that 95 per cent of the studies he reviewed from 1970 to 1976, 91 per cent from 1976 to 1980, and 70 per cent from 1983 to 1987, used some form of control group. He observes: 'This decrease may be due in part to research utilizing a variety of experimental designs that do not necessitate a defined control group' (Gazda, 1989, p. 318). Single-case research designs are increasingly used in counselling and psychotherapy research (Kazdin, 1982, 1986; Tracey, 1983). Kazdin writes: 'Single case experiments permit inferences to be drawn about intervention effects by using the patient as his or her own control. The impact of treatment is examined in relation to changes in the patient's dysfunction over time' (Kazdin, 1986, p. 39). He states that there are four main characteristics of single-case experiments: clear specification of goals, use of repeated observations, the delineation of time periods in which different conditions (baseline, treatment) apply, and relatively stable data – the more variable the data, the more difficult it is to draw conclusions about intervention effects (Kazdin, 1986).

Single-case designs and single-group designs are different but overlap. Single-group designs allow for the analysing and reporting of group data either with or instead of individual data. Useful inferences may be drawn from single-group designs without satisfying each of Kazdin's characteristics of single-case designs. For example, group data may still be of value despite Kazdin's condition of repeated observations, such as daily frequency counts of targeted behaviours, not being met. Also, in single-group designs, if use is not made of repeated measures, Kazdin's characteristic of stability of data cannot be assessed. When designing any training-group study, researchers must always consider the advantages and disadvantages of collecting repeated-measures data in addition to data from pre-test, post-test and follow-up administrations.

Below are a number of single-group designs for evaluating lifeskills groups:

1. *Pre-test/post-test design.* Group data can be analysed and reported with a pre-test/post-test design. Pre-test/post-test designs have the advantage of simplicity. However, pre-test/post-test designs without control groups have the disadvantage that researchers cannot make rigorous inferences about cause and effect.

2. *Waiting list control design.* A waiting list control design entails a minimum of three measurements. Take the example of an eight-week weight-loss group. The first measure might be eight weeks prior to the start of the group, the second measure at the group's start and the third measure at the group's end. The eight-week time interval before the group starts

is a no-treatment control period. The waiting list control design can be viewed as an experimental design. Researchers can compare changes taking place during the programme with any change that may have taken place with no treatment. However, the notion of no treatment is qualified by the fact that the expectancy of treatment may influence behaviour.

3. *Pre-test/post-test/follow-up test design.* In the pre-test/post-test/follow-up test design, instead of the no-treatment period being before the programme starts it takes place immediately after the programme ends. Again, the importance of collecting follow-up data is stressed. However, the use of a follow-up period for control purposes has distinct limitations. First, researchers cannot equate a no-treatment period with a period of withdrawal of treatment at the end of the group. In the former, participants have had no treatment, whereas in the latter they have experienced the intervention. Second, many lifeskills training groups heavily emphasize consolidating trained skills as self-help skills for when groups end. This emphasis makes the assumption of equivalency between a pre-group and a post-group control period even more problematic.

4. *Waiting list control/pre-test/post-test/follow-up test design.* Where possible, this is the optimum design for much single-group research. This design has the twin advantages of a reasonably 'pure' waiting list control period and the collection of follow-up data.

5. *Reversal design.* Inasmuch as the group intervention is withdrawn or reversed, the pre-test/post-test/follow-up test design can be viewed as a reversal design. However, probably the most popular reversal design in single-case research is the ABAB design (Thoresen & Mahoney, 1974). The ABAB design can be restricted to four administrations of measures: pre-treatment, end of first treatment period, end of reversal period, and end of second treatment period. However, often the ABAB design also entails taking repeated measures. For example, in a management-of-smoking lifeskills group, repeated measures of smoking behaviour might be taken during the following four periods: A, prior to the intervention; B, during the first administration of the intervention; A, during a period when the intervention is withdrawn; and B, during the period when the intervention is reinstated. The reversal to a no-treatment condition is meant to help show that any changes that take place are influenced by the treatment condition: their incidence falls off when treatment is withdrawn and increases when treatment resumes.

From a research viewpoint there are limitations to ABAB reversal designs. For example, performance frequently does not reverse to baseline levels in the reversal phase. Indeed, the whole emphasis in lifeskills training groups is that it should not. Consequently, assuming reversability in reversal control periods is questionable. Also, there are practical limitations to ABAB reversal designs. Training groups tend to be run continuously rather than on a start-stop-start-stop basis. Training groups with a no-treatment period in the middle may be difficult to organize and also contribute to participant drop-out. Furthermore, even participants who remain may feel that they are being used as research guinea-pigs and be resentful. Such resentment adversely affects the group's emotional climate and may create resistances to participation and learning. The use of repeated measures may be perceived by participants as more relevant for some training groups, for instance weight loss and managing smoking, than for others, for example managing conflict. In any event, to gain compliance, requests for repeatedly filling in self-observations need to be sensitively made. In addition, there are ethical reservations about withdrawing and then reinstating treatment unless, in the long run, this is to participants' advantage.

6. *Multiple-baseline design.* In multiple-baseline designs a minimum of two baselines are required. Thoresen and Mahoney (1974) give the example of baseline data being collected for four personal hygiene behaviours. The first, nail biting, is treated for several weeks, while the remainder remain untreated. Then toothbrushing is added to the currently-under-treatment category while the other two behaviours remain untreated. Ultimately, all four behaviours are treated. Multiple-baseline designs seek to demonstrate that targeted behaviours change only when interventions are applied. There are a number of limitations to multiple-baseline designs. First, the design assumes that the baselines are independent and that an intervention focused on one behaviour will not change others. This assumption of baseline independence is not always tenable. Second, in training groups, it is often desirable to teach general rules and thinking skills in addition to targeting specific behaviours. For instance, at the start of personal hygiene programmes, some general rules presented are relevant to most, if not all, personal hygiene behaviours, for example the need to assume responsibility for health. It is poor pedagogic practice to target specific hygiene behaviours alone. Third, ethical issues exist in withholding treatment for behaviours subject to a prolonged baseline period.

Leaders and researchers can evaluate single-group data in a number of ways. First, the data may be subjected to visual inspection. Changes and trends may be observed both for groups and individuals. Where individual as well as group data are reported, interesting observations may be made about the presence or lack of individual progress that might be disguised in group data. Second, the data may be evaluated statistically. Statistical analyses may entail use of conventional t and F tests, time series analysis, and randomization tests. Third, the data may be evaluated in terms of their practical validity for leaders and participants. Do the data make practical and therapeutic sense? Fourth, attempts may be made to replicate data from training group studies. Tracey uses Chassan's distinction between direct and systematic replication (Chassan, 1979; Tracey, 1983). In direct replication, leaders and researchers conduct and investigate second or third lifeskills training groups run like the first in as many ways as possible. In systematic replication, some variables of interest are changed in each subsequent single-group study.

When designing and leading lifeskills training groups, all leaders should regard themselves as hypothesis makers and testers. Leaders should be applied scientists doing their best to learn from both past and current experiences. At the very least, all training group leaders should engage in self-evaluation, invite participant evaluation of the group experience, and foster participant self-assessment. The degree to which leaders participate in more rigorous forms of evaluative research depends on numerous factors such as their current interests, the time available, their research skills, and what research support they can call on. Most leaders should be able to manage a straightforward single-group pre-test/post-test/follow-up test evaluative sequence in addition to collecting and analysing less formal evaluation questionnaires. Exercise 33 has been designed to develop your skills of evaluating lifeskills training groups.

Exercise 33   Evaluate a lifeskills training group

Either for the lifeskills training group you designed in Exercise 6 or for another training group, answer the following questions.

A. LEADER SELF-EVALUATION
What questions do you think it important to ask yourself to evaluate your work with the group?

B. PARTICIPANT EVALUATION
What questions do you think it important to ask participants so that they evaluate:
- their own progress
- the group experience
- your work as leader?

C. RESEARCH EVALUATION
Design a research study evaluating your lifeskills training group using either a comparison-group design or a single-group design. Make sure to specify:
- the goals for your research
- what measures you intend using
- when you will take measurements
- any scientific, practical or ethical problems with your research design.

CONCLUDING COMMENT

A continuing need exists for well-designed and well-conducted research studies on lifeskills-group processes and outcomes. Though much has been achieved, further creative and well-executed studies are still badly needed in all lifeskills training areas (Martin, 1990). Such studies are likely to go beyond the resources of most group leaders. Nevertheless, the need for high-quality applied research into training groups is great. Applied researchers and research funding bodies have a big role to play in creating a sound database for future lifeskills training practice.

CHAPTER HIGHLIGHTS

Effective training group leaders monitor and evaluate throughout their groups.

Leader self-evaluation after a group ends has numerous purposes: gaining perspective; assessing the degree of goal attainment; receiving affirmation; identifying what interventions work; and assessing your own strengths and weaknesses in leading training groups.

When self-evaluating, leaders must counteract tendencies to perceptual distortion.

Leaders can encourage participants to evaluate their group experience in two main ways: first, evaluating what they learned from the group and how helpful it was for attaining personal goals; second, evaluating group processes and leader skills.

Leaders require clear goals for any research that they conduct into their groups.

Clusters of variables, albeit somewhat interrelated, that training group researchers may investigate include: leader variables, participant variables, process variables and outcome variables.

Two main groupings of research designs for studying lifeskills training groups are comparison-group designs and single-group designs.

As a minimum, comparison-group designs require pre-tests and post-tests on both control and 'experimental' groups.

Variations in the basic comparison-group design include adding follow-up tests and using comparison groups with treatment modifications.

Single-case research designs and single-group research designs both overlap and are different. Single-group designs allow for the analysing and reporting of group data with or instead of individual repeated-measures data.

The optimum design for much single-group research is the waiting list control/pre-test/post-test/follow-up test design.

Single-group data may be evaluated by visual inspection, by statistical analyses, whether or not they make practical or therapeutic sense, and by attempts at replication.

Researchers into training groups should always be mindful of any scientific, practical and ethical limitations and issues in their studies.

A continuing need exists for well-designed and well-conducted research studies in training-group processes and outcomes.

THIRTEEN

How to Maintain and Develop Training Group Leader Skills

The toe of the star-gazer is often stubbed.
Russian Proverb

CHAPTER QUESTIONS

What is the current state of your training group leader skills?

How can leaders consolidate, maintain and develop lifeskills training skills?

REASSESS YOUR TRAINING GROUP LEADER SKILLS

Throughout this book, you have explored your training group leader skills. By now you have completed many, if not all, of the exercises. In addition, you may have practised training skills either in work or in other settings, for example voluntary agencies. Exercise 34 asks you to reassess your training group leader skills. Exercise 34 is the follow-up or post-test for Exercise 2, your initial assessment. Once you have completed Exercise 34, look back at your answers to Exercise 2 and note any differences. You may use Exercise 34 as a reassessment exercise both now and in the future. Unlike the leader self-evaluation questions listed in Chapter 12, Exercise 34 may be filled in prior to conducting training groups as well as after. Take your time over the exercise. Accurate self-assessment is vital for pinpointing strengths and weaknesses. Once you have clearly identified weaknesses, you are already part way to correcting them.

Exercise 34 Reassess your strengths and weaknesses as a training group leader

Using the following format, make a worksheet for reassessing your training group leader skills strengths and weaknesses. For more detail about a skills area, see the relevant chapter.

SKILLS AREA	MY STRENGTHS	MY WEAKNESSES
Prepare training groups		
Design lifeskills programme		
Assessment and help self-assessment		
Facilitate training groups		
Speak in public		
Demonstrate lifeskills		
Design and implement structured activities		
Prepare and manage individual training sessions		
Consolidate self-help skills and end training groups		
Evaluate and research training groups		

Make a list of your main skills strengths. Then make a list of the specific skills weaknesses you most need to work on. Set yourself goals and make and implement a plan to improve your training group leader skills.

CONSOLIDATE, MAINTAIN AND DEVELOP YOUR TRAINING GROUP LEADER SKILLS

You have now probably acquired some skills for leading lifeskills training groups. How can you consolidate, maintain and develop these skills? As with participants trying to consolidate trained skills as self-help skills, consolidating your leader skills does not automatically happen. You still need to work hard on the thinking and action skills of being effective group leaders. Many factors may interfere with your effectiveness. You must cope with them as best you can. Some of these factors are internal: for example, thinking skills weaknesses. Other factors are external: for instance, poor supervision or insufficient opportunity to lead groups.

Each of you has come to this book with a different set of group leader strengths and weaknesses. Furthermore, you have been exposed to different kinds of training. Also, your group leader experience varies. Some of you may be either enrolled in or have completed practicum courses in group leadership. These courses may or may not have emphasized leading training groups. Others may lead training groups without formal training. Still others may be both trained and experienced leaders. Whatever your current status, below are suggestions for how to consolidate, maintain and develop your trainer skills.

Clarify your values

What are the values by which you choose to lead your life? What ultimately is of worth to you? How can you develop and sustain the inner strength to be an effective training group leader? Some leaders may need to clarify their values before they can gain a genuine commitment to leading groups effectively. For example, instead of viewing training groups mainly in terms of either materialistic values, 'How much money is there in it for me?', or needs for approval, 'How can I be really popular in groups?', some leaders may need to access more fundamental human values. Such values include: a concern for developing participants' full humanity; prizing the uniqueness of each participant; being committed to working with participants for their sakes and not just for your own; and helping participants to make their own choices. Some leaders find inner strength and guidance from religious beliefs. The more committed leaders are to fundamental human values, the more they strive to consolidate and improve their training skills. Conversely, committed leaders are less likely to be sidetracked into superficial values and actions. Clarifying your values is partly a matter of self-help and of listening more deeply to yourself (Gendlin, 1981) and partly a matter of working with and learning from others.

Discipline your thinking

You need to discipline your thinking to keep growing as a training group leader. Thinking skills to work on include: attribute responsibility accurately for developing training skills; possess realistic rules and avoid perfectionism; accurately perceive feedback; use coping self-talk when faced with difficulties and setbacks; predict the future realistically; set realistic goals for yourself and your groups; use visualizing to rehearse and enhance strengths and cope with setbacks; and use managing-problems skills to think yourself through difficulties rather than reacting impulsively (Beck & Weishaar, 1989; Ellis, 1989; May & Yalom, 1989; Meichenbaum & Deffenbacher, 1988; Nelson-Jones, 1989). Like clarifying your values, disciplining your thinking is partly a matter of self-help and partly a matter of working with and learning from others.

Observe skilled leaders

In this book, I emphasize learning by observing. Learn by observing skilled leaders. The groups you observe need not necessarily be lifeskills training groups. For example, you may learn much about group facilitation by observing well-led person-centred groups. A number of ways exist to observe skilled leaders. In all instances, participants should consent to being observed. There is less resistance to observers where participants understand that such observation is for group leader training. However, participants require reassurance that observers maintain confidentiality. The following are some arrangements, not necessarily mutually exclusive, for observing lifeskills training groups.

- *Be present.* You may be allowed to sit in the room while a group is in progress. It may be easier for participants if you are unobtrusive. For instance, you sit outside the horseshoe and do not participate in discussions or structured activities.

- *Observe through a one-way mirror.* Observers may watch groups from behind one-way mirrors. A microphone and speaker system can provide sound. One-way mirror observation has the advantages of relative unobtrusiveness and of seeing proceedings both life-sized and as they happen.

- *View closed-circuit TV.* A video camera may be connected to a monitor in another room. Disadvantages of closed-circuit TV include the obtrusiveness of a camera in group rooms and a lessening of visual detail through problems of camera angle and monitor size.

- *Make video-recordings.* Watching your own video-recordings of groups has some of the disadvantages of using closed-circuit TV. In addition, participants may have more reservations about being recorded and observed than about being only observed. However, video-recordings have the advantage that leaders and observers can discuss and analyse tapes. Also, tapes can be stopped and played back to highlight specific 'do's' and 'don'ts'. Furthermore, videotapes may be reused for training purposes.

- *View videotapes and films recorded elsewhere.* Observing videotapes and films recorded elsewhere is another way to learn leader skills. Sources for purchasing films and videos include the American Association for Counseling and Development film library (5999 Stevenson Avenue, Alexandria, VA 22304, phone 703/823–9800) and Psychological and Educational Films (3334 East Coast Highway, Corona Del Mar, CA 92625, phone 714/494–5079). An advantage of films and tapes recorded elsewhere is that they are often of well-known leaders who portray a range of skills. Disadvantages can include price, the there-and-then nature of material, and the fact that observers do not view series of sessions.

Two important issues in observational learning are how many sessions observers watch and whether or not they engage in post-group discussions with the leaders of observed groups (Yalom, 1985). Observing single sessions can be very valuable. Nevertheless, added benefits accrue from observing one or more complete lifeskills training groups. Observers may see leaders use different skills for initial, working and ending stages. Also, observers may watch the development, or lack of development, of participants' skills. Where possible, observers should have the opportunity for post-session discussions with leaders. These discussions are best held shortly after group sessions when they are still fresh in people's minds.

Obtain supervision

Training group leaders require practice to develop competencies. You may build your skills by receiving supervision. Since the skills of leading lifeskills groups are varied, different approaches to supervision may suit different skills. The following are some approaches to supervision which may be used either singly or together.

- *Case study discussions of sessions.* The preparatory, initial, working and ending stages of each group that you lead can be discussed with supervisors as case studies. Supervisors may help you to design programmes and develop presentations. In addition, supervisors can be sounding boards as you work through problems and issues from sessions. An added strength of the group case study approach is that supervisors can focus on cognitive group leader skills (Biggs, 1988). A disadvantage is lack of videotape evidence to support discussion of how you actually behaved.

- *Supervisor views and then discusses live sessions.* Your supervisors may watch you leading sessions. Yalom states that an excellent supervision format, schedules permitting, is for supervisors to observe the last 30 minutes of psychotherapy group sessions and then hold supervisory discussions immediately afterwards (Yalom, 1985). Live viewing followed by supervision has the advantage of immediacy. However, if only viewing part of sessions, supervisors may not see the range of skills you used. Also, apart from recall, there is no evidence to illustrate specific points.

- *Supervisor views and discusses video-recorded sessions.* Viewing video-recordings is much preferable to viewing audio-recordings, since trainee leaders and supervisors can pick up body as well as verbal and voice messages. Broadly speaking, there are two main approaches to viewing supervision videotapes:

supervisor-centred and supervisee-centred. In the supervisor-centred approach there is an expert–neophyte relationship. Supervisors control the sessions and stop the video playback to point out good and poor use of skills. The supervisee-centred approach is represented by Kagan's Interpersonal Process Recall method (Kagan, 1984). Here supervisees control the proceedings and stop the video playback when they want. The supervisor's role is to facilitate the supervisee's recall by making inquiries: for example, 'What were you trying to do?', 'What were you feeling?', and 'Were there any risks for you?' Much supervision adopts a mixed model. A variation of the mixed model is to have supervisors control one session and supervisees control the next.

- *Co-lead with experienced leaders.* One of the best ways to learn trainer skills is to co-lead groups with more experienced leaders. In such instances, the experienced leaders may not be your supervisors. Nevertheless, they can always perform a supervisory function as you prepare groups, plan sessions, work together during sessions and discuss how you performed afterwards.

What characteristics make for effective supervision? Supervisors need to have a sound knowledge of the subject matter of your groups and also of how to put material across. The quality of the supervisory relationship is important. Supervisors are likely to be more effective if they demonstrate warmth, respect and empathy. In addition, supervisors should provide specific rather than general feedback. Furthermore, immediate post-group supervision is likely to be more effective than supervision delayed by several days (Matarrazo & Patterson, 1986).

Arrange peer supervision

Practising leaders should consider peer supervision in which you support and learn from each other. Co-counselling is one model of peer supervision. For instance, you may have 30 minutes each, reversing the supervisor/supervisee roles at the end of the first period. Furthermore, you can negotiate the role that you wish your supervisor to play – facilitator, trainer, personal support, etc. – so that you 'control' your supervision. Groups are another model of peer supervision. The group can decide how best to use the talents and resources of participants. Again, individual participants who present material can state what kind of assistance they require.

Practise and experiment

Training group leaders can build their training skills and confidence by rehearsal and practice. Furthermore, if they are prepared to take calculated risks, leaders can extend both the range of their interventions and the areas in which they lead groups. Effective group leadership is not just a matter of being safe all the time. Good leaders are flexible and creative in preparing groups, designing interventions, and responding to moment-to-moment session events. Also, leaders can increase the range of lifeskills groups that they offer. Broadening their training range may both increase leaders' skills and provide added stimulation and interest.

Participate in groups

Participant experience is often useful for learning about how to function in groups and also about how groups function (Corey & Corey, 1982; Rogers, 1970; Yalom, 1985). The accreditation committee of the American Group Psychotherapy Association has recommended a requirement of 60 hours of participation in groups (Yalom, 1985). There are two main, if overlapping, agendas for participating in well-led groups. First, there is the personal growth agenda. You may learn much about how you relate to people, including your defensive processes. You may also work through some of your anxieties about interacting in groups. Second, there is the professional growth agenda. You may have much more empathy for what it feels like to be a participant in groups if you participate yourself. Also, you may have more insight into the benefit of good facilitation if you have experienced it. Rogers states that, in the person-centred group leadership programme at La Jolla, about half of the programme's 150 hours were given over to direct experience as a participant in more than one small encounter group (Rogers, 1970). In addition, you may have a better grasp of didactic skills of leading training groups if you have experienced and observed them in a number of lifeskills groups.

Obtain counselling

Group leaders who are not at ease with themselves are likely to communicate tensions and anxieties to participants. An intensive group experience may not give the trainee leaders sufficient help with exploring specific problems and coping styles. Having individual sessions with competent and disciplined counsellors may be necessary. Training group leaders should be effective choosers who are in touch with their feelings, think effectively and act appropriately. Leaders should have worked through much of the emotional baggage and unfinished business from their upbringings, including self-defeating ways of feeling, thinking and acting. Such working through is often difficult to achieve without competent help.

Attend conferences, workshops and courses

There are no hard and fast distinctions between conferences, workshops and courses. However, training courses are usually spread out over a longer period, say a month or more, whereas workshops are ordinarily relatively intense experiences lasting from a day to a week. Some conferences are composed almost entirely of workshops. Other conferences have more of a focus on academic content. National professional associations in such areas as counselling, psychology, social work, teacher education, careers work, nursing, personnel work and business management are one source of information about lifeskills training courses and workshops. Also, professional associations may run sessions or workshops on group leadership at their conferences. Table 13.1 provides a checklist for assessing training courses and workshops.

Table 13.1   Checklist for assessing training courses and workshops

1. What are the goals?
2. What methods will be employed?
3. What is the pertinent training and experience of the group leader?
4. What is the size of the training course or workshop?
   Is there a screening process prior to entry?
5. When does the course or workshop start?
   How long is each session?
   Over what period will the course or workshop continue?
   Where will it be held?
   Are the facilities adequate?
6. What is the fee for the course or workshop, if any?
   Will it involve additional expenses?

If you are interested in building your group leadership skills in a particular area, you can also explore training opportunities in specialized agencies. For example, leaders wanting to direct role-plays can attend psychodrama courses or workshops run by psychodrama agencies. Leaders wishing to develop their group facilitation skills can attend courses and workshops run by experts in these skills. Developing your leader skills involves making use of a variety of learning opportunities.

Keep abreast of relevant literature

Effective group leaders keep up with the relevant literature. You can read books and journals about how to lead groups. By reading, you can increase your understanding of the theoretical and research underpinnings of group leadership. Furthermore, you can expand your understanding of the specific areas in which you lead groups, for example pain management skills or parenting skills.

How can you go about finding out about relevant books and training manuals? Here are some sources of information.

- *Name and subject catalogues in libraries.* Even if you do not know any names, you can still search for books under relevant key words, for example 'groups' or 'assertion'.

- *Publishers' catalogues.* If possible, find out which publishers specialize in books on helper training and structured groups. A well-known publisher of training material is Lifeskills Associates (Ashling, Back Church Lane, Adel, Leeds LS16 8DN).

- *Book reviews in journals.* You may subscribe to or get access to copies of *Contemporary Psychology*, a journal that publishes only book reviews. In addition, look up the book review sections in relevant professional and academic journals.

- *Master reference sources.* In North America, the master reference to currently available books, authors and publishers is the eight volumes of *Books in Print* (1989). Again, if you do not know the names of authors, you may conduct searches using key words. The similar source for books available in Britain is *Whitaker's Books in Print* (1989). There is an *Australian Books in Print* (1989). If possible, always use the most recent edition of the above sources.

- *Ask around.* If necessary, be prepared to ask what books other people read and which training manuals they use. If you operate as part of a team or are in a network of group leaders, you may help to keep each other up to date on reading suggestions.

You may also keep abreast of the literature by reading relevant professional and academic journals. Some journals focus specifically on group work; for example, the *International Journal of Group Psychotherapy*, the *Journal for Specialists in Group Work* and *Group Relations*. Other journals include research articles on group approaches to the training of different lifeskills, for example *Cognitive Therapy and Research* and *Behavior Therapy*. The main reference source for finding out about journals is *Ulrich's International Periodicals Directory 1989–1990* (1989). *Psychological Abstracts* is the main source of abstracts of psychological journal articles. A list of journals for articles relevant to leading lifeskills groups is provided as an Appendix.

Keep abreast of audiovisual training resources

Leaders also need to keep up with the latest training films, videotapes and audiocassettes. Some journals now review audiovisual material as well as books. Publishers' catalogues are another source of information. Distributors of self-help audiocassettes include: BMA Audio Cassettes (200 Park Avenue South, New York, NY 10003; phone, 1–800–221–3966 or in NY (212) 674–1900); Psychology Today Tapes (Dept 9101, Box 059073, Brooklyn, NY 11205–9061; phone (212) 337–6759); and Research Press (Box 3177, Champaign, IL 61826; phone (217) 352–3273). If you are interested, ask film, videotape and audiocassette distributors to send you their most recent catalogues.

Keep abreast of relevant information

Many training groups require leaders to have up-to-date information. For example, at the very least leaders of career education groups should have knowledge about current sources of occupational information and about occupational trends. Other examples of leaders providing information include: leaders of single-mothers' groups providing relevant legal and welfare information; leaders of pre-retirement groups providing financial planning, and occupational and leisure information; and leaders of health education groups providing relevant health care information.

Avoid burnout

Paraphrasing General MacArthur: 'Old lifeskills group leaders never die, they burn out long before.' Leading lifeskills groups can be stressful. When such stresses are added to other stresses that they may face, group leaders can become excellent candidates for burnout or breakdown. Freudenberger defines burnout: 'To deplete oneself. To exhaust one's physical and mental resources. To wear oneself out by excessively striving to reach some unrealistic expectation imposed by one's self or by the values of society' (Freudenberger, 1980, p. 17). Maslach and Jackson assess burnout as having three major components: emotional exhaustion, depersonalization and insufficient sense of personal accomplishment (Maslach & Jackson, 1981).

Many thinking and action skills weaknesses contribute to training group leaders feeling burned out. Relevant thinking skills weaknesses include: perfectionist personal rules; misattributing cause; undue pessimism; setting unrealistically high goals; and undue need for approval. Action skills weaknesses include: inability to set limits on workloads; poor time management; insufficient recreational outlets; and poor skills at looking after health and physical fitness.

Leaders who are punchdrunk with exhaustion lack the energy to lead groups competently. When thoroughly run down, you are not at your best. Your emotional depletion communicates itself to participants. Training group leaders have both professional and personal obligations not just to avoid burnout, but also to be positively psychologically well. Skills for managing stress and burnout include: negotiating a realistic workload both with others and yourself; muscular and visual relaxation; adequate recreational outlets; networking with supportive people; effective thinking; being assertive; and assuming more responsibility for your health. Take steps to prevent burnout where possible.

Exercise 35 helps you to assess methods of consolidating, maintaining and developing your training group leader skills.

Exercise 35 Consolidate, maintain and develop your training group leader skills

Listed opposite are different methods of consolidating, maintaining and developing your training group leader skills. Use the worksheet and assess both whether or not and how you might use each method.

DEVELOPING THE HUMAN POTENTIAL

Though nature may be indifferent to the survival of the human species, humans cannot afford this luxury. Furthermore, humans have the responsibility for making the most of their short sojourns on earth. Probably most people function well below their potential (Maslow, 1970). The lifeskills training movement represents an

METHOD	MY ASSESSMENT OF WHETHER AND HOW I CAN USE EACH METHOD
Clarify my values	
Discipline my thinking	
Observe skilled leaders	
Obtain supervision	
Arrange peer supervision	
Practise and experiment	
Participate in groups	
Obtain counselling	
Attend conferences, workshops and courses	
Keep abreast of relevant literature	
Keep abreast of audio-visual training resources	
Keep abreast of relevant information	
Avoid burnout	

Develop a plan to consolidate, maintain and improve your training group leader skills.

---

optimistic attempt to help people realize more of their potential. As training group leaders, you are part of an exciting attempt to improve the amount of happiness and well-being on this planet. May you have strength and skills in your endeavours.

CHAPTER HIGHLIGHTS

Effective training group leaders assume responsibility for consolidating, maintaining and developing their skills.

Leaders can periodically reassess their trainer strengths and weaknesses.

Suggestions for consolidating, maintaining and developing group leader skills include: clarify your values; discipline your thinking; observe skilled leaders; obtain supervision; arrange peer supervision; practise and experiment; participate in groups; obtain counselling; attend conferences, workshops and courses; keep abreast of relevant literature; keep abreast of audiovisual training resources; keep abreast of relevant information; and avoid burnout.

The lifeskills training movement represents an optimistic attempt to help people fulfil more of their potential. As group leaders you are part of this exciting endeavour.

Appendix

Some academic and professional journals for articles relevant to leading lifeskills training groups.

BRITAIN

Behaviour Research and Therapy
British Journal of Clinical Psychology
British Journal of Guidance and
  Counselling
British Journal of Social Psychology
Counselling
Counselling Psychology Quarterly
Group Relations
Journal of Occupational Psychology
Journal of Social and Personal
  Relationships
Personnel Review
The Psychologist

ASIA

Asian Journal of Psychology and
  Education
Japanese Journal of Behavior Therapy

AUSTRALASIA

Australian Counselling Psychologist
Australian Psychologist
Australian Journal of Psychology
Bulletin of the Australian Psychological
  Society
New Zealand Journal of Psychology

NORTH AMERICA

American Journal of Family Therapy
American Psychologist
Applied Cognitive Psychology
Behavior Modification
Behavior Therapy
Canadian Journal of Counselling/Revue
  Canadienne de Counselling
Canadian Journal of Psychology/Revue
  Canadienne de Psychologie
Canadian Psychology
Career Development Quarterly
Counselor Education and Supervision
The Counseling Psychologist
Journal for Specialists in Group Work
Journal of Abnormal Psychology
Journal of Counseling Psychology
Journal of Consulting and Clinical
  Psychology
Journal of Counseling and Development
Journal of Marital and Family Therapy
Journal of Personality and Social
  Psychology
Journal of Vocational Behavior
Personnel Journal
Personnel Psychology
Psychology Today

INTERNATIONAL

International Journal for the
  Advancement of Counselling

International Journal of Group
  Psychotherapy

In addition, academic and professional journals in such areas as teacher education, social work, nursing and management may publish articles of interest to training group leaders.

BIBLIOGRAPHY

Abramowitz, I. A. & Coursey, R. D. (1989). Impact of an educational support group on family participants who take care of their schizophrenic relatives. *Journal of Consulting and Clinical Psychology*, **57**, 232–6.

Acock, A. C. & Hurlbert, J. S. (1990). Social network analysis: A structural perspective for family studies. *Journal of Social and Personal Relationships*, **7**, 245–64.

Alberti, R. E. & Emmons, M. L. (1986). *Your Perfect Right: A Guide to Assertive Living* (5th edn). San Luis Obispo: Impact Publishers.

Allen, V.B., Sampson, J.P. & Herlihy, B. (1988). Details of the AACD Ethical Standards. *Journal of Counseling and Development*, **67**, 157–8.

Allred, G. B. (1988). Sensitizing nursing home staff to residents' needs: A workshop. *Journal of Counseling and Development*, **66**, 248–9.

Alpert, R. & Haber, R. N. (1960). Anxiety in academic achievement situations. *Journal of Abnormal and Social Psychology*, **61**, 204–15.

Amatea, E. S. & Cross, E. G. (1983). Coupling and careers: A workshop for dual career couples at the launching stage. *Personnel and Guidance Journal*, **62**, 48–52.

Amatea, E. S., Clark, J. E. & Cross, E. G. (1984). Life-styles: Evaluating a life role planning program for high school students. *Vocational Guidance Quarterly*, **32**, 249–59.

American Association for Counseling and Development (1988). *Ethical Standards*. Alexandria, VA: American Association for Counseling and Development.

American Psychological Association (1973). *Guidelines for Psychologists Conducting Growth Groups*. Washington, DC: American Psychological Association.

American Psychological Association (1981). Ethical principles of psychologists. *American Psychologist*, **36**, 633–8.

American Psychological Association (1985). *Standards for Educational and Psychological Testing*. Washington, DC: American Psychological Association.

American Psychological Association (1987). General guidelines for providers of psychological services. *American Psychologist*, **42**, 724–9.

Anastasi, A. (1988). *Psychological Testing* (6th edn). New York: Macmillan.

Arbuckle, D. S. (1976). Comment on A. E. Ivey's paper 'The counselor as teacher'. *Personnel and Guidance Journal*, **54**, 434.

Argyle, M. (1983). *The Psychology of Interpersonal Behaviour* (4th edn). Harmondsworth, Middlesex: Penguin.

Argyle, M. (1984). Some new developments in social skills training. *Bulletin of the British Psychological Society*, **37**, 405–10.

Argyle, M. (1986). Rules for social relationships in four cultures. *Australian Journal of Psychology*, **38**, 309–18.

Arlow, J. A. (1989). Psychoanalysis. In R. Corsini & D. Wedding (eds), *Current Psychotherapies* (4th edn), pp. 19–62. Itasca, IL: Peacock.

Australian Books in Print (1989). Melbourne: R. Thorpe.

Azrin, N. H., Flores, T. & Kaplan, S. J. (1975). Job-finding club: A group-assisted program for obtaining employment. *Behaviour Research and Therapy*, **13**, 17–27.

Azrin, N. H. & Philip, R. A. (1979). The Job Club method for the job handicapped: A comparative outcome study, *Rehabilitation Counselling Bulletin*, **23**, 144–5.

Bandura, A. (1969). *Principles of Behavior Modification*. New York: Holt, Rinehart & Winston.

Bandura, A. (1976). Effecting change through participant modeling. In J. D. Krumboltz & C. E. Thoresen (eds), *Counseling Methods*, pp. 248–65. New York: Holt, Rinehart & Winston.

Bandura, A. (1977). *Social Learning Theory*. Englewood Cliffs, N J: Prentice-Hall.

Bandura, A. (1986). *Social Foundations of Thought and Action: A Social Cognitive Theory*. Englewood Cliffs, N J: Prentice-Hall.

Bandura, A., Grusec, J. E. & Menlove, F. L. (1966). Observational learning as a function of symbolization and incentive set. *Child Development*, **37**, 499–506.

Barnette, E. L. (1989). A program to meet the emotional and social needs of gifted and talented adolescents. *Journal of Counseling and Development*, **67**, 525–8.

Barrow, J. C. & Moore, C. A. (1983). Group interventions with perfectionist thinking. *Personnel and Guidance Journal*, **61**, 612–15.

Beck, A. T. (1976). *Cognitive Therapy and the Emotional Disorders*. New York: New American Library.

Beck, A. T. (1988). *Love Is Never Enough: How Couples Can Overcome Misunderstandings, Resolve Conflicts, and Solve Relationship Problems through Cognitive Therapy*. New York: Harper & Row.

Beck, A. T. & Emery, G. (1985). *Anxiety Disorders and Phobias: A Cognitive Perspective*. New York: Basic Books.

Beck, A. T. & Greenberg, R. L. (1974). *Coping with Depression*. New York: Institute for Rational Living.

Beck, A. T. & Weishaar, M. E. (1989). Cognitive therapy. In R. Corsini & D. Wedding (eds), *Current Psychotherapies* (4th edn), pp. 285–320. Itasca, IL: Peacock.

Beck, A. T., Rush, A. J., Shaw, B. F. & Emery, G. (1979). *Cognitive Therapy of Depression*. New York: John Wiley.

Bem, S. L. (1974). The measurement of psychological androgeny. *Journal of Consulting and Clinical Psychology*, **42**, 155–62.

Bem, S. L. (1981). Gender schema theory: A cognitive account of sex typing. *Psychological Review*, **88**, 354–64.

Bernstein, D. (1988). *Put It Together, Put It Across: The Craft of Business Presentation*. London: Cassell.

Beutler, L. E., Crago, M. & Arizmendi, T. G. (1986). Research on therapist variables in psychotherapy. In S. L. Garfield & A. E. Bergin (eds), *Handbook of Psychotherapy and Behavior Change* (3rd edn), pp. 257–310. New York: Wiley.

Biggs, D. A. (1988). The case presentation approach in clinical supervision. *Counselor Education and Supervision*, **27**, 240–8.

Blanchard, M. (1989). Wellness programs produce positive results. *Personnel Journal*, **68**, 30.

Blatner, A. (1989). Psychodrama. In R. J. Corsini & D. Wedding (eds), *Current Psychotherapies* (4th edn), pp. 561–71. Itasca, IL: Peacock.

Bloch, S. & Crouch, E. (1985). *Therapeutic Factors in Group Psychotherapy*. Oxford: Oxford University Press.

Bloom, D. E. (1986). Women and work. *American Demographics*, **8**, 25–30.

Books in Print (1989). Vols 1–8. New York: R. R. Bowker.

Bowlby, J. (1979). *The Making and Breaking of Affectional Bonds*. London: Tavistock.

Bradford, L. P., Gibb, J. R. & Benne, K. D. (eds), (1964). *T-Group Theory and Laboratory Method: Innovation in Re-education*. New York: John Wiley.

Brammer, L. M. (1985). *The Helping Relationship: Process and Skills* (3rd edn). Englewood Cliffs, NJ: Prentice-Hall.

Brehm, S. S. & Smith, T. W. (1986). Social psychological approaches to psychotherapy and behavior change. In S. L. Garfield & A. E. Bergin (eds), *Handbook of Psychotherapy and Behavior Change* (3rd edn), pp. 69–115. New York: John Wiley.

British Association for Counselling (1990). *Code of Ethics and Practice for Counsellors*. Rugby: British Association for Counselling.

British Psychological Society (1991). *Code of Conduct, Ethical Principles & Guidelines*. Leicester: British Psychological Society.

Brolin, D. E. & Gysbers, N. C. (1989). Career education for students with disabilities. *Journal of Counseling and Development*, 68, 155–9.

Brown, A. (1986). *Groupwork* (2nd edn). Aldershot, England: Gower.

Brown, R. A. & Lewinsohn, P. (1984). A psychoeducational approach to the treatment of depression: Comparison of group, individual and minimal contact procedures. *Journal of Consulting and Clinical Psychology*, 52, 774–83.

Bundy, M. L. & White, P. N. (1990). Parents as sexuality educators: A parent training program. *Journal of Counseling and Development*, 68, 321–3.

Butler, P. E. (1981). *Self-assertion for Women*. New York: Harper & Row.

Carkhuff, R. R. (1971a). *The Development of Human Resources: Education, Psychology and Social Change*. New York: Holt, Rinehart and Winston.

Carkhuff, R. R. (1971b). Training as a preferred mode of treatment. *Journal of Counseling Psychology*, 18, 123–31.

Cautela, J. R. (1967). Covert sensitization. *Psychological Reports*, 20, 459–68.

Cautela, J. R. (1976). The present status of cover modeling. *Journal of Behavior Therapy and Experimental Psychiatry*, 6, 323–6.

Chassan, J. B. (1979). *Research Designs in Clinical Psychology and Psychiatry*. New York: Wiley.

Christoff, K. A., Scott, W. O. N., Kelley, M. L., Schlundt, D., Baer, G. & Kelley, J. A. (1985). Social skills and social problem-solving training for shy young adolescents. *Behavior Therapy*, 16, 468–77.

Clifford, T. (1987). Assertiveness training for parents. *Journal of Counseling and Development*, 65, 552–4.

Combs, A. W., Richards, A. C. & Richards, F. (1976). *Perceptual Psychology: A Humanistic Approach to the Study of Persons*. New York: Harper & Row.

Conn, M. K. & Peterson, C. (1989). Social support: Seek and ye shall find. *Journal of Social and Personal Relationships*, 6, 345–58.

Cook, J. P. (1986). Training: A five-step program that keeps training on target. *Personnel Journal*, 65, 106–14.

Cooper, A. & Stoltenberg, C. D. (1987). Comparison of a sexual enhancement and a communication training program on sexual and marital satisfaction. *Journal of Consulting and Clinical Psychology*, 34, 309–14.

Corey, G. (1990). *Theory and Practice of Group Counseling* (3rd edn). Pacific Grove, CA: Brooks/Cole.

Corey, G. & Corey, M. S. (1982). *Groups: Process and Practice* (2nd edn). Grove, CA: Brooks/Cole.

Corey, G., Corey, M. S., Callanan, P. J. & Russell, J. M. (1988a). *Group Techniques* (revised edn). Pacific Grove, CA: Brooks/Cole.

Corey, G., Corey, M. S. & Callanan, P. J. (1988b). *Issues and Ethics in the Helping Professions* (3rd edn). Pacific Grove, CA: Brooks/Cole.

Cormier, W. H. & Cormier, L. S. (1985). *Interviewing Strategies for Helpers: Fundamental Skills and Cognitive Behavioral Interventions.* Pacific Grove, CA: Brooks/Cole.

Corrigan, J. D., Dell, D. M., Lewis, K. N. & Schmidt, L. D. (1980). Counseling as a social influence process: A review. *Journal of Counselling Psychology*, 27, 395–441.

Costley, D. L. & Moore, F. A. (1986). The subliminal impact and hidden agendas of training. *Personnel Journal*, 65, 101–5.

Daws, P. P. (1973). Mental health and counselling: Counselling as prophylaxis. *British Journal of Guidance and Counselling*, 1, 2–10.

Deffenbacher, J. L., Story, D. A., Stark, R. S., Hogg, J. A. & Brandon, A. D. (1987). Cognitive-relaxation and social skills interventions in the treatment of general anger. *Journal of Counseling Psychology*, 34, 171–6.

Deffenbacher, J. L., Story, D. A., Brandon, A. D., Hogg, J. A. & Hazaleus, S. L. (1988). Cognitive and cognitive-relaxation treatments of anger. *Cognitive Therapy and Research*, 12, 167–84.

Dorn, N. & South, N. (1986). Developing work-related education on alcohol and drugs. *British Journal of Guidance and Counselling*, 14, 88–96.

Downing, N. E. & Walker, M. E. (1987). A psychoeducational group for adult children of alcoholics. *Journal of Counseling and Development*, 65, 440–2.

Dyer, W. W. (1976). *Your Erroneous Zones.* London: Sphere.

D'Zurilla, T. J. & Goldfried, M. R. (1971). Problem solving and behavior modification. *Journal of Abnormal Psychology*, 78, 107–26.

Egan, G. (1977). *You and Me: The Skills of Communicating and Relating to Others.* Pacific Grove, CA: Brooks/Cole.

Egan, G. (1990). *The Skilled Helper: A Systematic Approach to Effective Helping* (4th edn). Pacific Grove, CA: Brooks/Cole.

Egan, G. & Cowan, M. A. (1979). *People in Systems: A Model for Development in the Human-Service Professions and Education.* Pacific Grove, CA: Brooks/Cole.

Eidelson, R. J. & Epstein, N. (1982). Cognition and relationship maladjustment: Development of a measure of dysfunctional relationship beliefs. *Journal of Consulting and Clinical Psychology*. 50, 715–20.

Ekman, P., Friesen, W. W. & Bear, J. (1984). The international language of gestures. *Psychology Today*, May, 64–9.

Elliott, S. N. & Gresham, F. M. (1987). Children's social skills: Assessment and classification practices. *Journal of Counseling and Development*, 66, 96–9.

Ellis, A. (1962). *Reason and Emotion in Psychotherapy.* New York: Lyle Stuart.

Ellis, A. (1980). Overview of the clinical theory of rational-emotive therapy. In R. Grieger & J. Boyd (eds), *Rational-Emotive Therapy: A Skills Based Approach*, pp. 1–31. New York: Van Nostrand Reinhold.

Ellis, A. (1985). *Overcoming Resistance: Rational-Emotive Therapy with Difficult Clients.* New York: Springer.

Ellis, A. (1987). The impossibility of achieving consistently good mental health. *American Psychologist*, 42, 364–75.

Ellis, A. (1989). Rational-emotive therapy. In R. Corsini & D. Wedding (eds), *Current Psychotherapies* (4th edn), pp. 197–238. Itasca, IL: Peacock.

Emery, G. (1982). *Own Your Own Life.* New York: New American Library.

Feindler, E. L., Marriott, S. A. & Iwata, M. (1984). Group anger control training for junior high school delinquents. *Cognitive Therapy and Research*, 8, 299–311.

Fischer, R. L. (1972). *Speak to Communicate: An Introduction to Speech.* Encino, CA: Dickenson Publishing Company.

Forster, E. M. (1951). Sayings of the week. *Observer*, October 7.

Frankl, V. E. (1959). *Man's Search for Meaning.* New York: Washington Square Press.

Frankl, V. E. (1969). *The Doctor and the Soul.* Harmondsworth, Middlesex: Penguin Books.

Fremouw, W. J. & Zittler, R. E. (1978). A comparison of skills training and cognitive restructuring-relaxation for the treatment of speech anxiety. *Behavior Therapy*, **9**, 248–59.

French, J. & Raven, B. (1959). The bases of social power. In D. Cartwright (ed.), *Studies in Social Power*, pp. 150–67. Ann Arbor: University of Michigan Press.

Freud, A. (1936). *The Ego and Mechanisms of Defense*. New York: International Universities Press.

Freudenberger, H. J. (1980). *Burnout: The High Cost of High Achievement*. London: Arrow Books.

Gallwey, W. T. (1974). *The Inner Game of Tennis*. London: Pan Books.

Ganger, R. E. (1989). Computer-based training improves job performance. *Personnel Journal*, **6**, 116–23.

Garfield, S. L. (1986). Research on client variables in psychotherapy. In S. L. Garfield & A. E. Bergin (eds), *Handbook of Psychotherapy and Behavior Change* (3rd edn), pp. 213–56. New York: Wiley.

Garis, J. W. & Niles, S. G. (1990). The separate and combined effects of SIGI or DISCOVER and a career planning course on undecided university students. *The Career Development Quarterly*, **38**, 261–74.

Gazda, G. M. (1989). *Group Counseling: A Developmental Approach* (4th edn). Boston: Allyn and Bacon.

Gendlin, E. T. (1981) *Focusing* (2nd edn). New York: Bantam Books.

Georges, J. C. (1989). The hard reality of soft-skills training. *Personnel Journal*, **68**, 41–5.

Gilbert, T. F. (1978). *Human Competence: Engineering Worthy Performance*. New York: McGraw-Hill.

Glasser, W. (1965). *Reality Therapy*. New York: Basic Books.

Glasser, W. (1984a). *Control Theory: A New Explanation of How We Control Our Lives*. New York: Harper & Row.

Glasser, W. (1984b). Reality therapy. In R. J. Corsini (ed.), *Current Psychotherapies* (3rd edn), pp. 320–53. Itasca, IL: F. E. Peacock.

Glick, B. & Goldstein, A. P. (1987). Aggression replacement training. *Journal of Counseling and Development*, **65**, 356–62.

Glick, P. C. (1984). How American families are changing. *American Demographics*, **6**, 20–5.

Goddard, R. W. (1989). Use language effectively. *Personnel Journal*, **68**, 32–6.

Goldfried, M. R. (1971). Systematic desensitization as a training in self-control. *Journal of Consulting and Clinical Psychology*, **37**, 228–34.

Goldfried, M. R. & Davison, G. C. (1976). *Clinical Behavior Therapy*. New York: Holt, Rinehart and Winston.

Goldstein, A. P. & Keller, H. (1987). *Aggressive Behavior: Assessment and Intervention*. New York: Pergamon.

Goldstein, I. L. & Gilliam, P. (1990). Training system issues in the year 2000. *American Psychologist*, **45**, 134–43.

Gonzalez, G. M. (1990). Effects of a theory-based, peer-focused drug education course. *Journal of Counseling and Development*, **68**, 446–9.

Gordon, T. (1970). *Parent Effectiveness Training*. New York: Wyden.

Graf, R. W., Whitehead, G. I. & LeCompte, M. (1986). Group treatment with divorced women using cognitive-behavioral and supportive-insight methods. *Journal of Counseling Psychology*, **33**, 276–81.

Gratton, L. (1985). Assessment centres: Theory, research and practice. *Human Resource Management Australia*, **23(3)**, 10–14.

Greenberg, I. A. (1975). Moreno: Psychodrama and the group process. In I. A. Greenberg (ed.), *Psychodrama: Theory and Therapy*, pp. 11–28. London: Souvenir Press.

Gregory, S. & Lee, S. (1986). Psychoeducational assessment of racial and ethnic minority groups: Professional implications. *Journal of Counseling and Development*, **64**, 635–7.

Gresham, F. M. & Elliott, S. N. (1986). *How I Act towards Others* (unpublished test). Baton Rouge, LA: University of Lousiana.

Grieger, R. (1989). A client's guide to rational-emotive therapy (RET). In W. Dryden & P. Trower (eds), *Cognitive Psychotherapy: Stasis and Change*, pp. 99–120. London: Cassell.

Guerney, B., Stollak, G. & Guerney, L. (1971). The practicing psychologist as educator – an alternative to the medical practitioner model. *Professional Psychology*, 2, 276–82.

Hains, A. A. & Szyjakowski, M. (1990). A cognitive stress-reduction intervention for adolescents. *Journal of Counseling Psychology*, 37, 79–84.

Hamilton, L. S. (1984). Developing game plans for entry into the post-secondary world: An intensive teaching approach. *Vocational Guidance Quarterly*, 33, 82–8.

Hatch, E. J. & Guerney, B. (1975). A pupil relationship enhancement program. *Personnel and Guidance Journal*, 54, 103–5.

Havighurst, R. J. (1972). *Developmental Tasks and Education* (3rd edn). New York: David McKay.

Haynes, L. A. & Avery, A. W. (1979). Training adolescents in self-disclosure and empathy skills. *Journal of Counseling Psychology*, 26, 526–30.

Heimberg, R. G., Dodge, C. S., Hope, D. A., Kennedy, C. R., Zollo, L. J. & Becker, R. E. (1990). Cognitive behavioral group treatment for social phobia: Comparison with a credible placebo control group. *Cognitive Therapy and Research*, 14, 1–23.

Heppner, P. P., Neal, G. W. & Larsen, L. M. (1984). Problem-solving training as prevention with college students. *Personnel and Guidance Journal*, 62, 514–29.

Herr, E. L. & Watts, A. G. (1988). Work shadowing and work-related learning. *Career Development Quarterly*, 37, 78–86.

Higgins, W., Ivey, A. & Uhlemann, M. (1970). Media therapy: A programmed approach to teaching behavioral skills. *Journal of Counseling Psychology*, 17, 20–6.

Holland, J. L. (1987). *Self-Directed Search: 1987 Manual Supplement*. Odessa, FL: Psychological Assessment Resources.

Homans, G. C. (1950). *Social Behavior: Its Elementary Forms*. New York: Harcourt, Brace & World.

Homans, G. C. (1961). *Social Behaviour: The Elementary Forms*. New York: Harcourt, Brace & World.

Hopson, B. & Hough, P. (1973). *Exercises in Personal and Career Development*. Cambridge, England: CRAC.

Hopson, B. & Hough, P. (1976). The need for personal and social education in secondary schools and further education. *British Journal of Guidance and Counselling*, 4, 16–27.

Hopson, B. & Scally, M. (1981) *Lifeskills Teaching*. London: McGraw-Hill.

Hosford, R. E. & Johnson, M. E. (1983). A comparison of self-observation, self-modeling, and practice without video feedback for improving counselor interviewing behaviors. *Counselor Education and Supervision*, 23, 62–70.

Hosford, R. E., Moss, C. S. & Morrell, G. (1976). The self-as-a-model technique: Helping prison inmates change. In J. D. Krumboltz & C. E. Thoresen (eds), *Counseling Methods*, pp. 487–95. New York: Holt, Rinehart and Winston.

Huey, W. C. & Rank, R. C. (1984). Effects of counselor and peer-led assertive training on black adolescent aggression. *Journal of Counseling Psychology*, 31, 95–8.

Ivey, A. E. (1976) Counseling psychology, the psychoeducator model and the future. *The Counseling Psychologist*, 6, 72–5.

Ivey, A. E. & Authier, J. (1978). *Microcounseling: Innovations in Interviewing, Counseling, Psychotherapy and Psychoeducation* (2nd edn). Springfield, IL: Charles C. Thomas.

Ivey, A. E., Ivey, M. B. & Simek-Downing, L. (1987). *Counseling and Psychotherapy: Integrating Skills, Theory and Practice* (2nd edn). Englewood Cliffs, NJ: Prentice-Hall.

Jacobs, E. E., Harvill, R. L. & Masson, R. L. (1988). *Group Counseling: Strategies and Skills*. Pacific Grove, CA: Brooks/Cole.

Jacobson, E. (1938). *Progressive Relaxation* (2nd edn). Chicago: University of Chicago Press.

Jacobson, N. S. (1989). The maintenance of treatment gains following social learning-based marital therapy. *Behavior Therapy*, **20**, 325–36.

Jeffrey, R. W. (1976). Reducing fears through participant modeling and self-directed practice. In J. D. Krumboltz & C. E. Thoresen (eds), *Counseling Methods*, pp. 301–12. New York: Holt, Rinehart and Winston.

Johnson, D. W. (1986). *Reaching Out: Interpersonal Effectiveness and Self-Actualization* (3rd edn). Englewood Cliffs, NJ: Prentice-Hall.

Johnson, D. W. & Johnson, F. P. (1987). *Joining Together: Group Theory and Group Skills* (3rd edn). Englewood Cliffs, NJ: Prentice-Hall.

Johnson, R. G. (1985). Microcomputer career exploration. *Vocational Guidance Quarterly*, **33**, 296–304.

Jones, J. E. & Pfeiffer, J. W. (1972–1981). *The Annual Handbook for Group Facilitators* (Vols 1–10). San Diego, CA: University Associates.

Jourard, S. M. (1971). *The Transparent Self* (revised edn). New York: Van Nostrand Reinhold.

Kagan, N. (1984). Interpersonal process recall: Basic methods and recent research. In D. Larsen (ed.), *Teaching Psychological Skills*, pp. 261–9. Pacific Grove, CA: Brooks/Cole.

Kalodner, C. R. & De Lucia, J. L. (1990). Components of effective weight loss programs: Theory, research and practice. *Journal of Counseling and Development*, **68**, 427–33.

Kanfer, F. H. & Gaelik, L. (1986). Self-management methods. In F. H. Kanfer & A. P. Goldstein (eds), *Helping People Change: A Textbook of Methods* (3rd edn.), pp. 283–345. New York: Pergamon Press.

Karoly, P. & Harris, A. (1986). Operant methods. In F. H. Kanfer & A. P. Goldstein (eds), *Helping People Change: A Textbook of Methods* (3rd edn), pp. 111–44. New York: Pergamon Press.

Katz, A. H. (1981). Self-help and mutual aid: An emerging social movement? *American Review of Sociology*, **7**, 129–55.

Kazdin, A. E. (1976). Developing assertive behaviors through covert modeling. In J. D. Krumboltz & C. E. Thoresen (eds), *Counseling Methods*, pp. 475–86. New York: Holt, Rinehart and Winston.

Kazdin, A. E. (1982). *Single-case Research Designs: Methods for Clinical and Applied Settings*. New York: Oxford University Press.

Kazdin, A. E. (1986). Research designs and methodology. In S. L. Garfield & A. E. Bergin (eds), *Handbook of Psychotherapy and Behavior Change* (3rd edn) pp. 23–68. New York: Wiley.

Keefe, F. J., Caldwell, D. S., Williams, D. A., Gil, K. M., Mitchell, D., Robertson, C., Martinez, S., Beckham, J. C., Crisson, J. E. & Helms, M. H. (1990). Pain coping skills training in the management of osteoarthritic knee pain: A comparative study. *Behavior Therapy*, **21**, 49–62.

Kendall, P. C. (1989). The generalization and maintenance of behavior change: Comments, considerations, and the 'No-cure' criticism. *Behavior Therapy*, **20**, 357–64.

Kendall, P. C. & Hollon, S. D. (1989). Anxious self-talk: Development of the anxious self-statements questionnaire (ASSQ). *Cognitive Therapy and Research*, **13**, 81–93.

Keyser, D. J. & Sweetland, R. C. (1984–1987). *Test Critiques* (Vols 1–4). Kansas City, MO: Test Corporation of America.

Klingman, A., Melamed, B. G., Cuthbert, M. I. & Hermecz, D. A. (1984). Effects of participant modeling on information acquisition and skill utilization. *Journal of Consulting and Clinical Psychology*, **52**, 414–22.

Kruger, A. N. (1970). *Effective Speaking: A Complete Course*. New York: Van Nostrand Reinhold.

Lazarus, A. (1977). *In the Mind's Eye*. New York: The Guilford Press.

Lazarus, A. (1989). Multimodal therapy. In R. J. Corsini & D. Wedding (eds), *Current Psycho-therapies* (4th edn), pp. 503–44. Itasca, IL:

F. E. Peacock.

Leduchowicz, T. & Bennett, R. (1983). Improving trainer effectiveness. *Personnel Review*, **12**, 19–25.

Lovett, S. & Gallagher, D. (1988). Psycho-educational interventions for family care-givers: Preliminary efficacy data. *Behavior Therapy*, **19**, 321–30.

Mahler, C. A. (1969). *Group Counseling in the Schools*. Boston: Houghton Mifflin.

Marlatt, G. (1980). Relapse prevention: A self-control program for the treatment of addictive behaviors. Invited address presented at the International Conference on Behavior Modification, Banff, Alberta, March.

Martin, J. (1983). Curriculum development in school counseling. *Personnel and Guidance Journal*, **61**, 406–9.

Martin, J. (1990). Confusions in psychological skills training. *Journal of Counseling and Development*, **68**, 402–7.

Martin, P. R., Nathan, P. R., Milech, D. & Van Keppel, M. (1989). Cognitive therapy vs. self-management training in the treatment of chronic headaches. *British Journal of Clinical Psychology*, **28**, 347–61.

Marx, R. (1982). Relapse prevention for managerial training: A model for maintenance of behavior change. *Academy of Management Review*, **7**, 433–41.

Maslach, C. & Jackson, S. (1981). The measurement of experienced burnout. *Journal of Occupational Behavior*, **2**, 99–113.

Maslow, A. H. (1962). *Toward a Psychology of Being*. New York: Van Nostrand.

Maslow, A. H. (1970). *Motivation and Personality* (2nd edn). New York: Harper & Row.

Masters, W. H. & Johnson, V. C. (1975). *The Pleasure Bond*. New York: Bantam.

Matarazzo, R. G. & Patterson, D. (1986). Research on the teaching and learning of therapeutic skills. In S. L. Garfield & A. E. Bergin (eds), *Handbook of Psychotherapy and Behavior Change* (3rd edn), pp. 821–43. New York: Wiley.

May, R. & Yalom, I. D. (1989). Existential psychotherapy. In R. Corsini & D. Wedding (eds), *Current Psychotherapies* (4th edn), pp. 363–402. Itasca, IL: Peacock.

McCarthy, P. R. (1982). Differential effects of counselor self-referent responses and counselor status. *Journal of Counseling Psychology*, **29**, 125–31.

McDonald, P. (1988). Families in the future: The pursuit of personal autonomy. *Family Matters*, **22**, 40–7.

Meichenbaum, D. H. (1977). *Cognitive-behavior Modification: An Integrative Approach*. New York: Plenum.

Meichenbaum, D. H. (1983). *Coping with Stress*. London: Century Publishing.

Meichenbaum, D. H. (1985). *Stress Inoculation Training*. New York: Pergamon Press.

Meichenbaum, D. H. (1986). Cognitive-behavior modification. In F. H. Kanfer & A. P. Goldstein (eds), *Helping People Change: A Textbook of Methods* (3rd edn), pp. 346–80. New York: Pergamon Press.

Meichenbaum, D. H. & Deffenbacher, J. L. (1988). Stress inoculation training. *The Counseling Psychologist*, **16**, 69–90.

Meichenbaum, D. H. & Goodman, J. (1971). Training impulsive children to talk to themselves: A means of developing self-control. *Journal of Abnormal Psychology*, **77**, 115–26.

Meichenbaum, D. H., Gilmore, J. B. & Fedoravicius, A. (1971). Group insight versus group desensitization in treating speech anxiety. *Journal of Consulting and Clinical Psychology*, **36**, 410–21.

Merta, R. J., Stringham, E. M. & Ponterotto, J. G. (1988). Simulating culture shock in counselor trainees: An experiential exercise for cross-cultural training. *Journal of Counseling and Development*, **66**, 242–5.

Miles, J. R. (1988). Selecting a video firm that produces results. *Personnel Journal*, **67**, 114–18.

Mitchell, J. V. (ed.), (1983). *Tests in Print 111: An Index to Tests, Test Reviews, and the Literature on Specific Tests*. Lincoln, NE: University of Nebraska Press.

Mitchell, J. V. (ed.) (1985). *Ninth Mental Measurements Yearbook* (Vols 1 & 2). Lincoln, NE: University of Nebraska Press.

Moore, D. & Haverkamp, B. E. (1989). Measured increases in male emotional expressiveness following a structured group intervention. *Journal of Counseling and Development*, **67**, 513–17.

Moracco, J. (1981). A comprehensive approach to human relations training for teachers. *Counselor Education and Supervision*, **19**, 119–35.

Morawetz, D. (1989). Behavioral self-help treatment for insomnia: A controlled evaluation. *Behavior Therapy*, **20**, 365–79.

Moreno, J. L. (1934). *Who Shall Survive?* Washington, DC: Nervous and Mental Disease Publishing Company.

Moreno, Z. T. (1959). A survey of psychodramatic techniques. *Group Psychotherapy*, **12**, 5–14.

Moreno, Z. T. (1975). A survey of psychodramatic techniques. In I. A. Greenberg (ed.), *Psychodrama: Theory and Therapy*, pp. 85–99. London: Souvenir Press.

Morgan, C. (1984). A curricular approach to primary prevention. *Personnel and Guidance Journal*, **53**, 467–9.

Morin, C. M. & Azrin, N. H. (1987). Stimulus control and imagery training in treating sleep-maintenance insomnia. *Journal of Consulting and Clinical Psychology*, **55**, 260–2.

Morrill, W. H., Oetting, E. R. & Hurst, J. C. (1974). Dimensions of counselor functioning. *Personnel and Guidance Journal*, **52**, 354–9.

Mosher, R. L. & Sprinthall, N. A. (1970). Psychological education in secondary schools: A program to promote individual and human development. *American Psychologist*, **25**, 911–24.

Mosher, R. L. & Sprinthall, N. A. (1971). Psychological education: A means to promote personal development during adolescence. *The Counseling Psychologist*, **2(4)**, 3–82.

Murgatroyd, S. (1985). *Counselling and Helping*. London: Methuen.

Murphy, A. I., Lehrer, P. M. & Jurish, S. (1990). Cognitive coping skills training and relaxation training as treatments for tension headaches. *Behavior Therapy*, **21**, 89–98.

National Board for Certified Counselors (1987). *Code of Ethics*. Alexandria, VA: National Board for Certified Counselors.

National Training Laboratory (1967). *Feedback and the Helping Relationship*. Washington DC: NTL Institute for Applied Behavioral Sciences.

Nelson, R. O., Hayes, S. C., Felton, J. L. & Jarrett, R. B. (1985). A comparison of data produced by different behavioral assessment techniques with implications for models of social-skills inadequacy. *Behaviour Research and Therapy*, **23**, 1–11.

Nelson-Jones, R. (1984). *Personal Responsibility Counseling and Therapy: An Integrative Approach*. New York: Hemisphere, and Milton Keynes, UK: Open University Press.

Nelson-Jones, R. (1986). Relationship skills training in schools: Some fieldwork observations. *British Journal of Guidance and Counselling*, **14**, 292–305.

Nelson-Jones, R. (1988a). The counselling psychologist as developmental educator. *The Australian Counselling Psychologist*, **4**, 55–66.

Nelson-Jones, R. (1988b). *Practical Counselling and Helping Skills: Helping Clients to Help Themselves* (2nd edn). London: Cassell.

Nelson-Jones, R. (1989). *Effective Thinking Skills: Preventing and Managing Personal Problems*. London: Cassell.

Nelson-Jones, R. (1990). *Human Relationship Skills* (2nd edn). London: Cassell.

Newman, J. L. & Fuqua, D. R. (1988). A comparative study of positive and negative modeling in counselor training. *Counselor Education and Supervision*, 28, 121–9.

Nomellini, S. & Katz, R. C. (1978). Effects of anger control training on abusive parents. *Cognitive Therapy and Research*, 7, 57–68.

Office of Population Census and Surveys (1987). Editorial: A review of 1986. *Population Trends*, 50, 1–12.

Ohlsen, M. M. (1977). *Group Counseling* (2nd edn). New York: Holt, Rinehart & Winston.

Ohlsen, M. M., Horne, A. M. & Lawe, C. F. (1988). *Group Counseling* (3rd edn). New York: Holt, Rinehart & Winston.

Osipow, S. H. (1982). Counseling psychology: Applications in the world of work. *The Counseling Psychologist*, 10(3), 19–25.

Osipow, S. H., Walsh, W. B. & Tosi, D. J. (1984). *A Survey of Counseling Methods* (revised edn). Homewood, IL: The Dorsey Press.

Paul, G. L. (1968). Two-year follow-up of systematic desensitization in therapy groups. *Journal of Abnormal Psychology*, 73, 119–30.

Paul, G. L. & Shannon, D. T. (1966). Treatment of anxiety through systematic desensitization in therapy groups. *Journal of Abnormal Psychology*, 71, 124–35.

Peale, N. V. (1953). *The Power of Positive Thinking*. Kingswood, Surrey: The World's Work (1913) Ltd.

Pease, A. (1981). *Body Language: How to Read Others' Thoughts by Their Gestures*, Sydney: Camel.

Pentz, M. A. & Kadzin, A. E. (1982). Assertion modelling and stimuli effects on assertive behaviour and self-efficacy in adolescents. *Behaviour Research and Therapy*, 20, 365–71.

Perry, M. A. & Fukuhara, M. J. (1986). Modeling methods. In F. H. Kanfer & A. P. Goldstein (eds), *Helping People Change: A Textbook of Methods* (3rd edn), pp. 66–110. New York: Pergamon.

Peterson, L. & Ridley-Johnson, R. (1980). Pediatric hospital response to survey on pre-hospital preparation of children. *Journal of Pediatric Psychology*, 5, 1–7.

Peterson, L., Schultheis, K., Ridley-Johnson, R., Miller, D. J. & Tracy, K. (1984). Comparison of three modeling procedures on the presurgical and postsurgical reactions of children. *Behavior Therapy*, 15, 197–203.

Pfeiffer, J. W. & Jones, J. (1969–1985). *Structured Experiences for Human Relations Training* (Vols 1–10). San Diego, CA: University Associates.

Pfeiffer, J. W., Heslin, R. & Jones, J. E. (1976). *Instrumentation in Human Relations Training* (2nd edn). La Jolla, CA: University Associates.

Plesma, D. & Flanagan, M. (1986). Human relations training for the elderly. *Journal of Counseling and Development*, 65, 52–3.

Poole, M. E. & Evans, G. T. (1988). Life skills: Adolescents' perceptions of importance and competence. *British Journal of Guidance and Counselling*, 16, 129–44.

Pretzer, J. L., Fleming, B. & Epstein, N. (1983). *Cognitive Factors in Marital Interaction: The Role of Specific Attributions*. Paper presented at the World Congress of Behavior Therapy, Washington; DC.

Priestley, P., McGuire, J., Flegg, D., Helmsley, V. & Welham, D. (1978). *Social Skills and Personal Problem-solving: A Handbook of Methods*. London: Tavistock Publications.

Professional Affairs Board (1980). Technical recommendations for psychological tests. *Bulletin of the British Psychological Society*, 33, 161–4.

Pryor, E. & Norris, D. (1977). Canada in the eighties. *American Demographics*, 5, 25–29, 44.

Ralph, A. (1988). Social skills training: How can we tell if it works? *Australian Psychologist*, 23, 305–14.

Raskin, N. J. & Rogers, C. R. (1989). Person-centered therapy. In R. Corsini & D. Wedding (eds), *Current Psychotherapies* (4th edn), pp. 155–94. Itasca, IL: Peacock.

Ratigan, B. (1986). Counsellors and staff development: Models of tutor training in tertiary educational settings. *British Journal of Guidance and Counselling*, **14**, 140–53.

Raue, J. & Spence, S. H. (1985). Group versus individual applications of reciprocity training for parent–youth conflict. *Behaviour Research and Therapy*, **23**, 177–86.

Resnik, J. L., Resnik, M. B., Packer, A. B. & Wilson, J. (1978). Fathering classes: A psychoeducational model. *The Counseling Psychologist*, (**4**), 56–60.

Riordan, R. J. & Beggs, M. S. (1987). Counselors and self-help groups. *Journal of Counseling and Development*, **65**, 427–9.

Robey, B. & Russell, C. (1984). Trends: All Americans. *American Demographics*, **6**, 32–5.

Roessler, R. T. (1988). Implementing career education: Barriers and potential solutions. *Career Development Quarterly*, **37**, 22–30.

Rogers, C. R. (1957). The necessary and sufficient conditions of therapeutic personality change. *Journal of Consulting Psychology*, **21**, 95–103.

Rogers, C. R. (1959). A theory of therapy, personality and interpersonal relationships as developed in the client-centred framework. In S. Koch (ed.), *Psychology: A Study of Science*, Vol. 3, *Formulations of the Person and the Social Context*, pp. 184–256. New York: McGraw-Hill.

Rogers, C. R. (1961). *On Becoming a Person*. Boston: Houghton Mifflin.

Rogers, C. R. (1969). *Freedom to Learn: A View of What Education Might Become*. Columbus, Ohio: Charles E. Merrill Publishing Co.

Rogers, C. R. (1970). *Encounter Groups*. London: Allen Lane, The Penguin Press.

Rogers, C. R. (1980). *A Way of Being*. Boston: Houghton Mifflin.

Rogers, G. T. (Producer) (1984). *My Father's Son: The Legacy of Alcoholism* (Film). Skokie, IL: Gerald T. Rogers Productions.

Romano, J. L. (1984). Stress management and wellness: Reaching beyond the counselor's office. *Personnel and Guidance Journal*, **62**, 533–7.

Rose, S. D. (1986). Group methods. In F. H. Kanfer & A. P. Goldstein (eds), *Helping People Change: A Textbook of Methods* (3rd edn), pp. 437–69. New York: Pergamon.

Russell, C. & Exter, T. G. (1986). America at mid-decade. *American Demographics*, **8**, 22–9.

Ryan, C. W., Jackson, B. L. & Levinson, E. M. (1986). Human relations skills training in teacher education: The link to effective practice. *Journal of Counseling and Development*, **65**, 114–16.

Sacks, S. & Gaylord-Ross, R. (1989). Peer-mediated and teacher-directed social skills training for visually impaired students. *Behavior Therapy*, **20**, 619–38.

Sampson, D. E. & Liberty, L. H. (1989). Textbooks used in counselor education programs. *Counselor Education and Supervision*, **29**, 111–21.

Sarason, I. G. (1973). Text anxiety and cognitive modeling. *Journal of Personality and Social Psychology*, **28**, 58–61.

Sarason, I. G. (1976). Using modeling to strengthen the behavioral repertory of the juvenile delinquent. In J. D. Krumboltz & C. E. Thoresen (eds), *Counseling Methods*, pp. 56–66. New York: Holt, Rinehart and Winston.

Saskatchewan Newstart (1973). *Life Skills Coaching Manual*. Prince Albert, Saskatchewan: Department of Manpower and Immigration.

Savikas, M. L. (1990). The career decision-making course: Description and field test. *The Career Development Quarterly*, **38**, 275–84.

Schlichter, K. J. & Horan, J. J. (1981). Effects of stress inoculation on the anger and aggression management skills of institutionalized juvenile delinquents. *Cognitive Therapy and Research*, **5**, 359–65.

Schmidt, J. R., Brown, P. T. & Waycroft, A. M. (1988). Developing the individual: Life skills and family therapy. *British Journal of Guidance and Counselling*, **16**, 113–28.

Shaw, C. (1988). Latest trends of ethnic minority populations. *Population Trends*, **51**, 5–8.

Skinner, B. F. (1953). *Science and Human Behavior*. New York: Macmillan.

Skinner, B. F. (1971). *Beyond Freedom and Dignity*. Harmondsworth, Middlesex: Penguin Books.

Smith, M. L. & Glass, G. V. (1977). Meta-analysis of psychotherapy outcome studies. *American Psychologist*, **32**, 752–60.

Spanier, G. B. (1976). Measuring dyadic adjustment: New scales for assessing the quality of marriage and similar dyads. *Journal of Marriage and the Family*, **38**, 15–28.

Sprinthall, N. A. (1973). A curriculum for secondary schools: Counselors as teachers for psychological growth. *The School Counselor*, **20**, 36–9.

Sprinthall, N. A. (1980). Psychology for secondary schools: The saber-tooth curriculum revisited? *American Psychologist*, **35**, 336–47.

Sprinthall, N. A. & Scott, J. R. (1989). Promoting psychological development, math achievement, and success attribution of female students through deliberate psychological education. *Journal of Counseling Psychology*, **36**, 440–6.

Steiner, C. M. (1974). *Scripts People Live*. New York: Bantam Books.

Steiner, C. M. (1981). *The Other Side of Power*. New York: Grove Press.

Stewart, C. G. & Lewis, W. A. (1986). Effects of assertiveness training on the self-esteem of black high school students. *Journal of Counseling and Development*, **64**, 638–41.

Stokes, T. F. & Osnes, P. G. (1989). An operant pursuit of generalization. *Behavior Therapy*, **20**, 337–55.

Strong, S. R. (1968). Counseling: An interpersonal influence process. *Journal of Counseling Psychology*, **15**, 215–24.

Strong, S. R. (1978). Social psychological approach to psychotherapy research. In S. L. Garfield & A. E. Bergin (eds), *Handbook of Psychotherapy and Behavior Change: An Empirical Analysis* (2nd edn), pp. 101–35. New York: John Wiley.

Stuart, R. B. (1980). *Helping Couples Change: A Social Learning Approach to Marital Therapy*. New York: Guilford Press.

Suinn, R. M. & Deffenbacher, J. L. (1988). Anxiety management training. *The Counseling Psychologist*, **16**, 31–49.

Sullivan, H. S. (1953). *The Interpersonal Theory of Psychiatry*. New York: W. W. Norton.

Swain, R. (1984). Easing the transition: A career planning course for college students. *Personnel and Guidance Journal*, **62**, 529–32.

Sweetland, R. C. & Keyser, D. J. (eds) (1986). *Tests: A Comprehensive Reference for Assessments in Psychology, Education and Business*. Kansas City, MO: Test Corporation of America.

Thoresen, C. E. & Mahoney, M. J. (1974). *Behavioral Self-control*. New York: Holt, Rinehart and Winston.

Thorne, B. & Da Costa, M. (1976). A counselling service as a growth centre. *British Journal of Guidance and Counselling*, **4**, 212–17.

Toomer, J. E. (1982). Counseling psychologists in business and industry. *The Counseling Psychologist*, **10**(3), 9–18.

Tracey, T. J. (1983). Single case research: An added tool for counselors and supervisors. *Counselor Education and Supervision*, **22**, 185–96.

Troy, W. G. & Magoon, T. M. (1979). Activity analysis in a university counseling center: Daily time recording or time estimates? *Journal of Counseling Psychology*, **26**, 58–63.

Thurman, C. (1984). Cognitive-behavioral interventions with Type A faculty. *Personnel and Guidance Journal*, **62**, 358–62.

Thurman, C. W. (1985). Effectiveness of cognitive-behavioral treatment in reducing Type A behavior among university faculty – one year later. *Journal of Counseling Psychology*, **32**, 445–8.

Turner, J. A. & Clancy, S. (1988). Comparison of operant and cognitive-behavioral group treatment for chronic low back pain. *Journal of Consulting and Clinical Psychology*, **56**, 261–6.

Twentyman, C. T. & McFall, R. M. (1975). Behavioral training of social skills in shy males. *Journal of Consulting and Clinical Psychology*, **43**, 384–95.

Ulrich's International Periodicals Directory 1989–1990 (1989). 28th edn., Vols 1–3. New York: R. R. Bowker.

Valenti, J. (1982). *Speak up with Confidence: How to Prepare, Learn, and Deliver Effective Speeches.* New York: William Morrow.

Watkins, C. E., Lopez, F. G., Campbell, V. L. & Himmell, C. D. (1986). Contemporary counseling psychology: Results of a national survey. *Journal of Counseling Psychology*, **33**, 301–9.

Webster-Stratton, C. (1989). Systematic comparison of consumer satisfaction of three cost-effective parent training programs for conduct problem children. *Behavior Therapy*, **20**, 103–15.

Webster-Stratton, C., Kolpacoff, M. & Hollinsworth, T. (1988). Self-administered videotape therapy for families with conduct-problem children: Comparison with two cost-effective treatments and a control group. *Journal of Consulting and Clinical Psychology*, **56**, 558–66.

Webster-Stratton, C., Hollinsworth, T. & Kolpacoff, M. (1989). The long-term effectiveness and clinical significance of three cost-effective training programs for parents with conduct-problem children. *Journal of Consulting and Clinical Psychology*, **57**, 550–3.

Wehrenberg, S. B. (1985). Management training games: The play's the thing. *Personnel Journal*, **64**, 88–91.

Wehrenberg, S. B. (1988). Learning contracts. *Personnel Journal*, **67**, 100–2.

Weishaar, M. E. & Beck, A. T. (1986). Cognitive therapy. In W. Dryden & W. Golden (eds), *Cognitive-behavioral Approaches to Psychotherapy*, pp. 61–91. London: Harper & Row.

Weissman, S. (1985). Preparing incarcerated youth for employment. *Journal of Counseling and Development*, **63**, 524–5.

Whitaker's Books in Print (1989). Vols 1–4. London: J. Whitaker & Sons.

Whitaker, D. S. (1985). *Using Groups to Help People.* London: Routledge & Kegan Paul.

Wilbur, C. S. & Vermilyea, C. J. (1982). Some business advice to counseling psychologists. *The Counseling Psychologist*, **10**(3), 31–2.

Wild, B. & Kerr, B. A. (1984). Training adolescent job-seekers in persuasion skills. *Vocational Guidance Quarterly*, **33**, 63–9.

Wilkinson, J. & Canter, S. (1982). *Social Skills Training Manual: Assessment, Programme Design and Management of Training.* Chichester, England: John Wiley.

Wolpe, J. E. (1982). *The Practice of Behavior Therapy* (2nd edn). New York: Pergamon Press.

Wolpe, J. & Lazarus, A. A. (1966). *Behavior Therapy Techniques: A Guide to the Treatment of Neurosis.* New York: Pergamon Press.

Wragg, J. (1986). Drug and alcohol education: The development, design and longitudinal evaluation of an early childhood programme. *Australian Psychologist*, **21**, 283–98.

Yalom, I. D. (1980). *Existential Psychotherapy.* New York: Basic Books.

Yalom, I. D. (1985). *The Theory and Practice of Group Psychotherapy* (3rd edn). New York: Basic Books.

Yamauchi, K. T. (1987). Self-help audiocassette tapes: Adjunct to psychological counseling. *Journal of Counseling and Development*, **65**, 448–50.

Zelko, H. P. (1986). Better seminars and workshops for both sponsor and participant. *Personnel Journal*, **65**, 32–4.

Zemore, R. (1975). Systematic desensitization as a method of teaching a general anxiety-reducing skill. *Journal of Consulting and Clinical Psychology*, **43**, 157–61.

Zimbardo, P. G. (1977). *Shyness: What It Is and What to Do about It.* Reading, MA: Addison-Wesley.

NAME INDEX

SUBJECT INDEX